Society of Ship-Owners Great Britain

Collection of interesting and important reports and papers on the navigation and trade

Society of Ship-Owners Great Britain

Collection of interesting and important reports and papers on the navigation and trade

Inktank publishing, 2018

www.inktank-publishing.com

ISBN/EAN: 9783747768761

COLLECTION

OF

INTERESTING AND IMPORTANT

REPORTS AND PAPERS

ON THE

NAVIGATION AND TRADE

OF

GREAT BRITAIN, IRELAND, AND THE BRITISH COLONIES IN THE WEST INDIES AND AMERICA,

WITH TABLES OF TONNAGE AND OF EXPORTS AND IMPORTS,

&c. &c. &c.

——— Some people he understood had been at infinite pains *to condemn* the framers of the *Navigation Act*, and to ridicule those who were weak enough to look up to it as beneficial to the country, notwithstanding which, he would confess *himself* one of those weak beings who *admired* its construction, and would gladly see it preserved *inviolate*. Lord *Loughborough's* Speech, Feb. 22, 1785.

——— At present, amongst European nations, a *naval* strength, which is the portion of Great Britain, is *more than ever* of the greatest importance to sovereignty, as well because most of the kingdoms of Europe are *not* continents, but, in a good measure, surrounded by the sea; as because the treasures of both *Indies* seem but an accessory to the *dominion* of the seas. Lord *Bacon*.

——— It is good not to try *experiments* in states, except the necessity be urgent, or the utility evident; and well to beware that it be the reformation that draweth on the change, and not the desire of change that pretendeth the reformation; and lastly, that the novelty, though it be not rejected, yet be held for *a suspect*, and as the scripture saith—" That we make a stand upon the *ancient way*, and then " look about us, and discover what is the straight and right way, and so to walk in " it." *Ibid.*

PRINTED BY ORDER OF

" *THE SOCIETY OF SHIP OWNERS OF GREAT BRITAIN.*"

AND SOLD BY

J. STOCKDALE, PICCADILLY; J. BUTTERWORTH, FLEET-STREET; AND J. AND J. RICHARDSON, CORNHILL.

1807.

TO

THE RIGHT HONOURABLE

JOHN LORD SHEFFIELD,

&c. &c. &c.

THE FOLLOWING COLLECTION

OF IMPORTANT PAPERS

ON NAVIGATION AND TRADE,

IS MOST RESPECTFULLY DEDICATED

By the Society of Ship-Owners

OF

GREAT BRITAIN,

IN TESTIMONY OF THEIR GRATEFUL SENSE

OF THE EMINENT SERVICES RENDERED

BY HIS LORDSHIP TO THE SHIPPING INTEREST

OF THE UNITED KINGDOM;

AND OF HIS ZEALOUS EXERTIONS,

ON ALL OCCASIONS, TO MAINTAIN,

UNIMPAIRED,

THE MARITIME STRENGTH OF THE EMPIRE.

In the Press, and in a few Days will be published in Octavo,

A COLLECTION of DEBATES in Parliament, on the Act of Navigation, on the Trade between Great Britain and the United States of America; and the Intercourse between the latter and the British West-India Islands, on the Tortola Free Port Bill, &c. from 1783 to 1807, both inclusive; with Notes and an Appendix, containing a variety of important Documents illustrative of those interesting Subjects.

CONTENTS.

b

APPENDIX, (A) annexed to the last Report.

Appendix (B.)

Appendix (C.)

Appendix (D.)

SUPPLEMENT TO THE VOLUME CONTAINING MISCELLANEOUS PAPERS, &c.

CONTENTS.

ERRATA, &c.

Supplement—p. xl *dele* twice the words "*and of*" after "*before*."
p. xcii The resolution of the 6th June, 1805, should have been inserted in p. civ *before* the 5th Sept. [illegible].
p. xcix *dele* the word "*then*" after *Secretary*.
Ibid. For 1806 in *note*, read 1807.
p. cix To the note *add*, "but which was *refused* by the Lords of the Treasury, in the *autumn* of 1806."
p. cxxi For "*general*" owners, read "*original*."
p. cxxii in *note*, for 1806, read 1807.
p. clxxi In rate of freight for 1795, from *Riga*, for 36*s*. *read* 45*s*.
p. ccv In *third* column, for "amount of *increase*," read "of *tonnage*."
p. ccvi *Dele* at the bottom of the table, "*ought to be* 42,562."
p. cclxv *should be* ccxlv.
p. ccl for *lead*, read *led*.
p. cclxxv *Dele* "*mechanics*," and insert "Do."
Ibid. After ironfounder, &c. *dele* "*manufacturers*," and insert "Do."

ON

THE NAVIGATION AND TRADE

OF

GREAT BRITAIN,

&c. &c.

INTRODUCTION.

THE following Reports of the Privy Council framed by that able and long experienced Statesman the Earl of LIVERPOOL, in the years 1784 and 1791, when President of the Committee of his Majesty's most honourable Privy Council for the Affairs of Trade and Foreign Plantations, contain a complete, satisfactory, and accurate Investigation of the important question respecting the Intercourse in *American* Ships, between his Majesty's Colonies in the West Indies and the *United States* of *America*, and they will be found, on an attentive perusal, to prove that the Complaints of the West India Planters, on the Restrictions therein recommended, were utterly unfounded; that *Great Britain* and *Ireland* and the remaining *British* Colonies in North America were fully adequate to the Supply in *British* Ships of all the necessary articles for the West India Colonies; and that the Ship-owners of *Great Britain* and *Ireland* instead of rejecting the Navigation between the American Continent and the West India Islands, on account of the Expence of the circuitous voyage, had every inducement of Profit, *if the Navigation Laws were inviolably maintained*, to enter fully and effectually into that Trade; and in further corroboration of this assertion the Society of Ship-owners not only refer to the Debates* which took place in Parliament between the years 1783 and 1789 on the Trade with *Ame-*

* See the Collection of Debates in Parliament on the Trade to and from America—Navigation Act, &c. Octavo Edition, 1807.

C

rica, and the Sentiments *then* expressed by some of his Majesty's *present* Ministers on the Subject, but also to their admision at the interviews which took place with them last Summer, namely, *that in time of peace** the Mother Country and its dependencies were adequate to all the necessary Supplies in *British* Ships of the West India Colonies, which consequently narrowed the subject so as to make it a mere question of *Price*.

The great body of *British* Ship-owners opposed the American Intercourse Bill of last Session from a thorough Conviction not only of its impolicy, but its ruinous tendency to the vital interests of the Empire, and in the hope that an *Inquiry* would have been instituted by Parliament on that subject, and into the *actual* State of the Shipping and Navigation of the Country, as the Increase of Shipping and the Improvement of Navigation were objects that had in *former* days frequently engaged the attention of THE LEGISLATURE, and various provisions had been made from time to time, by which it was endeavoured to *confine*, as much as possible, the Trade to and from this Country and its dependencies, the employment of the Fisheries, and the conveyance coastwise, to the *Shipping and Mariners of this country alone*.

" The Laws which the Legislature has provided for " the encouragement and increase of British Shipping " and Navigation are a Series of restrictions and prohi- " bitions, and tend to the establishing of a Monopoly, but " it is a plan of regulation which our ancestors, who were " more versed in the *practical* philosophy of life than " the *speculative* one of the closet, thought necessary " for the welfare and safety of the kingdom; reasoning " from the self-preservation of an individual to the self-pre-

* See also the American Intercourse Bill of last Session, as it was *first* printed.

" servation of a people, they considered the *defence* of this " Island from *foreign invasion* as the *first* law in the na- " tional Policy; and judging that the *dominion* of the *land* " *could not be preserved* without possessing that *of the Sea*, " they made every effort to procure to the Nation a *mari-* " *time* power of its own. They wished that the Merchants " should *own* as many Ships, and employ as many *native* " Mariners, as possible. To *induce*, and sometimes to " *force* them, to this application of *their Capitals*, restric- " tions and prohibitions were devised. These affected " not only Foreigners but Natives; the *interests of com-* " *merce* were often *sacrificed* to this object. *Trade* was " considered principally as the means for *promoting* the " employment of *Ships*, and was encouraged chiefly as it " conduced to the one great national object, the *naval* " *strength* of the country.

" This policy was pursued by those who came after " them in directing the public Councils; and in the last " century, when many institutions of our Ancestors fell " a sacrifice to the rage of reformation, *the wisdom of the* " *navigation system was respected*: measures were even taken " for rendering it more narrow and restrictive. The " foreign war which those measures then brought upon " us, and the odium *which they have never ceased* to " cause, to the present* day, among neighbouring nations, " have not induced the Legislature to give up any one of " its main principles.

" *Experience has shewn the advantage of adhering to this* " *maritime policy*. The inducement and obligation to " employ *British* Ships had the effect of *increasing* their " number. The increase of their number became a " spur to seek out employment for them. Foreign " Trade and the Fisheries were, by various expedients,

* 1792.

"made *subservient* to advance the *interests of Shipping*. "Trade and Shipping thus *reciprocally* contributed to "advance each other; and thus combined, they con-"stituted very considerable sources of national wealth. "Having been at first encouraged for the sake of the "*Navy*, they were afterwards encouraged for *their own*. "From being subordinate and auxiliary to another "subject, they are now become principal objects them-"selves in the *national* policy; and in the mean time the "*naval* power of the Country is sure of supply and sup-"port, without being directly in contemplation."

"If the wisdom of any scheme of policy is to be "measured by its effects and consequences, our Naviga-"tion system is entitled to the praise of having attained "the end for which it was designed. Whether we regard "the primary or inferior objects in this system, whether "it is the increase of Shipping, the extension of our "Foreign Trade, or the strength of our Navy, they have "all advanced to a degree of consideration unexampled; "and they owe that advancement to THIS SYSTEM.

"With regard to our Shipping, it is well known that "we enjoy a greater share in what may be properly "called our own navigation; that is, in the navigation "by which our own Trade is carried on, than any other "Nation in *Europe*; and that after we have furnished "these demands of our own commerce, we are able to "supply *with Ships* the Trade of Foreign Nations. This "extensive employment has gradually increased the "*mercantile* Shipping of Great Britain to upwards of "1,365,000 Tons, which is (i. e. in 1792) valued at the "Sum of £11,466,000.

"That this increase in our Shipping is to be ascribed "to *our Navigation System* may be made appear from re-"cent experience, in the application of it to the Trade

" *of the United States*. When those Countries were part " of our Plantations, a great portion of their Produce " was transported to *Great Britain*, and our West India " Islands, in *American Bottoms*, they had a share in the " Freight of Sugars from those Islands to Great Britain. " But since the independence of those States, since their " Ships have been *excluded* from our Plantations, and that " Trade is *wholly confined* to *British-built Ships*, we have " gained that share of our carrying Trade from which " they are *now excluded*, and we moreover enjoy a con- " siderable proportion in the carriage of the produce " of the *United States*.

" The increase of our Trade and Naval strength has " kept pace with that of our Shipping and Navigation. " We can reflect with pride that our Foreign trade, com- " bined with our Manufactures and domestic industry, " enables us to raise annually sixteen millions of money " with more ease than four millions were raised during " the reign of *King William*, and this upon a People, who, " in their different ranks, enjoy more riches, more com- " petency, and more comforts, than any People *in Europe*, " and who are more industrious, because they are better " protected by a constitution which has been progressively " improving, both in the theory and practice of it, to " the present time.

" It was chiefly owing to the effects of *this wise system* " *of navigation* that, during the late* war, we were en- " abled, notwithstanding the defection of our Colonies, " to maintain an arduous contest against *France*, *Spain*, " and *Holland*, till in the end the Fleets of this Country " might be said to have triumphed over the *Naval powers* " of *Europe*.

* American War.

"After *this experience* no one can doubt but that it is "the Policy of *Great Britain* to give her principal attention to *maritime* affairs: to carry on *her own* Trade, "*in her own Ships*, directly to all parts of the World; "and to encourage her Fisheries in every Sea; and from "these sources she may always hope to obtain a *Naval* "force adequate to guard her shores from *hostile invasion*, "and to secure domestic felicity, both public and private, "firm and unshaken as the foundations of the Island."

Such were the observations of a learned and elegant writer on this *momentous* subject in 1792, but who has now, in common with the public, to deplore the destructive and calamitous consequences which are *daily* resulting from the *suspension* of the Act of Navigation and the *gratuitous* concessions made to *Neutral* Nations, and, too fatally in particular, to *America*, which has become of late the great carrier of the world.

The Act of the 23d George 3. c. 39, was for a *limited* period, and was then *tolerated* only from the peculiar situation in which *Great Britain* was placed by the final separation of the *American* States from *Great Britain* by the Peace then concluded. It will appear by reference to the Reports of the Board of Trade in 1784 and 1791, that the same with the continuations were intended, as a *temporary* expedient, *not* warranted even by the *then actual* situation of the Navigation and Trade of the Mother Country; that Act therefore could not fairly be adduced as an authority for the *enormous extension* of the *suspending* powers by the Intercourse Bill of last Session, which was to authorise the King and his Successors, with the advice of his and their Privy Council, to suspend, during the *present* or *any future* War, all the provisions of the *Act of Navigation* in the *British* settlements in the West Indies and South America, both as to exports and imports;

which in effect places the whole of the *Colonial* trade, in all its branches, in the hands of the King's Ministers, and thereby renders the *Shipping* and *Mercantile* interests of the Nation entirely *dependant* on the will and pleasure of the officers of the Crown. On that as well as on *constitutional* grounds the Bill appeared to the Ship-owners to be highly objectionable, they therefore felt no common degree of surprise that, in so *early* a period of *their* Administration, such rapid strides should have been made towards *narrowing* the *legislative* functions of *Parliament*. Indeed the Bill was truly described by some of the friends of the *present* Ministers, to be an attempt to increase the power of the Privy Council, although the ostensible and avowed object of it was alledged to be merely for the purpose of securing at all times a regular, steady, and cheap supply of provisions and lumber for the Inhabitants of the *British West India Islands*. The various classes of petitioners against the Bill, with a degree of moderation highly commendable at all times, but especially under the present critical and alarming situation of the Navigation and Trade of the Empire, urged the necessity of *an inquiry* on the subject before a Committee of the House of Committee; but all their entreaties in that respect were unavailing, and the promoters of that ruinous measure *denied to them* that, which had hitherto, in all *other branches of Trade*, been considered *a matter of course*, if not *of Right*, namely, the appointment of a Committee, to inquire into the nature and true merits of their respective cases.

The reasons alledged by his Majesty's Ministers in favour of the Bill were that the Governors of the *British* West India Islands, on entering into office, *swear* to observe and maintain, in the exercise of their functions, the Laws of the Mother Country; and that the Privy

Council sitting in *London* are much more proper Judges when the Laws of Navigation should be suspended in the West India Islands *than the Governors on the spot!* The fact of the existence of any *necessity* for the measure, in justification of it, as alledged in the preamble of the Bill, was evidently *abandoned:* it could not, indeed, with propriety, have been persisted in, as the petitioners against the Bill expressed an anxious desire *to take issue* upon the facts advanced by the *resident* West India Planters in support of a *free intercourse with America*, urging, at the same time, that they were ready to prove the converse of them; and it is remarkable there should have been on that occasion so much anxiety for the *moral* feelings of the Governors of the West India Islands, when, almost *daily*, the Act of Navigation and other Statutes relating to Trade are broken, relaxed, and suspended, at *home*, by Orders of Council, Treasury Instructions, and other Instruments, issued by Government, and for whose indemnity an Act has for some years been annually passed*.

In consequence of the *suspensions* of the Act of Navigation since 1793, there has been a *gradual decrease* of *Ship Building* in the *British* Empire, and a *depreciation* in the value of *British* Shipping; those which were formerly employed in the *circuitous* Trade from the Mother Country to *America*, and from thence to the *British* West India Settlements have been *entirely driven out* of it, which has since been carried on by *Neutrals*, to the manifest injury of this Country. The *facility* † with which Licences are granted to *Neutrals* affords a just and strong ground of complaint to *British* Ship-

* See Lord Sheffield's Strictures, p. 216.

† Ibid. p. 222, et seq.

owners not only in the *European* Trade, which is principally carried on by them, but *generally*; it was from the experience which they had dearly bought in that respect they were so anxious the Bill should not pass into a Law.

On a firm reliance that the *maritime* principles of the Country, established by the Act of Navigation, would always be *religiously adhered to*, the great body of *British* Ship-owners embarked their property: the *frequent relaxations* of the provisions of that statute have been considered as *so many instances of violated faith*, that it may be difficult to persuade them such impolitic and temporary expedients will *not again* be resorted to, so as to induce them *extensively* again to venture their Capitals in such *hazardous property*: it is, in truth, of the utmost consequence to persons in trade, independent of the common contingencies attached to it, that *legislative* regulations on the subject should be permanent, and not temporary or fluctuating, otherwise no person can with prudence enter into it with a rational prospect of success, which result ought always to be held out to him as an inducement to risk his money, not only with respect to his individual advantage, but also to the ultimate general benefit which the Country must derive from its Trade and Commerce, when prosperously carried on.

The *alarm* which has justly gone forth, excited by the Sentiments of his Majesty's *present* Ministers, expressed in the course of the debates on the *American* Intercourse Bill, cannot be wondered at, especially under the Circumstances in which the Ship-owners of *Great Britain*, and the Merchants trading to and residing in the *British* American Colonies, are now placed, from the injurious consequences which they have felt under the relaxations of the Navigation Laws: it would therefore be the extreme of *injustice* to impute to the Ship-owners *party motives*, to which every one of them was utterly a stranger in the Cause for which they contended; they felt that the question involved not only their *particular* interest, but the *future existence of the Maritime Power of Great Britain.* The only possible ground, indeed, on which such motives could be suspected, would not be *discreditable* to them, namely, that the *late* Administration had given the strongest assurances of an intention *to confine* the suspensions of the provisions of the Navigation Act as to *Europe*, to the transit of *those articles necessary in our Manufactures* which can only be procured from the Enemies' Countries, and considerably *to narrow* the *deviations* from the Rule of 1756, as to the *Colonies* of the *Enemy*.

The Ship-owners have thought it necessary to state the grounds on which they opposed that Bill, in order to prove, that so far from being *inimical* to the Interests of the British West India *Planters*, their views have been *equally* directed to them as to their own; by shewing the ruin which must result to *our* Colonies in that part of the World by the *continued relaxation* of the principles of the Navigation and Colonial System of *Great Britain*, to which we are, most indisputably, indebted for our Maritime and Commercial Greatness, and, consequently, for our independence as a Nation.

The Society of Ship-owners avail themselves of this opportunity to communicate to the Public their proceedings since the establishment of the Institution, in order that it may be *generally* known they have not been actuated, in any measure entertained by them, by *partial* or *interested* motives, but by a *constant* and *anxious solicitude* to avert, if possible, those ruinous consequences which will inevitably ensue from the frequent suspensions of the Navigation Act, and from the *present* system of *gratuitous* concessions to other Nations; with a view, if possible, *before it is too late*, to impress on the *Public Mind* the absolute necessity of endeavouring *to prevent*, by every constitutional means, the *Confirmation* of those *Concessions*, which it is rumoured are *now* unhappily *contemplated*.

The Society do not presume to offer any observations on the other points which are supposed to have led to such Concessions; they cannot, however, resist expressing their *painful apprehensions* on the subject, which they are led to entertain from the *sentiments avowed*, by the King's *present* Ministers, in the Debates on the *American* Intercourse Bill of last Session, and from the *yielding* influence which appears, unfortunately, to pervade, *at this time*, the *British* Government.

In all points of minor consequence which have been presented to their notice, the Society of Ship-owners have always acted on general principles, not only to obtain an amelioration of the *depressed* state of *British* Shipping, but with a due regard to the *other Interests* of the Empire: they court an investigation of their principles and views, and an inquiry into their conduct and its motives; they are desirous the *Public* should be apprized of the evil consequences which must arise from the adoption of the *New* System, and they venture to direct the *public attention* to their proceedings and statements, convinced that the Nation will see the necessity of adhering to the *wise System* of OUR FOREFATHERS, rather than give *further* effect to the *theoretical* speculations of *modern* writers on political Œconomy, or the principles of that *New Philosophy* which has entailed so much misery on other *European* Nations.

They might, though perhaps not without some appearance of affectation, refer to innumerable authorities in support and justification of their principles and conduct, and among them to Lord Bacon, Sir Walter Raleigh,

Sir William Temple, Sir Josias Child, Mr. Lediard, Mr. Addison, Mr. Gee, Mr. Missisippi Law, Dr. Campbell, and many other writers of former times, as well as to several eminent writers of the present day; but ABOVE ALL *they rely* on the principles *constantly* recognised by the LEGISLATURE up to the year 1793, and which are so admirably illustrated in the *two* Reports of the Privy Council *now* presented to the Public.

The Shipping Interest had for several years forborne to represent to Government the apprehensions they entertained of the evil consequences which would arise from the suspension of the Act of Navigation, and such forbearance, they trust, will appear justifiable, when the circumstances in which the Country was placed between the years 1793 and 1801 are recollected; but immediately on the *appearance* of Peace they availed themselves of the opportunity, and in the *short* period which intervened between the *late* and the *present* War, they made *frequent* applications to Government during *Mr. Addington*'s administration, which proving ineffectual, they *reluctantly* petitioned, in 1802 and 1803, the Legislature against any *further* suspension of the Navigation Act, but *unsuccessfully*: no enquiry was then instituted on the subject, and the Navigation Act continued during the remainder of Mr. *Addington*'s Administration to be more *generally suspended* than before under the Act of the 43 George 3. c. 153. which authorises, under Orders in Council, the Importation, in *Neutral* Ships, of *any* goods from *any* place belonging to *any* State, *not* in Amity with the King, during the present war, and for six months afterwards. The Shipping Interest was thus circumstanced on Mr. PITT's return to Power, in the summer of 1804. The Shipowners in *London* and at the *Out Ports* then lost no time in renewing their applications *for Relief*, and several interviews took place; after which the expectation was held out, which has already been alluded to, with respect to the *European* and *Colonial* Trade: very little doubt indeed could be entertained of such an intention on the part of the *then* Administration, as Mr. PITT expressed HIS CONVICTION of the necessity of some alteration being *gradually* made in the *Relaxations* which had taken place in the Navigation and Colonial System of Great Britain. The Ship-owners had indeed good grounds, for confidence in that intention, from the measures* *actually* taken by the *then* Ministers, on the recommendation from the *Committee for Trade*, for *confining*, as far as circumstances would immediately permit, to *British* Bottoms the *whole of the Colonial Trade*, and of *reclaiming* that most salutary principle, that all *Supplies*, from whatever Country they came, should be conveyed to the West India Settlements in *British* Ships, as well as from HIS AVOWED INTENTION to *except* the bringing brandies † and other spirits from the general importation in *Neutral* Vessels *direct* from *Enemies Countries*, which would not only have materially relieved the British West India *Planters*, but have considerably benefited British *Ship-owners* without any loss to the Revenue, which surely may be much more effectually secured and protected whilst Trade is carried on in *British* than in *Foreign* Bottoms. This acknowledgment is an Act of mere Justice due to the Public Merits of the *most transcendant* STATESMAN that ever adorned the Councils of this Nation, not more conspicuous for his Talents, inflexible Integrity, and Firmness,

* See Earl Camden's Letters, in September 1804 and January 1805, to the Governors of the West India Islands, and Lord Castlereagh's Letter in September 1805, and various Minutes of the Board of Trade.

† See a Letter on this subject, dated London, April 1806, in Yorke's Political Review, vol. i. p. 917. Also other Letters and Essays in that work.

than for HIS CANDOUR *in retracing* HIS OWN MEASURES, when it appeared to him to be necessary to do so.

The Ship-owners are desirous also of expressing the obligations they are under to LORD SHEFFIELD, for his excellent " Strictures on the Necessity of inviolably " maintaining the Navigation and Colonial Syetem of " Great Britain,"—and to JOHN STEPHENS, Esq. for his learned, animated, and patriotic Work, intitled " *War in Disguise*;" both which they beg leave, *at this important crisis*, most earnestly to recommend to the *serious* attention and consideration of THEIR COUNTRYMEN: for unless the principles so fully elucidated and so ably defended by these eminent writers are in future *strictly adhered to* " We cannot rear or retain our Seamen, the grand " support of our present pre-eminence, nor preserve our " Country from falling below the level of surrounding " Nations."—It has been justly observed by Sir *William Temple*, that " the numbers and courage of *our Men*, " with the strength *of our Shipping*, have for many ages " past made us *a match* for the greatest of our Neighbours " *at Land*, and an *over-match* for the strongest *at Sea**."

The Society of Ship-owners think it important to state, that the *numerous body of Men* whose Capitals are

* " If we wisely keep at home the Army, which may be *essential* to our " domestic safety, act only on the defensive on shore, and *assert firmly* " *our belligerent Rights on the Ocean*, we shall find it more *frugal* by far to " continue at *open* War, than to suspend hostilities again, for a year or " two, by an anxious and dangerous Peace. Such a Use of our *maritime* " power as the State of Europe and the World would abundantly justify, " and as the *late* Conduct of the Enemy invites, would *give us means* of " maintaining the Contest for fifty years, if necessary, without an *ad-* " *ditional* tax, except such as France, her Allies and States under her " influence, would pay." See " *The Dangers of the Country*," page 97—also *ibid*, pages 5, 6, 98, 108, 109, &c.

embarked, at this time, in *British* Shipping, are not engaged in *other* Mercantile pursuits, but depend wholly on the returns they expect to receive from their property so employed. This observation is considered the more necessary from *recent inquiries* which have been made to ascertain who the Ship-owners *were*, they never having been before considered *distinct* from the *Merchants*, and that the property in Shipping had generally belonged to that very respectable and intelligent class of his Majesty's Subjects. It was evidently from the experience *the latter* had acquired, of *no profit* being to be derived from *Ship-owning*, that they withdrew their capitals from such concerns: it will be seen by the comparative* Statement of the expences incurred in the outfit of Ships, extracted from Accounts of *actual* disbursements and receipts in the years 1780, 1795, and 1805, being *periods of war*, that Provisions of all kinds have, on an average, *advanced* £84. 8*s.* 2*d.* per cent.; that Materials and Stores of all kinds have *advanced* in like manner £122. 10*s.* 2*d.* per cent.; and that Seamens' Wages have, on an average of the different classes of Seamen, *advanced* £39. 7*s.* 1*d.* per cent.; whilst *the Rates of Freight* have, on an average, *decreased* £6. 10*s.* 4*d.* per cent. †

* *Vide post*, Supplement, page clxxviii.

† *Vide* post, ibid, page lxvii. for a *similar* statement in periods of *peace*. These and the other Statements in the Supplement shew the *Loss actually sustained* on Capital embarked in *British* Shipping. It is with great concern the Ship-owners *understand*, it is *contemplated* by his Majesty's *present* Ministers to make the Duties on the *Tonnage* of Shipping PERPETUAL, although it was expressly stated in *Lord Sidmouth's* Administration, when *first* proposed, that it should be a WAR TAX, and *cease* with it; *Vide post*, Supplement, xci, and the Debates in Parliament in 1802 and 1803: indeed, it was declared, at that time, by the *then* Administration, to be a *Tax of Experiment*, and an Assurance was even held out, that if the Ship-owners could prove that the Payment of the Tonnage

The Society of Ship-Owners pledge themselves to substantiate these statements, and also the various other accounts adduced by them, in order to shew the *inadequacy* of the employment of *British* Shipping, arising *principally* from the *increased* competition of *Foreign* Vessels, by the impolitic admission of them into the Trade of this Country, and the ultimate depression it will produce on the *naval* power of Great Britain.

As the Account of the number of Ships and Vessels built in Great Britain between the 5th January, 1806, and the 5th January, 1807, distinguishing the Tonnage of *each* Ship and Vessel, and the Ports or Places where built, has not yet been produced, and laid before Parliament, the Society of Ship-Owners forbear to comment, further than in stating *they are apprehensive* it will appear that there has been a *very alarming decrease in Ship-building* throughout the Empire, and that the number of average sized Ships built in the last two years is *not equal* to the *actual consumption* of that class of shipping within that period.

London,
January, 1807.

Tonnage Duty was *adding* to their *Losses*, instead of *taking* from their *Gains*, the Tax should be abandoned. This fact can be proved by testimony the most credible, and which must be within the Recollection of many of the eminent Persons who supported, at that time, the Shipping Interest.

ERRATUM.

Page six, line 23, for House of Committee, read *House of Commons*.

A

STATE

OF THE

ALLEGATIONS AND EVIDENCE

PRODUCED, AND

OPINIONS OF *MERCHANTS* & OTHER *PERSONS*

GIVEN, TO THE COMMITTEE OF COUNCIL;

Extracted from their Report of the 31st of May, 1784,

ON HIS MAJESTY'S ORDER OF REFERENCE OF THE EIGHTH OF MARCH LAST,

Made upon the REPRESENTATION of the *West-India* PLANTERS and MERCHANTS, purporting to shew the distressed State of His Majesty's SUGAR COLONIES by the Operation of His Majesty's Order in Council of the 2d of *July*, 1783, and the Necessity of allowing a free Intercourse between the Sugar Colonies and the United States of *America*, in *American* Bottoms.

PRINTED IN THE YEAR MDCCLXXXIV;
AND
Reprinted by Order of the Society of Ship-owners of Great-Britain.

1806.

A

STATE

OF THE

ALLEGATIONS and EVIDENCE produced, and Opinions of Merchants and other Persons given, to the Committee of Council; extracted from their Report of the 31st of *May*, 1784, on His Majesty's Order of Reference, of the 8th of *March* last, made upon the Representation of the *West-India* Planters and Merchants, purporting to shew the distressed State of His Majesty's Sugar Colonies, by the Operation of His Majesty's Order in Council of the 2nd of *July*, 1783, and the Necessity of allowing a free Intercourse between the Sugar Colonies and the United States of *America*, in *American* Bottoms.

THE said representation contains the four following allegations, *viz.*

First.—That His Majesty's Sugar Colonies are at present in so great distress for want of a free intercourse between them and the United States of *America*, by *American* ships, that not a moment should be lost in granting further relief.

Second.—That the supplies derived to the said Sugar Colonies from the dominions of the said United States are in many instances, and at many seasons of the year, not to be had from any other country, at any price whatever; and that in many other inftances fuch fupplies are not to be had from any other places, but at prices wholly ruinous.

Third.—That the navigation between the North American Colonies, and His Majefty's Sugar Colonies, cannot be effectually carried on by Britifh fhips, on account of the heavy expence, uncertainty, and delay of fuch circuitous navigation, beyond that which would attend the direct navigation in American fhips.

Fourth.—That the planters in his Majesty's Sugar Colonies can no otherwife pay for the fupplies received from the dominions of the faid United States, than by the produce of their eftates; which produce, in many inftances, does not find any adequate vent in Great Britain, and if not taken off by the North Americans, would remain a dead weight upon all the reft of the produce of the faid Sugar Colonies.

Proofs in Support of the Firft Allegation.

IN fupport of the firft allegation, the planters and merchants laid before the committee an addrefs of the affembly of Jamaica, to the governor of the faid ifland, of the 19th November, 1783, ftating—That in confequence of the order in council of 2d July, ftaves, pine-boards, plank, and building-timber, had been carried to a moft exorbitant price; and that they had the jufteft reafons to fear, that, after every exertion they could make, their produce would perifh on their hands for want of the requifite package; and praying, therefore, that the governor would permit the importation from the United States of America, in American bottoms, of the articles enumerated in his Majefty's faid order in council; and alſo to permit the produce of the iſland to be exported in return; for the ſpace of nine months: which requeſt the governor had refuſed to comply with.—They alſo produced three letters from the ſaid iſland of Jamaica, complaining, in ſtrong but general terms, of the diſtreſs of the ſaid iſland, in conſequence of the reſtrictions laid on their trade with the United States, by the ſaid order in council; and they brought evidence to prove, that ſlaves had been ſold, on the 23d of December laſt, at 28*l*. currency, P. M. in ſome parts of the iſland; and about 40*l*. currency, P. M. in the north part of the iſland (the general price in time of peace having been from 10*l*. to 12*l*. P. M.)—They produced alſo the votes of the aſſembly of Jamaica, of the 6th of November, 1783, to ſhew that a meſſage had been ſent to the governor of the ſaid iſland, ſtating—That there were at that time in the town of Kingſton about 4,300 barrels of flour, beſides 700 barrels on board a veſſel in the harbour, which was not permitted to be landed; that a regular adequate ſupply of periſhable articles could alone prevent apprehenſion of ſcarcity; that the uncertainty of ſuch ſupply occaſioned the then high price of flour; and that a renewal of permiſſion for importation appeared to be the only remedy for the evil.

They further produced an addreſs of the aſſembly of Antigua to the governor, of the 9th October, 1783, complaining in ſtrong terms of the reſtriction laid on their commerce with the United States by the ſaid order in council; and ſtating that it appeared, from the beſt information, that the proviſions then at market would not anſwer the conſumption of the ſaid iſland, for more than two months; and that the prices of the ſaid proviſions were riſen nearly 50*l*. per cent.; and praying that permiſſion might be given to import the produce of the United States, and to export the produce of the ſaid iſland, in veſſels belonging to the ſaid States, until his Majeſty's pleaſure ſhould be known, or until a commercial treaty ſhould be definitively ſettled between Great Britain and the ſaid States: which requeſt the governor of Antigua had refuſed to comply with. They produced alſo a letter, dated 28th of December, from the ſaid iſland, ſtating, in general terms, that the negro proviſions and lumber were at a very high price, and that the ſmalleſt eſtates in the ſaid iſland muſt ſink under the accumulated diſadvantage they were loaded with, and all others muſt be leſſened in their value.—They alſo produced evidence to prove, that upon the arrival of the order in council in the iſland of Barbadoes, lumber roſe inſtantly from about 7*l.* to 25*l.* currency per 1,000 feet; but had ſince fallen to about 12*l.*, in conſequence of importation from the iſlands which were then in the poſſeſſion of the French.

They further alledged, That the iſlands which had been conquered by the French had, during the time they were under the French-government, been provided with ſupplies by the veſſels of the United States; and, having been but juſt ſurrendered to his Majeſty, were not, therefore, in the ſame diſtreſs for want of theſe articles as his Majeſty's other iſlands.

In addition to the foregoing evidence, the planters and merchants repreſented—That in Jamaica the ſeveral articles of ſupply were ſtill very near at the war price, owing to the uncertainty of procuring them; and that accounts had been received from the Leeward Iſlands of the high prices of thoſe articles there; and they alledged, that a great part of the ſupply they had of late received was brought by ſhips carrying on a contraband trade. They alſo produced a letter from Grenada, dated February 28th, 1784, ſtating, that every article of lumber was at a war price there; and another from Saint Chriſtopher's, of the 4th March, 1784, ſtating, that almoſt every article was very high; and another from Tortola, dated 31ſt March, 1784, ſaying, " At preſent we cannot buy a ſtave, hoop, or board in our iſland, and what we have by us coſt five joes; when in my time I have frequently bought ſuch lumber at $1\frac{1}{2}$ or 2 joes* per thouſand.

They alſo tranſmitted to the committee, at their deſire, the following abſtract of the prices current of lumber and proviſions at Kingſton in Jamaica, as publiſhed in the Kingſton Gazette, from the 20th of September 1783, to the 20th of March laſt, both incluſive; and alſo an account of the prices of the ſaid articles in time of peace.

* A joe is the thirty-six ſhilling piece.

ABSTRACT of the Current Caſh Prices at *Kingſton* in *Jamaica*, taken from the Royal Gazette, publiſhed by Authority.

	Flour per Barrel of 196 lb.	Staves per Hund.		Boards per plank, per 1,000 feet.				Pitch Pine Scantling per 1,000 feet	Shingles.		Wood Hoops.
		White Oak.	Red Oak	Common.	Cedar.	Cy-preſs.	Yellow Pine.		Boſton.	Cedar.	
1783.	l. s. l. s.	l.	l.	l.	l.			l.		l. s.	l.
September 20th —	3 10 to 4 —	12 to 15	13 —	10	30	—	—	15 —	l.2 to 2 15	5 10	10
24 { Proclamation publiſhed.											
October 18th —	6 15 to 7 —	35	20 —	18 to 20	35 to 40	28 —	25 —	30 —	3 15	7 10	10
November 8 —	3 5 to 3 15	35	25 —	18 to 20	35 to 40	28 —	25 —	30 —	3 15	7 10	10
1784. January 31 —	1 15 to 2 5	25	16 —	10 to 12	35 to 40	12 —	12 —	15 —	2 —	5 —	10
February 21 —	1 15	25	16 —	10 to 12	35 to 40	12 —	12 —	15 —	2 —	5 —	10
28 —	1 15	25	16 —	10 to 12	35 to 40	12 —	12 —	15 —	2 —	5 —	10
March 20 —	1 15	15	12 —	12 to 15	35 to 40	12 —	14 —	18 —	2 10	5 —	18
N. B. The Common Peace Prices are about	l. s. l. s. 1 5 to 2 5	l. l. 10 to 12	l. 8 to 10	5 to 10	—	6 to 12	6 to 12	8 to 12	2 5	2 15 to 3 10	10

And in the letter of the chairman, tranfmitting this account, it is faid, "That provifions of all kinds are of fo perifhable a nature in the Weft Indies, and the confumption both of provifions and lumber fo immenfe, that, unlefs the authorized channels of fupply are opened, the clandeftine ones are not to be relied upon as fufficient to protect the iflands from being again reduced to diftrefs in the courfe of a very few weeks."

PROOFS E CONTRA, TO THE FIRST ALLEGATION.

IN oppofition to the facts and obfervations before ftated, particularly in what regards the prefent ftate of the ifland of Jamaica, there was evidence laid before the committee, to the following effect.

That from the return made of the imports into the feveral ports of the ifland, previous to the month of November, 1783, the apprehenfions of want in the articles of lumber, &c. by no means warranted the pofitive and ftrong affertions, contained in the addrefs of the affembly of Jamaica, to the governor of that ifland. And that the governor of Jamaica had made early and repeated applications to the governors of Nova Scotia, and Canada, for an immediate fupply of fuch of the articles as were at that time wanted in the ifland, but which could not be expected to arrive there to anfwer the then demand.

The diftrefs which enfued upon the publication of his Majefty's aforefaid order in council, was ftated to be principally owing to the planters not having expected that any reftriction in this refpect would take place, and having omitted, therefore, to make provifion of thofe feveral articles by other means: for that it is evident from the abftract of prices current, as before ftated, as well as from other evidence, that

C

in the ſpace of about ten weeks the prices of lumber and proviſions began gradually to fall in the iſland of Jamaica, and continued falling very conſiderably to the 20th of March laſt. And further, that from the 12th of December to the 17th of March, incluſive, ſeventy-five Britiſh veſſels, navigated according to law, (the names of which are inſerted in the Appendix, N° 1) had arrived at Kingſton, with cargoes of lumber and proviſions; all which veſſels, except about ten, came from the ports of the United States—That theſe ſhips brought to Kingſton 18,000 barrels of flour, 559,050 ſtaves and heading, 796,253 feet of boards, ſcantling, &c. and 1,450,790 ſhingles.—And it was obſerved, that the quantity of flour before mentioned, viz. 18,000 barrels, is, according to what was imported in the year 1773, equal to the conſumption of the iſland for nine months.

Letters of various correſpondents laid before the committee, poſitively aſſert, that the iſland was in no diſtreſs for want of any of the articles before mentioned.—One, dated the 10th of January laſt, ſays, "We are almoſt as well ſupplied already as before the diſturbance took place, and a few more veſſels will make every thing very reaſonable."—Another, dated the 18th January, encloſing an account of prices current, ſays, "We have received ample ſupplies for this crop; the prices are nearly as reaſonable as they were ſold at this market before the war."—Another, dated Kingſton, the 22d February, ſays, "Never was this market ſo overſtocked with flour, as it is at preſent; Philadelphia flour can be purchaſed under 30s. per barrel, and from there being upwards of 20,000 barrels for ſale in Kingſton, good and bad, none are inclined to ſpeculate in ſo dangerous an article: two thirds muſt be unfit for uſe, before the other third can be uſed, unleſs a foreign demand takes place, which at preſent is not likely."—Another, dated Kingſton, the 29th of February, ſays, "Proviſions of all kinds, and every ſpecies of goods from America, are in the utmoſt plenty."

There was alſo laid before the committee, an account of prices current at Kingſton, on the 20th of March, as tranſmitted from thence; which is as follows:

ARTICLES.	Prices Current.			Prices Sterling.		
	£.	s.	d.	£.	s.	d.
Superfine Philadel. flour, per barrel	1	10	—	1	1	5
Common ditto per ditto	1	7	6	—	19	7$\frac{1}{2}$
Ship Bread, per cwt. - - - -	1	5	—	—	17	10$\frac{1}{4}$
White Oak Staves & Heading, per M.	13	—	—	9	5	8$\frac{1}{2}$
Red Oak Staves - - - - - -	10	—	—	7	2	10$\frac{1}{4}$
Pitch Pine Boards - - - - - -	12	—	—	8	11	5$\frac{1}{8}$
Yellow Pine ditto - - - - - -	10	—	—	7	2	10$\frac{1}{4}$
Common Boards - - - - - -	8	—	—	5	14	3$\frac{1}{4}$
Common Shingles - - - - - -	1	5	—	—	17	10$\frac{1}{4}$
Meſs Beef and Pork - - - - -	3	—	—	2	2	10$\frac{1}{4}$
Butter, per lb. - - - - - - -	—	1	—	—	—	8$\frac{1}{2}$
Spermaceti Candles - - - - -	—	3	6	—	2	6

And evidence was given to the committee, by two eminent merchants, who had reſided many years in Jamaica, that they never recollected the article of flour being ſo cheap; and that many of the other articles, even before the war, would have been thought pretty reaſonable, particularly ſtaves; and, as the prices of theſe articles at Philadelphia, particularly of white and red oak ſtaves, have ariſen, during and ſince the war, more than double, it was inferred, that, in proportion to the firſt coſt in America, they are now cheaper at Jamaica than they were before the war.

The committee examined the gentlemen laſt mentioned, in order to learn their opinion of what were the average prices of lumber and proviſions at Kingſton, for ten years before the war; and they obtained from them the following account, in which they all agreed.

		l.	s.		l.	s.	Medium.
Superfine Flour, per Barrel, ſuppoſed to be 200 lb.	from	2	9	to	2	19	£. 2 14
White Oak Staves from Philadelphia, per 1,000 —	from	10	—	to	14	—	12 —
Red Oak Staves, per 1,000 — —	from	8	—	to	12	—	10 —
Common Boards, per 1,000 feet. —	from	7	—	to	10	—	8 10
Cypreſs and Yellow Pine Boards —	from	8	—	to	11	—	9 10
Pitch Pine Scantlings and Boards —	from	9	—	to	12	—	10 10
Boſton Shingles, per 1,000 feet —	from	—	15	to	1	5	1 —
Cedar and Cypreſs Shingles, per 1,000 feet — —	from	3	—	to	3	10	3 5
Wood Hoops, from America, per 1,000	from	5	—	to	8	—	6 10
Ditto from Great Britain — —	from	10	—	to	15	—	12 10

N. B. The prices of the before-mentioned articles are very variable in Jamaica:—the above are the medium prices; the retail prices would be proportionably higher.

Flour, before the war, was uſually ſold by the 100 lb.—it was never under 20*s.* the 100 lb. frequently as high as 35*s.* and 40*s.* and ſometimes 45*s.*

White oak ſtaves from Philadelphia, with proportion of heading, the long M. 1,200.—They have been known as low as 8*l.* and as high as 22*l.*

Red oak ſtaves, the long M.—They have been known as low as 7*l.* and as high as 20*l.*

Common Boards, per 1,000 feet:—They have been known as low as 5*l.* and as high as 15*l.*

Cypreſs and Yellow pine boards, per 1,000 feet:—They have been known as low as 6*l.* and as high as 15*l.*

Pitch pine ſcantling and boards:—They have been known as low as 8*l.* and as high as 18*l.*

Cedar and cypreſs ſhingles, per 1,000 feet:—They have been known as low as 2*l.* 15*s.* and as high as 3*l.* 15*s.*

Wood hoops from America, the long M. 1,200.

Ditto from Great Britain, the long M. 1,200.

To ſhew at one view the difference in the prices current of lumber and proviſions at Kingſton, on the 20th of March, and the prices of the ſaid articles prior to the war, as ſtated in the foregoing accounts, the committee inſerted in their report the following tables.

COMPARATIVE STATE of the Prices Current of Lumber and Provifions, at *Kingfton* in *Jamaica*, on 20th *March*, according to the Two Accounts delivered in to the Committee.

FIRST ACCOUNT.

		l.	s.	d
Superfine Flour, per Barrel of 196 lb		1	15	0
White Oak Staves, per 1,000		15	0	0
Red Oak Ditto, per Ditto		12	0	0
Common Boards, per 1,000 feet	12*l.* to	15	0	0
Cedar	35*l.* to	40	0	0
Cypress		12	0	0
Yellow Pine		14	0	0
Pitch Pine Scantling, per 1,000 feet		18	0	0
Shingles, Boston		2	10	0
Cedar		5	0	0
Wood Hoops, per 1,000		18	0	0

SECOND ACCOUNT.

	l.	s.	d
Superfine Philadelphia Flour, per Bushel	1	10	0
White Oak Staves and Heading, per M.	13	0	0
Red Oak Staves	10	0	0
Common Boards	8	0	0
Yellow Pine	10	0	0
Pitch Pine Boards	12	0	0
Common Shingles	1	5	0

COMPARATIVE STATE of the Average Prices of Lumber and Provifions, at *Kingfton* in *Jamaica*, before the War, according to the Two Accounts delivered in to the Committee.

First Account.

	l.	s.		l.	s.	Medium. l.	s.	d.
Superfine Flour, per Barrel of 196 lb. -	1	5	to	2	5	1	15	0
White Oak Staves, per 1,000 - - -	10	0	to	12	0	11	0	0
Red Oak Staves, per do.	8	0	to	10	0	9	0	0
Common Boards, per 1,000 feet - -	5	0	to	10	0	7	10	0
Cypress and Yellow Pine, per ditto - -	6	0	to	12	0	9	0	0
Pitch Pine Scantling, per ditto - - -	8	0	to	12	0	10	0	0
Shingles, Boston -	2	5						
Ditto, Cedar - -	2	15	to	3	10	3	2	6
Wood Hoops, per 1,000	10	0						

Second Account.

	l.	s.		l.	s.	Medium. l.	s.	d.
Superfine Flour, per Barrel -	2	9	to	2	19	2	14	0
White Oak Staves, Phila.	10	0	to	14	0	12	0	0
Red Oak Staves -	8	0	to	12	0	10	0	0
Common Boards -	7	0	to	10	0	8	10	0
Cypress and Yellow Pine Boards - -	8	0	to	11	0	9	10	0
Pitch Pine Scantling and Boards - -	9	0	to	12	0	10	10	0
Shingles, Boston -	0	15	to	1	5	1	0	0
Do. Cedar and Cypress	3	0	to	3	10	3	5	0
Wood Hoops from America - - -	5	0	to	8	0	6	10	0
Do. from Great Britain	10	0	to	15	0	12	10	0

FURTHER PROOFS.

TO throw ſome light on theſe two contradictory accounts, and to obtain ſuch information as might aſſiſt his Majeſty's judgment in deciding to which of the two the greateſt attention ought to be paid, the committee thought it right again to examine the ſaid two merchants; who ſaid, they never conſidered the prices current, as publiſhed in the Kingſton Royal Gazette, as very exact—That they are apt to continue them from one paper to another; and that they have known the actual prices to vary during the time that the prices have appeared in the Gazette to be the ſame—That, beſides, they are generally the higheſt retail prices, and at the longeſt credit, which is commonly about twelve months—That the retailer is generally paid for the ſeveral articles in produce; and that the American factor or ſupercargo is paid in produce, if he will take it, if not, money, or bills of exchange, which is generally the caſe, and he has a right to make his option—That the aforeſaid prices current of the 20th of March were agreeable to the prices ſent from their houſe at Kingſton in Jamaica, which they ſaid undoubtedly deſerved the moſt credit, in preference to thoſe publiſhed in the Kingſton Gazette, being prices taken from real ſales, and ſent over to them for their conduct in trade. And being aſked, If they could aſſign the cauſe of the difference between the ſaid prices current ſent them, and thoſe publiſhed in the Kingſton Gazette? they ſaid, They imagined that the former were the cargo prices, paid for in caſh; the latter, the retail prices, with profit and credit.—The truth of the prices current on the 20th March, and the average prices before the war, laſt ſtated, and the reſt of the evidence of the ſaid two merchants, was confirmed by the teſtimony of another merchant of great experience in this trade.

The committee ſtate, That they have not been able to procure the ſame ample information of the condition of his Majeſty's other iſlands in the Weſt Indies, with reſpect to lumber and proviſions, as of the iſland of Jamaica; nor have the planters and merchants produced any account of prices current in Barbadoes or any of the Leeward Iſlands—That in reſpect to the addreſs of the aſſembly of Antigua, of the 9th of October 1783, to the governor of that iſland, the miſchiefs and calamities which they apprehended would follow from the reſtrictions of his Majeſty's order in council have been thought only imaginary; and, as a proof that their fears were not founded in reaſon, an account hath been produced to the committee, of what American produce had been imported into that iſland in the ſpace of one month after the publication of the ſaid order in council; by which it appears, that from the 6th of October to the 12th of November laſt, twenty-one veſſels had entered there, with ſundry articles of American produce, containing, among other things, 1,679 barrels of flour, 606 barrels and 174 kegs of biſcuit, 580 buſhels of corn, 256,000 feet of lumber, 34,650 ſtaves and heading, 1,928,000 ſhingles, and 484 cedar poſts, beſides other ſmaller articles.

Information was alſo given to the committee, that by letters from Barbadoes, dated the 21ſt of March, it appears that there were no particular complaints there, at that time, for want of any of the articles they are ſupplied with from America—That lumber was ſelling for about 9*l.* currency per thouſand, and flour pretty reaſonable—That ſeveral ſhips had arrived at Barbadoes from America, and others were expected—That one ſhip belonging to Briſtol had arrived from Piſcataqua a ſhort time before, laden with lumber.— A merchant, who had two brigs going from Virginia with lumber and flour, informed the committee, that his correſpondent in Virginia wrote to him, on the 13th of March,

D

"that he was afraid the flour imported into Barbadoes would be a loſing article."

An account has been alſo received from Roſeau in Dominica, dated February 3, 1784, giving an aſſurance, that there were then more merchant veſſels there, than there were during the five years the French were in poſſeſſion of that iſland.

And it was repreſented, that great numbers of the ſhips before mentioned, which had brought plenty of lumber and proviſions to Jamaica, had firſt touched at the ſeveral ports in the Leeward Iſlands, in their way down to Jamaica; and, as they had brought part of their cargoes from thence unſold, it was inferred they muſt have left plenty there.

The following account of prices current at London, on the 2d of December laſt, and at Philadelphia on the ſame day, of the following articles, was produced to the committee.

	At London.	*At Philadelphia.*
Fine flour, per 100lb.	£.0 16 0	£.0 15 9
Common, do. per do.	0 14 0	0 13 0
Meſs beef, per barrel -	2 2 6	2 2 6
Ditto pork, per do. -	2 8 0	3 0 0
Herrings, per do. -	1 5 0	0 18 0
White oak ſtaves, per M.	6 5 0	6 0 0
Sterling -	£.13 10 6	Ster. £.13 9 3

By this account it appears, that an aſſortment of the foregoing goods could at that time have been purchaſed very near as cheap at London as at Philadelphia; and they could have been carried cheaper from London than from Philadelphia; for the price of freight from England to the Weſt Indies is 30 per cent. leſs than from Philadelphia: But it was obſerved, that this account could not be depended on as a ſtandard of prices for the future.

Information was alſo given to the committee, That a great part of the rum caſks lately made uſe of in Jamaica were puncheons, that carried out dry goods from Great Britain, or puncheon packs.

That the price of puncheon packs here at preſent, is from 13 to 14*s.* ſterling, which is equal to 18 or 19*s.* currency; and that, including freight and the charge of ſetting them up in Jamaica, they can be afforded there at the rate of from 25 to 30 ſhillings currency; and that, during the time lumber and ſtaves were cheapeſt at Jamaica, puncheons never ſold for leſs than from 25*s.* to 30*s.* currency; at which rate the planter generally ſells the puncheon with the rum in time of peace.

Proofs in Support of the Second Allegation.

IN ſupport of the ſecond allegation, viz. " That the ſupplies which the ſugar colonies receive from the dominions of the United States of America, are in many inſtances, and at many ſeaſons of the year, not to be had from any other country, at any price whatever; and that, in many other inſtances, ſuch ſupplies are not to be had from any other places, but at prices wholly ruinous;"

The planters and merchants produced to the committee, an account of the total import from North America, into the Britiſh Weſt India iſlands, in the years 1771, 1772, and 1773, diſtinguiſhing the quantities imported from the United States of America, from the quantities imported from Canada, Nova Scotia, and Newfoundland; which account is inſerted in the Appendix, No. 2.—One of the objects for producing this account was, to ſhew the great value of theſe imports, which they eſtimated to amount annually to above 700,000*l.* ſterling. Another object was, to ſhew how very ſmall a proportion of theſe imports were brought from Canada, Nova Scotia, and Newfoundland (the only colonies in North America that now remain under the dominion of Great Britain). And, in order to prove that the Weſt India iſlands could not be ſupplied with corn from Canada, the planters and merchants alledged, that there was then a ſhip loading in the river Thames for Canada, which actually carried out flour—That during the late war, the army in Canada amounted to no more than 15,000 men, and that the province could not ſupply them, but the whole ſupply was ſent from England—That in one year the army was diſtreſſed, becauſe the contractor relied upon the produce of the province for their ſupply.

They alſo alledged, that the crops of wheat in Canada are always uncertain, and that Canada is at this time nearly in the ſame ſtate of cultivation as when it firſt came into our poſſeſſion—That no Britiſh ſubjects have ſettled there, one family alone excepted—That the number of its inhabitants may amount to 100,000, moſtly Catholics, and not poſſeſſing any ſpirit of induſtry. They acknowledged, however, that in the years 1772, 1773, and 1774, when the ſouthern parts of Europe were in great diſtreſs for corn, a large exportation from Canada had been made, and in one of thoſe years to the amount of 400,000 buſhels.

In order to ſhew, that the Weſt India iſlands could not receive a proper ſupply of lumber from Canada, they alledged, that though the white oak from Canada is very good for ſtaves, the other ſpecies of lumber were of an inferior quality, and always ſold in the Weſt Indies at a lower price than that imported from other parts—That they want hands in that colony to get wood, the price of labour being from half a dollar to a dollar per day.—With reſpect to Nova Scotia, they alledged, that though the increaſe of inhabitants lately gone there may in time lead to ſome ſupply of grain, lumber, and other articles from that colony, yet at present Nova Scotia is supplied with these from other parts —That the loyalists sent to Nova Scotia carried provisions with them, and are themselves, for the most part, men of a different description from labourers—That there was in the colony also a want of hands, and that the price of lumber was greatly raised, in the countries bordering on Nova Scotia, in consequence of the demand for it from thence; and that, in short, neither Nova Scotia nor Canada were in a better condition to furnish the islands with supplies than before the war.

THE Committee, after having heard all that the planters and merchants thought fit to offer in evidence on this head, judged it expedient to proceed to a further investigation of this subject.

It appeared, by the information received from numerous respectable authorities, as well as by the accounts laid before the committee, that the province of Canada is able to export great quantities of wheat and flour for the consumption of the British West India islands—That in the years 1771, 1772, 1773, there were imported annually, from all parts of America, into the British West India islands, at an average, 132,750 barrels of flour: during nearly the same period, that is, from 1771 to 1775, inclusive, there was exported from Canada *annually*, at an average, 265,000 bushels of wheat; and that the common price of the grain, before the war, did not exceed 3*s*. per bushel.—They observe, that soon after the year 1775, the exportation wholly ceased, in consequence of the war, when great numbers of the inhabitants of the province were employed in the public service, either as batteaux men to transport provisions in their boats, or as waggoners to convey them by land, or as seamen employed upon the lakes—That this diminished the cultivation of the country, and was the caufe that fo much corn was not produced—That the enemy's troops were fometimes in poffeffion of a part of the country, and that at other times the inhabitants were in apprehenfion of them—That in the year 1778, the governor prohibited the exportation of grain, and that the prohibition was ftill in force on the 21ft day of September laft; but that the committee hath been affured, no flour was imported during the war, except for the ufe of the troops and Indians.

It was further reprefented, that this prohibition operated as a great difcouragement to the induftry of the farmer; but all the witneffes agree, that the exportation of grain from Canada will in future revive and increafe, *efpecially if the Weft India market is fecured to them;* and that feveral perfons of great experience are of opinion, that an annual export of 300,000 bufhels may be depended upon—That before the war, the trade of Canada, in flour, was checked for want of proper mills to grind their corn, and they frequently fent grain to Philadelphia for that purpofe; but fince the peace, proper mill ftones have been imported, and new mills have been erected at a great expence, in convenient places; fo that their flour in future will be much finer, more free from bran, and fitter for exportation, and the commerce of the province in this article will be thereby greatly improved and extended.—And the committee have been affured, by a perfon of very refpectable authority, who from his long refidence there muft be beft acquainted with the nature of the climate, that he never knew the crop of grain materially fail till laft year, which happened to be unufually rainy.

It alfo appeared, that great quantities of lumber can be furnifhed from Canada, and the market of Quebec, where it will be exchanged for Britifh manufactures; and that the Canadians have learnt to cut their lumber to great advantage, by floating mills, of a new conftruction, built at a third of the expence of ordinary mills.

It was obferved, that the navigation of the river Saint Lawrence, which is frozen a confiderable part of the year, is a great impediment to the trade of this country. But though this may materially affect lumber, the freight of which, as a bulky article, is a material confideration, yet it cannot much injure the trade in flour, which, if properly packed, is not liable to damage in a fhort time.

It was further ftated, that Nova Scotia will foon be able to fupply great quantities of lumber; and that, if grants of lands are properly made, and fecured to the inhabitants, they will, in about three years, be able to furnifh, at moderate prices, moft of the articles which the Weft India iflands can want from North America. And, though the fea coaft, from Cape Canfo to Cape Sable, is rocky and barren, and produces nothing but fir-trees, the interior parts of the country, and the banks of all the rivers that empty themfelves into the Bay of Fundy, have as fine a foil as any part of the world: The peninfula is fitted for dairy farms; and there are immenfe tracts of good land on the other fide of the Bay of Fundy, and on the river St. John's, Pedicodiack, and others of lefs note, which are proper for every fort of tillage: and that the whole country produces the fineft garden vegetables in the world, particularly potatoes.

Affurance was given to the committee, that the climate of Nova Scotia is fine and healthy, and that the number of new fettlers there amount to near 30,000; are induftrious, and extremely anxious to cultivate the land allotted to them— That the neutral French, who ftill remain, were always an induftrious people; and that, before the year 1754, fuch of them as were fettled at Beaux Sejiours, Tintamarre, and other places of the province, fupplied Canada, and other French fettlements in North America, with a confiderable quantity of grain; and that they and all the old inhabitants, when they are no longer in a precarious ftate with refpect to the government under which they are to live, will follow the example of the new fettlers, and will learn from them to improve the country to great advantage, efpecially if encouragement is given to their induftry, *by fecuring to them proper markets.*—And the committee were affured, from good authority, that upon the like encouragement the population of Nova Scotia will be increafed.

It appeared alfo, that great parts of this country abound with lumber, particularly white oak; and that a number of faw mills are already erected in that province, and that more will be erected as foon as the grants are fettled.

It alfo appeared to the committee, that there are 1,500,000 acres in the ifland of Cape Breton, capable of producing any fort of European grain, and remarkably fit for garden vegetables; and, though the coaft is very much fubject to fogs, the air in the center is dry, and fit for the produce of grain —That it abounds alfo with great quantities of lumber, pine of every dimenfion, oak of various kinds, white and red (the former in plenty), afh and elm, beech, birch, and maple, which grow to great fcantlings—That thefe woods lie contiguous to the coaft, or on navigable rivers; and that there are a great number of ftreams in the ifland fit to erect faw-mills thereon; and it is not doubted but that lumber fufficiently proper for every purpofe may be procured in Canada, Nova Scotia, and Cape Breton; and that the difadvantage to which Canada is fubject in point of navigation, is reverfed with refpect to Nova Scotia and Cape Breton, the navigation from thefe countries to the Weft India iflands being performed in a lefs time than from the ports of the United States.

Befides thefe articles, which are the ftaple commodities of thefe countries, there are others, of which the Weft India iſlands ſtand in need: two of theſe are rice and India corn. The conſumption of the firſt, in the Weſt India iſlands, is very ſmall, amounting, at an average of three years, to no more than 20,563 barrels annually.—It is certain that theſe articles cannot be produced either in Canada or Nova Scotia. India corn is a more neceſſary article; and the quantity imported into our Weſt India iſlands, at an average of three years, is 401,464 buſhels annually.—And the committee were informed there is a great deal of India corn now grown in Nova Scotia, and that a great deal more will be planted this ſpring on Saint John's river, provided the grants are confirmed to the new ſettlers and provincials in due time; and that parts of Canada are capable alſo of producing it.—It was obſerved, that the grain of this India corn may poſſibly not be ſo large and fine as that which is produced in the ſouthern parts of America; but that it may anſwer for the ſame uſes nearly as well—That it is certain that Canada and Nova Scotia can and will produce all the ſubſtitutes for India corn, viz. beans, peas, barley, oats, and potatoes, at the moſt reaſonable rates; with which ſubſtitutes, except potatoes, the planters during the laſt war fed their negroes—That there is alſo no doubt, but in a ſhort time great quantities of India corn, of the fineſt ſort, may be produced in the iſlands of Bahama, where there is a ſoil and climate perfectly fitted for it; to which a large colony are already gone, and more are expected to arrive; and that from theſe iſlands the navigation to the Weſt India iſlands is very eaſy and ſhort.

Another article of which the Weſt India iſlands ſtand in need, is live ſtock, and ſalted beef and pork. Live ſtock can be furniſhed in great quantities from Nova Scotia. It furniſhed the Britiſh army, whilſt it was at Boſton, with a plentiful ſupply of it, though it was not then peopled with half the inhabitants it is at preſent; and the ſhortneſs of the

E

navigation from this country to the West India islands, is a favourable circumstance with respect to this supply.

The committee also state, that besides salted beef and pork, which may be supplied from both Canada and Nova Scotia, the West Indies can be furnished *with those articles in plenty*, and of a superior quality, from Great Britain, and *particularly from Ireland:* And it was stated to the committee, that the salted beef and pork from America is of a *loose* and *open* texture, and *easily goes to decay* in hot climates; so that, all circumstances considered, those articles may be had on *cheaper* terms (in the opinion of several witnesses) from Great Britain and Ireland, *than from any part of North America.*

The last important article of provision which the West India islands stand in need of, is dried and pickled fish; and there were stated sufficient reasons for believing, that the whole supply *can be furnished* by one or other of the fisheries of Great Britain and Ireland, and those of Newfoundland, Canada, and Nova Scotia.—The quantity imported into the British West India islands, according to the account the committee have received, is 159,669 quintals of dried fish annually.

The cod fish imported into the islands is of an inferior quality to that which is sent to the European market, being principally for the food of negroes: something more than nine tenths of this quantity was imported into his Majesty's islands by ships belonging to the New England provinces; but a considerable part of this, that is 67,000 quintals, the New Englanders annually purchased of the fishermen at Newfoundland; *so that of this they were merely the carriers.* The price of cod at the ports of exportation in New England, was considerably *dearer* than at Newfoundland, nearly as 9 to 7; but it assisted the traders of New England in making up their assortments for the West India markets;

and, as they purchafed this fifh with rum of their own diftilling, at Newfoundland, fo they fold it in the Weft Indies, for rum of a finer quality, and for fugar and melaffes, and made thereby a profitable trade.—Newfoundland alone is faid to be fufficient for the fupply of dried and pickled cod; but the fituation of Nova Scotia is fo favourable for carrying on the fifheries, being much nearer the fifhing banks than the ports of New England, that there is no doubt but they will have a confiderable fhare in this commerce; and it appeared, that great advantages will be derived from *a free intercourfe* between Newfoundland, Nova Scotia, and the Weft India iflands, for the exchange of their refpective produce.—That in addition to the dried and pickled cod, the Weft India market requires a fupply of falted mackarel, herrings, and other fmall fifh: that part of thefe, particularly the herrings, *may be exported from Great Britain and Ireland*, which are of a fuperior quality to any fifh of this fort in America; and, by accounts laid before the committee, can be fupplied in great quantities. Pickled mackarel and falmon may be furnifhed from the fifheries on the coafts and in the rivers of Nova Scotia and Labrador, where they may be catched in great plenty.

Proofs in Support of the Third Allegation.

IN fupport of the Third Allegation; viz. " That the navigation between the North American colonies, and the fugar colonies, cannot be effectually carried on by Britifh fhips, on account of the heavy expence, uncertainty, and delay of fuch circuitous navigation, beyond that which would attend the direct navigation in American fhips;"—the planters and merchants urged, that before the laft war, more than three parts in four of the ſhips employed in carrying on the commerce between the Britiſh Weſt India iſlands and North America, were American; and they produced two accounts, by which it appeared, that the number of ſhips ſo employed in the year 1772, amounted to 1208; of which only 13 came from the colonies now under the dominion of his Majeſty; that is, 5 from Canada, 6 from Newfoundland, and 2 from Nova Scotia. They inferred alſo, from the number of veſſels being ſo great, that their tonnage muſt have been ſmall, and conſequently they could not be Britiſh ſhips employed in the American trade, which are ſcarce ever *of leſs burthen* than 250 or 300 tons. They produced alſo another paper, to ſhew, that of 561 ſail, which entered at the port of Kingſton in Jamaica in the year 1774, 131 were Britiſh built, and 422 American built. They ſaid, that upon an experiment made for 2 or 3 ſucceſſive years, of carrying on the trade by a circuitous voyage, that is, by ſending ſhips from England to America to take in lumber, and carry the ſame from thence into the iſlands, it was found not to anſwer—That the ſhips did not ſave themſelves in point of expence; and that it could never anſwer to a merchant to employ ſhips in ſuch circuitous voyage upon ſpeculation.—And being aſked, Whether there was any number of ſhips, belonging to the Weſt India iſlands, employed in the trade between the iſlands and America? they anſwered, It was believed there were none.

E CONTRA.

UPON this ſubject the committee examined a number of eminent merchants trading to North America and the Weſt Indies, as well as other perſons who had been employed in his Majeſty's ſervice in America; and, upon the whole of the evidence laid before the committee, it appeared to them, that there never was a period *in which this country was better prepared* than it is at prefent, to enter into any new branch of the carrying trade.—Many feamen have lately been difcharged from the fhips of war, and many mercantile veffels, with their crews, difmiffed from the public fervice; and the committee have been affured, that, from the circumftances before mentioned, there is at prefent in this country *an overftock of fhipping* which wants employment; fo that the price of freight from Great Britain to America has fallen as low as it was in the laft peace; that is, from 8*l.* per ton to about 3*l.* to about Quebec, and about 2*l.* to other parts of America—and that there is no doubt that the freight from America to the Weft Indies will fall as low as it was in the laft peace, *though confined* to Britifh fhipping.

The committee alfo ftate, that it has been obferved to them that the owners of Britifh veffels, concerned in the Weft India trade, have long laboured *under great difadvantages* from the difficulty of procuring *outward freights* for their veffels; but that now, by going firft to North America, and from thence to the Weft Indies, and fo home, they will be fure of two freights, and perhaps three, inftead of little more than one: And it is alledged, that they will reap this benefit with *very fmall additional charges* in the payment of feamen's wages and port duties. And it has been proved to the committee, that though the fhips employed in the Weft India trade from the port of London, called eftablifhed fhips, have not hitherto engaged in this circuitous commerce—and, being large fhips, of great expence, might not, upon trial, find it for their advantage—yet that fhips from *the out ports frequently engaged in it*, fometimes by going firft to North America, taking a cargo of lumber from thence for the iflands in the Weft Indies, and running home freighted with fugar and other Weft India produce; and that at other times they went firſt for the Weſt India iſlands, with ſupercargoes, who employed their veſſels in a trip to the continent for lumber, while they were purchaſing rum and other produce of the iſlands for their homeward voyage—That, in particular, ten or twelve ſhips have been known to come to Georgia in a year, that were employed in this trade, and others to the Carolina's for the ſame purpoſe; and it has been proved to the committee, that there are *ten large ſhips* from the port of London already deſtined for this circuitous trade, and three others intended to be employed in the like manner, whoſe chief object is the freight from America to Jamaica; and that theſe ſhips will go from hence even in ballaſt, in caſe a freight outward cannot be obtained, becauſe they will, perhaps, make, by freight from America to Jamaica, 2,000*l.* or 2,500*l.* whereas, in all probability, (as was the caſe laſt year) they would not make above 800*l.* or 900*l.* from London to Jamaica.

On this head, the committee obſerve, that the number of Britiſh ſhips which ſeized the opportunity of going from North America to the Weſt India iſlands, with lumber and proviſions, on the *firſt notice* of the order in council (as already ſtated) is a clear proof *that this branch of commerce is profitable*; and, as a further proof of the value of this commerce, the freight from North America to the Weſt Indies is from 30*l.* to 40*l.* per cent. more than from Great Britain to the Weſt Indies.

Information was alſo given to the committee, that, beſides the ſhips before mentioned, there are 12 ſail of Britiſh ſhips eſtabliſhed at Jamaica, for carrying on the trade between that iſland and the continent of America, beſides others intended to be fitted out; to which may be added the ſhips of Canada and Nova Scotia, which will be employed in this trade; And it has been proved to the committee, that many ſhip-carpenters have ſettled in Nova Scotia, for the purpoſe of ſhip building; and, if the trade to the Weſt India iſlands is confined to Britiſh ſhipping, it is expected that many more perſons of that deſcription will be induced to ſettle in Nova Scotia, where they will find timber of every ſort fit for ſhip-building; and, as the tide in the Bay of Fundy riſes very high, the harbours of that country are better fitted for building ſhips than any of the continent of North America. —Information has been alſo given to the committee, that before the war, ſhips of between 200 and 300 tons were built in Canada, for which they have timber in great plenty; and that, beſides what have been mentioned, the intercourſe between the Weſt Indies and America will be carried on by ſloops *belonging* to the Bermuda and Bahama iſlands, which have always had a principal ſhare of this trade.

The accounts produced by the Weſt India planters and merchants, before ſtated, ſhew, that the number of veſſels which entered the ports of the Britiſh Weſt India iſlands in 1772, with the produce of North America, was 1208; and that, on an average of three years preceding the war, the number of veſſels that entered thoſe ports with the produce of North America was 1610, containing 115,634 tons, and navigated by 9,718 men: but, as the veſſels employed in this trade were generally able to make 3 trips in the year, the above numbers muſt be divided by 3, in order to ſhew the number of ſhips or veſſels, the quantity of tonnage, and the number of men actually ſo employed; the real number, therefore, will turn out to be 533 ſhips, containing 38,544 tons, and navigated by 3,339 men: and it has been ſhewn, by three different calculations laid before the committee, that the *value of this freightage*, in a commercial light, is not leſs than 245,000*l.* a year.

Proofs in Support of the Fourth Allegation.

IN ſupport of the fourth allegation; viz. "That the planters in his Majeſty's Sugar Colonies can no otherwiſe pay for the ſupplies received from the dominions of the ſaid United States, than by the produce of their eſtates; which produce, in many inſtances, does not find any adequate vent in Great Britain, and, if not taken off by the North Americans, would remain a dead weight upon all the reſt of the produce of the ſaid Sugar Colonies;"—the planters and merchants produced accounts to ſhew, that, beſides ſmaller articles, there was exported to North America,

In the Years			
1773.	Sugar,	3,776	Hhds.
	Rum,	32,265	Puncheons.
1774.	Sugar,	5,325	Hhds.
	Rum,	43,488	Puncheons.

They alledged, that the Americans then took, from the Britiſh Weſt India iſlands, their produce in payment for nearly the amount of what they imported. They admitted, that the rum exported to North America was for American conſumption only, and none of it afterwards re-exported. They alledged, that before the war, no foreign rum was conſumed in North America, except ſome ſmuggled from particular places, none being permitted to be made in the French iſlands until lately, that the governor of Martinique had iſſued a proclamation, giving licence to American merchants to erect a rum diſtillery at the Bay of Gallery, and proper ciſterns for keeping melaſſes near the town of St. Pierre—That the Americans took melaſſes from the French iſlands, which they diſtilled into a rum of very inferior quality, known by the name of *New England Spirit*; that a trifling quantity of the ſame was exported to Africa, and ſome uſed to be ſent to Canada, until diſtilleries were eſtabliſhed in that province.—And the planters and merchants informed the committee, that, it was univerfally underftood at Jamaica that a gentleman, formerly of London, was gone from Jamaica to the French iflands, with a view of pufhing to the utmoft extent the diftilleries for rum eftablifhed in the French iflands, and improving the manufacture of that commodity; and they obferved that the bringing thofe diftilleries to a condition proper for fupplying the demand for rum from the United States muft be a work of time; and that the true rule whereby to form a judgment of the effect the faid diftilleries might have upon the export of rum from the Britifh Weft Indies, was not either from the prefent price, or the prefent demand; but that we ought to look forward to a future period.—The planters and merchants brought with them no account of the prefent prices of rum, either at Jamaica or the other iflands; and letters were produced to fhew the low prices and fmall demand for rum, in February and March laft, at Granada and Saint Chriftopher's, being fo low as 3*s.* and 2*s.* 6*d.* per gallon; and it was agreed, by all whom the committee have examined on this head, that rum was the principal article which the Britifh Weft India iflands fent to America before the war, in return for the produce of that continent.

The price of fugar in the Britifh iflands is fo much higher than in the other iflands, that the Americans always preferred going to the latter for the purchafe of that article. The quantity of rum fent from the Britifh Weft India iflands to North America, on an average of three years, was, according to the account of imports and exports in North America, 2,800,000 gallons in a year; and the quantity of the melaffes 250,000 gallons—This laft may be confidered as fo much additional rum, as it is probable the greateft part of it was diftilled into that fpirit in America. The whole quantity of rum, therefore, the produce of our iflands, which the Americans took from them, may be fairly ftated at 3,050,000

F

gallons. This quantity, great as it is, is but a part of the rum neceſſary for the conſumption of North America; for it is ſaid, that almoſt all the melaſſes of the French iſlands were imported into it, and diſtilled into rum, chiefly in the New England provinces; and this is probable, as the price of melaſſes in the French iſlands has of late years very much increaſed, in conſequence of the great demand for it.

It was alſo ſhewn to the committee, that the conſumption of rum in North America was not annually leſs than 7,000,000 gallons; and there is no reaſon to ſuppoſe that this conſumption will be leſs in future; and if the French diſtil their own melaſſes, it can make no difference in the quantity of rum diſtilled.

BY an account of prices current of ſugar, rum, and coffee, at Kingſton in Jamaica, on the 18th day of January laſt laid before the committee, it appeared that thoſe articles then ſold at prices at leaſt as high as they were, on an average, between the years 1770 and 1775; and the committee have been informed, that by accounts lately received, dated 20th March, the produce of that iſland had riſen, in the courſe of the laſt month, nearly ten per cent. This riſe is alledged to be owing to the preſent demand for the American market.

A correſpondent at Savanna la Mar, in a letter to a merchant of London, doubts whether he can execute the orders he had received from London for rum within the time appointed; becauſe there were at Savanna la Mar ſeveral purchaſers for rum and ſugar from Kingſton, for the American market.—Rum had broke, at Savanna la Mar, at 2*s.* 6*d.* per gallon, which is as high as any purchaſed at that port during the laſt five years, and higher than it uſually broke at in times of peace.—Rum ſold at Kingſton, upon the 20th of March, at 2*s.* 9*d.*;

and, by the laſt accounts from the Leeward Iſlands, dated in February, the price of new rum was expected to be at 2*s.* 3*d.* and ſtrong Granada rum at 2*s.* 6*d.*; which, the committee are informed, is at leaſt as high as rum uſually broke at in thoſe iſlands in times of peace. And, from the preſent price of rum, and the demand for it, there is no reaſon to apprehend that there will be any want of a ſufficient vent for this article of produce.

It appeared by the account of imports and exports produced to the committee, that there were imported into Canada, Nova Scotia, and Newfoundland, before the war, 998,672 gallons in a year; and that in the year 1774, 748,491 gallons of rum were imported from the Weſt Indies, and from the continent of America, into that colony only.

By another account produced, it appeared, that in ſome years there has been a large importation of rum into Canada from Great Britain; but it is probable that a conſiderable portion of this might be for the uſe of his Majeſty's troops. This, however, was but part of the conſumption of thoſe provinces: great quantities were ſmuggled, particularly into Canada, where there was a high duty; and ſtill more into Newfoundland, where there was not only a high duty on rum imported from the American continent, but where there was one cuſtom-houſe only; and great quantities were ſold by the Americans, out of their veſſels, to the fiſhermen on the banks.—When it is conſidered, therefore, that the people of Nova Scotia have in the laſt year been more than doubled by the new ſettlers, and that the people of Canada are alſo much increaſed, there can be little doubt that the conſumption of rum will be greatly increaſed in the remaining Britiſh colonies, eſpecially if all duties upon the rum of our iſlands, imported into Canada, be taken off, or at leaſt greatly diminiſhed, and foreign veſſels allowed as little intercourſe as poſſible with our fiſhermen at Newfoundland.—What the quantity consumed in such case may be, it is impossible to say; but it will probably leave no greater quantity to be imported into other parts of America, than such as will find an easy market.

It was suggested to the committee, that the confining the intercourse with our West India islands to British ships, will be a means of securing to the planters a greater export of their produce, than if the ships of the United States were allowed to come, as formerly, to the ports of our islands; for, though the West India planters and merchants seemed to imagine, that before the war the Americans took from the British West India islands their produce in payment for nearly the amount of what they imported, the accounts of imports and exports state the value of the produce of the continent of North America, imported into the islands, as valued at the port of importation at 720,000*l.* annually, including freight; and the amount of the produce of our islands, imported into North America, valued in like manner at the port of importation, at 420,000*l.*, including freight; which makes a balance of 300,000*l.* in favour of the Americans: and it has been asserted, by merchants well versed in that commerce, who have appeared before the committee, that the Americans never took, in payment of their cargoes, more than a small part of the produce of our islands; one, in particular, has informed the committee, that the Americans trading to Jamaica, before the war, used to take produce of that island, in payment for provisions and lumber imported there, in nearly the following proportions:

The Southern Provinces, about one half, or rather more; —the balance in dollars.

The Middle Provinces, about one fourth;—balance, dollars and sterling bills of exchange.

The Northern, or New England Government, not above one tenth;—balance in dollars.

And ſo unwilling were the Americans to take the produce of the Britiſh iſlands, that, when they ſold their lumber and proviſions in exchange for produce, and not for caſh, they generally demanded a higher price. With the caſh thus procured, whatever it might be, they went down to the foreign iſlands, and purchaſed ſugar, melaſſes, and coffee, much cheaper than our iſlands could afford them.

It is therefore argued, that, when the trade is confined to our own ſhips, it is more probable that there will be a greater exchange of produce for produce.

THE planters and merchants, in offering their evidence to the committee, adverted to two other material and important points, in order to induce his Majeſty to comply with their requeſt viz.

Firſt.—The policy which the French are purſuing, for the purpoſe of opening an intercourſe between their iſlands and the United States,

Secondly.—The meaſures which the United States, and the ſeveral provinces of which they are compoſed, have taken in conſequence of his Majeſty's order in council of the 2d of July.

In reſpect to the firſt of theſe points, it appears that an arrêt had been publiſhed at Saint Domingo, which puts the trade between the United States and that iſland upon the ſame footing as before the war; but by a proclamation publiſhed at Martinique, and the French Windward Iſlands, for opening the ports of the French iſlands to the United States, permiſſion is given to the veſſels of the United States, to load with the produce of the French iſlands, without any limitation; but the permiſſion which is given to bring the produce of the United States to the French iſlands, is confined to ſuch articles only as France cannot ſupply her colonies with;— and this has been ſince explained to admit the importation of lumber of all ſorts, ſtaves and heading, ſhingles, rice, horſes, cattle, live ſtock, and all fiſh but cod (which are to be ſupplied from their own fiſheries), to the excluſion of the three great articles of American produce, viz. European and Indian grain, ſalted beef and pork, and pickled cod; but it is ſaid, that permiſſion is to be given, occaſionally, to import ſalted proviſions, and other articles, when the iſlands are in want of them. And the committee were informed, that what is thus permitted to be imported, is little more than what the French allowed to the Americans before the war, by ſpecial permiſſion to particular ſhips, when the neceſſity of their iſlands required it.

With reſpect to the ſecond point, viz. "The meaſures which the United States, and the provinces of which they are compoſed, have taken in conſequence of his Majeſty's order in council of 2d of July"—the committee find, that the State of Maryland has, on this account, impoſed a duty of five ſhillings per ton on Britiſh ſhipping, at their entrance or clearance in the ports of that State (which is ſaid to be two ſhillings more than they have laid on all *other* ſhipping), and two per cent. *ad valorem*, over and above what is now paid, or may hereafter be paid, by the citizens of the ſaid State, upon all merchandize and manufactures the growth and produce of Great Britain, or any colony or other place under the dominion of Great Britain, imported in any *Britiſh ſhip* or other veſſel owned or belonging, in part or wholly, to any Britiſh ſubject or ſubjects.

And the aſſembly of Georgia, now ſitting, has prohibited all intercourſe with the Britiſh Weſt India iſlands, until the orders of his Majeſty in council are revoked.

It does not appear that any of the other ſtates have yet paſſed any legiſlative acts to the like purpoſe; but in the aſſembly of Penſylvania, which was ſitting when the laſt accounts came away, an act had been read a ſecond time, for impoſing duties on every ton of Britiſh ſhipping, and on Britiſh manufactures and commodities, in like manner as thoſe impoſed by the ſtate of Maryland, with the addition, that the aſſembly of Penſylvania propoſed to augment the duty on Britiſh manufactures and commodities, imported in Britiſh ſhipping, to 2½ per cent. *ad valorem*; and there is intelligence received of a general ferment in all the ſouthern and middle ſtates, on account of the reſtriction laid by his Majeſty's order in council.

The aſſembly of New York had addreſſed the governor on this ſubject, in terms of reſentment to Great Britain; and the aſſembly of Virginia have unanimouſly reſolved, "That the United States, in congreſs aſſembled, ought to be impowered to prohibit Britiſh veſſels from being the carriers of the growth or produce of the Britiſh Weſt India iſlands to the ſaid ſtates, ſo long as the order in council ſhall be continued; or to concert ſuch other meaſures as ſhall be thought effectual to counteract the deſigns of Great Britain with reſpect to the American commerce."

The province of South Carolina has laid duties on Britiſh Weſt India produce, from 50*l*. to 100*l*. per cent. higher than on that of foreign iſlands: but it appears that this duty was impoſed *before* they had any knowledge of his Majeſty's order in council of 2d July.

Whether the congreſs, or the ſeveral legiſlatures of the American States, will perſiſt in this policy, is impoſſible to be known. But the committee have examined many reſpectable perſons, perfectly informed of the ſtate of America, and of the nature of its commerce;—who all agree in opinion, that by prohibiting or obſtructing the intercourſe between the continent of America and the Weſt India iſlands, the people of the United States will ſuffer much more than any of his Majeſty's ſubjects; and that, for want of a ſufficient vent, their lumber and proviſions muſt periſh on their hands.

APPENDIX.

No. I.

An ACCOUNT of all the Flour and Lumber imported in British-built Vessels, navigated according to Law, and entered at the Port of Kingston in Jamaica, from 12th December 1783, to 17th March 1784.

Arrival at Kingston.	Vessels.	Barrels of Flour	Staves and Heading.	Feet of Boards, Scantling, &c.	Shingles.	Packed or shaken Hds.	From
1783							
Dec. 12	Schooner Hope, Smart	—	—	21,250	36,300	—	East Florida
	Brig. Mars	210	—	34,465	204,600	—	Philadelphia
	Brig. Recovery, Grimes	260	25,000	—	30,000	—	Virginia
	Ship Qu. of England, Campbell	209	98,000	20,000	44,000	—	Philadelphia
	Schooner Sally	250	1,500	—	—	—	New York
14	Sloop Patty, Killy	250	—	—	—	—	Tortola
15	Sloop Betsey, Wainwright	762	—	—	—	—	Philadelphia
16	Brig. Polly and Harriot	—	3,608	15,000	70,000	—	Georgia
	Schooner Rose, Brunton	—	—	4,000	—	—	New York
	Schooner Betsey, Lear	456	2,000	—	30,000	—	Philadelphia
18	Ship Robina, Maniel	1,280	4,800	—	—	—	Do.
22	Sloop Industry, Darrat	193	2,000	1,000	—	—	New York
23	Ship Maria, Jones	1,139	6,500	—	—	—	Philadelphia
	Ship Cormorant, Hutchinson	900	70,000	—	—	—	Virginia
	Ship Yorick, Anderson	—	—	60,000	—	—	Quebec
29	Brig. Lord Howe, Maclean	—	2,000	30,000	18,000	100	Penobscot
1784							
Jan. 2	Brig. Agnes, Bailiff	—	5,000	22,000	47,000	—	Massachusets
3	Brig. Pirgey	—	—	300	—	—	Maryland
	Brig. Bermudian, Smillie	—	2,000	40,000	—	—	Philadelphia
	Ship Harford, Folger	1,625	2,200	—	42,000	—	Do.
	Sloop Rover, Stuart	—	—	800	—	31	Quebec
	Sloop Perseverance, King	201	5,900	—	9,600	—	Virginia
6	Brig. Arrow, Cruickshanks	—	—	—	211,000	—	S. Carolina
8	Brig. Glasgow, Patrick	1,307	4,700	—	—	—	Virginia
9	Brig. Atalanta, Stanton	923	1,300	—	—	—	Philadelphia
	Brig. Dart, Tyrie	557	1,500	—	—	—	Maryland
	Brig. Hawke, Coupland	—	6,600	147,000	100,000	50	Massachusets
12	Sloop Liberty, Dunscomb	300	10,000	—	—	—	Maryland
	Brig. Admiral Rowley	—	3,000	68,000	—	—	Massachusets
13	Schooner Betsey, Wilson	170	15,000	—	—	30	Philadelphia
15	Sloop Sally, Alboury	150	—	4,500	—	—	Bermuda
	Brig. Liverpool, Darcun	540	4,000	—	—	—	Maryland
17	Schooner Betsey, Braine	—	—	4,000	58,000	—	S. Carolina
	Schooner Providence	224	2,300	—	—	—	Philadelphia
	Carried forward	12,275	280,908	522,315	904,500	212	

G

No. I. *Continued.*

Arrival at Kingston.	Vessels.	Barrels of Flour.	Staves and Heading.	Feet of Boards, Scantling, &c.	Shingles.	Packed or shaken Hds.	From
1784	Brought forward —	12,275	180,908	522,315	904,500	211	
Jan. 21	Ship Fame, Aldis —	39	—	—	—	—	London
	Brig. Swift — —	480	25,000	—	—	—	New Yor
	Ship Bristol, Kinsley —	500	—	—	—	—	Grenada
22	Brig. Duncan, Craig —	110	—	—	—	—	Antigua
25	Brig. Renown, Darrel —	—	—	—	40,000	—	S. Carolin
	Brig. Porcupine, Stubins —	—	15,000	40,000	20,000	60	Kennebu
	Schooner Abigail, Pattes —	—	2,000	—	8,000	—	New Yor
30	Ship St. Cuthbert, Wright —	—	8,000	20,592	10,690	—	Ditto
	Sloop Polly and Sally, Paterson — —	20	—	—	—	—	Ditto
	Ship Commerce, Blake —	100	—	—	—	—	Bristol
	Snow Industry, Nelson —	—	78,400	—	—	—	Bermuda
Feb. 2	Brig. Active, Bateman —	—	—	5,000	3,000	—	St. Thom
	Brig. Penelope, Williams —	150	11,600	—	2,000	100	Massachu
4	Brig. Porgey — —	—	—	—	50,000	—	Bahamas
	Snow Tygress, Christian —	—	2,000	25,000	—	—	Tortola
6	Ship Findlay, Farrie —	173	—	—	—	—	Glasgow
7	Brig. Dispatch, Luscombe —	225	—	—	—	—	Bristol
9	Brig. Newry, Clarke —	—	11,000	11,000	—	120	Tortola
	Snow Judith, Shutter —	1,162	2,500	—	—	—	Philadelph
11	Ship Sally, Darrel —	—	—	44,541	51,000	—	S. Carolin
	Lady Juliana, Sayle —	160	—	—	—	—	London
	Ship Two Brothers, Swift —	1,900	7,000	—	43,000	—	Grenada
16	Brig. Sally, Gates —	63	—	40,000	44,000	—	N. Caroli
20	Brig. Loyalist, Bishop —	—	500	16,000	40,000	—	E. Florida
22	Schooner Betsey, White —	—	4,000	—	6,000	—	Connectic
	Schooner Batchelor —	300	—	—	—	—	New York
25	Brig. Sally, Albro —	470	5,000	—	—	—	Grenada
28	Brig. Port Roseway, Shannon—	—	3,500	10,000	—	91	Connectic
	Sloop Sally — —	—	10,600	—	—	—	St. Thoma
29	Ship Anne — —	103	—	—	—	—	Bristol
	Ship Friendly Adventure —	—	60,652	16,680	118,600	—	Virginia
Mar. 5	Sloop Relief, Bachop —	—	—	4,000	—	—	E. Florida
7	Brig. Carolina, Camplin —	—	—	23,000	70,000	—	Ditto
8	Sloop Two Brothers —	—	—	3,360	—	—	Bahamas
9	Brig. Swallow, Hook —	—	13,000	—	—	—	S. Carolina
11	Brig. Elizabeth, Barington —	—	18,390	12,265	10,000	—	Georgia
16	Brig. Æolus, Wright —	560	—	—	—	—	Glasgow
	Schooner Nancy, Newbold —	—	—	—	30,000	50	Bermuda
17	Schooner Scorpion, Kemp —	—	—	2,500	—	—	Bahamas
	Total in Three Months —	18,800	559,050	796,253	1,450,790	632	

No. II.

An ACCOUNT of the Total Import from North America into the Britifh Weft India Iflands, in the Years 1771, 1772, and 1773; taken from an official Account figned by Mr. Stanley, Secretary to the Commissioners of the Cuftoms in London, dated 15th March, 1775.

LUMBER.		From the United States	From Canada and Nova Scotia.	From Newfoundland.
Boards and Timber —	Feet —	76,767,695	231,040	2,000
Shingles —	N° —	59,586,194	185,000	
Staves —	N° —	57,998,661	27,350	
Hoops —	N° —	4,712,005	16,250	9,000
Corn —	Bufhels —	1,204,389	24	
Peafe and Beans —	Ditto —	64,006	1,017	
Bread and Flour —	Barrels —	396,329	991	
Ditto —	Kegs —	13,099		
Rice —	Barrels —	39,912		
Ditto —	Tierces —	21,777		
Fifh —	Hogfheads -	51,344	449	2,307
Ditto —	Barrels —	47,686	646	202
Ditto —	Quintals —	21,500	2,958	11,764
Ditto —	Kegs —	3,304	609	
Beef and Pork —	Barrels —	44,782	170	24
Poultry —	Dozens —	2,739	10	
Horfes —	N° —	7,130	28	
Oxen —	N° —	3,647		
Sheep and Hogs —	N° —	13,815		
Oil —	Barrels —	3,189	139	118
Tar, Pitch, and Turpentine —	Ditto —	17,024		
Mafts —	N° —	157		
Spars —	N° —	3,074	30	
Shook Casks —	N° —	53,857	40	141
Soap and Candles —	Boxes —	20,475		
Ox Bows and Yokes —	N° —	1,540		
Houfe Frames —	N° —	620		
Iron —	Tons —	399½		

A

REPORT

OF

THE LORDS OF THE COMMITTEE OF PRIVY COUNCIL,

Appointed for all Matters relating to Trade and Foreign Plantations,

ON

The Commerce and Navigation between his Majesty's Dominions, and the Territories belonging to the United States of America.

28th January, 1791.

Reprinted by Order of the Society of Ship-owners of Great-Britain.

1806.

At the Council Chamber, Whitehall, the 28th January, 1791.

By the Right Honourable the Lords of the Committee of Council appointed for the Confideration of all Matters relating to Trade and Foreign Plantations.

YOUR Majefty having been pleafed, by your order in council of the 30th September, 1789, to refer to this committee an act paffed by the congrefs of the United States of America on the 4th July preceding, entitled, "*An act for* "*laying a duty on goods, wares, and merchandize, imported into* "*the United States*;" and alfo, another act paffed by the faid congrefs on the 20th of the faid month of July, entitled, "*An act impofing duties on tonnage*;" and your Majefty having directed the committee to confider the faid acts, and report their opinion on the fame to your Majefty; the Lords of the committee loft no time in calling for fuch accounts, and collecting fuch other information, as might beft enable them to form an opinion on the probable effects of the faid acts, and of the meafures which, in confequence thereof, it might be proper, under all the prefent circumftances, to purfue for the fecurity of the Britifh commerce and navigation. With this view, the committee referred feveral queftions to a committee of merchants of the city of London, concerned in the trade to the United States of America, and to the merchants and fhip-owners of Briftol, Liverpool, and

Glaſgow, concerned in the ſame trade: for as this trade is principally carried on from the ports before mentioned, the merchants and ſhip-owners reſiding therein were, in the opinion of the committee, beſt qualified to judge of the effects which any regulation made by the government of the ſaid States is likely to produce on the commerce, the manufactures, and the ſhipping-intereſt of your Majeſty's dominions.

The lords of the committee thought it right alſo to apply to your Majeſty's conſuls, ſtationed in the United States, for ſuch information as they, from their reſidence, were beſt able to afford on many parts of this ſubject.

Some time of courſe elapſed before the merchants and ſhip-owners of the ports before mentioned could return anſwers to the queſtions propoſed to them; and it was neceſſary to allow ſtill further time to your Majeſty's conſuls, reſident in America, to collect and tranſmit the information required of them.

And the committee muſt confeſs that, even after they had received all the neceſſary information, they found great difficulty in forming a deciſive opinion on the ſubject referred to them; eſpecially as, in diſcuſſing the various points ariſing out of it, they were unavoidably led to enter into a full conſideration of this branch of commerce in all its parts; and the difficulty was increaſed, when they obſerved in the anſwers of the merchants and ship-owners before mentioned (who appear to have paid great attention to the queſtions propoſed to them), that they expreſſed their ſentiments with much heſitation, and ſome difference, concerning the meaſures beſt calculated to promote their intereſts: It happened alſo, that other circumſtances afterwards occurred, which induced the committee to think that ſome ſuſpenſion in making their report might not be inexpedient:—But as the duke of Leeds, one of your Majeſty's principal ſecretaries of ſtate, has lately acquainted this committee, that it is your Majesty's intention forthwith to send to America a person, authorised on the part of your Majesty, to treat with the government of the United States on commercial as well as other matters; and as his grace has signified your Majesty's commands, that this committee should take into consideration, and report, what are the proposals, of a commercial nature, proper to be made by the government of this country to the said United States; the Lords of the committee have thought it their duty to resume the consideration of this business, and to proceed without delay in making their report on the whole of this extensive subject.

As it may be of use to be informed of all that the merchants and ship-owners, trading to America, have urged in support of their respective opinions, the Lords of the committee will place in the Appendix to this Report the whole of the answers* given by the said merchants and ship-owners to the questions proposed to them, availing themselves in the Report, which they now present to your Majesty, of such facts, stated in the said answers, as appear to the committee to be important and well authenticated; and of such arguments and calculations as appear to be well founded, particularly such as have contributed in any degree to assist the committee in forming their judgment on this occasion.

The connection which had so long subsisted between Great Britain and the countries now forming the United States of America, was finally dissolved by the acknowledgment of their independence in the year 1783; the ancient commercial system, arising out of that connection, *of course ended with it*; and the laws, by which the trade of these countries, con-

* See the answers of the merchants and ship-owners of London, Bristol, Liverpool, and Glasgow, to the questions referred to them, in the Appendix (A).

H

fidered as colonies, had hitherto been regulated, ceafed to have effect :—It was neceffary therefore to adopt new principles, on which a new fyftem of commerce might be founded. But thefe States, for feveral years fubfequent to their independence, were governed in all commercial matters by feparate and diftinct legiflatures, which were independent of each other, and had different interefts to purfue :—For fo long it was thought wife by the government of this country to fufpend the confideration of a complete commercial arrangement between the faid States and your Majefty's dominions, and to make only provifional regulations.—For this purpofe, the Britifh legiflature, in each feffion fince the year 1783, has vefted in your Majefty, with the advice of your privy council, powers fufficient for making fuch provifional regulations: but as a new conftitution has of late been formed for the general government of the United States, to which all the thirteen States have now acceded; and as the fundamental articles of this conftitution have vefted in a prefident, in a senate, and a houfe of reprefentatives, the powers requifite for regulating the commercial concern of all thefe States, which are in this refpect now to be confidered as one body politic, it is certainly become neceffary to determine, by what principles the commerce between the faid States, and the different parts of your Majefty's dominions, fhould in future be regulated.

The committee think it right to begin by laying before your Majefty a fhort ftate of the meafures purfued by the government of this country, from the conclufion of the late war in 1783 to the prefent time, for the purpofe of regulating the commerce carried on by the fubjects of the United States with your Majefty's dominions; and, *vice verfâ*, of the meafures purfued by the legiflatures of the faid States, from the year 1783 to the opening of the firft feffion of the prefent congrefs, for the purpofe of regulating the commerce carried on in their dominions by the subjects of your Majesty.—The committee will next endeavour to shew the effects which the independence of the United States, as well as the measures before mentioned, have hitherto produced on the commerce and navigation of your Majesty's dominions.

CONDUCT OF GREAT BRITAIN.

Your Majesty, by your orders in council, has been pleased to make the following regulations:

First—That any goods, the importation of which into this kingdom is not prohibited by law, being the growth or production of any of the territories of the United States of America, may be imported directly from thence into any of the ports of this kingdom, not only in British ships, owned by your Majesty's subjects, and navigated according to law, but also in ships built in the countries belonging to the United States of America, and owned by the subjects of the said States, and whereof the master and three-fourths of the mariners, at least, are subjects of the United States.

OBSERVATION.

The permission thus given for importing the before mentioned articles into Great Britain from the countries in America belonging to the United States, in any other ships than those which are built in your Majesty's dominions, owned by your Majesty's subjects, and navigated according to law, is directly contrary to the provisions in an ancient statute of this kingdom; which had never, till on this occasion, been dispensed with, in favour of any foreign nation, or the colony of any such nation in America: for by the 12*th Cha.* 2. *ch.* 18. *sect.* 3. " No goods or commodities whatsoever of the " growth, production, or manufacture of any part of America,

"are to be imported into any of your Majesty's European do-
"minions in any other ship or vessel, *than such as do truly*
"*belong to your Majesty's subjects*, and are navigated ac-
"cording to law in the manner therein described, under the
"penalty of forfeiting all such goods, and the ship or vessel
"in which they are brought."—By the foregoing regulation, made in favour of the commerce of the United States, your Majesty has put the said commerce, as far as relates to the ships in which any merchandize of the growth or production of the said States may be imported, upon the same footing on which the commerce of every independent European nation, carried on with this country, is now allowed to stand.

Secondly—Your Majesty, by the said orders in council, has been pleased to permit, that any goods, being unmanufactured (except fish-oil, blubber, whale-fins, and spermaceti,) and also any pig-iron, bar-iron, pitch, tar, turpentine, resin, pot-ash, pearl-ash, indigo, masts, yards, and bowsprits, being the growth or production of any of the territories of the United States of America, may be imported directly from thence into any of the ports of this kingdom, upon payment of the same duties, as the like sorts of goods are or may be subject to, if imported from any British island or plantation in America;—and that fish-oil, blubber, whale-fins, and spermaceti, and also all other goods, not herein before enumerated or described, being the growth, production, or manufacture of any of the territories of the said States, may be imported from thence into the ports of this kingdom, upon payment of such duties of customs and excise, as are payable on the like goods upon their importation into this kingdom from countries not under the dominion of your Majesty, according to the tables marked A, D, and F, annexed to the Consolidation Act; and in cases where different duties are therein imposed upon the like goods imported from different foreign countries, then upon payment of the lowest of such duties.

OBSERVATION.

Your Majesty by this regulation has thought fit to grant to the commerce of the United States, with respect to certain articles above enumerated and described (being those in which the commerce of the said States is principally carried on), the same preference as is granted to the commerce of the islands and plantations in America, remaining under your Majesty's dominion: And, in many of these articles, the commerce of the said States derives great benefit from *the preference*, thus given, to the detriment of the commerce of other foreign nations, as will be seen by the following table:

		Duties payable if imported from the United States.			Duties payable if imported from other foreign countries.		
		l.	*s.*	*d.*	*l.*	*s.*	*d.*
Pot-ash . . .	per cwt.	free			0	2	3
Pearl-ash . .	per cwt.	free			0	2	3
Iron, bar . .	per ton	free			2	16	2
Pitch . . .	per last	0	11	0	0	12	5
Tar . . .	per last	0	11	0	0	12	4½
Skins, beaver	each	0	0	1	0	0	8¼
Tobacco . .	per lb.	0	1	3	0	3	6

It is proper to add, that all woods, the produce of the countries belonging to the United States, except masts, yards, and bowsprits, may be imported from thence *duty free*; whereas the like woods imported from other foreign countries are subject to various high duties, which produce a revenue of more than 250,000*l.* per annum to Great Britain.

And, with respect to all other articles, either of produce or manufacture, not so enumerated or described in the said order, your Majesty has been pleased to put the commerce of the United States upon the footing of the most favoured nation, except such nations only with which your Majesty has made treaties of commerce, founded on the principles of reciprocity and mutual advantage.

Thirdly—Your Majesty, by the said orders in council, has allowed the goods and merchandize, being the growth, production, or manufacture of the territories of the United States, though imported in ships belonging to the subjects of the said States, to be *exempted* from the aliens-duty.

OBSERVATION.

The goods imported in ships belonging to all other foreign nations are subject to the aliens-duty; and the government of this country has received frequent complaints from other foreign nations of the distinction thus made, to their prejudice, in favour of the commerce of the United States.

Fourthly—Your Majesty, by the said orders in council, did think fit to permit to be imported into the colonies or islands belonging to your Majesty in America or the West Indies, *in British ships only*, navigated according to law, all such articles of the growth, production, or manufacture of any of the territories of the said United States (except salted provisions, and the produce of their fisheries), as might by law before the declaration of independence have been imported from the countries belonging to the said States into any of the said colonies or islands; but your Majesty, at the same time, thought fit to prohibit any commercial intercourse between the countries belonging to the United States of America, and the colonies or islands belonging to your Majesty in America or the West Indies, in ships belonging to the subjects of the said United States.

OBSERVATION.

This last regulation, first established by order in council, has since been adopted and confirmed by act of parliament;

and, though the people of the United States complain of this regulation more than of any other, *it is not new*, but is founded on the ancient law of this country, " which forbids any goods " to be imported into, or exported from, any of the colonies " belonging to your Majesty in Asia, Africa, or America, " except in ships belonging to your Majesty's subjects, and " navigated according to law:"—It is founded also on a principle of public law approved and adopted by all European nations, who have ever claimed a right of restraining the trade and navigation of their colonies, in such manner as, in their judgment, will be most conducive to their respective interests.—It might be proved, if it were necessary, that the policy of Great Britain, in this respect, is much more liberal than that of France or Spain.

CONDUCT OF THE UNITED STATES.

The committee will proceed, in the next place, to lay before your Majesty a short abstract of the laws affecting the commerce of your Majesty's subjects, passed by the several legislatures of the said States, between the year 1783, and the first session of the present congress.

The merchants and ship-owners, concerned in the trade to America, have repeatedly laid before your Majesty's ministers an account of the losses to which their property and commerce have been exposed by laws of this description.

PROHIBITIONS.

By laws, made in the provinces of New Hampshire, Massachusett's Bay, and Rhode Island, vessels owned, in whole or in part, by the subjects of Great Britain, were prohibited from taking on board in those provinces any goods or merchandize of the growth or manufacture of those States, or of any other of the United States; and such vessels, so loaded, were, together with their cargoes, made subject to seizure and condemnation.—The legiſlature of Pennſylvania thought fit to inveſt congreſs with a power for fifteen years to prohibit the importation or exportation of all merchandize in veſſels belonging to, or navigated by, the ſubjects of any nation with whom congreſs ſhall not have formed treaties of commerce, provided congreſs have the conſent of nine ſtates to carry ſuch act into execution. This law, as well as all others of the ſame deſcription, pointed in terms againſt the commerce of every nation with which congreſs had not formed treaties of commerce, had principally, if not ſolely, in view the commerce and navigation of Great Britain.—By laws made in Maſſachuſett's Bay and Rhode Iſland, congreſs was impowered to prohibit the importation of Britiſh Weſt India produce in Britiſh veſſels, whenever all the ſtates compoſing the union ſhould have veſted congress with a ſimiliar power.

Tonnage duties, giving a preference to the ſhips of the United States, and of other nations, over thoſe of Great Britain.

By a law made in Pennſylvania, a duty of 4*s*. 6*d*. per ton for every voyage was impoſed on the veſſels of every nation with which congreſs had not made treaties of commerce.—By a law made in Maryland, a duty of 1*s*. per ton was impoſed on all foreign ſhipping, except Britiſh; and a duty of 5*s*. per ton on Britiſh ſhipping.—By a law paſſed in Virginia, in 1788, a duty of 6*s*. per ton was impoſed on Britiſh veſſels, and 3*s*. per ton on all other foreign veſſels.—By a law made in North Carolina, a duty of 5*s*. per ton was impoſed on Britiſh veſſels; and a duty of 1*s*. per ton on all other veſſels.

Duties on import, giving a preference to the ſhips of the United States, and of other nations, over thoſe of Great Britain.

By laws paſſed in the provinces of New Hampſhire, Maſſachuſett's Bay, and Rhode Iſland, in 1785, a duty of *6d.* currency, being equal to $4\frac{1}{4}$*d.* ſterling, was impoſed on every buſhel of ſalt imported in ſhips owned, in whole or in part, by Britiſh ſubjects; and by laws paſſed in the provinces of New York and Maryland, the cargoes of Britiſh ſhips are, in every caſe, to pay double the duties impoſed on thoſe of other nations.—By a law of Virginia a tariff was eſtabliſhed, to commence in March, 1788, by which an additional duty was impoſed on all merchandize imported in Britiſh ſhips.

Duties on import, giving a preference to the produce and manufactures of other nations over thoſe of Great Britain.

By laws made in the provinces of New Hampſhire, Maſſachuſett's Bay, and Rhode Iſland, a duty of *6s.* ſterling per hundred weight is laid on cordage of Britiſh manufacture, and only half that duty if it be of the manufacture of any other foreign nation.—By a law paſſed in the province of Maryland, a duty of *2s.* per cwt. was impoſed on brown and clayed ſugars imported from the Britiſh Weſt India iſlands; and a duty of *1s. 6d.* per cwt. on the like articles imported from the plantations of France, Spain, Holland, Denmark, and Sweden; and a duty of *1d.* per lb. on refined ſugar imported from Great Britain; and a duty of $\frac{1}{2}$*d.* per lb. on the like article imported from the dominions of France, Spain, Holland, Denmark, and Sweden.—By a law paſſed in South Carolina, in 1784, higher duties were impoſed on the produce of the Britiſh Weſt India iſlands than were payable on

I

the like produce of the Weſt India iſlands of other foreign nations; and in Georgia ſimilar acts were paſſed for the ſame purpoſes. The committee believe that the laws before mentioned are by no means all that have been paſſed for the purpoſes before ſtated. The regulations made in theſe reſpects by the legiſlatures of the ſeveral ſtates are ſo various, that it is hardly poſſible to obtain a complete account of them. The merchants of Glaſgow eſtimate the tonnage duty * impoſed in the period above mentioned on Britiſh ſhipping through all the United States, to have been on an average 2*s.* 3*d.* more per ton than on American ſhips, and that this charge on a ſhip of 200 tons amounts to 22*l.* 10*s.* for each voyage; and they eſtimate the duty, impoſed during the ſame period, on goods imported in Britiſh ſhips through all the United States, to be upon an average 2 per cent. more than on the like goods imported in American ſhips, and that this charge on a cargo of the value of 2000*l.* amounts to 40*l.*

The laws hitherto enumerated, particularly thoſe that gave a preference to the merchandize and ſhips of other nations over thoſe of Great Britain, were certainly unfriendly; and your Majeſty's ſubjects have a right to complain of them: but there is another deſcription of laws paſſed, during the ſame period, by the legiſlatures of many of theſe ſtates, for the expreſs purpoſe of preventing or poſtponing the recovery of juſt debts, and of obliging creditors to take, as a legal tender in payment of them, depreciated paper, or other property, inſtead of caſh: ſuch laws muſt be conſidered as deſtructive of all mercantile confidence and credit, and as contrary to every principle of honour and juſtice.

* The committee have thought it right to rely in theſe reſpects very much on the calculations made by the merchants of Glaſgow, who, from the trade they carry on, are certainly competent to judge of the accuracy of ſuch calculations. They appear alſo to have paid great attention to the queſtions referred to them.— The merchants of this city have differed upon many points, and have made ſeparate reports; but they appear to agree nearly in their calculations.

A pretence was taken to justify these laws by alledging that the debts to which they relate were contracted before the late war, and might, therefore, be considered as cancelled by it.—Nothing can be more unjust than to suppose that the conduct of any sovereign (in whatever light it may be viewed) can cancel mercantile contracts, or other private and personal obligations, by which the subjects of one country may have previously bound themselves to the subjects of another country, though hostilities between the two countries may happen afterwards, from any cause, to ensue. But even this pretence was removed by the *4th and 5th articles* of the late definitive treaty of peace between your Majesty and the United States: for by the *4th article* it was stipulated, "That creditors on either side should meet with no law- "ful impediment to the recovery of the full value in sterling "money of all *bonâ fide* debts heretofore contracted:" and by the *5th article* it was stipulated, "That congress shall "earnestly recommend to the several states a reconsideration "and revision of all acts and laws regarding the premises, "so as to render them perfectly consistent, not only with "justice and equity, but with that spirit of conciliation "which, on the return of the blessings of peace, should "universally prevail."—The legislature of Great Britain has acted in full conformity to these just and honourable principles: the persons and property of American subjects have uninterruptedly enjoyed, in every part of your Majesty's dominions, the same protection as the subjects of your Majesty; and no distinction has ever been made in this respect, either by the British legislature, or by your Majesty's courts of justice, to the disadvantage of the subjects of the United States.

A particular account of the laws before described, passed by the legislatures of many of the states of North America, has, from time to time, been laid before your Majesty's ministers by such of your subjects as have severely suffered by these unjust transactions:—It is sufficient, therefore, at present to observe to your Majesty, that in many of the states laws have been passed enacting, that in some cases debts should be paid only by installments, postponing the last of these installments to a very distant period;—that in other cases no suits should be permitted to be instituted for a debt contracted by a citizen of the United States till a distant period;—that in other cases no execution should be levied till after the expiration of a certain number of years: and these rules have, in some instances, been applied not only to debts contracted before the war, or during its continuance, but even to debts contracted since the peace. Laws have also been passed in some of the states making a depreciated paper-currency legal tender, and even authorising debtors to tender land at a certain valuation in satisfaction of their debts; and yet it has been held by the courts of justice in some of the states that British subjects are aliens, and, as such, not capable of holding lands; so that the land, thus assigned to a British creditor in payment of his debt, by this rule of law reverted to the state, as forfeited by the alienage of the possessor.—To delay the recovery of debts it was enacted by a law in one of these states, that no suit should be commenced till the creditor had made application, in writing, from himself to his debtor for payment.—In another of these states the governor made an order (which for a short time subsisted), compelling all British subjects and factors, who had arrived there for the purpose of collecting and recovering the debts belonging to their employers, forthwith to depart the territories of that state.

In almost all these states, laws have passed precluding British creditors from claiming interest, which had accrued during the continuance of the war, on any debts then owing to them.—In one of the ſtates all demands of intereſt were declared unlawful till after the firſt of May, 1786.

As late as the month of July, 1787, it was laid down by the chief juſtice of Pennſylvania, in his direction to a jury, that the laws of particular ſtates were ſufficient to ſet aſide the uſage which had hitherto prevailed between Britiſh and American traders, as far as related to the payment of intereſt that had accrued during the continuance of the war: and when one of the jurors aſked him, whether the late treaty of peace ought not to have ſome influence on the queſtion, the chief juſtice anſwered, that the treaty of peace only ſecured the mutual recovery of debts, when the amount was aſcertained; but that the amount of the debt was to be aſcertained by the law of the land: the jury in this caſe accordingly deducted intereſt for ſix years and a half. Juries have in other caſes deducted eight years intereſt and a half.

It is but juſtice, however, to the late congreſs to obſerve, that at the ſame time that they publiſhed an account of the ratification of the late treaty of peace, they came to a reſolution to recommend to the ſeveral ſtates to conform to every part of the fifth article before mentioned; and by a letter written by the ſaid congreſs in April 1787, addreſſed to the governors of the ſeveral ſtates, they acknowledged with regret that in ſome of the ſtates too little attention had been paid to the public faith pledged by the late treaty of peace. They obſerved, that not only the obvious dictates of religion, morality, and national honour, but alſo the firſt principles of good policy demand a punctual compliance with engagements conſtitutionally made;—that the legiſlatures of individual ſtates have no right to accept ſome articles of a treaty and reject others, or to decide in what ſenſe the citizens and courts of juſtice of ſuch ſtate ſhall underſtand or interpret any particular ſtipulation;—that if any doubt ſhould ariſe concerning the meaning of any fuch article, the fovereigns only, who are parties to the treaty, have a power, by mutual confent, to interpret and explain it;—that a contrary conduct would ferve only to introduce confufion at home, and to raife new difputes with thofe nations with whom treaties have been formed, which might probably terminate in open hoftilities; they then refolved in fubftance as follows:

1ft, That treaties, conftitutionally made, are a part of the law of the land, and are not only independent of the will and power of particular legiflatures, but alfo binding and obligatory upon them.

2dly, That all acts, or parts of acts, which are now exifting in any of the ftates, repugnant to the treaty of peace, ought to be forthwith repealed; as well to prevent their continuing to be executed in violation of that treaty, as to avoid the difagreeable neceffity there might otherwife be, of raifing and difcuffing queftions touching their validity and obligation.

3dly, That it be recommended to the feveral ftates to repeal all acts repugnant to the treaty of peace between the United States and his Britannic Majefty, and to declare that the courts of law and equity, in all cafes and queftions arifing from or touching the faid treaty, fhall decide and adjudge according to the true intent and meaning of the fame.

None of the foregoing recommendations, made by the late congress, were ever fully complied with by any of the individual ftates to whom they were addreffed. The affembly of Virginia paffed an act which had the appearance of conforming to the laft of thefe recommendations, but annexed conditions which rendered their compliance of no effect.

The committee will now proceed to ſhow the effects which the independence of the United States, as well as the laws and proceedings before ſtated, have hitherto produced on the commerce and navigation of your Majeſty's dominions.

In order to ſhow the effects ſo produced on the commerce and navigation of your Majeſty's dominions, the Lords of the committee will inſert in this place the beſt account they have been able to procure of the ſtate of the commerce carried on with the countries now belonging to the United States of America, and with your Majeſty's remaining colonies in America, and with your Majeſty's iſlands in the Weſt Indies; and alſo of the number and tonnage of the veſſels employed therein, for ſix years preceding the laſt war, and for ſix years ſince. The trade carried on with the countries now belonging to the United States was, before the war, and is ſtill, ſo connected with the trade carried on to the remaining Britiſh colonies in America and the Britiſh iſlands in the Weſt Indies, that it is impoſſible to form a true judgment of the paſt and preſent extent of the firſt of theſe trades, and the changes that have happened in it, without taking a comprehenſive view of all theſe trades, as they are connected with, and influence each other.

The committee will ſtate; *Firſt*, the value of the exports from Great Britain to theſe ſeveral countries; and *Secondly*, the value of the imports into Great Britain from theſe ſeveral countries.

Compariſon of the exports from Great Britain to the countries belonging to the United States of America, before and ſince the war.

Value of the Britiſh manufactures yearly exported to the countries belonging to the United

States upon an average of six years before the War, ending with 1774 - - 2,216,970

Ditto, of six years since the war, ending with 1789 - - - 2,119,837

Annual decrease since the war - - £97,133

Value of the other articles yearly exported to these States from Great Britain, upon an average of six years before the war, ending with 1774 - - - - 515,066

Ditto, of six years since the war, ending in 1789 - - - - 213,806

Annual decrease since the war - - £301,260

Total annual decrease since the war of British manufactures and other articles exported from Great Britain to the countries belonging to the United States - - - £398,393

Comparison of the exports from Great Britain to the remaining British colonies in North America, before and since the war.

Value of British manufactures yearly exported to the remaining British colonies in North America, on an average of six years before the war, ending with 1774 - - 310,916

Ditto, on an average of six years since the war, ending with 1789 - - - 603,928

Annual increase since the war - - £293,012

Value of the other articles yearly exported from Great Britain to these British colonies, upon an average of six years before the war, ending with 1774 - - - - -	68,495
Ditto, on an average of six years since the war, ending with 1789 - - -	225,160
Annual increase since the war - -	£156,665

Total annual increase, since the war, of British manufactures and other articles exported from Great Britain to the remaining British colonies in North America - - -	£449,677

Comparison of the exports from Great Britain to the British islands in the West Indies, before and since the war.

Value of British manufactures yearly exported to the British islands in the West Indies, on an average of six years before the war, ending with 1774 - - - -	1,182,379
Ditto, on an average of six years since the war, ending with 1789 - - -	1,297,275
Annual increase since the war - -	£114,896

Value of other articles yearly exported from Great Britain to the British islands in the West Indies, on an average of six years before the war, ending with 1774 - -	167,240

K

Ditto, on an average of ſix years ſince the war, ending with 1789 - - -	167,145
Annual decreaſe ſince the war - -	£ 95
Total annual increaſe, ſince the war, of Britiſh manufactures, and other articles, exported from Great Britain to the Britiſh iſlands in the Weſt Indies - - - -	£114,801

It appears from the foregoing compariſons, that though the value of the exports to the countries belonging to the United States has annually diminiſhed ſince the war to the amount of 398,393*l*. yet this diminution is more than compenſated by the increaſed value of the annual exports, ſince the war, *to the remaining Britiſh colonies in North America*, and *to the Britiſh iſlands in the Weſt Indies*, this increaſe amounting upon an average to 564,478*l*. per ann.; ſo that upon the whole, the value of the exports from Great Britain to all the countries before mentioned has increaſed, upon an average of ſix years ſince the war, compared with the value thereof upon an average of ſix years before the war, in the ſum of 166,085*l*.:—It appears alſo, that the increaſe has been *wholly in Britiſh manufactures*, and that the decreaſe has been in other articles, principally foreign merchandize ſent from Great Britain; for the value of Britiſh manufactures, ſo exported, has annually increaſed ſince the war 310,775*l*., and the value of other articles, principally foreign merchandize, has, during the ſame period, annually decreaſed 144,690*l*.

Comparison of the imports into Great Britain from countries belonging to the United States of America, before and since the war.

Value of merchandize imported yearly into Great Britain from the countries belonging to the United States, upon an average of six years before the war, ending with 1774	1,752,142
Ditto, on an average of six years since the war, ending with 1789 - - -	908,636
Annual decrease since the war - -	£ 843,506

Comparison of the imports into Great Britain from the remaining British colonies in North America, before and since the war.

Value of merchandize imported yearly into Great Britain from the remaining British colonies in North America, on an average of six years before the war, ending with 1774 -	123,372
Ditto, on an average of six years since the war, ending with 1789 - - -	220,358
Annual increase since the war - -	£ 96,986

Comparison of the imports into Great Britain from the British islands in the West Indies, before and since the war.

Value of the merchandize imported yearly from the British islands in the West Indies, on an average of six years before the war, ending with 1774 - - - -	3,232,119

Ditto, upon an average of fix years fince the war, ending with 1789 - -	3,903,185
Annual increafe fince the war	£ 671,966

It appears from the three comparifons laft ftated, that the decreafe in the value of the imports fince the war, from the countries belonging to the United States of America, annually amounting to 843,506*l.*, has not been wholly compenfated by the increafe of the value of the imports, during the fame period, from the remaining Britifh colonies in North America, and from the Britifh iflands in the Weft Indies, amounting together annually to 768,052*l.* but that on the whole there has been a decreafe in the annual value of the imports from all thefe countries, fince the war, of 75,454*l.* The beforementioned great decreafe in the value of the imports from the countries belonging to the United States of America, is nearly accounted for, by the decreafed quantity of *tobacco and rice* annually imported, fince the war, into Great Britain.

The quantity of tobacco fo imported, has, upon an average of fix years annually, decreafed	lbs. 44,774,458		
Being in value - £582,987 : 6 : 0			
And the quantity of rice fo imported has, in like manner, annually decreafed	cwt. 259,035	qrs. 3	lb. 9
Being in value - £196,526 : 5 : 4			
Total decreafe, fince the war, in the value of rice and tobacco annually imported,	£. 779,514	*s.* 1	*d.* 4

As long as the countries belonging to the United States were fubject to the laws that regulate the trade of Britifh colonies, the two commodities before mentioned could be brought from thence only to Great Britain: they may be now carried directly to any other country that has occafion for them. Four-fifths of the whole quantity of tobacco and rice, imported before the war into Great Britain, were afterwards re-exported for the confumption of other countries; and the value of thefe commodities, fo exported, was included in the annual amount of the exports from Great Britain to all countries: it was natural therefore to expect, that by the lofs of this branch of commerce, the ftate of our exports in general might be greatly affected. During the three years immediately fubfequent to the war, the value of the annual exports from Great Britain to all countries was not quite fo great as it had been before the war; but in the three years 1787, 1788, and 1789, the value of the annual exports from Great Britain was much greater than it had been before the war; and the exports in the year 1789 greatly exceeded thofe of any former year. Since 1783, there has been from year to year a regular increafe of exports from Great Britain; and the value of the exports of 1789 exceeds the value of the exports of 1784 £4,400,609 : 10 : 1.

It appears from the foregoing comparifons of exports and imports, that, as the value of the exports to the countries now belonging to the United States has exceeded the value of the imports from thence fince the war in a much greater proportion than before the war, the balance of trade between Great Britain and the faid countries, is now much more in favour of Great Britain than it was before the war.

It is proper in this place to take notice, that all the foregoing comparifons relate folely to the trade of Great Britain; and that they do not include the trade of Ireland with any of the countries before mentioned; and it is right to obferve, that both the exports and imports of Ireland, to and from all the faid countries in America and the Weft Indies, have greatly increafed fince the war, as well in confequence of the independence of the United States, as of the permiſſion given in 1780 to the people of Ireland to carry on a direct trade in the ſame manner as the people of Great Britain with the Britiſh colonies in North America, and the Britiſh iſlands in the Weſt Indies.

The committee will proceed, in the next place, to lay before your Majeſty the beſt account they have been able to procure of the number and tonnage of the veſſels employed in the different branches of commerce, reſpectively carried on between Great Britain and the countries belonging to the United States of America, and the remaining Britiſh colonies in North America, and the Britiſh iſlands in the Weſt Indies.

There are many difficulties in ſtating this account:—

Firſt—The account of the number of veſſels employed in this commerce, was not kept with the ſame accuracy before the war as it is at preſent; and the account of their tonnage, as kept before the war, is ſtill leſs accurate. Before the paſſing of the act, *For the further encreaſe and encouragement of ſhipping and navigation*, Britiſh veſſels were not ſurveyed with ſufficient accuracy; and the account of their tonnage was taken from no better authority than the declaration of the maſter: it was then alſo for the intereſt of the maſter to diminiſh the number of tons of which his veſſel conſiſted; as he was in conſequence thereof charged with a ſmaller ſum for pilotage and light-houſe duties. It is ſuppoſed, that the amount of the tonnage of a ſhip aſcertained in this manner was in general one-third leſs than the real tonnage.

Secondly—As before the war the countries now under the government of the United States were Britiſh colonies, the veſſels belonging them were conſidered as Britiſh veſſels: in the account therefore of veſſels employed in theſe ſeveral branches of commerce before the war, there was no diſtinction made between the veſſels belonging to the people of the countries now under the dominion of the United States, and ſuch as belonged to the other parts of the Britiſh dominions. All theſe veſſels were equally conſidered as Britiſh ſhips.

Thirdly—The committee have not been able to procure accounts of the number of veſſels, and their tonnage, employed in this trade for the ſix years before the war, and the ſix years ſince the war, on which they have formed the averages of the exports and imports as before ſtated: the accounts which they have been able to procure, and on which they have formed the following averages, are of the years 1770, 1771, and 1772, before the war, and of 1787, 1788, and 1789, ſince the war; and they have choſen the three years laſt mentioned, as theſe years are ſubſequent to the paſſing of the act, *For the further encreaſe and encouragement of ſhipping and navigation*; from which time the accounts of the number of veſſels, and their tonnage, have been kept with greater accuracy in every part of the Britiſh dominions.

Veſſels employed between Great Britain and the countries belonging to the United States.

	Ships.	Tons.
Number and tonnage of the veſſels clearing outwards, and employed yearly in the trade between Great Britain and the countries now belonging to the United States of America, on an average of the years 1770, 1771, and 1772, before the war, -	628	—81,951
Number of ditto ſo employed, entering inwards, on a like average - -	699	—91,540

	Ships.	Tons.				
Medium of the average-number, and tonnage of the veſſels entering inwards, and clearing outwards - - -	663	86,745				

	British.		American.		Total.	
	Ships.	Tons.	Ships.	Tons.	Ships.	Tons.
Number and tonnage of Britiſh veſſels, and of veſſels belonging to the United States, clearing outwards, ſo employed, on an average of the years 1787, 1788, and 1789, ſince the war, -	272	55,785	157	25,725	429	81,510
Number and tonnage of ditto, entering inwards, on a like average	251	49,405	169	27,403	420	76,808
Medium of the average - number, and tonnage, of Britiſh and American veſſels ſo employed, entering inwards, and clearing outwards	261	52,595	163	26,564	425	79,159

It appears from the foregoing averages, that the number of veſſels employed in the direct commercial intercourſe between Great Britain and the countries now belonging to the United States of America, has decreaſed ſince the war 238;

and that the quantity of tonnage has decreafed fince the war 7,586 tons. The decreafe of the tonnage appears to be much lefs than the decreafe of the number of the fhips, and the decreafe of the tonnage inwards is much greater than that of the tonnage outwards. The reafon that the quantity of the tonnage in general appears to be lefs decreafed than the number of fhips is:

Firft, That *larger* fhips are now employed in this, as well as in every other branch of commerce, than formerly.

Secondly, The imperfect manner of taking the account of the tonnage before the war, as before ftated, which was then eftimated, for the reafons before mentioned, about one third lefs than it really was.

The greater decreafe of the tonnage inwards, compared with that of the tonnage outwards, is to be imputed to the diminifhed importation of the bulky articles of rice and tobacco, as before ftated.

It appears, by the foregoing account of the veffels employed in this trade fince the war, that the number of Britifh veffels, fo employed, exceeds the number of American veffels, fo employed, 98 fhips; and the quantity of Britifh tonnage, fo employed, exceeds the quantity of American tonnage, fo employed, 26,031 tons.

As there was no diftinction before the war between fhips belonging to the inhabitants of the countries now under the dominion of the United States, and the other parts of the Britifh dominions, it is impoffible to ftate, with certainty, what was the proportion of each defcription of fhips then employed in this branch of commerce.

The veffels, fo employed, were then of three forts:

Firft—Veffels belonging to merchants refident in the Britifh European dominions.

L

Secondly—Veſſels belonging to Britiſh merchants, occaſionally reſident in thoſe colonies, that now form the United States.

Thirdly—Veſſels belonging to merchants, who were natives and permanent inhabitants of thoſe colonies, that now form the United States.

The following table will ſhew the proportion of each deſcription of veſſels, claſſed in the manner before mentioned, then employed in this branch of commerce, according to the beſt information that can be obtained :

	Proportion of vessels belonging to merchants resident in the British European dominions.	Proportion of vessels belonging to British merchants occasionally resident in those colonies that now form the United States.	Proportion of vessels belonging to merchants, who were natives and permanent inhabitants of those colonies that now form the United States.
New England	1-8th	1-8th	6-8ths
New York	3-8ths	3-8ths	2-8ths
Pennſylvania	2-8ths	3-8ths	3-8ths
Maryland and Virginia	6-8ths	1-8th	1-8th
North Carolina	5-8ths	2-8ths	1-8th
S. Carolina and Georgia	5-8ths	2-8ths	1-8th

From the foregoing table it is evident, that the proportion of veſſels, claſſed under the before-mentioned deſcriptions, varied according to the different colonies, now forming the United States, with which the commerce of Great Britain was then carried on; the quantity of ſhipping ſo employed which belonged, either to the inhabitants of Great Britain, or to Britiſh merchants occaſionally reſident in the ſaid colonies, being much greater in the commercial intercourſe, then carried on with the ſouthern colonies, than with the northern colonies, particularly thoſe of New England.—But, upon the whole, there is reaſon to believe, from calculations founded on the foregoing table, as well as from other information, that the proportion of tonnage, employed before the war in this branch of commerce, which belonged to the inhabitants of Great Britain, was about 4-8ths and an half; and the proportion, which belonged to Britiſh merchants, occaſionally reſident in the colonies now forming the United States, was about one-eighth and an half, making together nearly ſix-eighths of the whole; and that the proportion of tonnage ſo employed, which belonged to merchants, who were then natives and permanent inhabitants of the colonies now forming the United States, was rather more than two eighths of the whole. At preſent the proportion of tonnage, employed in this branch of commerce, belonging to the merchants of Great Britain, is nearly ſix-eighths of the whole; and the proportion of tonnage, belonging to the merchants of the United States, is rather more than two-eighths of the whole; ſo that, in this view of the ſubject, though the quantity of ſhipping, employed between Great Britain and the countries now under the dominion of the United States, has ſince the war decreaſed on the whole in the degree before ſtated, yet, allowing for this decreaſe, the *ſhare of the ſhipping which belongs to the merchants of Great Britain has increaſed* in the proportion of one-eighth and an half; (the ſhare of the ſhipping, which before the war belonged to Britiſh merchants, occaſionally reſident in the colonies now forming the United States, being transferred to merchants reſident in Great Britain), and the ſhare of the ſhipping ſo employed, which now belongs to merchants, ſubjects of the United States, and permanent inhabitants thereof, is nearly the ſame as it was before the war.

Veſſels employed between Great Britain and the remaining Britiſh colonies in North America.

	Ships. — Tons.
Number and tonnage of Britiſh veſſels clearing outwards, and employed yearly in the trade between Great Britain and the remaining Britiſh colonies in North America, on an average of the years 1770, 1771, and 1772, before the war - -	250—9,582
Number and tonnage of ditto, ſo employed, entering inwards, on a like average -	273—12,857
Medium of the average-number and tonnage of Britiſh veſſels entering inwards, and clearing outwards - - - -	261—11,219
Number and tonnage of Britiſh veſſels, clearing outwards, employed in this trade, on an average of the years 1787, 1788, and 1789, ſince the war - -	486—61,858
Number and tonnage of ditto ſo employed, entering inwards, on a like average -	249—30,355
Medium of the average-number and tonnage of Britiſh veſſels entering inwards, and clearing outwards - - - -	367—46,106

By the foregoing averages it appears, that the number of veſſels employed between Great Britain and the remaining colonies in North America, being all Britiſh ſhips, has increafed fince the war in the proportion of about one half, being 106 veffels more than it was before the war; and the quantity of tonnage has increafed 34,887 tons, being in the proportion of about four times more than it was before the war.

Veffels employed between Great Britain and the Britifh iflands in the Weft Indies.

	Ships. Tons.
Number and tonnage of Britifh veffels clearing outwards, and employed yearly in the trade between Great Britain and the Britifh iflands in the Weft Indies, on an average of the years 1770, 1771, and 1772, before the war - - - - -	420—75,143
Number and tonnage of ditto fo employed, entering inwards, on a like average -	563—85,821
Medium of the average-number and tonnage of Britifh veffels, entering inwards, and clearing outwards - - -	491—80,482
Number and tonnage of Britifh veffels clearing outwards, and employed yearly in the trade between Great Britain and the Britifh iflands in the Weft Indies, on an average of the years 1787, 1788, and 1789, fince the war - - - -	531—128,207
Number and tonnage of ditto, fo employed, entering inwards, on a like average	588—139,265

Medium of the average-number and tonnage of British vessels, entering inwards, and clearing outwards - - - 559—133,736

By these last averages it appears that the number of vessels employed between Great Britain and the British islands in the West Indies, being all British ships, is, since the war, 68 ships more than before the war, and has therefore increased in the proportion of about one-seventh; and that the quantity of tonnage is, since the war, 53,254 tons more than it was before the war, and has therefore increased in the proportion of more than five-eighths. It is of importance also to observe, that before the war a part of the ships annually employed in bringing to Great Britain the produce of the West India islands, was built in the countries now belonging to the United States of America. These ships were in general loaded in the northern states with lumber and provisions, and consigned to merchants in the West Indies, where their cargoes were sold, and being then freighted with sugar and other West India produce, they proceeded to Great Britain, where they were sold at a rate considerably under the price, for which vessels of the same dimensions could be built in Great Britain. Their number is supposed to have been about fifty annually; and it is for this reason that the number of ships entering inwards before the war appears, by the foregoing accounts, to have exceeded the number of ships clearing outwards, in a much greater proportion than it does at present. Since the war, *the ships employed in this branch of commerce are principally built in Great Britain*; and as these ships, and the sailors with which they are manned, *have a more immediate connection with the mother country*, it is certain that they contribute in a much greater degree than the ships which they have replaced, *to increase the efficient strength of Great Britain as a naval power*.

Vessels employed between the remaining British colonies in North America, and the countries belonging to the United States.

	Ships. — Tons.
Number and tonnage of British vessels clearing outwards, and employed yearly in the trade between the remaining British colonies in North America, and the countries which were then British colonies, but now form the United States of America, on an average of the years 1770, 1771, and 1772, before the war -	250—9,582
Number and tonnage of ditto, so employed, entering inwards, on a like average -	276—12,857
Medium of the average-number and tonnage of British vessels entering inwards and clearing outwards - - -	263—11,219
Number and tonnage of British vessels clearing outwards, and employed yearly in the trade between the remaining British colonies in North America, and the countries belonging to the United States, on an average of the years 1787, 1788, and 1789, since the war - - -	208—15,135
Number and tonnage of ditto, so employed, entering inwards, on a like average -	269—15,524
Medium of the average-number and tonnage of British vessels entering inwards and clearing outwards - -	238—15,329

The number of the veſſels ſo ſtated includes their repeated voyages; and it appears that the number has decreaſed, ſince the war, 25 veſſels, or about one-tenth.: but the quantity of the tonnage has increaſed 4,110 tons, or about one-third. The veſſels employed before the war in this branch of trade might lawfully belong to the inhabitants of the countries now under the dominion of the United States; it is certain they then owned much the greateſt ſhare of theſe veſſels: but veſſels ſo employed can now belong only to the inhabitants of the remaining colonies, or of ſome other part of the Britiſh dominions: *a great part of this branch of freight* may be conſidered, therefore, *as a new acquiſition*, and was obtained by *the wiſe policy* which your Majeſty thought proper to adopt by your order in council of 18th June, 1784.

Veſſels employed between the Britiſh iſlands in the Weſt Indies, and the countries belonging to the United States.

	Ships.	Tons.
Number and tonnage of Britiſh veſſels clearing outwards, and employed yearly in the trade between the Britiſh iſlands in the Weſt Indies, and the countries belonging to the United States, on an average of the years 1770, 1771, and 1772, before the war - -	2,172	103,540
Number and tonnage of ditto, ſo employed, entering inwards, on a like average - - - -	2,297	111,939
Medium of the average-number and tonnage of Britiſh veſſels, entering inwards, and clearing outwards -	2,234	107,739

	Ships.	Tons.
Number and tonnage of Britifh veffels clearing outwards, and employed yearly in the trade between the Britifh iflands in the Weft Indies, and the countries belonging to the United States, on an average of the years 1787, 1788, and 1789, fince the war - - -	510	—57,904
Number and tonnage of ditto, fo employed, entering inwards, on a like average	579	—67,573
Medium of the average-number and tonnage of Britifh veffels entering inwards and clearing outwards - -	544	—62,738

The account of the number of veffels from whence thefe averages are taken, includes their repeated voyages. It has decreafed fince the war 1690 fhips, or is three-fourths lefs than it was before the war. The quantity of tonnage has decreafed 45,001 tons, or rather lefs than half what it was before the war: but five-eighths of thefe veffels, before the war, belonged to merchants, permanent inhabitants of the countries now under the dominion of the United States; and three-eighths to Britifh merchants refiding occafionally in the faid countries. At that time very few veffels belonging to Britifh merchants, refident in the Britifh European dominions or in the Britifh iflands in the Weft Indies, had a fhare in this trade. The veffels employed in this trade can now only belong to Britifh fubjects refiding in the prefent Britifh dominions. *Many veffels now go from the ports of Great Britain, carrying Britifh manufactures to the United States; then load with lumber and provifions for the Britifh iflands in the Weft Indies, and return, with the produce of thefe*

M

islands, to Great Britain. The vessels so employed are much larger than those in which this trade was formerly carried on, and for this reason the tonnage employed in it has decreased much less than the number of the vessels. The whole of this branch of freight may also be considered as a new acquisition, and was obtained by your Majesty's order in council before mentioned, *which has operated to the increase of British navigation*, compared to that of the United States, in a double ratio; but it has taken from the navigation of the United States more than it has added to that of Great Britain.

Vessels employed between the remaining British colonies in North America, and the British islands in the West Indies.

	Ships.	Tons.
Number and tonnage of British vessels clearing outwards, and employed yearly in the trade between the remaining British colonies in North America and the British islands in the West Indies, on an average of the years 1770, 1771, and 1772, before the war - - - - - -	15	753
Number and tonnage of ditto, so employed, entering inwards, on a like average	23	1,240
Medium of the average-number and tonnage of British vessels entering inwards and clearing outwards - - -	19	996

Number and tonnage of British vessels clearing outwards, and employed yearly in the trade between the remaining British co-

	Ships.	Tons.
lonies in North America and the Britiſh iſlands in the Weſt Indies, on an average of the years 1787, 1788, and 1789, ſince the war - - -	142	12,696
Number and tonnage of ditto, ſo employed, entering inwards, on a like average -	171	16,331
Medium of the average-number and tonnage of Britiſh veſſels, entering inwards, and clearing outwards - - -	156	14,513

The account of the number of veſſels, from whence theſe averages are taken, includes their repeated voyages. The number of veſſels ſo employed has increaſed ſince the war 137 ſhips, being ſeven times more than it was before the war: and the quantity of tonnage has increaſed 13,517 tons, being thirteen times more than it was before the war. Many of theſe veſſels before the war belonged to the inhabitants of the countries which were then Britiſh colonies, but are now under the dominion of the United States: they can now only belong to Britiſh ſubjects reſident in ſome part of your Majeſty's preſent dominions: a part of theſe veſſels, therefore, may be conſidered as a new acquiſition in conſequence of the order in council before mentioned.

The great increaſe of theſe veſſels is to be imputed to the improvement of theſe *remaining* colonies, in conſequence of the great number of refugees who have reſorted thither: it is to be imputed alſo to the more frequent intercourſe that ſubſiſts at preſent between theſe colonies and the Britiſh iſlands in the Weſt Indies, and to the great number of ſhips belonging to theſe colonies, or to ſome other part of your Majeſty's preſent dominions, which go from Newfoundland to the Britifh iflands in the Weft Indies with fifh, a branch of freight which was almoft wholly engroffed before the war by merchants who were permanent inhabitants of the countries then Britifh colonies, but which are now under the dominion of the United States, and from which branch of freight the fubjects of thefe ftates are at prefent entirely excluded.

As the refult of the foregoing deduction, the committee have thought fit to caufe the following table to be prepared; allowance is therein made for the repeated voyages which the veffels employed in thefe different branches of trade are fuppofed to make in each year; and the number and tonnage of the veffels is reduced in due proportion. This table will fhow your majefty, at one view, the increafe and decreafe of veffels and tonnage employed in thefe various branches of navigation, and how far the balance on the whole is at prefent in favour of Great Britain.

		Since the War.			
	…nging to Mer- … were Natives …hent Inhabit- …he countries … then British …ut now form … States.	Vessels belonging to Subjects of the present British dominions.		Vessels belonging to Subjects of the United States.	
	Tons	Vessels	Tons	Vessels	Tons
Veffels, and their…	21,686	261	52,595	163	26,564
Veffels, and their… America	1,402	367	46,106	—	—
Veffels, and their…	5,030	559	133,736	—	—
(a) Veffels, and …	5,609	158	10,219	—	—
(b) Veffels, and … States	31,423	181	20,912	—	—
(c) Veffels, and … in the W…	249	52	4,837	—	—
	65,399	1,578	268,405	163	26,564

R…ned different Branches of Freight,

		American.	
		Veffels.	Tons.
		2	—
—	—	32	1,402
—	—	30	5,030
—	—	131	5,609
—	—	651	31,423
—	—	4	249
Total Decreafe	—	850	43,713
—	—	—	4,877
Balance of Decreafe	—	850	38,836

…t thefe veffels make 1½ voyage in a year.
…yages in a year.
… thefe veffels make three voyages in a year.

The committee think it will throw further light on this ſubject if they lay before your Majeſty an account of the veſſels that were built in the ports of the countries now forming the United States in the year 1772, compared with the number of veſſels that were building in the ports of the ſaid States in the year 1789. This compariſon will prove to your Majeſty how greatly the trade of ſhip-building has declined in theſe countries ſince they were no longer a part of your Majeſty's dominions, and conſequently how very much the number of ſhips belonging to them muſt have decreaſed.

*An Account of the Number of Ships and Brigs built in the Ports of the United States in the Year 1772, compared with the like Veſſels building in the ſaid States in 1789**.

STATES.	1772.		1789.	
	Veſſels.	Tons	Veſſels.	Tons.
New Hampſhire - -	—	—	6	—
Maſſachuſets - - -	—	—	5	—
Rhode Iſland - - -	—	—	—	—
Connecticut - - -	—	—	—	—
Total of the New Eng. Provin.	123	18,149	11	0
New York - - -	15	1,640	—	—
New Jerſey - - -	1	80	1	200
Pennſylvania - - -	18	2,897	14	2,966
Maryland - - - -	8	1,626	5	1,200
Virginia - - - -	7	933	—	—
North Carolina - - -	3	253	—	—
South Carolina - - -	2	213	—	—
Georgia - - - -	5	753	—	—
TOTAL	182		31	

* In the account of ſhips and brigs built in the ports of the United States in the year 1772, which has been laid before the committee, there is no ſpecification of the numbers built in each of the New England provinces, but a total only of the number and tonnage of veſſels built in all theſe provinces; and Mr. Bond, conſul at Philadelphia, who ſent the account of the veſſels building in 1789, has not given the tonnage of the eleven veſſels then building in the provinces of New Hampſhire and Maſſachuſet's Bay: ſo that it is not poſſible to make a compariſon of the quantity of tonnage of which the veſſels in the foregoing table conſiſts.

The committee have received from Mr. Bond, your Majesty's consul at Philadelphia, very accurate accounts of the number of vessels and quantity of tonnage, employed in the trade to and from the port of Philadelphia, where he resides, in the years 1773, 1774, and 1775, distinguishing the vessels and tonnage belonging to the inhabitants of Great Britain—those belonging to the inhabitants of Philadelphia—and those belonging to the inhabitants of the United States, including Philadelphia; and also a like account of the number of vessels and quantity of tonnage so employed in the years 1788 and 1789, distinguishing the vessels and tonnage belonging to the inhabitants of the present British dominions, and those belonging to the subjects of the United States.—As these accounts throw further light on this important subject, the committee will insert them in the Appendix.*

It appears by the first of these accounts, that the tonnage of the vessels belonging to the inhabitants of Great Britain, clearing out from the port of Philadelphia in the years 1773, 1774, and 1775, was not equal to one-fourth part of the tonnage of the vessels so clearing out, and belonging only to the inhabitants of Philadelphia; and that it was equal only to two-elevenths of the tonnage of the vessels belonging to the inhabitants of the countries now forming the United States, including Philadelphia.

It appears by the second of these accounts, that the tonnage of the vessels belonging to the inhabitants of the present British dominions, clearing out from the port of Philadelphia in the years 1788 and 1789, amounted to within one-fifth of the tonnage of all the vessels belonging to the inhabitants of the United States, including Philadelphia, which cleared out from the same port in the same years:—and Mr.

* See these accounts in the Appendix, (B).

Bond alledges, that the tonnage of the veſſels belonging to the inhabitants of the preſent Britiſh dominions, now employed in the port of Philadelphia, in that branch of trade which is called the over-ſea trade, is full four-fifths of the tonnage of all the veſſels ſo employed.

To complete the foregoing accounts, the committee thought it right to enquire what ſhare the ſhips of other European nations, beſides Great Britain, have obtained in the commerce carried on with the United States of America.—It is well known, that the expectation which theſe nations entertained of acquiring a conſiderable ſhare in this branch of trade, in caſe the Britiſh colonies, which now form the United States, could eſtabliſh their independence, operated as a ſtrong motive to induce many of them to be adverſe to the cauſe of Great Britain during the late war; and inclined ſome of them, by degrees, to take a part in the conteſt.

The following account is the beſt that the committee have been able to procure of the veſſels belonging to other European nations, beſides Great Britain, which entered the principal ports of the United States in the following years:

NEW YORK.

1789.	Ships.	Brigantines.	Schooners.	Sloops.	Suppoſed tonnage, according to the American admeaſurement.
Portugueſe - -	3	4	1	0	1,380
Spaniſh - - -	3	3	1	4	1,580
Dutch - - -	2	1	0	0	960
French - - -	1	5	0	0	1,000
Swedes - - -	0	2	0	0	400
Total -	9	15	2	4	5,320

PHILADELPHIA.

1788.	Ships.	Brigantines.	Schooners.	Sloops	Supposed tonnage, according to the American admeasurement.
French - - -	1	4	1	0	692
Dutch - - -	0	4	4	2	1,022
Spanish - - -	7	6	4	0	2,335
Portuguese - -	0	3	0	0	321
Swedish - - -	0	2	0	1	430
Danish - - -	0	1	0	0	157
Prussian - - -	0	2	0	0	388
Total -	8	22	9	3	5,345

CHARLES-TOWN.

1787.	Ships.	Brigantines.	Schooners.	Sloops	Supposed tonnage
Spain - - -	0	2	39	3	1,073
France - - -	0	4	2	2	715
United Netherlands -	1	4	0	0	799
Altona - - -	1	0	0	0	280
Bremen - - -	0	1	0	0	193
Denmark - -	0	1	0	0	164
Hamburgh - -	0	1	0	0	130
Austria - - -	0	1	0	0	127
Total -	2	14	41	5	3,481

The foregoing tables will show in what proportion the several European nations, therein mentioned, have acquired a share in the commerce carried on in three of the principal ports of the United States. The committee have not been able to procure like accounts of the ships belonging to those

European nations, which have been employed in the trade carried on in the other ports of the United States; but, from information laid before them, they have reafon to think that the tonnage of the veffels belonging to European nations, befides Great Britain, which traded to the ports of Virginia in the year 1789, amounted to 2,664 tons;—that the tonnage of the veffels of the like defcription, which traded to the ports of Maryland in the year 1789, amounted to 2,348 tons;—that the tonnage of the veffels of the like defcription, which traded to the ports of North Carolina in the year 1789, amounted to about 3,000 tons;—that the tonnage of the veffels of the like defcription, which traded to the ports of Georgia in the year 1789, amounted to about 2,500 tons;—that the tonnage of the veffels of the like defcription, which traded to the ports of Maffachufet's Bay in the year 1789, amounted to 1,758 tons.

The committee have no information of the veffels of the like defcription, which have been employed in the commerce carried on with the other United States; but if we add to the foregoing quantity of tonnage, amounting to 26,416 tons, one-fourth more for all the remaining ports of the United States of America, the whole of the tonnage of veffels of the defcription before mentioned, employed in the commerce with the United States, will in fuch cafe amount to 33,020 tons, which is but little more than one-fourth of the tonnage of the veffels belonging to Britifh merchants in all the different branches of this commerce, not making allowance in either cafe for repeated voyages.

Immediately after the peace, the merchants of foreign nations entered with great zeal into the trade which was then for the firft time laid open to them, with the countries belonging to the United States of America; but thefe merchants foon found that the great expectations they had entertained were not likely to be realized.—They learned by

N

experience that this trade was not to be carried on without trusting the Americans with their goods, and without giving them longer credit than is usually given in the trade carried on to European countries: many of them sent their vessels with supercargoes on board, who would not sell the goods with which they were entrusted but for ready money, or in barter for an immediate return in the produce of the country: several of these supercargoes met with an ill reception. To these circumstances it is owing, that the merchants before mentioned are now less disposed to engage in this branch of commerce, and that many British vessels are *now* * *actually employed* in carrying the produce of America directly to the markets of other European nations.

The lords of the committee have thought it right to push their enquiries, on all that relates to the commerce carried on with the United States, and to the shipping employed therein, to the utmost extent; as it appeared to them to be *of the greatest importance* to ascertain, with as much accuracy as possible, the effects which the late revolution in North America has hitherto produced on the commerce and navigation of your Majesty's present dominions.—To enable the committee to form a true judgment of what may be the probable effects of the two acts referred by your Majesty to their consideration, or of any other measures which the present congress may pursue, and to suggest, in consequence thereof, what system of policy it may be adviseable for your Majesty's government to adopt, in order to counteract the evil effects of such measures, it was absolutely necessary to be informed how far the acts and other proceedings of the late congress, or of the legislatures of the separate states, have hitherto operated to the disadvantage of British commerce and navigation.—It is true that the merchants and ship-owners of London, Bristol, Liverpool, and Glasgow, in the reports before mentioned,

* In 1791.

all agree in aſſerting that the commerce and ſhipping-intereſt of Great Britain have, in the direct intercourſe between Great Britain and the United States, ſuffered in a certain degree by the diſtinctions made to their diſadvantage in favour of the commerce and ſhipping of the United States, and of other foreign nations.—Theſe diſtinctions may perhaps have contributed to diminiſh the advantages which might otherwiſe have been derived from this trade: but it is evident, from the foregoing comprehenſive view of the various branches of commerce and navigation, to which theſe accounts refer, that the exports from Great Britain to all the countries before mentioned (which is the moſt valuable part of this commerce), have increaſed ſince the war, on an average 166,085*l.* per annum; and that the imports into Great Britain from the ſaid countries have decreaſed ſince the war, on an average, only 75,454*l.* per annum; and that the number of ſhips belonging to the merchants reſident in the preſent Britiſh dominions, employed in all theſe different branches of commerce, has increaſed ſince the war, on an average, annually, 256; and that the quantity of their tonnage has increaſed 111,638 tons; and in like manner, that the number of ſhips, belonging to the ſubjects of the United States, ſo employed, has decreaſed 850 ſhips, and the quantity of their tonnage has decreaſed 38,836 tons.—If indeed we ſuppoſe that the tonnage of the veſſels employed in theſe branches of commerce was eſtimated before the war at one-third leſs than it really was, as before ſtated, the increaſe of the tonnage of the veſſels, belonging to merchants reſident in the preſent Britiſh dominions, will in ſuch caſe be only 59,384 tons; and the decreaſe of the tonnage of veſſels belonging to merchants, that are ſubjects of the United States, will in ſuch caſe amount to 60,634 tons.—It is proper to add, that the inhabitants of the countries which now form the United States had before the war ſome ſhare in the circuitous commerce of Great Britain, by trading from one foreign port to another, and returning occafionally to a Britifh port: they have fince the war loft the benefit arifing from the freight employed in that circuitous trade, whatever the amount of it may have been; and the whole of it now belongs to the inhabitants of the prefent Britifh dominions:—it appears alfo, from what has been before ftated, that the inhabitants of the countries now belonging to the United States built, in the year 1772, 182 top fail-vessels; and that, in the year 1789, the number of fuch veffels, building in the ports of the United States, was only 31:—it appears laftly, that the tonnage of the veffels which belong to the fubjects of all the nations of Europe, befides Great Britain, now employed in the trade with the United States, in the whole amounts to but little more than one-fourth of the tonnage of the fhips, fo employed belonging to the fubjects of the prefent Britifh dominions*.

The lords of the committee will proceed, in the next place, to give an account of the new form of government lately eftablifhed in the United States, as far as it relates to the commerce of the faid ftates, and of the principles on which it is formed; and of fuch of the meafures, hitherto adopted by the faid government, as can have any influence on the commerce and navigation of the Britifh dominions.

A convention of delegates, deputed from all the ftates compofing the United States of America, affembled at Philadelphia on the 17th day of September, 1787.—This convention agreed upon a certain number of fundamental articles, which were to form the bafis of the new conftitution, and laid them before the congrefs of the United States, then affembled, advifing that thefe fundamental articles fhould be fubmitted to a convention of delegates chofen in each indivi-

* Subfequent to the time when this report was completed, and prefented to his Majefty, the government of the United States have publifhed a paper, which contains an account of the tonnage of the veffels entering the feveral ports of the Unit-

dual State by the people thereof, under the recommendation of its exifting legiflature, for their affent and ratification; and

ed States, from the 1ft October, 1789, to the 30th September, 1790. The account is as follows:

An Account of the Tonnage of Vessels entered into the United States of America, from the 1st October, 1789, to the 30th September, 1790, distinguishing each State according to the Magnitude of its Tonnage; and distinguishing the American from Foreign Vessels.

STATES.	AMERICAN.				EUROPEAN.		
	Coasting Vessels.	Fishing Vessels.	Vessels in the Oversea Trade.	Total Tonnage.	Vessels belonging to Gt. Britain, including Ireland.	Vessels belonging to other Nations.	Total Tonnage of the whole.
Massachusets	53,073	24,826	99,124	177,023	19,493	853	197,369
Pennsylvania	6,055	—	51,594	57,649	42,605	9,665	109,919
Virginia	9,914	55	33,560	43,529	56,273	4,092	103,894
New York	6,203	—	42,072	48,275	36,918	6,921	92,114
Maryland	16,099	60	39,272	55,431	23,339	9,485	88,255
*South Carolina	508	—	16,871	17,379	18,725	4,256	40,360
†North Carolina	5,723	—	24,219	29,942	4,941	244	35,127
Connecticut	6,330	—	24,286	30,616	2,556	—	33,172
Georgia	1,090	—	9,544	10,634	15,041	1,570	27,245
New Hampshire	1,670	473	11,376	13,519	3,458	34	17,011
‡Rhode Island	1,626	838	7,061	9,525	95	221	9,841
Delaware	1,061	—	3,080	4,141	1,783	—	5,924
New Jersey	3,429	—	2,085	5,514	267	79	5,860
TOTAL	112,781	26,252	364,144	503,177	225,494	37,420	766,091

RECAPITULATION.

Total Tonnage of each Country, viz.	Tons.	Tons.
United States - -		503,177
Great Britain	222,347	
Ireland -	3,147½	
		225,494½
France -	13,435½	
Holland -	8,815¼	
Spain -	8,551¼	
Portugal -	2,934	
Denmark -	1,619¾	
Germany -	1,668	
Prussia -	394	
Sweden -	311½	
		37,419½
TOTAL - -		766,091

* In the returns from Charles Town, one quarter is wanting, and not included.
† The returns from this state did not commence till 11th March, 1790.
‡ The returns from this state did not commence till 21st June, 1790.

NOTE.—This table contains an account of the tonnage of vessels entering the several ports of the United States, in a period subsequent to any of those years, on that, as ſoon as the conventions of nine ſtates ſhould have ratified the conſtitution, founded on the fundamental articles

which the averages stated in the report were formed. It contains an account of all the tonnage belonging to the subjects of the United States of America, employed in every part of their foreign trade, their coasting trade, and their fisheries, which entered their ports during that period, but does not distinguish what part of it was employed in their foreign trade with the British dominions. On the other hand, the account given in the report is only of so much of the tonnage of the United States as was employed during those years in the various branches of commerce with such parts of the British dominions with which they are allowed now to trade, in ships belonging to the said States. This table contains also an account of the tonnage of British vessels employed during that period in the trade with the United States, and makes the quantity thereof apparently much greater than that stated in the report, as employed therein, during the preceding years, on which the averages were formed.—But it should be observed, that in the period to which the table refers, many events happened, which would necessarily increase the quantity of tonnage employed in the various branches of commerce carried on with the United States. The great demand for corn in almost every country of Europe, during the latter part of the year 1789, and till the harvest of 1790, was the cause that many more ships were freighted during that period, for the purpose of bringing corn from America, than ever had been before. It is well known, that many ships sailed from Great Britain upon speculation for this purpose only; and that the demand for corn in Europe more than doubled the usual price of wheat in America; and that the price of freight from America was considerably raised on that account.—For these reasons, the quantity of American tonnage as well as the quantity of foreign tonnage, and particularly British, that entered the ports of New York, Pennsylvania, Virginia, and Maryland (which are the principal corn countries of the United States), was much greater in this period than in the years to which the report refers.—It happened also, that in this year, the revolution in France induced the several French colonies in the West Indies to open their ports for American ships in a much greater degree than they were opened before. *This circumstance must necessarily have increased the American shipping employed in the intercourse between the countries belonging to the United States and the French islands in the West Indies.*——It is proper also to observe, that the quantity of American as well as of British and other foreign tonnage, as stated in this table, appears to be greater than it actually was, for this reason, that the table which professes to contain an account of the tonnage of vessels entering the ports of the United States includes their repeated voyages, so that the quantity of these different descriptions of tonnage really existing, must be much less than it appears to be in the table.—It is proper further to observe, that many British ships may have entered the ports of the United States without having directly cleared out for the said ports from any British port, or without returning directly from the said ports to a British port;

before mentioned, and have ſignified the ſame to the United States in congreſs aſſembled, the ſaid congreſs ſhould appoint the time and place, purſuant to the ſaid articles, for com-

and in such case, they would not appear in the accounts furnished by the offices of government from which the averages stated in the report were taken. It is a known fact, and is stated as such in the report, that many British ships are employed in carrying on a direct commercial intercourse between the countries belonging to the United States and foreign European nations, and return only occasionally to a British port.

The foregoing observations are sufficient to account for many of the differences that will be found between the accounts of tonnage given in the said table, and the average accounts of tonnage stated by the lords of the committee of privy council in their report, which were taken either from accounts furnished by the public offices of this kingdom, or from information they had previously received from America.

The great superiority which British navigation enjoys in the commerce with the United States, is no less evident from the accounts stated in the foregoing table, than from the averages stated in the report of the committee. The quantity of the tonnage of British vessels which entered the ports of the United States in the period to which this table refers, appears thereby to be more than three-sevenths of the tonnage of all the vessels belonging to the United States, whether employed in their over-sea trade, their coasting trade, or their fisheries: it appears to be even more than three-fifths of all the American tonnage employed in their over-sea trade, which is the only branch of the trade with the United States in which British ships are allowed to have a share, and to enter into competition with the ships of the said states.—The tonnage of the vessels belonging to all other European nations entering the ports of the United States, as stated in the table during the period to which it refers, is in quantity but little more than that stated in the report of the committee; and it would probably not exceed the said quantity, if we had data sufficient to enable us to make the proper deductions; but compared with the tonnage of the British vessels which, according to this table, entered the ports of the United States during the same period, it is equal only to one-sixth part; though, according to the averages stated in the report, from accounts of the preceding years, it was then supposed to be equal to about one-fourth.

If congress continue to publish every year accounts of the tonnage of vessels entering their ports, in the same manner as they have done for the last year, we shall be able in time to form a more decisive and accurate judgment on this subject.——The reasoning of the lords of the committee in the subsequent parts of the report, *is rather confirmed and strengthened*, than in any degree weakened by the accounts stated in the before-mentioned table.

mencing the proceedings neceſſary to the formation and eſtabliſhment of the new federal government.

As ſoon as nine ſtates had acceded to the plan before mentioned, the late congreſs, in purſuance thereof, gave the neceſſary orders for the election of a ſenate and houſe of repreſentatives, of which the new federal government was to be compoſed. This ſenate and houſe of repreſentatives firſt began to ſit at New York on the 4th of March, 1789. They have already held two ſeſſions, and have made ſeveral laws for regulating the commerce of the United States:—A new commercial ſyſtem therefore is now formed, which it is the intention of this committee to lay before your Majeſty.

This commercial ſyſtem is founded; *Firſt*, in the fundamental articles of the new conſtitution, as ſettled by the convention of the 17th September, 1787:—And *Secondly*, in the laws which the new congreſs, aſſembled according to this conſtitution, have paſſed in the two ſeſſions already held by them.

By the firſt article of the new conſtitution, ſection 8, a power is given to the ſenate and houſe of repreſentatives (which the committee will in future call the congreſs) with the aſſent of the preſident of the United States, (which aſſent is to be given by him under certain regulations preſcribed by the ſaid fundamental articles) to lay and collect taxes, duties, impoſts, and exciſes; and it is declared, that all duties, impoſts, and exciſes, are to be uniform throughout the United States.

By the ſame article, ſection 9, no tax or duty is to be laid on articles *exported* from any of the ſtates; and no preference is to be given by any regulations of commerce or revenue to the ports of one ſtate over thoſe of another.

By the ſame article, ſection 10, no ſtate, without the conſent of congreſs, is to lay any duties on imports or exports, except what may be abſolutely neceſſary for executing the laws, called the inſpection laws*; and the net produce of all duties, laid by any individual ſtate on imports or exports, is to be for the uſe of the treaſury of the United States;—and all ſuch laws are to be ſubject to the reviſion and controul of congreſs; and no ſtate without the conſent of congreſs is to lay any duty of tonnage.

By the ſame article and ſame ſection, no ſtate is for the future to emit bills of credit, or coin money, or to make any thing but gold and ſilver coin, a tender in payment for debts:—and by the ſame article, ſection 8, congreſs is to have a power to coin money, and to regulate the value of ſuch coin, and to fix the ſtandard of weights and meaſures.

By article 1ſt, ſection 10, no ſtate is to paſs any *ex poſt facto* law, impairing the obligation of contracts.

By the ſame article, ſection 8, congreſs is to have a power to eſtabliſh uniform laws on the ſubject of bankruptcies throughout the United States.

By the ſame article and ſame ſection, congreſs is to regulate commerce with foreign nations:—and by article 6, all treaties made, or which ſhall be made, under the authority of the United States, are to be deemed the ſupreme law of the land; and the judges in every ſtate are to be bound thereby, any thing in the conſtitution or laws of any individual ſtate to the contrary thereof notwithſtanding: and laſtly, by article 3, ſection 1 and 2, congreſs is authorized, from time to time, to eſtabliſh one ſupreme court, and other inferior courts, in which the judicial power of the United States is to be veſted:—and this judicial power is to extend to all caſes in law and equity, ariſing under the preſent conſtitution, or under treaties made or to be made by the authority of the United States, and to all caſes affecting ambaſſadors or other

* The inſpection laws are laws paſſed by the legiſlatures of the ſeveral ſtates, for appointing inſpectors to aſcertain the quality of certain commodities exported.

O

public miniſters and conſuls, and to all caſes of admiralty and maritime juriſdiction.

It is evident, that many of theſe regulations, which are made fundamental articles of the new conſtitution, took their riſe from defects which had been perceived in the former ſyſtem of government. Theſe regulations are founded on principles of juſtice; and they are certainly favourable to commerce in general; and if the preſent congreſs carry them fully into execution, many of the laws made by the legiſlatures of individual ſtates, impoſing partial burthens on Britiſh commerce and Britiſh ſhips, as before ſtated, will be *ipſo facto* repealed.

In conſequence of the regulation, which declares, that all treaties, already made, or which ſhall hereafter be made, ſhall be deemed to be a part of the ſupreme law of the land, and that the judges in every ſtate ſhall be bound thereby, it may be expected, that Britiſh creditors will now reap the benefit of the 4th article of the late treaty of peace, which ſtipulates, that "Creditors, on either ſide, ſhall meet with no lawful impediment in the recovery of the full value in ſterling money of all *bonâ fide* debts heretofore contracted."

By the regulation, which declares, that no ſtate is to paſs any *ex poſt facto* law, impairing the obligation of contracts, all the laws, made by the legiſlatures of individual ſtates, to prevent Britiſh merchants from recovering the full value of their legal debts, muſt be conſidered as *ipſo facto* repealed.

By the regulation, which declares, that no ſtate ſhall make any thing but gold and ſilver coin a tender in payment of debts, and that congreſs alone ſhall coin money, and regulate the value of ſuch money, as well as of all foreign coin, the laws, paſſed by the legiſlatures of individual ſtates, which oblige Britiſh merchants to take, in payment of their debts, any thing beſides what is thus made legal tender, muſt be conſidered alſo as *ipſo facto* repealed.

And laſtly, the regulation which authoriſes congreſs to eſtabliſh judicatures for deciding all ſuits and controverſies ariſing under the preſent conſtitution, and under treaties, &c. affords juſt reaſon to expect that theſe fundamental articles will be carried into complete execution; and that in all theſe reſpects the legiſlatures of the individual ſtates, and the courts of judicature dependent on them, will no longer have the power of reſiſting, under any pretence, the ſupreme authority of congreſs.

In a word, many of the injuſtices and partialities hitherto practiſed by the legiſlatures of particular States have thus been condemned by the united voice of the people of America aſſembled in convention; and it is certainly reaſonable now to expect that the preſent congreſs, which is compoſed of a body of men aſſembled from every part of the United States, and who act upon a larger ſcale, and in ſupport of a more extenſive and general intereſt, will not commit the like acts of injuſtice, to which the legiſlatures of particular States were too frequently liable, in favour of the immediate and preſſing intereſts of the perſons by whom they were elected, and ſometimes even to relieve the diſtreſſes of the very individuals who compoſed theſe provincial legiſlatures.

The lords of the committee will now proceed to give an account of the ſeveral acts that have been paſſed by the preſent congreſs, in the two ſeſſions already held by them, as far as they relate to the commerce and navigation of your Majeſty's dominions.

The principal acts of this deſcription which were paſſed by congreſs in their firſt ſeſſion, were the two referred by your Majeſty to the conſideration of this committee. By the firſt of theſe acts, entitled, " An Act for laying duties on goods, wares, and merchandize imported into the United States," the duties on each ſort of merchandize, imported into every part of the United States, were made the same, from whatever country they are brought, and in whatever ships they are imported, except that a discount of 10 per cent. of all the said duties was allowed on such goods, wares and merchandize, as should be imported in vessels built in the United States, and which should be wholly the property of citizens thereof, or in vessels built in foreign countries, and, on the 16th day of May, 1789, wholly the property of citizens of the United States, and so continuing till the time of importation; and except, that goods imported from China or India, in ships built in the United States, and belonging to citizens thereof, or in ships built in foreign countries, and, on the 16th day of May 1789, wholly the property of citizens thereof, and so continuing till the time of importation, were made subject to a less duty than the like goods imported in ships of the same description from Europe; and except that all the said last-mentioned goods, if imported in any other manner, that is, in ships that are not of either of the descriptions before mentioned, and not directly from China or India, were made subject to a still higher duty.

The particular duties, so imposed on each sort of goods imported into the United States, will be seen in a copy of the said act annexed to this Report*. The merchants of Glasgow, who have had these duties under their consideration, estimate that they amount, on an assorted cargo, to 7½ per cent. of its value at most; and they estimate the distinction, made by the discount of 10 per cent. of the duties, in favour of goods imported in ships belonging to the subjects of the United States, to amount, on such a cargo, to three-fourths per cent. of its value at most.

By the second of these acts, entitled, "An act imposing

* See this act in the Appendix, (C.)

duties on tonnage," a duty was laid on all ſhips or veſſels built within the ſaid States, and belonging wholly to the citizens thereof; and on ſhips or veſſels, not being built within the ſaid States, but on the 29th day of May 1789, belonging wholly to the citizens thereof, during the time ſuch ſhip or veſſel ſhall continue ſo to belong—6 cents per ton.

On all ſhips or veſſels hereafter built in the United States, and belonging wholly, or in part, to the ſubjects of foreign powers—30 cents per ton.

On all other ſhips or veſſels—50 cents per ton.

On all ſhips or veſſels employed in the tranſportation of any of the produce or manufactures of the United States coaſtwiſe, except ſuch ſhip or veſſel be built within the ſaid ſtates, and belong to citizens thereof—50 cents per ton.

On all ſhips or veſſels built in the United States, and belonging to the citizens thereof, employed in the coaſting trade, or the fiſheries—6 cents per ton, to be paid once in each year.

A *cent* is the hundredth part of a Spaniſh dollar, and in value nearly equal to a halfpenny.

The preſent congreſs, in their ſecond ſeſſion, repealed the duties impoſed by the firſt of the before-mentioned acts; and, by an act then paſſed, entitled, "An act making further proviſion for the payment of the debts of the United States," they impoſed new duties, the amount of which will be ſeen in a copy of the ſaid act, which is annexed to this Report*.

By this act, congreſs have augmented the duties principally on wines, ſpirits, teas, ſalt, cables and cordage of all ſorts; and they have augmented them in a leſs degree on ſome few articles of manufacture, which may be con-

* See Appendix, (D.)

ſidered as objects of luxury; but on moſt other articles, either of produce or manufacture, the duties are continued the ſame*. There is reaſon to believe, that theſe duties

* The committee have inſerted the following table, in order to ſhew on what merchandizes, and in what proportions, the congreſs have thought it right to increaſe the duties of impoſt in the ſaid act. It will prove to what articles the preſent congreſs principally turn their attention, when they wiſh to increaſe the revenue of the United States by duties on goods imported.

			Old Duty	New Duty.	Increase of Duty.
			Cents.	Cents.	Cents.
Madeira Wine . . .		per gall.	18	—	—
London quality . .		ditto	18	35	17
Other Madeira . . .		ditto	18	30	12
All other Wines . . .		ditto	10	20	10
Sherry . . .		ditto	10	25	15
Spirits diſtilled, Jamaica proof .		ditto	10	—	—
All other Spirits . . .		ditto	8	—	—
If more than 10 per cent. below proof		ditto	8	12	4
If more than 5 and not more than 10 per cent. below proof , .		ditto	8	12½	4½
If of proof, and not more than 5 per cent. below proof . . .		ditto	8	13	5
If above proof, but not exceeding 20 per cent. . . .		ditto	8	15	7
If more than 20 and not more than 40 per cent. above proof . . .		ditto	8	20	12
If more than 40 per cent. above proof		ditto	8	25	17
Molaſſes . . .		ditto	2½	3	0½
Teas from India.					
In American veſſels.	Bohea	per lib.	6	10	4
	Souchong, and other black teas	ditto	10	18	8
	Hyſon .	ditto	20	32	12
	Other green teas	ditto	12	20	8
Teas from Europe.					
In American veſſels.	Bohea .	ditto	8	12	4
	Souchong, and other black teas	ditto .	13	21	8

are carried to the utmoſt extent which the people of the United States can at preſent bear ; for, in the debates of the

			Old Duty.	*New Duty.*	*Increaſe of Duty.*
			Cents.	*Cents.*	*Cents.*
	Hyſon .	per lib.	26	40	14
	Other green teas	ditto	16	24	8
	Teas from any other place.				
In any other veſſels.	Bohea .	ditto	15	15	—
	Souchong, and other black teas	ditto	22	27	5
	Hyſon .	ditto	45	50	5
	Other green teas	ditto	27	30	3
Coffee		ditto	2½	4	1½
Sugar, loaf		ditto	3	5	2
brown		ditto	1	1½	0½
Other ſugar		ditto	1½	2½	1
Indigo		ditto	16	25	9
Steel, unwrought . . .		per 112 lib.	56	75	19
Cables		ditto	75	100	25
Cordage, tarred . . .		ditto	75	100	25
Cordage, untarred, and yarn .		ditto	90	150	60
Twine and packthread .		ditto	200	300	100
Coal		per buſh.	2	3	1
Salt		ditto	6	12	6
Gold, ſilver, and plated ware, jewelery and paſtework		ad val.	7½ per ct.	10 per ct.	2½ per ct.
Clocks and watches .		ditto	5 per ct.	10 per ct.	5 per. ct.
Coaches, chariots, &c.		ditto	15 per ct.	15½ per ct.	0½ per ct.
Glaſs . . .		ditto	10 per ct.	12½ per ct.	2½ per ct.
Paper and parchment of all ſorts . . .		ditto	7½ per ct.	10 per ct.	2½ per ct.
Marble, bricks, tiles, ſlates, and other ſtones .		ditto	5 per ct.	10 per ct.	5 per ct.
Pictures and prints .		ditto	5 per ct.	10 per ct.	5 per ct.
Carpets and carpeting		ditto	5 per ct.	7½ per ct.	2½ per ct.
Velvets and velverets, cambrics, muſlins, lawns, laces, gauzes, chintzes, coloured calicoes, and nankeen		ditto	5 per ct.	7½ per ct.	2½ per ct.

houſe of repreſentatives, complaints have been ſince made of the amount of many of them; and it was on that account found neceſſary not to preſs the immediate payment of them on the delivery of the merchandize, but to allow longer credit than is uſually given to thoſe who pay public duties; for it appears, that the American retailer is frequently in want of caſh till he has ſold the goods on which the duties are to be paid.—A drawback is allowed of all the ſaid duties, with reſpect to ſuch merchandizes as ſhall be re-exported within twelve calendar months to any foreign port or place, except one per cent. of the amount of the ſaid duties, which is to be retained as an indemnification for any expence that may have accrued concerning the ſame.

In this laſt act, the congreſs have altered, and in ſome degree augmented, the diſtinction made in the duties on goods imported in ſhips belonging to the ſubjects of the United States, or built therein, and belonging in part to the ſaid ſubjects, and on ſhips belonging to foreign nations; for, inſtead of allowing a diſcount of 10 per cent. of the duties on all goods imported in American ſhips, as in the firſt of theſe acts, an addition of 10 per cent. of the duties now impoſed is made payable on all ſuch goods imported in any other than American ſhips, as before deſcribed, except in caſes where an additional duty is ſpecifically laid by the laſt act on any merchandizes imported in ſuch ſhips.

As the duties, ſo increaſed by this laſt act, do not affect many of the principal objects of Britiſh manufacture, they will not probably raiſe the duties on an aſſorted cargo from Great Britain to more than 1 or 1½ per cent. above what they were in the act of the firſt ſeſſion, that is, to about 8½ or 9 per cent. in the whole.

The ſecond of the acts referred to the committee by your Majeſty, entitled, " An act impoſing duties on tonnage," was alſo repealed by the preſent congreſs in their ſecond seſſion; and inſtead thereof another act was then paſſed for the like purpoſe.

A ſhort time after this ſecond ſeſſion commenced, an attempt was made in the houſe of repreſentatives to increaſe the tonnage duty to one dollar per ton on all foreign-built veſſels, belonging to nations which had not made treaties of commerce with the United States; and it was even propoſed, that this tonnage duty ſhould be raiſed ſtill higher, at ſome future period, when the citizens of the United States had built veſſels ſufficient for carrying their exports to foreign markets; and that, whenever that period arrived, veſſels belonging to nations, which had not made commercial treaties with the United States, ſhould not be permitted to export from the countries belonging to the ſaid States any unmanufactured article, being the growth or produce thereof; unleſs the nation, to which ſuch veſſels ſhould belong, ſhall permit the importation, into their territories, *of fiſh, and other ſalted proviſions*, as well as grain and lumber, in veſſels belonging to the ſubjects of the United States. The houſe of repreſentatives came to a reſolution, and ordered a bill to be brought in, for the purpoſes before ſtated: this bill had a firſt and a ſecond reading; but when it came into the committee, where it was much diſcuſſed, the purport of the bill was wholly altered:—the diſtinction between the veſſels belonging to foreign nations having treaties of commerce with the United States, and thoſe that have not, was rejected; and the new act came out of the committee, and was afterwards paſſed into a law, impoſing the ſame duties, and enacting nearly the ſame regulations, as the tonnage act of the laſt ſeſſion.

The preſent congreſs, in its firſt ſeſſion, paſſed an act for regulating, as well the collection of the duties before mentioned, as the manner of entering and clearing out veſſels:—

P

this act was alſo repealed in the ſecond ſeſſion; and inſtead thereof a new act was paſſed for the like purpoſes.

By this act, congreſs have permitted ſhips, belonging to the citizens of the United States, to enter at more ports and places than ſhips belonging to foreign nations:—they have confined the entry of ſhips, arriving from any country beyond the Cape of Good Hope, to a certain number of ports therein mentioned; allowing, however, every ſuch ſhip to enter at any port, in which ſhe may be owned, or from which ſhe may have ſailed on her voyage:—Congreſs have regulated alſo the mode of collecting the duties *ad valorem*, by enacting, that the value of all ſuch goods ſhall be eſtimated by adding twenty per cent. to the invoice price of ſuch of the ſaid goods as ſhall arrive from *beyond* the Cape of Good Hope, and ten per cent. on the invoice price of ſuch of the ſaid goods as ſhall arrive from any other foreign country.—A diſcount of ten per cent. for prompt payment was allowed by the firſt of theſe acts, but it is omitted in the ſecond:—This laſt act requires, however, that the tonnage duty be paid within ten days after the entry is made, and before the ſhip ſhall be permitted again to clear out: it is alſo required, that the regiſter of every ſuch ſhip be lodged, at the time of entry, in the office of the collector, and there remain till the time of her clearing out: and it is declared, that no merchandize of foreign growth or manufacture, ſubject to the payment of duties, ſhall be brought into the United States in any other manner than by ſea, or in any ſhip or veſſel leſs than thirty tons burthen, except within the diſtrict of Louiſbourg.

To enforce the due execution of the laws before mentioned, as well as all other laws, which derive their authority from the fœderal government now ſubſiſting, the preſent congreſs, in their firſt ſeſſion, paſſed an act for erecting courts of judicature for the trial of all ſuits ariſing under the new conſtitution, as well as under treaties, according to the fundamental article 3d, ſection the 1ſt and 2d, as before ſtated.

By this act, which is entitled, "An act to eſtabliſh the judicial courts of the United States," congreſs have created one ſupreme court, to conſiſt of a chief juſtice and five aſſociated juſtices: And in each of the thirteen diſtricts (into which the States are divided, for this as well as other purpoſes) they have eſtabliſhed a court, to be called "The Diſtrict Court," in which one judge is to preſide, who is to be called "The diſtrict judge."—They have claſſed the diſtricts into three circuits, and have appointed a court in each circuit, to be called "The Circuit Court," which is to conſiſt of two of the juſtices of the ſupreme court, and the judge of the diſtrict where they ſit.

The ſupreme court is to be holden twice a year, on the firſt Monday in February, and the firſt Monday in Auguſt.—The diſtrict judge is to hold four ſeſſions in the year.—The circuit courts are to be holden twice a year.

The laws of the ſeveral States (except where the fundamental articles of the conſtitution, the acts of the congreſs of the United States, or treaties made with foreign powers, ſhall otherwiſe require or provide) are to be regarded in theſe courts, as rules of deciſion in trials at common law, in all caſes to which they apply:—Iſſues in fact are to be tried by a jury in all caſes, except thoſe in equity, and thoſe of admiralty, and of maritime juriſdiction.

The ſeveral caſes, in which theſe courts have original juriſdiction, either concurrent or excluſive, are deſcribed in the act: the ſupreme court has original and excluſive juriſdiction in all ſuits and proceedings againſt ambaſſadors, and other public miniſters, and their domeſtic ſervants;—and it has original, but not excluſive, juriſdiction, in all ſuits brought by ambaſſadors or other public miniſters, or in which a conful or vice-conful fhall be a party: and it has a power to iffue writs of prohibition, and writs of mandamus, in cafes warranted by the principles and ufages of law, to any courts appointed, or perfons holding office under the authority of any of the United States: there are alfo in this act many fpecific provifions for regulating the proceedings of all the courts appointed by this act, and for supporting the exercife of their refpective jurifdictions. The prefent congrefs, in their fecond feffion, made no alteration in this act, except for the purpofe of extending the provifions of it to the State of North Carolina, and that of Rhode Ifland; which States had acceded to the fœderal government between the firft and fecond feffion of congrefs.

THE committee having thus brought into one view all the materials neceffary to affift them in forming their judgment, they will now proceed humbly to offer to your Majefty their opinion on the feveral points referred to them by your Majefty's order in council of the 30th September, 1789, and by the letter of his grace the duke of Leeds, one of your Majefty's principal fecretaries of ftate, dated the 12th November, 1790.

The committee will confider thefe points under the following heads:

First——Commerce.

Secondly—Navigation.

They will begin with the commerce of expõrt from Great Britain to the United States.

The extent and value of this branch of commerce has been already ftated; and it has been fhewn, that nine-tenths of the articles, exported from Great Britain to the faid United States, are Britifh manufactures.

It has alfo been fhewn, that goods of the fame fort, brought from any foreign European country, and imported into the United States, are now made fubject, by the acts of the prefent congrefs, to the fame duties, from whatever European country they may be brought, or in whatever foreign fhips they may be imported.

The merchants, who have been confulted, do not think that thefe duties on goods imported into the United States, amounting on an average to between eight and an half and nine per cent. of their value, are higher than thofe to which Britifh goods, fo imported, were made fubject by the legislatures of individual States before the eftablifhment of the new fœderal government :—and thefe duties are much lefs than the duties payable upon Britifh goods of the like forts imported into moft European countries : they are even lefs than the duties payable on the like forts of Britifh goods imported into France and Holland according to the late treaties of commerce made with thofe countries; Great Britain therefore can have no pretence to complain of the amount of thefe duties : the United States are now an independent nation, and have an undoubted right to impofe duties of the defcription before mentioned, either for the purpofe of raifing a revenue, or of encouraging the produce or manufactures of their own territories :—As long as the prefent congrefs fhall give no preference in this refpect to goods of the like forts imported from other European countries, Great Britain cannot complain of injuftice, nor has fhe any reafon to apprehend a competition :—the excellence and cheapnefs of the manufactures of Great Britain, and the credit which Britifh merchants are able and willing to give, will always enfure to them a greater fhare in the trade of export to the United States, than can be enjoyed by any other European nation. All new eftablifhed countries (and fuch are the United States) can trade only with thofe nations who are able to afford them an extenfive credit, and to incur the rifque refulting therefrom : if all the colonies belonging to European nations in America and the West Indies were to become independent, Great Britain would have undoubtedly the greatest share in the commerce carried on with them.—Even during the late war, the manufactures of Great Britain found their way in great abundance, by indirect courses, into the countries of the United States; and, notwithstanding the price of them was very much advanced by the circuitous mode, in which they were conveyed, great quantities were eagerly purchased by those who were then the enemies of Great Britain.

It is not probable that the commerce of Great Britain will suffer considerably (at least for a long course of years) from any encouragement, which the United States may give to their own manufactures, by laying high duties on those of foreign countries.—In the countries belonging to the United States, that are situated to the south of Pennsylvania, there are no manufactures whatsoever, except a few articles made of leather, which they are enabled to manufacture from the low price of the skins purchased by them.—The legislatures of the northern and middle States have passed laws for the encouragement of manufactures, and have established societies for the like purpose: the inhabitants of these States manufacture some coarse articles for their own use, but very few for exportation.—In the northern and middle States, there is some wool, but of an inferior quality, and much dearer than in Great Britain.—In the States of New England, linen of a coarse sort has been made; and some of it has been exported for the use of other States.—In New England and Pennsylvania there are many iron works; some of them were established before the late war: and the people of these States have manufactured nails and inferior sorts of iron tools, so as to *diminish* very much the importation of these articles from Europe.—In New England and New York, many sorts of houshold furniture are made, and every kind of carriage in very tolerable perfection, as well as some other articles, the materials of which are principally wood and iron.—In New England and Pennsylvania, attempts have been made to introduce cotton manufactures; but it appears from the specimens, that have been transmitted to the committee, that these manufactures are in general of the common sorts, and much inferior in quality, and dearer than those made at Manchester.—In Pennsylvania, paper-mills have been erected, in which paper is made of a tolerable quality, sufficient for their own consumption, and some even for exportation: And in this State, *sugar refineries* have also been established (some of them even before the war) with success; and they are now endeavouring to draw sugar from a particular kind of maple, which they have in great abundance, and thereby to diminish the quantity of sugar imported from the West India islands.—They brew porter in Pennsylvania, but of a very inferior quality.

From this account of the manufactures*, *at present* subsisting in the United States, nothing can be inferred, that ought to give the least apprehension to the manufacturers of Great Britain. The people of all countries, who live in temperate climates, will occasionally employ themselves in manufactures for domestic use during the winter months, or at such times as the cultivation of their lands does not require their attendance: but these domestic occupations seldom give rise to manufactures of any great extent. The people of the United States can apply their industry with more profit to the cultivation of the earth; and it is astonishing to what a degree the inhabitants of all these States prefer agriculture to manufacture: immediately after the peace, great numbers migrated from the northern States to the southern in search of new land, which they could obtain at a cheap rate in the uncultivated countries, that lie at the

* In the year 1791.

back of the ſouthern States: and of late, ſtill greater numbers have reſorted, and are ſtill reſorting, to the interior parts of the American continent beyond the mountains, where ſix new ſettlements are forming: and the people of two of theſe ſettlements are already as numerous as the inhabitants of ſome of the ancient States. In all the States to the ſouthward of Pennſylvania, the principal inhabitants are great landholders, and the inferior inhabitants ſlaves; neither of which are likely to direct their induſtry to manufactures. In countries circumſtanced like the United States, the price of labour will be always too high to enable them to enter largely into the buſineſs of manufactures: and, from the want of capital, they can never afford to give the credit, that is neceſſary to obtain a ſale of them in foreign markets.

From what has been ſaid, the committee are induced to think, that, with reſpect to this branch of commerce, there are but two propoſitions, which it may be proper for Great Britain to make to the preſent government of the United States, in any negotiation for a commercial treaty with them.

Firſt—That the duties on Britiſh manufactures, imported into the United States, ſhall not be raiſed above what they are at preſent.

It may be of uſe to bind the United States, not to raiſe theſe duties above what they are preſent, by obtaining an expreſs ſtipulation for that purpoſe: but if this conceſſion cannot be obtained, it may be ſufficient perhaps to ſtipulate, that the duties on Britiſh manufactures, imported into the United States, ſhall not at any time be raiſed above the duties now payable on the like manufactures imported from Great Britain into France and Holland, according to the commercial treaties with thoſe two powers: or at leaſt, that theſe duties ſhall not be higher than thoſe payable on the like manufactures imported into the United States from the most favoured European nation.

Secondly,—That the duties on all other merchandize, whether British or foreign, imported from Great Britain into the United States, shall not be raised higher at any time, than the duties payable on the like merchandize imported from any other European nation.

This equality of duties is founded in justice. Great Britain enjoys it by the laws of the present congress: But it may be of use to bind the United States to the observance of this rule *in future*, especially as the legislatures of the individual States very frequently departed from this rule before the establishment of the present fœderal government.

The committee will, in the next place, consider the commerce of import into Great Britain from the United States.

The extent and value of this branch of commerce have already been stated. It has been shewn, that the annual imports into Great Britain from the United States have diminished on an average since the war 843,506*l.*; and that this decrease is nearly accounted for by the decreased import of rice and tobacco. The imports from the United States consist principally of articles of food, of naval stores, and of materials of manufactures. All the articles so imported, except perhaps tobacco and grain, can be obtained from other foreign countries, at as low a price, and in as great perfection.

When these States were British colonies, the government of this country granted them favours on account of its connection with them, and encouraged the importation into Great Britain of many sorts of merchandize produced by them, by allowing them to be imported, either free of duty or by making them ſubject to lower duties than were paid on the like articles imported from foreign countries. Since theſe countries were declared independent, Great Britain has continued all the diſtinctions, to which they were before entitled in favour of ſeveral ſorts of merchandize, except as far as relates to oil, and the produce of their fiſheries: And in all other reſpects, the imports into this kingdom from the United States are put on an equal footing with thoſe of the moſt favoured European nation, except ſuch nations only with whom Great Britain has made commercial treaties, founded on reciprocal advantages. It has been ſhewn in a former part of this report, what the amount of the ſeveral before-mentioned diſtinctions is: if they were aboliſhed, it is probable that the imports from the United States would ſuffer a ſtill greater reduction; and it may well be doubted, whether any other ſufficient market could be found for the ſale of many of thoſe articles, which are now brought from thence to Great Britain. Even at preſent, great quantities remain on hand after plentiful crops: and this conſideration has induced ſome perſons to think that the commerce of the United States will in future decline, unleſs they can produce new ſtaples proper for the European market.

Tobacco is at preſent the moſt important ſtaple of the United States. The commerce of this article is ſtill of benefit to Great Britain, though the import of it has been greatly diminiſhed ſince the war. This diminution is owing to the loſs of the monopoly, which we enjoyed before the war, when the tobacco of theſe countries could, by the laws then in force, be imported only into Great Britain. And yet by continuing higher duties on the tobacco imported from other countries, Great Britain ſtill gives to the United States a monopoly *againſt herſelf* in the import of this article. If the tobacco of all countries was made ſubject, on importation, to equal duties, this commodity would be imported from the East Indies, from the Spanish and Portuguese colonies in America, either through Spain and Portugal, or through the British islands in the West Indies; and in a short time, it would probably be imported from the populous settlements now forming on the banks of the Ohio and Missisippi, where tobacco of the best quality is said to be produced: Great Britain would thereby obtain a greater variety of assortments, and her trade in tobacco would be considerably augmented.

Corn is another staple article. It is only in years of general scarcity that Great Britain has occasion to import from the United States corn for the consumption of its inhabitants. At all other times, the surplus quantity, which may be wanted for food, can be obtained, either from Ireland, from the province of Quebec, or from foreign European countries. It is certainly, however, advantageous to the commerce of Great Britain, to encourage the importation of tobacco, corn, and rice, and all other articles, into this country *as a deposit*: but it may be doubted, whether we *do not counteract* this policy, by *encouraging* the importation of any of these articles from the United States, in a manner that discourages the import of them from foreign countries. The British merchant will certainly be able to purchase all these commodities at a cheaper rate, and thereby to improve his trade in them, by having a greater number of markets, to which he can resort upon equal terms for the purchase of them.

After mature consideration of the foregoing circumstances, the committee think that, under this head, there is but one proposition, to which the government of Great Britain can *safely* give its assent in any negotiation for a commercial treaty with the United States, viz.

That no higher duties ſhall at any time be impoſed by the Britiſh legiſlature on any merchandize, the production or manufacture of the United States, imported from thence into Great Britain, than are now payable on the like article, imported from the moſt favoured European nations, even from France and Holland, according to the commercial treaties now ſubſiſting with theſe powers.

It will not be proper even to make this conceſſion, unleſs the United States will, in return, agree to ſtipulate, that the imports into the United States from Great Britain ſhall, in like manner, continue on the footing of the moſt favoured nation, as before propoſed.

The committee do not think it adviſeable that the government of Great Britain ſhould bind itſelf *to continue*, even for a limited time, the diſtinctions hitherto made in favour of certain ſorts of the merchandize of the United States imported into this country. Great Britain may find it for her intereſt, in her negotiations with other foreign powers, to make the duties on goods imported from thoſe countries the ſame as on the like ſort of goods imported from the United States, either by reducing the duties now payable on their importation from other foreign countries, or by raiſing the duties now payable on their importation from the United States. It is not, however, the opinion of the committee, that the preſent ſyſtem ſhould be diſturbed, unleſs in caſes where it is evident that ſome alteration is neceſſary for the general improvement of the commerce of Great Britain.

The commerce carried on with the United States, conſiſting for the moſt part of an exchange of Britiſh manufactures for naval ſtores, and raw materials, is entitled to ſome favourable diſtinctions (though not perhaps to the preſent extent), where ſuch diſtinctions do not interfere with the attention which Great Britain is bound to pay to other more effential interefts, or with the juftice which fhe owes to other foreign nations in alliance with her.

It is proper alfo to obferve, that this commerce is carried on * with Britifh capitals in a much greater degree, than the commerce carried on with any other foreign country; and in all commercial matters, the merchants of Great Britain continue ftill to have a clofe connection with the fubjects of the United States; fo that any great and fudden change would be feverely felt by thofe who, under the faith of the fyftem adopted by the Britifh government fince the declaration of independence, have engaged again in this branch of commerce, and embarked their property in it. Any change, which may be made, fhould be gradual: and there will be lefs ground of complaint, if it can be fo contrived, that without detriment to the public revenue, the duties on goods, imported from other foreign countries, fhould be reduced to the level of thofe now payable on the like forts of goods imported from the United States, and that thefe laft duties fhould in no cafe be augmented.

The committee will confider, in the next place, the commerce carried on by the remaining Britifh colonies in America and the Britifh iflands in the Weft Indies, with the countries belonging to the United States.

This branch of commerce is certainly diminifhed fince the laft war. The committee have not been able to obtain an accurate account of it. The imports into our colonies and iflands from the United States, confift of feveral forts of provifions,—and of ftaves, lumber, and all forts of timber fit for building, none of which are fubject to any duty; and confequently no accurate account can be obtained of the quantity of each fort fo imported: it is evident, however, from the great diminution in the fhipping employed in this branch of commerce, that thefe imports muft have

* In the year 1791.

greatly diminiſhed.—The exports from the Britiſh iſlands in the Weſt Indies to the United States, conſiſt principally of ſugar, rum, and coffee.—The following account will ſhew the quantities of each of theſe articles annually exported to the United States before and ſince the war on an average.

	Before the war.	Since the war.
	Gallons.	Gallons.
Rum	2,559,664	1,653,609
	Cwt.	Cwt.
Sugar	46,943	31,167
	Cwt.	Cwt.
Coffee	3,246	2,063

Though this branch of trade has diminiſhed both in imports and exports, *a proportionable increaſe has thereby been produced in the commerce carried on between the Britiſh iſlands in the Weſt Indies, and the colonies remaining to Great Britain in North America, and between the ſaid iſlands in Great Britain and Ireland.* This increaſe is evident from the increaſed quantity of ſhipping employed in theſe different branches of trade, as before ſtated. It has already been mentioned that, immediately after the peace, the commercial intercourſe between the *remaining* Britiſh colonies and iſlands, and the countries belonging to the United States, was regulated by your Majeſty's order in council, and that it is now regulated by act of parliament. This commerce, with reſpect both to imports and exports, is left nearly upon the footing on which it ſtood before the war, except that ſalted proviſions, and the produce of the fiſheries of the United States, are *not* allowed to be imported from thence into the Britiſh colonies and iſlands.

With reſpect to this branch of commerce, it may be proper for Great Britain to make the following propoſition in any negotiation for a commercial treaty with the United States, viz.

That the commercial intercourse between the remaining British colonies in North America, or the British islands in the West Indies, and the countries belonging to the United States, as far as relates to imports and exports, should continue on the present footing for *a limited number of years.*

The committee think that it would *not be adviseable* for Great Britain to enter into any engagement on this subject for *an unlimited number* of years. It has been found by experience, that the British islands in the West Indies become every year *less in want of the provisions and lumber*, which they have hitherto obtained from the countries of the United States: and a considerable quantity of provisions is now produced in some of these islands, particularly in the island of Jamaica.—Both provisions and lumber are now sent to a large amount *from Great Britain*, as well as *from the remaining British* colonies in America, and *provisions from Ireland*: and it cannot be doubted, that the provisions and lumber, imported from the United States into the West India islands, *tend to diminish the immediate intercourse*, as well between these islands and the British dominions in Europe, as between the said islands and the remaining British colonies in America.—Whether it may ever be proper, all circumstances considered, to put further restraints on the imports from the countries belonging to the United States into the West India islands, is a point, which it is not necessary at present to decide. The policy of Great Britain, in this respect, will depend on future contingencies: but it would be improper, by any stipulation in a commercial treaty, *to relinquish for ever* the right of taking this subject into consideration, as occasion may require.

The committee will now proceed to the second head,

NAVIGATION.

The ships of the United States, coming to the ports of Great Britain, have hitherto been permitted by the British government to continue upon the same footing as before the war. They do not pay the alien's duty, though the ships of all other foreign nations pay it, as before mentioned: They pay, however, Trinity dues, light-house duties, and pilotage, as foreign ships, in all the ports of Great Britain, except London, where they still continue to pay these only as British ships.

The only restriction, which the government of Great Britain has put on the ships of the United States, since the said States were declared independent, is in the trade carried on by them with the British colonies in America, and the British islands in the West Indies; in the commercial intercourse with these colonies and islands, the ships of the United States are now treated as the ships of all other foreign nations, and are not allowed to import or export any merchandize whatever.

In a former part of this report, an account has been given of the distinctions made, to the *disadvantage* of *British* ships, in the commerce with the United States, both before and since the establishment of the new fœderal government. These distinctions consisted, either of higher tonnage duties on British ships than on other ships, or of higher duties on goods imported in British ships than in other ships. It has been stated, that the tonnage duties, imposed by the legislatures of the several States before the establishment of the new fœderal government, were, upon an average, 2*s.* 3*d.* per ton more than were imposed on ships of the United States: and that the difference of duties on goods, imported in a British ship, was then two per cent. on their value more than the duties on the like goods imported in ſhips of the United States: So that a Britiſh veſſel of 200 tons would pay for each voyage 22*l.* 10*s.* tonnage duty; and for a cargo of the value of 2,000*l.* ſterling, 40*l.* import duty more than a ſhip of the United States of the ſame tonnage, and laden with goods of the ſame value.

It has alſo been ſtated, that the tonnage duty, impoſed by the preſent congreſs, on Britiſh or other foreign-built veſſels, is 2*s.* per ton more than is impoſed on ſhips of the United States; ſo that this diſtinction is leſs by 3*d.* per ton, than was impoſed on Britiſh ſhips by the legiſlatures of the ſeveral States, previous to the eſtabliſhment of the new fœderal government.

It has alſo been ſtated, that, by an act of the preſent congreſs, it is required that there ſhall be paid for the cargoes, imported in Britiſh or other foreign ſhips, an addition of 10 per cent. of the duties, payable on the like goods imported in a ſhip of the United States. The merchants of Glaſgow eſtimate this duty to be ¾ per cent. on the value of the cargo, and conſequently 1½ per cent. leſs than the diſtinction made in this reſpect by the legiſlatures of the ſeveral States before the eſtabliſhment of the new fœderal government; ſo that a Britiſh ſhip of 200 tons will now pay for each voyage 20*l.* tonnage duty, and for a cargo of the value 2,000*l.* ſterling, 15*l.* import duty, more than a ſhip of the United States of the ſame tonnage, and laden with goods of the ſame value.

The lords of the committee have thought it right to bring theſe facts and calculations once more under the view of your Majeſty, in order to ſhew that the diſtinction in tonnage and import duties, now made between a Britiſh ſhip and a ſhip of the United States of the ſame burthen, and laden with a cargo of merchandize of the ſame ſorts and

R

value, is about five-twelfths lefs than it was before the eftablifhment of the new fœderal government.

There is at prefent no diftinction between Britifh-built fhips and other foreign-built fhips.—Ships built in the United States, and owned in part by foreigners, pay 20 cents, or 10*d.* per ton lefs duty than foreign-built fhips, when they are employed in the over-fea trade, between the United States and foreign countries: In the coafting trade, Britifh fhips pay the fame tonnage duty as other foreign-built fhips. The effects produced by the diftinctions made by the government of the United States (even when they were five-twelfths more than they are at prefent, upon Britifh and American navigation, are fhewn in the table prepared for that purpofe, and inferted in a former part of this report: It will be there feen, that the navigation of Great Britain, notwithftanding all thofe diftinctions, has, upon the whole, greatly increafed *fince the war*:—It will there alfo be feen that, of fix different branches of freight, in which the veffels belonging to the inhabitants of the countries now forming the United States, had a confiderable fhare before the war, there are five of which they are now wholly deprived; and, in the fixth or remaining branch of freight, viz. "in the direct commerce carried on between Great Britain and the United States," they retain little more than the fame proportion they enjoyed before the war, though they have endeavoured, in the manner before ftated, to favour their own navigation, and *deprefs that of Great Britain.*

It is certain alfo, that the fhips of Great Britain enjoy other advantages fufficient, in a great meafure, to compenfate the unfavourable diftinctions before mentioned:

Firft—The premium of infurance on a fhip of the United

States, bound to and from America, is much greater * than the premium on a British ſhip:

Secondly—The difference between the port charges of all deſcriptions, ſuch as Trinity-dues, light-houſe duties, and pilotage, paid in the ports of Great Britain (though various according to the ports at which the ſhip arrives), is in every one of them very much in favour of a Britiſh ſhip:

Thirdly—The ſhips of Great Britain derive a conſiderable advantage from having a more univerſal and extended navigation, while the navigation of the United States is more confined, as their ſhips are not permitted to trade to the Britiſh iſlands in the Weſt Indies, and cannot venture with ſafety into the Mediterranean, or to the ſouthern parts of Europe, for fear of the Barbary corſairs.

But though theſe advantages may perhaps compenſate the diſtinctions made by the United States to the diſadvantage of Britiſh ſhips; yet it does not follow that no meaſures ought therefore to be purſued by the government of Great Britain *in ſupport of the ſhipping intereſt of this country*, ſo as to counteract the unfavourable diſtinctions to which Britiſh ſhips are now ſubject.—As the ſecurity of the Britiſh dominions principally depends on the greatneſs of your Majeſty's naval power, *it has ever been the policy of the Britiſh government*, to watch with a jealous eye every attempt that has been made by foreign nations to the detriment of its navigation: and even in caſes where the intereſts of commerce, and thoſe of navigation, could not be wholly reconciled, the government of Great Britain *has always given the preference to the intereſts of navigation*; and it

* In 1791.

has never yet ſubmitted to the impoſition of any tonnage duties by foreign nations on Britiſh ſhips trading to their ports, without proceeding immediately to retaliation.

In the year 1593, during the reign of Queen Elizabeth, the State of Venice, (which was then one of the firſt maritime powers of Europe,) made a diſtinction to the diſadvantage of Engliſh ſhips in the duties on merchandize imported into, or exported from, the Venetian territories: Queen Elizabeth, in a charter ſhe at that time gave to the Turkey company, forbade, for the twelve years during which the ſaid charter was to continue, the importation into England of currants, or the wine of Candia in Venetian ſhips, upon forfeiture of the ſaid ſhips and their cargoes, unleſs the State of Venice ſhould think fit to aboliſh the diſtinction before mentioned to the diſadvantage of the ſhips of England:—And in the year 1660, when the government of France impoſed a duty of 50 ſols per ton, payable in the ports of that kingdom, upon the ſhipping of all foreign nations, including therein the ſhipping of Great Britain, the legiſlature of this country, by the *12th Cha. 2. ch.* 18. immediately impoſed, by way of retaliation, a duty of 5*s.* per ton on all veſſels belonging to the ſubjects of France, which ſhould trade to the ports of this kingdom, and enacted, that this duty ſhould continue to be collected as long as the duty of 50 ſols per ton, or any part thereof, ſhould be charged on Britiſh ſhips trading to the ports of France, and three months longer.

As a further inducement to the government of Great Britain to pay due attention to the ſyſtem of policy which the congreſs of the United States appear now to have in view, the committee think it right to ſuggeſt, that, if the Britiſh legiſlature acquieſce in the diſtinctions already made by the preſent congreſs without remonſtrance, the congreſs of the United States may, in a future ſeſſion, be encouraged to increafe thefe diftinctions, fo as to make them, in the end, effectual for the purpofe for which they are intended. The houfe of reprefentatives, in the two laft feffions of congrefs, have certainly had fuch a meafure in contemplation: In the laft feffion they proceeded fo far in it, that a refolution was paffed, and a bill was twice read for that purpofe: the members returned from the northern States, ftrongly fupported this meafure; thofe of the fouthern States refifted it, as being contrary to their interefts: the more moderate members, both of the fenate, and houfe of reprefentatives, thought the time was not yet arrived when they might venture with fafety to take a ftep of this importance.

Four modes of retaliation have been fuggefted to the committee: *Firft*—It has been propofed to follow the fpirited example of the government of this country in the reigns of Queen Elizabeth and Charles II.; and with this view to impofe (as by the *12th Ch. 2. c.* 18.) on the fhips of the United States, coming to this country, a tonnage duty equivalent to the diftinctions made to the difadvantage of Britifh fhips trading to the ports of the United States: but it may be doubted, whether the precedents which are urged in fupport of this direct mode of retaliation, can properly be applied to the prefent cafe. The trade, which Great Britain carries on with the United States, is certainly of a very different nature from that which was carried on with the State of Venice in the reign of Queen Elizabeth, or with the kingdom of France in the reign of Charles II.: the prefent trade of the United States confifts principally of an exchange of Britifh manufactures for naval ftores and raw materials:—the trade with Venice and France, at the periods before mentioned, was directly the reverfe: Great Britain then imported from both thefe countries manufactures or articles of luxury, which were paid for principally by returns in raw materials.—The woollen manufacture was then the only one we poſſeſſed: any reſtraint put on a trade of this laſt deſcription, by way of retaliation, could, in no event, be very detrimental to the intereſts of this country; it might even operate for its benefit: but a reſtriction of the nature before mentioned, put on the preſent commerce with the United States, would tend to confine this trade to ſo much of it as can be carried on in Britiſh ſhips only, or to the importation of ſo much of the ſeveral articles of which it conſiſts, as may be neceſſary for our own conſumption, and would prevent their being brought here as a place of depoſit, at leaſt by American ſhips.—Theſe ſhips would, in ſuch caſe, find it their intereſt to carry their cargoes directly to other foreign countries.

It is the opinion of ſome of the merchants and ſhip-owners, who have been conſulted, that, even in the preſent ſtate of this trade, not only the ſhips of the United States, but Britiſh ſhips, have too many inducements to carry thoſe bulky articles to foreign ports, inſtead of bringing them to the ports of Great Britain as a place of depoſit; and that to this circumſtance it is to be imputed, that our trade in tobacco and rice has ſince the war declined in the manner before ſtated: and it is proper to add, that any meaſure which induces the American merchant to carry his commodities to foreign markets, inſtead of bringing them to Great Britain, may have the effect of diminiſhing, in return, the export of Britiſh manufactures to the countries of the United States.

The *ſecond* mode of retaliation is, that a duty be impoſed on all manufactures or merchandize laden in the ports of Great Britain, on board the ſhips of the United States, for the purpoſe of being carried to the countries of the ſaid States, equivalent to the diſtinctions made to the diſadvantage of Britiſh ſhips trading to the ports of the United States.—This propoſition, which is made by the merchants and ſhip-owners of Liverpool, will, if adopted, have this bad effect, that the manufactures and merchandize of Great Britain ſent from hence to the United States in Britiſh ſhips, or in ſhips of the ſaid States, will pay, either here or in America, higher duties than will be payable on the like goods imported into the United States from other foreign countries, in ſhips belonging to ſubjects of the ſaid States: and if congreſs ſhould in future raiſe the duties on theſe manufactures and merchandize imported in Britiſh ſhips, or ſhould make the diſtinctions in the tonnage duties greater than they are at preſent, it will be neceſſary for Great Britain, in purſuing this line of policy, to impoſe equivalent duties on Britiſh manufactures and merchandize exported in American ſhips; ſo that, in the end, the manufactures and merchandize ſent from this country, might be wholly excluded from the American market, to the benefit of the trade of other foreign countries.

The *third* mode of retaliation is, that the government of Great Britain ſhould allow a bounty on Britiſh ſhips trading to the ports of the United States, in proportion to their tonnage and cargo, equivalent to the diſtinctions made to the diſadvantage of Britiſh ſhips trading to the ſaid ports. If this propoſition is adopted, the legiſlature of Great Britain will be under the neceſſity of raiſing this bounty on Britiſh ſhips and their cargoes, in proportion as congreſs ſhall at any time increaſe the diſtinctions already made to the diſadvantage of Britiſh ſhips trading to the ports of the United States:—and congreſs will thus have it in its power to impoſe a charge on the revenues of Great Britain, by the very ſame meaſure which lays a burthen on the commerce of Great Britain, and increaſes the revenue of the United States.

The *fourth* mode of retaliation is, that a duty be impoſed on the merchandize of the United States imported into this country in ſhips of the ſaid States, equivalent to the diſtinctions made to the diſadvantage of Britiſh ſhips trading to the ports of the United States.—This propoſition, taken in its full extent, is liable to all the objections that have been ſtated againſt the firſt mode of retaliation: theſe objections it is not neceſſary here to repeat.

The merchants and ſhip-owners of Liverpool appear diſpoſed to proceed to immediate retaliation. They think that this mode of proceeding will lead to a negotiation, and oblige congreſs to conſent to reaſonable terms. They alledge, but without ſufficient foundation, that the act of the preſent congreſs, which makes a diſtinction to the diſadvantage of Britiſh ſhips, to the amount of 10 per-cent. of the duties payable on goods imported in them, bears harder upon Britiſh ſhips, than any of the diſtinctions enacted in the laws of particular States before the eſtabliſhment of the preſent fœderal government: and they add, that the diſtinctions before mentioned will prevent Britiſh ſhips from obtaining freights, while there are ſhips of the United States ready to receive them.

The merchants and ſhip-owners of London, Briſtol, and Glaſgow, are of opinion, not to proceed to immediate retaliation.—They think that it will be adviſeable to endeavour firſt, by negociation, to remove the preſent unfavourable diſtinctions; but if juſtice cannot in this way be obtained, that it will be neceſſary, in the end, to proceed to retaliation. It is clear, therefore, that all theſe merchants look forward, in certain contingencies, to a meaſure of this nature.—The committee thought it right, on this account, to ſtate all the modes of retaliation which have hitherto been propoſed to them, and the objections which may be urged againſt each of theſe modes.

After mature conſideration of this very difficult part of the ſubject, the Lords of the committee will venture humbly to ſuggeſt, that, if at length it ſhall be found abſolutely neceſſary, for the *ſupport* of the *navigation* of this country, to proceed to ſome meaſure of retaliation, the beſt that can be adopted is—to impoſe upon tobacco and rice, the produce of the United States, imported in the ſhips of the ſaid States for the conſumption of Great Britain, and upon ſuch other articles, the produce of the ſaid States, as can be obtained from other countries at as low a price, and in as great perfection, imported in the ſhips of the ſaid States for the like purpoſe, a higher duty than ſhall be payable on the like articles, imported from thence in Britiſh ſhips, or from other foreign countries—to allow all ſuch articles to be imported from the countries of the ſaid States, for the purpoſe of being warehouſed, ſubject to the preſent duties, even in ſhips belonging to the United States—and to grant a bounty of 15*s*. per hogſhead on tobacco, imported in Britiſh ſhips, on being taken out of the warehouſe for exportation.

It will be proper alſo, in ſuch caſe, to make the ſhips of the United States ſubject to the *aliens duty*, in the ſame manner as other foreign ſhips.—It is apprehended that this laſt meaſure muſt at all events be adopted; for there is reaſon to believe, that other foreign nations will not patiently ſubmit to this diſtinction, if the ſhips of the United States continue to be exempted from it: and it would be highly impolitic in Great Britain to give up this duty in all caſes, as it certainly affords eſſential protection to the ſhipping intereſt of this country, in the trade carried on with ſome of the northern nations of Europe.

The committee think, that the mode of retaliation, before ſuggeſted, will effectually anſwer all purpoſes for which it is intended; and it is probable that the members of congreſs, who repreſent the ſouthern States, being ſenſible how much it will tend to diminiſh the ſale of their ſtaple commodities, will be thereby induced to reſiſt any violent meaſures, to which the members of the northern States might on this account be inclined; and that a majority of congreſs will by

S

this means be brought to consent to a fair and reasonable settlement of this business.

The committee are of opinion, that this mode of retaliation will not, in any material degree, injure the commerce of Great Britain, at the same time that it will protect and support its navigation.—It will not raise the price of the before mentioned articles, imported from the United States for the consumption of this country, as a sufficient quantity may be imported in British ships for that purpose; and by encouraging the importation of the like articles from other foreign countries, it may tend even to diminish the price of them at the British market.

It is clear also, that this mode of retaliation will not tend to prevent the importation of any of those articles from the United States into this country, as a place of deposit, even in the ships of the said States: it lays no new burthens on these articles imported for that purpose in such ships; and it proposes to give a bounty on tobacco imported in British ships, whenever it shall be taken out of the warehouse for re-exportation: this measure may perhaps have the effect of restoring the trade of tobacco to the flourishing state in which it was before the war, when this commodity was necessarily brought from the United States to Great Britain, before it could be carried to foreign countries.

A bounty of 15*s*. per hogshead will probably be sufficient to answer the end for which it is proposed to be given.—The merchants of Glasgow estimate the charges of landing and re-shipping a hogshead of tobacco in the ports of Great Britain, and the freight and insurance of it from Great Britain to the ports of Holland and Germany, from 15*s*. to 20*s*. per hogshead.

Whether the before mentioned bounty may not be too heavy a charge on the revenue of Great Britain, it belongs not to this committee to decide: they will only observe, that the importation of tobacco into Great Britain, ſince the war, is about 50,000 hogſheads leſs than it was before the war.—If it is ſuppoſed that the bounty of 15*s.* will be paid even on 60,000 hogſheads, it will amount to 45,000*l.* per annum.—But the merchants of Glaſgow alledge, that a ſhip of about 200 tons, going to a foreign port, expends therein not leſs, on an average, than 4 or 500*l.* in every voyage, which is a gain to the foreign port, and a loſs in equal proportion to the ports of Great Britain: and it is certain, that the duties, which are now paid in every ſuch foreign port upon the cordage, ſailcloth, &c. employed in refitting the ſhip, and on wines, ſpirits, beer, cloth, candles, &c. conſumed by the crew, and by all thoſe to whom this buſineſs gives occupation, would, if ſuch ſhip came to a Britiſh port, be an addition to the revenue of Great Britain:—the merchants alſo obſerve, that many of the ſeamen ſo employed are in the end loſt to this country; for by navigating from one foreign country to another, they acquire foreign connections, particularly in America, where the Engliſh language is ſpoken, ſo that theſe ſeamen no longer retain their natural attachment to this country.

The mode of retaliation before ſuggeſted, and particularly the bounty before propoſed, will probably preſerve this country from another evil now impending, and likely to be very detrimental to its navigation. The committee have been informed, that there are merchants in this country, who are employing a part of their capitals in building ſhips in the United States for the purpoſe of carrying on their commerce with the United States in ſuch veſſels, and thereby avoiding the unfavourable diſtinctions to which Britiſh ſhips are now expoſed.—Though a project of this nature is not only detrimental but even hoſtile to the intereſts of this country, it is doubtful whether any legal proviſion can be deviſed, ſufficient to prevent it: the only manner in which it can be effectually prevented is, to make it no longer the intereft of any inhabitant of Great Britain to venture his property in fuch a fpeculation.

In giving their opinion on this fubject, the committee have thus far principally had in view the direct navigation between Great Britain and the countries belonging to the United States. On the navigation between the Britifh iflands in the Weft Indies, as well as the remaining Britifh colonies in North America, and the countries now under the dominion of the United States, the committee have already made fome obfervations in the preceding part of this Report: and in a former Report of the 31ft May, 1784, they humbly fubmitted to your Majefty their reafons for not allowing to the fhips of the United States the privilege of trading to the ports of your Majefty's faid colonies and iflands. *Your Majesty was pleased to approve of the advice then given:* many of the merchants and planters of the iflands in the Weft Indies, who formerly refifted this advice, *now acknowledge the wifdom of it:*—Parliament, by paffing an act for making permanent regulations, founded on this Report, have given their fanction to the fyftem of policy therein recommended.—*The great advantages, which have refulted from this meafure,* appear in the accounts ftated in the former part of this Report.

After full confideration of all that has been offered on the fubject of navigation, the committee think that there is but one propofition, which it will be advifable for the minifters of Great Britain to make on this head to the government of the United States, in any negociation for a commercial treaty between the two countries, viz.—That Britifh fhips, trading to the ports of the United States, fhall be there treated, with refpect to the duties of tonnage and import, in like manner as fhips of the United States fhall be treated in the ports of Great Britain.

If this principle of equality is admitted by the government of the United States, as the bafis of negociation, it will be proper then to confider, whether fhips of the United States, trading to the ports of Great Britain, ſhould not be made ſubject to the aliens duty, as well as other foreign ſhips; and in return that congreſs ſhould impoſe on Britiſh ſhips, trading to their ports, ſome diſtinction, equivalent to the amount of the aliens duty; or whether every diſtinction of this nature ſhould not be aboliſhed on both ſides.—The committee have offered, already, ſome reaſons, which induce them to think that the firſt of theſe alternatives ſhould be adopted.

If congreſs ſhould propoſe to apply the rule of aboliſhing all diſtinctions to Trinity dues, light houſe duties, and pilotage, ſuch a propoſition cannot be complied with. Theſe ſeveral ſorts of charges are of ancient eſtabliſhment, and are the property of private perſons, or of corporate bodies; and the funds ariſing from them, are, in many inſtances, applicable to public works or charitable purpoſes.—An attempt to equalize them would affect the intereſts of many of the ports of this kingdom, and alter their relative ſituations:—in conſideration of the diſtinction which time and accident have made in all theſe reſpects, docks, magazines, and other buildings, have been erected in ſeveral ports of the kingdom at the charge of individuals: any change of this nature would have the effect of increaſing the great advantages, which the capital of Great Britain already enjoys, in carrying on its commerce, over many of the other ports of the kingdom: And laſtly, if this favour was granted to the ſhips of the United States, other nations would be induced to claim the like equality, which it is impoſſible to grant, conſiſtently with the intereſts of this country.

If congreſs ſhould propoſe (as they certainly will) that this principle of equality ſhould be extended to *the ports of our colonies and iſlands*, and that the ſhips of the United States ſhould be *there* treated as Britiſh ſhips, it ſhould be anſwered, that this demand *cannot be admitted*, even as a ſubject of negociation: by the public law of Europe, every nation has a right to regulate the commerce which it carries on with its own colonies, in the manner that ſhall appear to be the moſt conducive to the intereſt of the mother country :—in regulations of this ſort, *no foreign government has any right to interfere*:—this branch of freight is of the ſame nature with the freight from one American State to another ; congreſs has made regulations to confine the freight, employed between different ſtates, to the ſhips of the United States ; and Great Britain does not object to this reſtriction.—The United States at preſent enjoy all the rights and privileges of an independent nation ; and, as ſuch, *they now have no pretence to claim the privileges* which they once enjoyed as Britiſh colonies.

If, in the courſe of this negociation, it ſhould be propoſed to treat on maritime regulations, the committee are of opinion, that the government of Great Britain may conſent to inſert in a commercial treaty with the United States, all the *articles* of maritime law which have of late been inſerted in our commercial treaties with other foreign powers ; except that any article allowing the ſhips of the United States to protect *the property of the enemies of Great Britain in time of war*, ſhould on no account be admitted :—it would be more dangerous to concede this privilege *to the ſhips of the United States*, than to thoſe of any other foreign country :—from their ſituation the ſhips of theſe States would be able to cover the whole trade of France and Spain with *their iſlands and colonies* in America and the Weſt Indies, whenever Great Britain ſhall be engaged in a war with either of thoſe powers ; and *the navy of Great Britain* would, in ſuch caſe, be deprived of the means of *diſtreſſing* the enemy, by deſtroying his commerce, and thereby diminiſhing his reſources.

The Lords of the committee agree in opinion with the merchants of London, Briſtol and Glaſgow, that before any meaſure of an adverſe nature is adopted, it is proper that attempts ſhould be made by negociation to induce the congreſs of the United States to consent to some fair and equitable plan of accommodation, and to a liberal system of commerce and navigation, founded on reciprocal advantages.—It has been shewn, in a former part of this Report, that, from the time that peace was concluded, and that the United States were acknowledged by treaty to be independent, the government of this country have never taken any hostile step to mark their resentment on account of the many oppressive and even unjust laws to which the merchants of Great Britain were made subject by the legislatures of the several States, previous to the formation of the present fœderal Government.—After an angry contest of seven years continuance, it was not to be supposed that all resentment would at once be extinguished in the minds of the people of the United States: in such a state of things, forbearance, on the part of Great Britain, in every thing not essential, was a prudent as well as dignified line of conduct: there was reason to hope that the spirit which had produced many of the before-mentioned acts of commercial hostility, would in time subside, and that ancient habits, and the recollection of former connections, might bring back the people of these States to a more favourable disposition to Great Britain:—circumstances might also occur, which would tend to detach them from their new connections, and make the people of the two countries, though no longer fellow-subjects, friends at least, as they were before the war:—the government of Great Britain has not been wholly mistaken in its expectations:—the new system adopted by the congress, is certainly much more favourable to the navigation and commerce of this country, than that which subsisted under the laws of particular states; and there can be no doubt, from the proceedings of congress already stated, and from all that passed in their debates during the two last sessions, particularly in the American senate, that a party is already formed in favour of a connection with Great Britain, which, by moderation on our part, may perhaps be ſtrengthened and increaſed, ſo as to bring about in a friendly way, all the objects we have in view.—It would indeed be extraordinary if, after having ſubmitted for the laſt ſeven years to a ſituation more diſadvantageous than the preſent, the government of Great Britain ſhould at once proceed to acts of retaliation, or commercial hoſtility, juſt at the time that the powers, who now govern the United States, appear to be more favourably diſpoſed to this country:—On the other hand, it would be imprudent to place, as yet, too much confidence in the ſuppoſed intentions of the new government, till we have learned from experience whether congreſs is likely to perſiſt in the principles it has hitherto adopted, and will have influence or power ſufficient to carry the laws, founded on theſe principles, into execution, through all the different ſtates.

For theſe reaſons, the committee are inclined to think, that it may be adviſeable for your Majeſty to conſent to open a negociation with the United States for the purpoſe of making a commercial treaty, eſpecially as congreſs appears inclined to this meaſure: but it will be right, in an early ſtage of this negociation, explicitly to declare that Great Britain can *never ſubmit*, even to treat on what appears to be the *favourite object* of the people of theſe States, that is, *the admiſſion of the ſhips of the United States into the ports of your Majeſty's colonies and iſlands*: it may be proper alſo to make them underſtand, that Great Britain has meaſures in view ſufficient for the protection and ſupport of its own commerce and navigation, in caſe congreſs ſhould proceed to make further diſtinctions to the detriment of theſe important objects, and ſhould refuſe to conſent to a fair and equitable plan of accommodation. The proper mode of retaliation, which, in ſuch an emergency, may be purſued, has already been ſtated.

There can be no doubt, that the commercial intercourſe which at preſent ſubſiſts between Great Britain and the United States is highly beneficial to both countries; but it is equally certain, that the United States have much more to apprehend from any interruption of this intercourſe, than Great Britain has to apprehend from any reſtriction which the government of the United States may put upon it:—it has been ſhewn, that the commerce of theſe ſtates with the other nations of Europe has hitherto been of no great extent; and there are circumſtances which make the further augmentation of it very difficult:—it has been ſhewn alſo that the merchants of Great Britain alone are inclined to run the riſk, and to give the credit which are eſſential to the ſupport of a commercial connection with all newly eſtabliſhed countries:—the articles which the people of the United States now ſend to the European markets are but few, and can be obtained in equal perfection from other countries: and it is more likely, that the demand for them from thence ſhould in future diminiſh, than increaſe:—when the crops of grain in Europe happen at any time to fail, the people of the United States will have an opportunity of exporting (as in the courſe of laſt year) great quantities of corn to the markets of Europe; but there is no trade ſo precarious as that of corn; and no ſyſtem of foreign commerce, permanently profitable, can be founded upon it; and new ſettlements are forming in the neighbourhood of the United States, which will ſoon rival them in this and in every other ſtaple commodity which they produce:—the fiſheries of the United States, once ſo proſperous, are now greatly declined, becauſe there is no longer any ſufficient market for the ſale of the produce of them; the former ſucceſs of theſe fiſheries is principally to be imputed to the ſhare which the produce of them had before the war in the markets of the Britiſh dominions:—Since the peace, the merchants of the

T

United States have endeavoured, by means of the cheapneſs of the rum, diſtilled from molaſſes, to carry on a trade to the coaſt of Africa, but with little ſucceſs:—at the ſame time, they launched alſo into a trade with the countries to the eaſt of the Cape of Good Hope, particularly China, which was at firſt profitable; but this trade ſoon found its limit, and has of late very much declined; the people of the United States have not wealth ſufficient to ſupport any large conſumption of Aſiatic luxuries, ſo that thoſe who have engaged in this trade, now found their hopes on the profits to be derived from ſmuggling theſe articles into other countries:—it muſt be acknowledged, that the commercial intercourſe between the United States and the French iſlands in the Weſt Indies has of late been greatly increaſed; and it is alſo probable, that the merchants of theſe ſtates have found opportunities to open illicit and profitable connections with the ſubjects of the Spaniſh dominions in America; but as theſe ſorts of commercial connection, though perhaps encouraged by the people of the French and Spaniſh colonies, are highly detrimental to the intereſts of their reſpective mother countries, and contrary to the laws by which the commerce of thoſe colonies has hitherto been regulated, the continuance of the advantages which the people of the United States may derive from theſe ſources of wealth, muſt be precarious, and will depend on circumſtances.—Such is the preſent ſtate of the commerce of the United States; the lords of the committee have thought it right thus to collect theſe conſiderations, which have been ſtated more at large in the former parts of this report, and to bring them once more under the view of your Majeſty, in order to ſhew that your Majeſty may ſafely reſiſt any unreaſonable pretenſions, but not to prevent a commercial arrangement with the United States, founded on terms which are conſiſtent with the eſſential intereſts of the commerce and navigation of the Britiſh dominions.

Accounts received ſince the Report was printed, with Obſervations on them.

FIRST ACCOUNT.

THE following abſtract of the exports from the countries belonging to the United States of America, from Auguſt 1789 to the 30th September 1790, was received after the foregoing report was printed.—It contains an account of the exports from the ſaid ſtates for about thirteen months, amounting in value to 20,415,966 dollars 84 cents, which, eſtimating the dollar at 4*s.* 6*d.* is equal to 4,593,592*l.* ſterling. —For twelve months, or one year, the export therefore would amount to 4,240,239*l.*—But the amount of the exports from the United States for this year, is probably conſiderably more than in a common year.—The great want of grain in Europe during the latter part of the year 1789 and the beginning of 1790, occaſioned a vaſt export of grain from the territories of the United States, ſo as to raiſe the price of wheat and flour in thoſe countries to nearly double what it is in an ordinary year.—The great increaſe of exports from the United States during the before mentioned period is proved by the ſtate of the exchange.—The par of exchange with Philadelphia is 66⅔ per cent. From the year 1783 this exchange had been, upon an average, at about 70, which is between 3 and 4 per cent. above par. From November 1789, when the great export of grain commenced, the exchange began to fall, firſt to 50, then to 45, and, at laſt, to as low as 40; because there were then bills on this country in great plenty, and the balance of trade between Great Britain and Philadelphia (which is uſually in favour of Great Britain) was, during that period, in favour of Philadelphia, owing to the unuſual export of grain: but in the month of July 1790, when the export of grain from the United States began to decline, the exchange roſe again to par, and is likely ſoon to be above par, as it was before November 1789.

It appears, by this abſtract, that the exports from the United States to the dominions of Great Britain are nearly one half of the whole of their exports.—To the dominions of France, the exports of the United States during this period were leſs than one half of the exports to the dominions of Great Britain; and it is probable that the increaſe of the exports to the French dominions, above the common average, was greater during this period, than the increaſe of the exports to Great Britain, or to any other country, as the dearth of corn in the years 1789 and 1790 affected France much more than any other European nation. It was leſs felt in Great Britain than in any country with which the United States have a commercial intercourſe.—About this period alſo the government of the Fren chiſlands, by regulations of their own, firſt opened their ports, almoſt without reſtriction, to the importation of lumber, fiſh, grain, live ſtock, and proviſions, from the United States, contrary to the intereſts and intentions of the mother country.—It appears that the value of the lumber, fiſh, grain, live ſtock, and proviſions, exported from the United States during this period, amounted to 10,968,049 dollars, or £.2,467,811 : 0 : 6

ſterling, being more than one half of the whole of their exports.

It is ſingular how ſmall the value is of the produce of the whale fiſhery exported from the United States: it amounts only to 252,591 dollars, or £. 56,832 : 19 : 6 ſterling.

This abſtract does not diſtinguiſh the exports to the ſeveral nations of Europe, from the exports to their reſpective colonies; ſo that it is impoſſible to determine what proportion the firſt bears to the latter.

Letter from the Secretary of the Treasury of the United States, transmitting to the House of Representatives an Abstract of the Exports of the United States from August 1789 to the 30th of September 1790.

TREASURY DEPARTMENT,
" SIR, Feb. 15, 1791.

" I do myself the honour to transmit through you to the house of representatives, a general return of the exports of the United States, abstracted from custom house returns, commencing on the various days in August, 1789, whereon they were respectively opened, and ending on the 30th of September last. From inadvertence in some of those offices, the space of time prior to the 1st of October, 1789, was blended with the quarter following, which prevented an uniform commencement of this abstract on that day; and there is yet a deficiency of many of the returns for the last quarter of the year 1790, which confines the abstract to the 30th of September last. The progress which was made in this form of statement of the exports, prior to the order of the house, and the impossibility of having it completed in the form directed by them before the fourth of March next, have occasioned me to offer it in its present shape.

" I am, &c.

" ALEXANDER HAMILTON,

" *Secretary of the Treasury.*

To the Honourable the SPEAKER
Of the House of Representatives of the United States.

Abstract of the Exports of the United States, from the Commencement of the Custom-Houses in the several States, which where at different Times in August, 1789, *to the* 30*th Day of September,* 1790.

Species of Merchandise, EXPORTED.		*Quantity.*		*Value.* Dollars.	Cts.
ASHES Pot, -	tons	7,050	10	661,634	
Ashes Pearl, -	do.	1,548	55	177,459	50
Apples, - -	barrels	5,898		6,318	
Boats, - -	-	8		372	
Bomb Shells, -	tons	10		100	
Bricks, - -	-	870,550		2617	50
Beer and Porter, -	casks	472		4,612	
Brandy, -	do.	97		3,016	
Cordials, -	boxes	236		637	
Cordage, -	-			5,739	
Carriages, -	-	220		28,017	
Candles Tallow,	lbs.	149,680		14,876	
Candles Wax, -	do.	5,274		2,461	
Candles Myrtle, -	do.	249		52	
Cyder, -	barrels	442		849	
Cotton, - -	bales	2,027		58,408	
Coffee, - -	lbs.	254,752		45,753	
Chocolate, -	do.	29,882		3,537	
Cocoa, - -	do.	10,632		950	
Cassia and Cinnamon,	do.	9,392		9,715	
Deer Skins, -	-			33,009	
Duck American, -	bolts	77		777	
Duck Russia, -	do.	220		2,200	
Earthen and Glass Ware				1,990	
Essence Spruce, -	boxes	115		600	
Flax Seed, -	casks	40,019		236,072	
Flax, - -	lbs.	21,970		1,468	

Species of Merchandize, EXPORTED.		Quantity.	Value. Dollars. Cts.
Furs, - - - -			60,515
Furniture, - -			8,351
FISHERY.			
Fish dried,	quintals	378,721	828,531
Fish pickled,	barrels	36,804	113,165
Oil Whale, -	do.	15,765	124,908
Oil Spermaceti,	do.	5,431	79,542
Candles do. -	℔s.	70,379	27,724
Whale-bone, -	do.	121,281	20,417
GRAIN.			
Buck-wheat, -	bushels	7,562	2,572
Corn, -	do.	2,102,137	1,083,581
Oats, - - -		98,842	20,900
Rye, - -	do.	21,765	13,181
Wheat, - -	do.	1,124,458	1,398,998
Genseng, - -	casks	813	47,024
Gunpowder, -	℔s.	5,800	861
Gin, - - -	gals.	18,025	16,989
Grindstones, -	-	203	450
Hair-powder, -	℔s.	12,534	1,687
Hats, - -	-	668	1,392
Hay, - -	tons	2,126	12,851
Horns, - -	-		1,052
Ironmongery, -	-		7,878
Iron Pig, - -	tons	3,555	91,379
Iron Bar, - -	do.	200	16,723
Indigo, - -	℔s.	612,119	537,379
LIVE STOCK.			
Horned Cattle, -		5,406	99,960
Horses, - -		8,628	339,516
Mules, - -		237	8,846
Sheep, - -		10,058	17,039
Hogs, - -		5,304	14,481
Poultry, -	doz.	3,704	6,263
LUMBER.			
Staves and Heading,		36,402,301	463,229
Shingles, - -		67,331,115	120,151

Species of Merchandize, EXPORTED.	Quantity.	Value. Dollars.	Cts.
Shook Hogſheads,	52,558	32,002	
Hoops, - -	1,908,310	19,598	
Boards, - -	46,747,730	260,213	
Handſpikes, - doz.	2,361	1,505	
Caſks, - -	2,423	3,697	
Scantling, - feet	8,719,638	95,368	
Lumber of different kinds, - do.	-	128,503	
Timber of ditto, do.	-	139,328	
Leather, - lbs.	22,698	5,302	
Logwood, - tons	264	3,911	
Lignumvitæ, - do.	176	1,760	
Lead and Shot, - do.	6	810	
Mahogany, -	-	18,531	
Medicine and Drugs, -	-	1,735	
Merchandize, - -	-	28,156	
Molaſſes, - gallons	15,537	3,904	
Muſkets, - -	100	500	
Nankeens, - bales	11	2,315	
Oil Linſeed, - barrels	119	1,962	
PROVISIONS.			
Flour, - barrels	724,623	4,591,293	
Bread, - ditto	75,667	209,674	
Meal, - ditto	99,973	302,694	
Peas and Beans bushels	38,752	25,746	
Beef, - barrels	44,662	279,551	
Pork, - ditto	24,462	208,099	
Hams and Bacon, lbs.	253,555	19,728	
Butter, - firkins	8,379	48,587	
Cheeſe, - lbs.	144,734	8,830	
Potatoes, - barrels	5,318	6,009	
Tongues, - do.	641	1,598	
Onions, Vegetables,	-	22,936	
Hogs Lard, - firkins	6,355	31,475	
Honey, - do.	165	990	
Oyſters pickled, kegs	272	272	
Pimento, - bags	715	4,928	
Pepper, - lbs.	6,100	1,440	
Paper, - reams	169	381	

U

Species of Merchandize, EXPORTED.		Quantity.	Value.
			Dollars. Cts.
Paint, -	lbs.	4,650	963
Pitch, -	barrels	8,875	17,488
Raw Hides, -	-	230	485
Raw Silk, -	lbs.	177	489
Rosin, -	barrels	316	778
Rice, -	tierces	100,845	1,753,796
Rum American,	gallons	370,331	135,403
Rum West India,	ditto	12,623	5,795
Raisins, -	casks	213	1,205
Salt, -	bushels	31,935	8,236
Sago, -	lbs.	2,319	455
Soap, -	boxes	597	3,967
Snuff, -	lbs.	15,350	5,609
Seeds and Roots, -	-	-	2,135
Shoes and Boots,	pairs	5,862	5,741
Saddlery, -	-	-	5,541
Starch, -	-	-	1,125
Sugar, Loaf, -	lbs.	16,429	3,432
Sugar, Brown, -	do.	33,358	2,237
Sassafras, -	do.	49,504	555
Steel, -	bundles	163	978
Stones sawed -	-	170	550
Tallow, -	lbs.	200,020	20,722
Tobacco, -	hhds.	118,460	4,349,567
Tea -	chests	1,672	121,582
Tar, -	barrels	85,067	126,116
Turpentine, -	do.	28,326	72,541
Ditto Spirits, -	do.	193	1,032
Tow Cloth, -	pieces	67	1,274
Vinegar, -	casks	24	106
Wines, -	pipes	1,074	83,249
Wax, -	lbs.	231,158	57,597
			20,194,794
To the North-west coast of America -			10,362
Amount of several returns received since the 15th February, 1791, - - -			210,810:84
		Total,	20,415,966:84

RECAPITULATION.

	Dollars.	Cts.	
Provifions, -	5,757,482		
Grain, - -	2,519,232		
Fifh, - -	941,696		
Lumber, -	1,263,534		
Live Stock, -	486,105		
	10,968,049		
Other articles, -	9,447,917	84	
			Total, 20,415,966:84

A Summary of the Value and Destination of the Exports of the United States, agreeably to the foregoing Abstract.

	Dollars.	Cts.
To the dominions of France, -	4,698,735	: 48
To the dominions of Great Britain, -	9,363,416	: 47
To the dominions of Spain, -	2,005,907	: 16
To the dominions of Portugal, -	1,283,462	
To the dominions of the United Netherlands,	1,963,880	: 9
To the dominions of Denmark, -	224,415	: 50
To the dominions of Sweden, -	47,240	
To Flanders, - - -	14,298	
To Germany, - - -	487,787	: 14
To the Mediterranean, - -	41,298	
To the African Islands and Coast of Africa,	139,984	
To the East Indies, - - -	135,181	
To the North West coast of America,	10,362	
	20,415,966	: 84

In addition to the foregoing, a considerable number of packages have been exported from the United States, the value of which being omitted in the returns from the custom-houses, could not be introduced into this abstract.

Treasury Department, February 15th, 1791.

TENCH COXE, Assistant Secretary.

SECOND ACCOUNT

Received ſince the Report was printed.

THE following account (which is publiſhed by Mr. Jefferſon, ſecretary of ſtate to the United States of America, in the Appendix to his Report of the 1ſt February 1790, on the cod and whale fiſheries, carried on by the ſubjects of the ſaid States) has alſo been received ſince the foregoing Report was printed.—It contains an account of the quantity of rice, flour, wheat, rye, and barley, imported into the ports of France from the United States of America, in the year 1789; being a part of that period in which a dearth prevailed in France, for want of proviſions of this nature.—This account being only for the year 1789, does not correspond in point of time with the preceding abſtract of exports from the United States, which contains an account of the ſaid exports from Auguſt 1789, to the 30th September 1790.—If the periods to which theſe two accounts refer had been the ſame, it would have been poſſible to have ſtated with accuracy what proportion of the whole of theſe articles, which appear by the firſt of theſe accounts to have been exported from the countries of the United States, were imported, according to the ſecond of theſe accounts, into the ports of France. But though theſe periods are in part different, it has been thought right to add, at the foot of this account, a comparative ſtate of the quantities of each of theſe articles exported from the United States, in the period to which the firſt account refers; and of the quantities of each of the ſaid articles which were imported into the ports of France, in the period to which the ſecond of theſe accounts refers.

It will ferve to fhew, generally, how large a proportion of the feveral forts of grain, exported from the United States, was fent to France during the time that there was fo great a want of them in the markets of Europe.

It is proper to obferve, that as the produce of the feveral forts of grain in France is fuppofed to be, in common years, fufficient for the confumption of the inhabitants of that kingdom, the trade of the United States with France, in all thefe articles, except rice, muft always depend on the feafon, and confequently be very precarious.

Grain and Flour imported from the United States of America into the ports of France, in the year 1789; *from an official ftatement.*

Articles.	Total exported to France.			
	French Quintals.	lb.		
Rice	123,401	69	equal to	Tierces of 500 French Pounds each. 24,680
Flour	256,545	94	equal to	American Barrels. 140,959
Wheat	2,015,297	3	equal to	American Bufhels. 3,664,176
Rye	307,390	96	equal to	558,891
Barley	260,131	53	equal to	520,262

Comparative State of the Quantities of each of the above Articles exported from the United States, in the Period to which the first Account refers; and of the Quantities of each of the said Articles imported into the Ports of France in the Period to which the second Account refers.

Total of the following Articles exported from the United States to all Countries, from August 1789, to the 30th September 1790, according to the first Account.	Articles.	Total of the following Articles exported to France from the United States of America in the Year 1789, according to the second Account.		
Tierces.		French Quintals. lb.		Tierces of 500 French lbs. each.
100,845	Rice	123,401 69	equal to	24,680
Barrels.				Amer. Barrels.
724,623	Flour	256,545 94	equal to	140,959
Bushels.				Amer. Bushels.
1,124,458	Wheat	2,015,297 3	equal to	3,664,176
21,765	Rye	307,390 96	equal to	558,891
	Barley	260,131 52	equal to	520,262

THIRD ACCOUNT,

Received since the Report was printed.

THE following account of the number of vessels which entered the ports of France, from the United States of America, in the year 1789, taken from the before mentioned Report of Mr. Jefferson, has also been received since the foregoing Report was printed.—This account will serve to prove, what is cautiously suggested in the Report of the Lords of the committee for trade and plantations, viz. that British vessels have a considerable share in the commercial intercourse carried on between the United States and the several nations of Europe;—for, according to this account, the British vessels that entered the ports of France from the United States, are above three times as many as the French vessels that entered the said ports from the United States, in 1789; and above eight times more than the vessels of all the other nations of Europe, and about one-fourth of the vessels of the United States that entered the ports of France during that period.—It is probable, that the share which British vessels have in the commercial intercourse between the United States and other nations of Europe to the south of France, is more considerable than the share they have in the intercourse between the United States and France.

Statement of the Vessels entered in the Ports of France, from the United States of America, in the Year 1789.

	Vessels.	Tons.
French,	13	2,105
Imperial,	3	370
English,	43	4,781
Dutch,	1	170
Hanseatic,	1	200
American,	163	24,173
	224	31,799

APPENDIX.

(A.)

N° I.

QUESTIONS referred on the 15th October 1789, by the Lords of the Committee of Privy Council, appointed for all Matters relating to Trade and Foreign Plantations, to a Committee of Merchants of the City of LONDON, *and to the Merchants and Ship-Owners of* BRISTOL, LIVERPOOL, *and* GLASGOW, *concerned in the Trade to the United States of America.*

QUESTION I.

HAVE the commerce and shipping interest of this country suffered by the distinctions, which have been hitherto made by the different legislatures of the States composing the United States of America, in the duties imposed by them on British or other foreign goods, or in the duties imposed on the tonnage of British, or other foreign ships, or American ships, previous to the passing the late Impost and Tonnage act by Congress; and in what respect and degree?

QUESTION II.

Will the commerce and navigation of this country be upon a worse footing under the general duties imposed by the late Impost and Tonnage acts of Congress, than they have hitherto been under the duties imposed by the legislatures of the particular States composing the United States of America?

QUESTION III.

If it should be thought proper to subject goods, brought in American ships, to the duties payable generally on goods brought in foreign ships, from which American ships only have hitherto been exempted, and further to impose a duty on the tonnage of American ships coming to this country, equal to the difference they have made in their tonnage act between American and foreign shipping coming to their ports, that is, forty-four cents of a dollar; would these measures have the effect of securing to the shipping of

[A]

this country the share it ought to enjoy in the trade between Great Britain and the countries belonging to the United States of America? or would such measures be the means of inducing the Americans to carry their produce in their own ships to the ports of other countries, instead of bringing it to those of Great Britain?

QUESTION IV.

If this country should now acquiesce in the distinctions made by the American Congress in favour of their own shipping, to the detriment of ours, is there *any security*, from the nature and circumstances of the trade between the two countries, that Congress will not be encouraged to *encrease* the duties imposed for this purpose, till they have succeeded *in driving our shipping* out of this trade, though the duties hitherto imposed may not wholly have that effect?

QUESTION V.

Do not American ships at present prefer carrying the produce of America, particularly tobacco and rice, to the ports of other countries rather than to those of Great Britain and Ireland; and to what causes is this preference to be imputed?

QUESTION VI.

Do not British ships, employed in the American trade, carry the before-mentioned American produce to foreign rather than to British ports? and in what degree, and to what causes, is this preference to be imputed?

N° II.

Report of the Committee of Merchants trading from LONDON *to America, in Answer to the foregoing Questions.*

ANSWER TO QUESTION I.

UNDOUBTEDLY, both the commerce and the shipping interest *of this country did suffer* by the distinctions made by the United States in favour of *other* foreigners, from the opening of the trade with the said States in 1783, until those distinctions were done away by the law passed under the present form of government, which took place on the first of August 1789. In what degree these distinctions were made, have been fully set forth in various memorials to administration;—they varied in the different States.

ANSWER TO QUESTION II.

The commerce and navigation of these kingdoms we do not conceive to be on a *worse* footing by the late imposed duties on goods imported, and on the tonnage of shipping, than they were under the laws of the different legislatures of the States.—In some of the States they are actually benefited by the new law of tonnage imposed under the present form of government.

ANSWER TO QUESTION III.

The right of government to bring forward the duties payable in general on goods brought hither in American bottoms, as are paid by other foreigners, cannot be denied; but it is submitted, whether the imposition of these duties (laying dormant as they have for years past) should not be dispensed with yet for a time. The United States are proceeding fast in a regular form of government, and the ancient attachment of the people to this country gaining ground, they must wish and seek a treaty with us, when it appears probable advantages would arise by a temporary forbearance.—Were a duty of tonnage to be imposed on American bottoms arriving in this kingdom, equal to the difference of duties on shipping laid in the United States between their own navigation and ours, it might, it would for the moment, operate no doubt in our favour, but must inevitably soon be retaliated by America, who would have an equal right to discriminate and lay an overbalance of tonnage duty on the shipping of these kingdoms.—The difference in favour of our shipping in the ports of America, and what American shipping pay here, is already considerable.

An American ship of 160 tons pays	£.	s.	d.
Light money - - - - - - -	21	15	0
Trinity dues - - - - - - -	5	4	2
Entry inward and outward, and clearing -	8	7	0
	35	6	2
But 9d. per ton pierage laid on the cargo is again restored to the ship - - - - -	6	0	0
	29	6	2
A British ship of the same burthen in the ports of the United States, 50 cents per ton, equal to 2s. 3d. - - - - - - - -	18	0	0
Entry inward and outward, and clearing, not more than - - - - - -	2	0	0
	20	0	0

Besides this difference in favour of British shipping, pilotage, and other port charges, are much less in America than they are in the port of London.—British shipping enjoy a very considerable share of the carrying trade, particularly from Maryland, Virginia, and South Carolina, nearly to the exclusion of other foreigners; and it is more than probable, should this country lay a heavier duty of tonnage on the shipping of America, it would be productive of the very measure suggested by the question,—" be the means of " inducing the American government to cause their produce to be " carried in their own ships to the ports of other countries, instead " of bringing it to those of these kingdoms."

ANSWER TO QUESTION IV.

The duties hitherto, or at present, imposed on British shipping and on British goods by the United States, we find, by experience, have not produced the effect of driving the former out of the trade between the two countries.—America, in laying her new imposts, makes no discrimination to the prejudice of our shipping, which heretofore she did to a considerable degree: but that partiality to other foreigners being now extinct, America would no doubt feel much irritated at any *new* impositions on the part of this country; and she certainly has it in her power to retaliate. We should not complain of the partiality of America to their own navigation, since Great Britain sets her the example. If the submission of government, without remonstrance on the business, in the distinction now made by the United States in favour of their own shipping, may be called acquiescence in the measure, it is not possible to say how this silence may hereafter operate, and induce America to increase the duties already imposed on British goods and shipping: but it is conceived it would not have that effect.

ANSWER TO QUESTION V.

American ships assuredly do prefer carrying the produce of the United States to the ports of other countries: the cause seems clear—expectation of better markets,—shorter voyages;—but one great temptation is, much less expence on shipping and their cargoes.—The charges on tobacco and rice, particularly the latter, in the ports of this country, are severely felt, and unquestionably occasion those and other articles to be often carried by American shipping, as well as our own, to foreign ports. To invite them to those of her kingdom, France gives great indulgencies—Free ports, both in the bay, and in the English Channel, where the contingent charges are also small.

ANSWER TO QUESTION VI.

This question may be answered nearly as the preceding; British shipping, like all others, unless in particular cases, prefer going to those places where the port charges are easy.—The proportion of

British ships, carrying the produce of the United States to foreign markets, cannot here be easily ascertained.—Few American vessels venture within the streights of Gibraltar, or in the track of the Barbary cruizers;—of consequence, in these voyages, foreign ships are employed; and in this, we have no doubt, the British have the preference.

The Committee are not sufficiently informed to be able to give satisfactory answers to the questions with respect to the out ports.

By order of the Committee,

13th November, 1789.

(Signed) EDW. PAYNE, Chairman.

N° III.

Report of the Merchants and Ship Owners of BRISTOL, *in Answer to the foregoing Questions.*

ANSWER TO QUESTION I.

WHEN America treated Great Britain with those impolitic distinctions of partial duties and restrictions, different from the goods and ships of other nations (as was the case in some of the provinces,) our commerce, and especially shipping, suffered in a considerable degree.

ANSWER TO QUESTION II.

The commerce of this country will now be on a better footing under the general duties imposed by the late acts of the States United, than under the duties imposed by the legislatures of the particular States, the impost being more equal, and alike on all foreigners; and though the tonnage duty is both heavy, and calculated to give a preference in the carrying trade to their own ships, yet our navigation being put upon *the same footing* with other foreign nations, our superiority over other countries will probably be evinced by our abilities and more extensive connections with America.

ANSWER TO QUESTION III.

If duties are laid by Great Britain upon American produce brought by their ships, equal to those from foreign states, together with a tonnage duty, equal to the difference between what is laid on British and their own vessels in America, it might perhaps increase the carrying trade in British ships, but would manifestly injure the American trade to this country, and induce them to prefer sending their produce in their own ships to the markets of all other nations. The balance of the American trade is importantly in our favour; and that balance will increase, as long as America continues in a peaceable and prosperous situation: We therefore wish to see the trade cherished by government; and are of opinion, it would be more to the advantage of Great Britain to continue her indulgence to the returns in produce made us by America, most of which are very necessary to our manufactures.

ANSWER TO QUESTION IV.

The settled form of government, which America has now assumed, gives fair ground to presume, that a commercial treaty may soon be negotiated between Great Britain and those States, which might be some security against any increase in the American duties on tonnage and merchandize, with respect to us. The advantages of commerce between two independent states must be in some measure reciprocal, or cannot be lasting: Our markets are as necessary to America as theirs to us. The power we have of retaliation will therefore awe America, and deter her from excessive impositions on our trade or shipping.

ANSWER TO QUESTION V.

The articles of rice and tobacco have a greater consumption in other European markets than in England; consequently, the Americans will, from interest, prefer carrying direct, rather than by bringing such produce to our ports, to make Great Britain the grand repository, where they complain of being subject to much expence, and perplexing inconvenience, in the discharging and re-exporting of such cargoes.

ANSWER TO QUESTION VI.

British ships, employed in that trade, prefer carrying American produce direct to other countries from the same causes; and it is probable, the severities exercised under some of the late acts and regulations have a tendency to induce British ships to prefer foreign voyages.

N° IV.

Report of the Merchants and Ship Owners of LIVERPOOL, *in Answer to the foregoing Questions.*

ANSWER TO QUESTION I.

THE commerce and shipping interest of this country have undoubtedly suffered by the distinctions which have been made by the different legislatures of the American States, in the duties imposed by them on British ships, by way of tonnage duties, and upon British merchandize, previous to the passing of the late general Impost and Tonnage act; inasmuch as American vessels have obtained a preference in consequence of them in British ports, and to such a degree, that British ships could procure no freights, whilst American ships were in the way to receive them, except in the trade to Pennsylvania, where neither restrictions nor distinctions did exist, and British vessels had even a decided preference.

ANSWER TO QUESTION II.

Though the duties imposed by the late Impost and Tonnage act of Congress may not be higher upon an average than those exacted under the legislatures of the different States; yet that clause in the late act of Congress, which remits ten per cent. of the duties upon wares and merchandizes imported in American vessels, bears harder upon British ships than any thing which existed in the American laws before, and *will prevent them from obtaining freights from Great Britain,* whilst American vessels offer to receive them.

ANSWER TO QUESTION III.

It is believed, that a duty upon goods imported from America in American ships to Great Britain would not be found to answer the intention to equalize the bounty of ten per cent. allowed on the duty on goods imported into America in American shipping:—Additional duties upon naval stores, timber, &c. would check the importation of those articles, and operate to lessen the consumption of British manufactures in those places, particularly in North Carolina, where they have scarcely any thing else to pay for them;—Additional duties in general would be a heavy clog upon the re-export of American produce from Great Britain.—To meet the ten per cent. bounty allowed on the duty on goods imported into America in American bottoms, the two following schemes are, with all due deference, submitted:

First—That a duty be laid upon all goods shipped on board of American vessels bound to America, equal to the ten per cent. bounty allowed on the duty in America, to be paid by the shipper of such goods, whose correspondent in America will have the same allowed to him there.

Or,

Secondly—That all goods entered outwards on board American vessels, bound to America, be entered free of any new duty to the shipper of such goods; such shipper or exporter of them specifying very exactly the contents of his entry; and in case they be goods which pay duty *ad valorem* in America, he to ascertain the value of such goods upon oath; that, on such American vessel *clearing out, the captain* shall pay the exact amount of the bounty, which will be allowed in America by the discount of ten per cent. on the duty payable inwards; this to be paid, exclusive of the tonnage, to be paid as hereafter specified.—To meet the tonnage duty imposed by the Americans, a tonnage duty might be imposed on American vessels, equal to that laid extra upon British shipping by Congress, say forty-four cents of a dollar, which is exactly equal to two shillings sterling per ton, and will perfectly countervail that duty.

We may here, perhaps, be allowed, with all due submission, to observe, that the nearer British shipping and that of the United States can be put upon *a state of equality*, the greater is the probability that the trade between the two countries will be cemented by a friendly and lasting intercourse; and that for this purpose, it might possibly be found very expedient to put the shipping of the American States, which resort to the British dominions in Europe, and return to the United States, upon the same footing as British vessels in regard to all port charges, whether of light money, river dues, dockages, pilotage, or by whatever other name such duties or payments are called, asked, and received by law from shipping, and which the American vessels pay at present in a greater proportion, being considered as foreigners; provided always, that such American vessels return direct to the United States, and not, if they proceed to ports or places not belonging to the American States.—Such measures as these, we humbly presume, might lead to a treaty of commerce mutually advantageous, and secure to the shipping interest of this country the share it ought to enjoy in the trade between Great Britain and the United States of America; and we conceive, that the Americans by this means would not be induced to carry their produce to other places in preference to this country, or to seek in foreign countries those articles of merchandize, which they are accustomed to procure from Great Britain.

ANSWER TO QUESTION IV.

We conceive that the acquiescence of this country in those distinctions now made by Congress in favour of American shipping, is no security against a future increase of the tonnage duty on British vessels in America: for this tonnage duty is imposed there, purposely to give the northern States a monopoly of the carrying trade of the southern ones, which the present duties are not sufficient to effect; and they are only preparatory to higher duties which will inevitably be imposed, if not prevented by contravening duties here, which alone can deter them from the object they have in view, and is part of their system to increase their naval power.

ANSWER TO QUESTION V.

The Americans, who, previous to the late revolution, were precluded from going direct with their tobacco and rice to foreign markets, have since been tempted to make the experiment; but these speculations have in general proved fatal adventures, and would have been more checked ere now, had not the late distressing famine in France, for a time, caused a brisk demand there for all the rice that arrived: As to tobacco, the quantity sent direct to foreign ports bears a small proportion to that sent to Great Britain.

ANSWER TO QUESTION VI.

We conceive that British ships, employed in the American trade, do not carry American produce to foreign ports in any considerable degree; nor do they carry it in preference, unless from the temptation of a much higher freight or a better market.

N° V.

Report of the Merchants and Ship Owners of GLASGOW, *in Answer to the foregoing Questions.*

Glasgow, 27th October, 1789.

AT a meeting, in the city hall, of the merchants and ship owners of Glasgow, concerned in the trade to the United States of America, called by public advertisement, the lord provost of Glasgow laid before the meeting a letter to him from William Fawkener, esq. secretary to the lords of the committee of privy council for trade and foreign plantations, together with two acts of the said United States, imposing duties of impost and tonnage, and also sundry queries for the consideration of the said merchants and ship owners of Glasgow; to every part of which their lordships desire that full and particular answers may be returned them by the said merchants and ship owners. And the meeting having taken these papers into consideration, resolved, that Messrs. James Ritchie, Alexander Oswald, Henry Riddel, and Robert Findlay, merchants in Glasgow, and William Fullarton, merchant in Greenock, be appointed a committee to prepare answers to said queries, and to report; of which committee the said Robert Findlay to be convener.

(Signed) John Campbell, jun. Provost.

Glasgow, 26th November, 1789.

The committee, appointed as above, having this day met to consider the queries from the lords of the committee of privy council for trade and foreign plantations, to the merchants and ship owners of Glasgow, concerned in the trade with the United States of America; and there being present Messrs. James Ritchie, Alex-

[B]

ander Oswald, Henry Riddel, and Robert Findlay, sundry opinions were delivered upon the subjects of these queries; and the said committee resolve to submit these different opinions to the consideration of the whole merchants and ship owners of Glasgow, concerned in the trade to the United States of America, for their final decision, as to the answers to be returned by them to the lords of the committee of privy council for trade and foreign plantations.

(Signed) Ro. Findlay, Convener.

Glasgow, 10th December, 1789.

At a meeting, in the city hall, of the merchants and ship owners concerned in the trade to the United States of America, called by public advertisement, to receive the report of their committee, appointed on the 27th October last, two reports were delivered to the meeting by said committee; which reports being read and considered, and the question being put, it was resolved by a majority, that Report, No. I. hereto annexed, be approved of by this meeting, and transmitted accordingly by the lord provost to William Fawkener, esq. secretary to the lords of the committee of privy council for trade and foreign plantations:—Resolved also, that Report, No. II. should likewise be transmitted by the lord provost to the said William Fawkener, esq. that the lords of the committee of privy council for trade and foreign plantations may have an opportunity of judging of the different arguments made use of by the merchants and ship owners of this city upon the subject of these queries.

(Signed) John Campbell, jun. Provost.

REPORT I.

ANSWER TO QUESTION I.

NO doubt the merchants and ship owners of Great Britain, who carried on trade to the United States of America, have sustained a loss in proportion to the additional duties of impost and tonnage, which were laid upon British ships, and goods imported in them, by the different American States, more than were laid upon American ships and goods imported therein.

These additional duties varied in the different States, and therefore we cannot say with precision what may have been the loss upon the whole; but, in general, there was a difference of $1\frac{1}{2}$ to $2\frac{1}{2}$ per cent. *of Impost*, in favour of goods imported into the United States in American ships.

As to the *Tonnage* duty again, the variation was more considerable in many of the different States.

In Pennsylvania, the Tonnage Duty on American ships was only about *4d.* sterling—on foreign ships *in treaty*, *8d.*—on foreign ships *not in treaty*, *2s. 1d.*

In Maryland, the Tonnage Duty on their own ships was *8d.* sterling—on foreign ships in treaty, *1s.*—on British ships, *3s. 6d.* —and on other foreign ships not in treaty, *1s. 7d.*

In Virginia, the Tonnage Duty on American ships was about *1s. 3d.* sterling; and on British ships it was *4s. 6d.*

In New York again, the Tonnage Duty on British ships was no more than *4d.* or *5d.* and on their own ships we believe it was the same; though we are not certain as to this point.

Upon the whole, however, we suppose that, *upon an average* of all the United States, British ships were subjected to a duty of *2s.* to *2s. 6d.* sterling per ton more than American ships.—— Say *2s. 3d.*

As to the *degree*, therefore, that the merchants and ship owners of British ships have suffered by the distinction of the duties of Impost and Tonnage against them in the United States, it can be only guessed at; but it may perhaps be nearly as follows:

Suppose 600 British ships annually employed in the trade to and from the United States—these may be estimated at 200 tons burthen each, which is 120,000 tons in all, and at *2s. 3d.* per ton, is -	£. 13,500
Suppose again, that each of these British ships carried, *at an average*, 2,000*l.* value of goods into the United States, this would be 1,200,000 value of goods, which, at 2 per cent. the average distinction of the impost is - - - -	£. 24,000
In all	£. 37,500

Upon this estimate, therefore, the annual loss to the merchants and ship owners of Great Britain, previous to the late Impost and Tonnage Acts of Congress, was 37,500*l.* or 62*l.* 10*s.* sterling upon each British ship on every voyage to the United States.

ANSWER TO QUESTION II.

British ships will be upon a better footing under the late general Impost and Tonnage Acts of Congress, than they have hitherto been upon an average in the United States; because the comparative duties betwixt them and American ships are thereby reduced.

For instance, the difference betwixt the Tonnage on American and British ships in the United States is now only 44 cents. of a dollar, which may be reckoned *2s.* sterling per ton; whereas formerly it was on an average about 2*s*. 3*d*. per ton, according to the estimate in the answer to the preceding question. Again—The Impost duties on goods imported into the United States in *all* ships are now the same, only with this distinction in favour of those imported in American ships, that these have a discount of 10 per cent. from the amount. These impost duties are various upon different articles; but upon an average of an assorted cargo, imported into the United States, will amount to from 6 to 7½ per cent.—and therefore, from 2-3ds to 3-4ths per cent. against those imported in British or other foreign ships.

The total additional duties to be annually paid by British more than by American ships, and on goods imported in the former, will therefore now stand as follows, according to the estimate in the answer to the preceding query:

On 120,000 tons of British shipping, at 2*s*. per ton	£. 12,000
On 1,200,000*l*. value of goods imported therein at ¾ per cent. - - - - -	£. 9,000
In all	£. 21,000

The difference therefore in favour of British ships under the late Impost and Tonnage Laws of Congress is 16,000*l*. sterling per annum; because it has been previously remarked, that, under the former laws of the particular States, they paid 37,000*l*. annually; whereas now, they will only pay 21,000*l*. or 35*l*. sterling on each ship on every voyage. Now this extra tax or duty upon British ships in the United States is, in our opinion, fully counterbalanced by the advantages which British ships possess over American ships in other respects.

ANSWER TO QUESTION III.

The British shipping, notwithstanding all the disadvantages under which it has laboured in America, has hitherto certainly enjoyed a very large share of the trade of the United States since the peace; nor is there any just grounds for present apprehension, that now, when these disadvantages are lessened, they will not retain an equal share as formerly. It must be acknowledged, however, that an equalization of duties of impost and tonnage, to be paid by American ships when they come into the ports of this country, would be just and right according to the law and custom of mutual reciprocity betwixt nations.—At same time, we are more doubtful as to the policy or expediency of at once enacting such a retaliating or equalizing law in this instance, at least at present.—The trade to and from the United States is of very great importance to the navigation, to the ship owners, as well as to the mercantile interest of this country, by reason of the bulky commodities which these States produce, and which of course employ, as we have already mentioned, many British ships in transporting them to a market.—Was an equalizing law, therefore, of impost and tonnage to be immediately passed in this country on American ships, it is not improbable that, *however contrary to the true interest of the United States*, the American Congress would at its next subsequent meeting enact a law, not only to impose still heavier duties upon British ships and their cargoes, but also to make an invidious unfavourable distinction betwixt these and the shipping of other foreign nations, for which indeed there was a large party, even in the late Congress, though by the firmness of the Senate it was at last over-ruled, and all foreign ships were put upon a footing.

No doubt Great Britain could again follow up and equalize, nor have the British merchants any reason to apprehend that the legislature of this country would not in all probability ultimately prevail; yet still this trial of strength or of skill would, in the mean time, cramp the trade betwixt this country and the United States, and be the cause of continuing or keeping alive that animosity which has unhappily so long prevailed, and of preventing that return of harmony and good understanding, which would be so comfortable and so beneficial for both.—It might also have a tendency to divert the trade of the United States into other channels more than at present, from whence it might not be so easily recovered. For all these reasons, we are of opinion, that it would at present be rather impolitic to enact an immediate law for equalizing the duties on American ships in this country with those now paid by British ships in the United States; especially considering that American ships do in fact, in common with other foreign ships, pay about 1*s.* 9*d.* per ton in this country, for light houses and the Trinity-house, more than British ships pay.

But though we are of opinion, that it would at present be rather impolitic to enact such an equalizing law, yet certainly these extra impost and tonnage duties on British ships in America are a *considerable grievance* to the British merchants, while the American ships pay no such extra duties in this country; and therefore we would, with all submission, recommend it to the committee of council for trade, to use their endeavours to have them removed *by negotiation* with the American Congress: this would be a more amicable mode, and in all probability more for the commercial interest of Great Britain, than by enacting an immediate retaliating law. *If negotiation* fails, it will then be time enough to bring forward such a measure; and it is in the mean time proper to remark, that every additional duty imposed upon American ships in the ports of Great Britain has a tendency most assuredly to induce the Americans, more than they now do, to carry their produce in their own ships to the ports of other countries, instead of bringing it into the ports of Great Britain; and of course to prevent this country from being the depôt of the bulky commodities of the United States.

ANSWER TO QUESTION IV.

There is certainly no *absolute security*, from the nature and circumstances of the trade betwixt this country and the United States, that Congress will not encrease the tonnage or impost duties, or perhaps both, with the view of *diminishing* the *British* ships now employed in that trade; but as Congress can never be wild enough to conclude, that it is fear, or any similar motive, which induces this country to acquiesce for the present in the late impost and tonnage duties, and as it is assuredly the interest of the people of the United States, especially of those in the *southern* States, to cultivate a connection with Great Britain, by enjoying the credits which its merchants give, and by employing its shipping for their bulky commodities, in rivalship to the American ships belonging to the northern or eastern States; we say that, for these reasons, we do not think it probable that a majority will be found in Congress to increase the duties on British ships, so as to drive them out of the trade, especially if the reconciliating mode of negotiation is adopted, which is pointed out in the answer to the preceding question:—But, at all events, if Congress should ever be so unwise as to impose duties with that view, Great Britain will have it always in her power to retaliate, by equalizing such duties on American ships and their cargoes in this country, and thus soon check the evil.

ANSWER TO QUESTION V.

We do not know that American ships at present *prefer* carrying tobacco and rice, or such produce of America, to other countries rather than to Great Britain: but as these are bulky commodities, and cannot support the expence of landing, agency, &c. in this country, and then reshipping and insuring them to the country of ultimate consumpt, and as it is not a very large proportion of these American productions which Great Britain and Ireland consume, it is for these reasons extremely natural to transport them direct from America to the probable country of consumpt; especially at a time when the British market has a sufficiency for its internal use, and when there is no encouragement in such a case from the British legislature to carry it to, and land it in, that market.—It is therefore a certain fact, that a greater proportion of the bulky produce of the United States goes direct from America to the ports of other countries than Great Britain in American ships—and it will still continue so, unless some encouraging measures are adopted for making the ports of Great Britain an emporium or depôt for such bulky produce; because every merchant, where he legally can, will most undoubtedly pursue his own interest; and it is in general his interest at present to carry the produce of the United States to the probable ports of consumpt at once, instead of depositing it, in the first instance, in the ports of Great Britain.

ANSWER TO QUESTION VI.

For the very same reasons which are set forth in the answer to the preceding question, it is most assuredly a fact, that even British ships carry a greater proportion of the bulky produce of America, directly from thence to the ports of other countries than Great Britain, and which their owners or freighters think may be ultimately the ports of consumpt;—perhaps, fully 2-3ds of the whole bulky produce of America, which falls to the share of British ships, may be in this manner transported to the ports of other countries. If this was not done, the British merchants could not pretend to compete, either with the merchants of America, or with those of other foreign countries, in the sale of those bulky articles at such ultimate ports of consumpt.—This necessity of sending British ships to foreign ports, instead of bringing them into Great Britain, is much regretted by every merchant in the trade; but if he did not, he must, for the reasons above-mentioned, relinquish the business altogether—The bulky article of tobacco alone from the United States, employs annually from 200 to 250 ships of all nations, of which, at least, three-fourths are British: and well do we remember, that, before the unhappy American war, the merchant, who imported tobacco into Great Britain, although he could not then legally carry it in the first instance any where else, had an allowance of 10lbs. of tobacco per hogshead *free of duty*, and had also an allowance of a halfpenny per lb. for all damaged tobacco cut off at the king's scale and burnt:—the master of the ship likewise had a small allowance in name of portage bill, provided he made a faithful report of his cargo. These allowances were a considerable assistance to the merchant, by enabling him to transport his tobacco at a small additional expence to any foreign market; and such transportation gave employment to a multitude of coasting vessels and their seamen; but, unhappily, these encouragements are now wholly withdrawn, even although there does not now exist any necessity of bringing this article in the first instance to Great Britain. The consequence is, of course, that it goes directly to the probable port of consumpt, and there the ship is again fitted out, the seamen's wages expended, both amounting to not less upon an average than 4 to 500*l.* on every voyage, and all the duties on cordage, sailcloth, wine, spirits, beer, candles, &c. in such outfit and expenditure, not only lost to the revenue of this country, but also the circulation of the whole money, and the employment of tradesmen in the above articles, are lost to one or other of the sea ports of Great Britain; and probably, likewise, many of the seamen themselves, who, by habitually navigating from one foreign country to another, lose their natural attachment to Great Britain,

N° VI

REPORT II. *of the Merchants and Ship Owners of* GLASGOW, *in Answer to the foregoing Questions.*

ANSWER TO QUESTION I.

THE commerce and shipping interest of this country have certainly suffered by the distinctions that have been hitherto made by the different legislatures of the States of America, in the duties imposed by them on British and foreign goods, to the extent of the difference of the duties when imported in British or American ships; that is to say, the importers of goods in British ships must sell their goods so much cheaper; and it is obvious, that the importers will prefer American to British ships.—The difference of those duties have been different in the different States; but, on an average, they may be supposed equal to two per cent. on the first cost of the goods.—In the same manner, the *American* ships have been enabled to serve for *less freight*, or which is the same thing, to gain more than the British ships by the difference of the tonnage duties, all other circumstances being supposed equal.—This difference in the tonnage duties has also been very different in the different States; but, on an average, may be supposed equal to two shillings and three pence per ton.—It is supposed there are 600 British ships, on an average, of 200 tons burthen, employed in carrying the produce of the United States to the West Indies, to our colonies in North America, to Britain, and to all the ports in Europe. But to illustrate what has been said in the case of a British ship of 200 tons burthen trading to the States of Virginia and Maryland, and carrying their produce to Britain, and making three voyages in two years, which is equal to one and a half voyage in one year, and supposing every voyage she carries out £2,000 sterling value of goods, the yearly disadvantage of a British ship, compared with that of an American ship, will stand as follows:

Difference of duty on 200 tons, at 2s. 3d. is -	22	10	0
Ditto ditto on £2,000 sterling, at 2 per cent. as above, is - - - - - - -	40	0	0
	£.62	10	0
Add one half for the half-yearly voyage - -	31	5	0
Total difference	£.93	15	0

between a British and an American ship, and which is equal to $6\frac{1}{4}$ per cent. per annum on a ship supposed worth £1500 sterling. Such has been the state of the trade between Britain and America since the peace, until the late regulations of Congress.—It has proved a very great encouragement to American shipping, and an equal discouragement to British. The number of American ships have increased, and are increasing—Many of them built in America by means of British capitals, and owned by British merchants, but navigated by American seamen.

ANSWER TO QUESTION II.

The commerce and navigation of this country will not be on a worse footing under the general duties lately imposed by Congress, but, on the contrary, will be on a better footing; because those duties are in most of the states considerably less than they were formerly.—The difference of the tonnage duty being now only two shillings per ton, and the duty on goods about $7\frac{1}{2}$ per cent. on the value, from which American ships have a discount of 10 per cent. equal to $\frac{3}{4}$ per cent. on the value of the goods:—So that now the disadvantage that a British ship of 200 tons, making three voyages in two years, and carrying the same value of goods, as supposed in the preceding answer, will stand as follows:

Difference of duty on a ship of 200 tons, at 2s. per ton	20	0	0
Ditto ditto on £2,000 sterling value of goods, at $\frac{3}{4}$ per cent.	15	0	0
	35	0	0
Add one half for the half-yearly voyage	17	10	0
Total	£52	10	0

Yearly difference between a British and an American ship, and which is equal to $3\frac{1}{2}$ per cent. per annum on £1,500, the supposed worth of the ship as above; this is a difference, though greatly lower than the duties formerly imposed by the different States, *which will in time give a decided superiority to the American shipping;* and it has been found by experience since the peace, that the shipping, employed in the trade to the United States, has been a very bare, if not an unprofitable, trade.—There are other circumstances, *which will contribute to the decay of our carrying trade*, and the diminution of our merchants, ships, and seamen, and of *consequence to the naval power of Great Britain.*—Such as these; 1st. Before the unhappy war with America, ships built in America were held as British ships, and great numbers of ships were built there by the British merchants, rather than in Britain, because they were much cheaper; and it is believed it will be allowed, that, after long experience and practice, the British merchants in general may be supposed to understand their true interest.—Now they are restricted to build in Britain alone; and though it must be allowed that a British ship will last longer, she is much dearer.—2dly. British ships are subjected to a heavy duty on hemp, and to duties on iron, timber, pitch, and tar, employed in ship-building, *far exceeding those in other parts of Europe and in America;* for instance, the duty on hemp imported into Britain is £3 : 13 : 4 sterling per ton : In America, five shillings sterling per ton, to take place in May 1790! even though she grows, and will in time be capable of raising excellent hemp! It is true, similar duties were imposed before the American war; but our situation then in the American trade was different from what it is now—Britain had a monopoly of the American trade—She must now compete, not only with America, but all Europe.——These observations are thrown out for the consideration of Government.

ANSWER TO QUESTION III.

If it should be thought proper to subject goods brought in American ships to the duties payable generally on goods brought in foreign ships, and also to equalize the tonnage duties, it will be a discouragement to American shipping, and *an encouragement to British shipping*, to the extent of the present difference of the duty; and such measures will not prevent the same quantity of American produce being brought into this country—more will be brought in British ships—less in American ships.——Since the unhappy separation of America from Britain, our share of the tobacco trade must necessarily be confined to what is wanted for the consumption of Britain and Ireland, or for the supply of the ports of the Baltic, who cannot afford to be direct importers,—the tobacco wanted by France, Holland, and the ports of Germany, will generally be sent directly to these ports, their consumption being equal to about two thirds of the whole tobacco of the growth of America.—The consumption of rice in Britain must be inconsiderable: But Britain will import tar, pitch, turpentine, lumber, &c. equal to her consumption and no more :—Wheat and flour will also be imported, when our ports are open.

ANSWER TO QUESTION IV.

There is no security, that Congress will not be encouraged to increase the duties on British and other foreign ships.—It is probable that they will increase these duties as their shipping increase, and British capitals can be easily transported to America for that purpose.—Foreigners have no title to complain of what Congress have done or may do in this respect—they may equalize, if they think proper.—*Congress have, in this instance, acted with true political wisdom, and on sound principles of navigation-laws,* and they will not be disposed to alter so wise a system.

ANSWER TO QUESTIONS V. AND VI.

Both British and American ships prefer carrying the produce of America, particularly tobacco and rice, to the ports of other countries, rather than to those of Great Britain and Ireland, excepting so far as tobacco and rice is wanted for the consumption of Britain and Ireland, because it will cost fifteen to twenty shillings on every hogshead of tobacco which shall be sent from Britain to France, Holland or Germany, for the consumption of those countries; and therefore the tobacco and rice, wanted by foreign countries, will generally be sent directly from America to the countries of consumption. Merchants are guided by their interest; and, in a fair and lawful trade, when they consult their interest, they best consult that of the public. An American merchant does not purchase British manufactures, merely *because they are British*, but on account they are better suited to the taste and fashion of America, and are better in quality, and cheaper.—On the other hand, he does not dislike the manufactures of France, merely because they are *French*, but on account of their being worse in quality and dearer, and less suited to the taste and fashion of America.

It is very true, that since the peace, more tobacco has been imported into Britain than was necessary for the consumption of Britain and Ireland: This has probably arisen from former habits, and from an allowance of ten pounds of tobacco free of duty on every hogshead of tobacco, which was equal, at the present duties, to twelve shillings and six-pence sterling per hogshead; and which was a bounty granted when it was unnecessary, perhaps improper, and has been withdrawn about four years ago:—But it is probable, that the importation into Britain will be diminished nearly to the extent of the British and Irish consumption, and what may be wanted for the ports in the Baltic, who cannot afford to be direct importers.

It is obvious, that a merchant, who imports tobacco into Britain, and afterwards sends it to Holland, cannot carry on that trade in competition with a merchant who sends tobacco directly from America to Holland, because it will cost from fifteen to twenty shillings per hogshead, as has been already stated, in landing and re-shipping charges, freight, and insurance to Holland.

(B.)

List of such vessels (and the respective tonnage of each denomination) as entered the port of Philadelphia from the 1st day of September, 1772, to the 1st day of September, 1775, distinguishing each year, and also distinguishing those which were owned in Great Britain, Ireland, and such parts of the British dominions as are not now comprehended within the United States (No. I.); those which were owned in the port of Philadelphia alone (No. II.); and those which were owned in the thirteen colonies which now compose the United States of America (No. III.)

No. I. BRITISH.

1772 to 1773.			1773 to 1774.			1774 to 1775.		
No.		Tons.	No.		Tons.	No.		Tons.
23	Ships	3,508	28	Ships	4,304	35	Ships	5,590
30	Brigantines..	2,925	33	Brigantines..	2,853	33	Brigantines..	3,170
4	Snows	370	12	Snows	1,246	7	Snows	730
22	Sloops	1,043	24	Sloops	1,142	22	Sloops	1,006
18	Schooners ..	822	22	Schooners	962	17	Schooners ..	842
97		8,668	119		10,507	114		11,338

No. II. PHILADELPHIA.

1772 to 1773.			1773 to 1774.			1774 to 1775.		
No.		Tons.	No.		Tons.	No.		Tons.
109	Ships......	16,385	116	Ships......	17,569	146	Ships......	23,406
140	Brigantines	12,148	176	Brigantines	15,749	205	Brigantines	17,802
25	Snows	2,902	18	Snows	2,092	17	Snows	1,972
39	Sloops	1,806	42	Sloops	1,844	36	Sloops	1,844
63	Schooners..	3,226	54	Schooners..	2,959	35	Schooners..	1,834
376		36,467	406		40,213	439		46,858

No. III. AMERICA.

1772 to 1773.			1773 to 1774.			1774 to 1775.		
No.		Tons.	No.		Tons.	No.		Tons.
5	Ships	700	6	Ships	860	7	Ships	902
46	Brigantines..	3,856	28	Brigantines..	2,224	30	Brigantines..	2,576
1	Snow	160		....		1	Snow	80
139	Sloops......	6,503	135	Sloops......	5,876	130	Sloops......	5,843
80	Schooners ..	3,899	81	Schooners ..	3,962	78	Schooners ..	4,025
271		15,118	250		12,922	246		13,426

A Table shewing what proportion the tonnage of Great Britain employed out of the port of Philadelphia bore to the tonnage employed out of that port, and owned therein, upon an average of three years antecedent to the war; and what proportion the tonnage of Great Britain so employed then bore to the tonnage of Philadelphia, united with the tonnage of the other twelve American colonies so employed.

Shewing also, what proportion the British tonnage now employed in the trade of Philadelphia bears to the tonnage of all the United States employed out of that port, upon an average of the last two years.

	1773.	1774.	1775.	Total.
	Tons.	Tons.	Tons.	Tons.
British	8,668	10,507	11,333	30,508
Philadelphia	36,467	40,213	46,858	123,538
American	15,118	12,922	13,426	41,466
Philadelphia and America combined	51,583	53,135	60,284	165,004

By the foregoing table it appears, that the tonnage of Great Britain employed out of the port of Philadelphia in the above years was not equal to 1-4th part of the tonnage employed out of and owned in the port of Philadelphia; and that the tonnage of Great Britain then so employed, bore only a proportion as 2 does to 11 to the tonnage of Philadelphia and the other twelve colonies combined so employed.

	1788.	1789.	Total.
	Tons.	Tons.	Tons.
British	23,004	29,372	52,376
American	28,028	37,728	65,756

By the above table it appears, that the tonnage of Great Britain employed out of the port of Philadelphia in the years 1788 and 1789, amounted to within 1-5th part of the tonnage of all the thirteen United States combined so employed.

A List of British Vessels which entered the Port of Philadelphia the following Years, viz. from 5th September, 1787, *to 5th September,* 1788.

From Great Britain.		Ireland.		British West Indies.		British American Colonies.	
Vessels.	Tons.	Vessels.	Tons.	Vessels.	Tons.	Vessels.	Tons.
16 Ships - -	3,748	4 Ships - -	1,021	1 Ship - -	174	1 Ship - -	160
19 Brigantines -	2,907	1 Brig - -	135	52 Brigs - -	6,229	6 Brigantines -	462
3 Snows - -	456	1 Snow - -	90	64 Sloops - -	5,597	1 Schooner - -	47
3 Sloops - -	198			24 Schooners -	1,696		
1 Schooner - -	85						
42 Sail.	7,394	6 Sail.	1,246	141 Sail	13,695	8 Sail.	669

Total.
22 Ships
78 Brigantines
4 Snows
67 Sloops
26 Schooners

} 197 Sail Vessels — 23,004 Tons.

Ditto, from 5th September, 1788, *to 5th September*, 1789.

From Great Britain. Vessels.	Tons.	Ireland. Vessels.	Tons.	British West Indies. Vessels.	Tons.	British American Colonies. Vessels.	Tons.
23 Ships - -	5,967	15 Ships - -	2,961	3 Ships - -	600	1 Ship - -	162
19 Brigantines -	2,936	5 Brigantines -	631	48 Brigantines -	6,010	10 Brigantines -	1,060
1 Snow - -	104	1 Snow - -	108	69 Sloops - -	5,586	2 Sloops - -	106
4 Sloops - -	223			29 Schooners -	2,332	7 Schooners -	544
1 Schooner - -	42						
48 Sail.	9,272	21 Sail.	3,700	149 Sail.	14,528	20 Sail.	1,872

Total
42 Ships
82 Brigantines
2 Snows
75 Sloops
37 Schooners
} 238 Sail Vessels — 29,372 Tons.

(C.)

An ACT *for laying a* DUTY *on* GOODS, WARES, *and* MERCHANDIZES *imported into the* UNITED STATES.

[Repealed by Sess. 2. ch. 39. New Duties to commence 1 Jan. 1791.]

SECTION I. Whereas it is necessary for the support of Government, for the discharge of the debts of the United States, and the encouragement and protection of manufactures, that duties be laid on goods, wares, and merchandizes imported,

Be it enacted by the SENATE *and* HOUSE *of* REPRESENTATIVES *of the United States of America in Congress assembled,* That from and after the first day of August next ensuing, the several duties herein after mentioned shall be laid on the following goods, wares, and merchandizes imported into the United States, from any foreign port or place, that is to say:

On all distilled spirits of Jamaica proof, imported from any kingdom or country whatsoever . . per gallon, ten cents.
On all other distilled spirits . . per gallon, eight cents.
On molasses . . . per gallon, two and a half cents.
On Madeira wine . . . per gallon, eighteen cents.
On all other wines . . . . . per gallon, ten cents.
On every gallon of beer, ale, or porter in casks . five cents.
On all cyder, beer, ale, or porter in bottles per dozen, five cents.
On malt . . . . per bushel, ten cents.
On brown sugars . . . . . per pound, one cent.
On loaf sugars . . . . . per pound, three cents.
On all other sugars . . per pound, one and a half cents.
On coffee . . . per pound, two and a half cents.
On cocoa . . . . . . per pound, one cent.
On all candles of tallow . . . . per pound, two cents.
On all candles of wax or spermaceti . per pound, six cents.
On cheese . . . . . . per pound, four cents.
On soap . . . . per pound, two cents.
On boots . . . . per pair, fifty cents.
On all shoes, slippers, or goloshes, made of leather . . . . . . per pair, seven cents.
On all shoes or slippers made of silk or stuff per pair, ten cents.
On cables, for every one hundred and twelve pounds . . . . seventy-five cents.
On tarred cordage, for every one hundred and twelve pounds . . . . . seventy-five cents.
On untarred ditto, and yarn, for every one hundred and twelve pounds . . . . ninety cents.

On twine or packthread, for every one hundred and twelve pounds . . two hundred cents.
On all steel unwrought, for every one hundred and twelve pounds . . . fifty-six cents.
On all nails and spikes . . . per pound, one cent.
On salt . . . . per bushel, six cents.
On manufactured tobacco . . per pound, six cents.
On snuff . . . . . . per pound, ten cents.
On indigo . . . . . . per pound, sixteen cents.
On wool and cotton cards . . . per dozen, fifty cents.
On coal . . . . . . per bushel, two cents.
On pickled fish . . . per barrel, seventy-five cents.
On dried fish, ... per quintal, fifty cents.

On all teas imported from China or India in ships built in the United States, and belonging to a citizen or citizens thereof, or in ships or vessels built in foreign countries, and on the sixteenth day of May last wholly the property of a citizen or citizens of the United States, and so continuing until the time of importation, as follows:

On bohea tea . . . . . . per pound, six cents.
On all souchong, or other black teas, per pound, ten cents.
On all hyson teas . . . per pound, twenty cents.
On all other green teas . . per pound, twelve cents.

On all teas imported from Europe in ships or vessels built in the United States, and belonging wholly to a citizen or citizens thereof, or in ships or vessels built in foreign countries, and on the sixteenth day of May last wholly the property of a citizen or citizens of the United States, and so continuing until the time of importation, as follows:

On bohea tea . . . . per pound, eight cents.
On all souchong, or other black teas per pound, thirteen cents.
On all hyson teas . . . per pound, twenty-six cents.
On all other green teas . . per pound, sixteen cents.

On all teas imported in any other manner than as abovementioned, as follows:

On bohea tea . . . . . per pound, fifteen cents.
On all souchong, or other black teas per pound, twenty-two cents.
On all hyson teas . . . per pound, forty-five cents.
On all other green teas . per pound, twenty-seven cents.

On all goods, wares and merchandizes, other than teas, imported from China, or India, in ships not built in the United States, and not wholly the property of a citizen or citizens thereof, nor in vessels built in foreign countries, and on the sixteenth day of May last wholly the property of a citizen or citizens of

[D]

the United States, and so continuing until the time of importation, twelve and a half per centum ad valorem.

On all looking-glasses, window and other glass (except black quart bottles)	ten per cent. ad valorem.
On all China, stone and earthern ware	
On gun-powder	
On all paints ground in oil	
On shoe and knee-buckles	
On gold and silver lace, and	
On gold and silver leaf	
On all blank books	seven and a half per centum ad valorem.
On all writing, printing, or wrapping paper, paper hangings, and pasteboard	
On all cabinet wares	
On all buttons	
On all saddles	
On all gloves of leather	
On all hats of beaver, fur, wool, or mixture of either	
On all millinery ready made	
On all castings of iron, and upon slit and rolled iron	
On all leather tanned or tawed, and all manufacture of leather, except such as shall be otherwise rated	
On canes, walking-sticks and whips	
On clothing ready made	
On all brushes	
On gold, silver and plated ware, and on jewellery and paste work	
On anchors, and on all wrought tin and pewter ware	
On playing cards	per pack, ten cents.
On every coach, chariot, or other four-wheel carriage, and on every chaise, solo, or other two-wheel carriage, or parts thereof	fifteen per centum ad valorem.

On all other goods, wares and merchandize, five per centum on the value thereof, at the time and place of importation, except as follows: Salt-petre, tin in pigs, tin-plates, lead, old pewter, brass, iron and brass wire, copper in plates, wool, cotton, dying woods and dying drugs, raw hides, beaver, and all other furs, and deer skins.

SEC. 2. *And be it further enacted by the authority aforesaid,* That from and after the first day of December which shall be in the year one thousand seven hundred and ninety, there shall be laid a duty on every one hundred and twelve pounds weight of hemp imported as aforesaid, of sixty cents; and on cotton per pound three cents.

SEC. 3. *And be it enacted by the authority aforesaid,* That all the duties paid, or secured to be paid upon any of the goods, wares, and merchandizes as aforesaid, except on distilled spirits, other than brandy and geneva, shall be returned or discharged upon such of the said goods, wares or merchandizes, as shall within twelve months after payment made, or security given, be exported to any country, without the limits of the United States, as settled by the late treaty of peace; except one per centum on the amount of the said duties, in consideration of the expence which shall have accrued by the entry and safe-keeping thereof.

SEC. 4. *And be it enacted by the authority aforesaid,* That there shall be allowed and paid on every quintal of dried, and on every barrel of pickled, fish, of the fisheries of the United States, and on every barrel of salted provision of the United States, exported to any country without the limits thereof, in lieu of a drawback of the duties imposed on the importation of the salt employed and expended therein, viz.

On every quintal of dried fish . . . . five cents.
On every barrel of pickled fish, . . . five cents.
On every barrel of salted provision . . . five cents.

SEC. 5. *And be it further enacted by the authority aforesaid,* That a discount of ten per cent. on all the duties imposed by this act shall be allowed on such goods, wares and merchandizes as shall be imported in vessels built in the United States, and which shall be wholly the property of a citizen or citizens thereof, or in vessels built in foreign countries, and on the sixteenth day of May last wholly the property of a citizen or citizens of the United States, and so continuing until the time of importation.

SEC. 6. *And be it further enacted by the authority aforesaid,* That this act shall continue and be in force until the first day of June which shall be in the year of our Lord one thousand seven hundred and ninety-six, and from thence until the end of the next succeeding session of congress, which shall be held thereafter, and no longer.

FREDERICK AUGUSTUS MUHLENBERG,
Speaker of the House of Representatives.

JOHN ADAMS, *Vice President of the United States, and President of the Senate.*

APPROVED, June 1, 1789.

GEORGE WASHINGTON, *President of the United States.*

(D.)

An ACT *making further Provision for the* PAYMENT *of the* DEBTS *of the* UNITED STATES.

WHEREAS, by an act, intituled, "An act for laying a duty on goods, wares and merchandizes imported into the United States," divers duties were laid on goods, wares and merchandize so imported, for the discharge of the debts of the United States, and the encouragement and protection of manufactures: and whereas the support of government and the discharge of the said debts render it necessary to encrease the said duties:

SEC. I. *Be it enacted by the* SENATE *and* HOUSE *of* REPRESENTATIVES *of the United States of America in Congress assembled,* That from and after the last day of December next, the duties specified and laid in and by the act aforesaid, shall cease and determine; and that upon all goods, wares and merchandize (not herein particularly excepted) which after the said day shall be brought into the United States, from any foreign port or place, there shall be levied, collected and paid the several and respective duties following, that is to say: Madeira wine of the quality of London particular, per gallon, thirty-five cents; other Madeira wine, per gallon, thirty cents; Sherry wine, per gallon, twenty-five cents; other wines, per gallon, twenty cents; distilled spirits, if more than ten per cent, below proof, according to Dycas's hydrometer, per gallon, twelve cents; if more than five, and not more than ten per cent. below proof, according to the same hydrometer, per gallon, twelve and an half cents; if of proof, and not more than five per cent. below proof, according to the same hydrometer, per gallon, thirteen cents; if above proof, but not exceeding twenty per cent. according to the same hydrometer, per gallon, fifteen cents; if of more than twenty and not more than forty per cent. above proof, according to the same hydrometer, per gallon, twenty cents; if of more than forty per cent. above proof, according to the same hydrometer, per gallon, twenty-five cents; molasses, per gallon, three cents; beer, ale and porter in casks, per gallon, five cents; beer, ale and porter in bottles, per dozen, twenty cents. Teas from China and India, in ships or vessels of the United States, bohea, per pound, ten cents; souchong and other black teas, per pound, eighteen cents; hyson, per pound, thirty-two cents; other green teas, per pound, twenty cents; teas from Europe, in ships or vessels of the United States; bohea, per pound, twelve cents; souchong and other black teas, per pound, twenty-one cents; hyson per pound, forty cents; other green teas, per pound, twenty-four cents: teas from any other place, or in any other ships or vessels, bohea per pound, fifteen cents; souchong and other black teas per pound, twenty-seven cents; hyson per pound, fifty cents; other green teas per pound, thirty cents; coffee per pound, four cents; cocoa per pound, one cent; loaf sugar per pound, five cents; brown sugar per pound, one and an half cent; other sugar per pound, two and an half cents; candles of tallow per pound, two cents; candles of wax or spermaceti per pound, six cents; cheese per pound, four cents; soap per pound, two cents; pepper per pound, six cents; pimento per pound, four cents; manufactured tobacco per pound, six cents; snuff per pound, ten cents; indigo per pound, twenty-five cents; cotton per pound, three cents; nails and spikes per pound, one cent; barr and other lead per pound, one cent; steel unwrought per one hundred and twelve pounds, seventy-five cents; hemp per one hundred and twelve pounds, fifty-four cents; cables per one hundred and twelve pounds, one hundred cents; tarred cordage per one hundred and twelve pounds, one hundred cents; untarred cordage and yarn per one hundred and twelve pounds, one hundred and fifty cents; twine and packthread per one hundred and twelve pounds, three hundred cents; salt per bushel, twelve cents; malt per bushel, ten cents; coal per bushel, three cents; boots per pair, fifty cents; shoes, slippers and goloshoes, made of leather, per pair, seven cents; shoes and slippers made of silk or stuff, per pair, ten cents; wool and cotton cards, per dozen, fifty cents; playing cards, per pack, ten cents; all china ware, looking glasses, window and other glass, and all manufactures of glass (black quart bottles excepted), twelve and an half per centum ad valorem; marble, slate and other stones, bricks, tiles, cables, mortars and other utensils of marble or slate, and generally all stone and earthen ware, blank books, writing paper, and wrapping paper, paper hangings, paste-boards, parchment and vellum, pictures and prints, painters colours, including lampblack, except those commonly used in dying, gold, silver and plated ware, gold and silver lace, jewellery and paste work, clocks and watches, shoe and knee buckles, grocery (except the articles before enumerated), namely, cinnamon, cloves, mace, nutmegs, ginger, aniseed, currants, dates, figs, plums, prunes, raisins, sugar-candy, oranges, lemons, limes, and generally, all fruits and comfits, olives, capers and pickles of every sort, oil, gunpowder, mustard in flour, ten per centum ad valorem; cabinet-wares, buttons, saddles, gloves of leather, hats of beaver, felt, wool, or a mixture of any of them, millinery ready made, castings of iron, and slit and rolled iron, leather tanned or tawed, and all manufactures of which leather is the article of chief value, except such as are herein otherwise rated, canes, walking-sticks and whips, clothing ready made, brushes, anchors, all wares of tin, pewter, or copper, all or any of them, medicinal drugs, except those commonly used in dying, carpets and carpeting, all velvets, velverets, satins and other wrought silks, cambrics, muslins, muslinets, lawns, laces, gauzes, chintzes, and coloured calicoes, and nankeens, seven and an half per centum ad valorem. All goods, wares and merchandize imported directly from China or India in ships or vessels not of the United States, teas excepted, twelve and an half per centum ad valorem. All coaches, chariots, phaetons, chaises, chairs, solos or other carriages, or parts of carriages, fifteen and an half per centum ad valorem; and five per centum ad valorem upon all other goods, wares and merchandize, except bullion, tin in pigs, tin plates, old pewter, brass, tutanag, iron and brass wire, copper in plates, salt petre, plaster of Paris, wool, dying woods, and dying drugs, raw hides and skins, undressed furs of every kind, the sea-stores of ships or vessels, the clothes, books, household furniture, and the tools or implements of the trade or profession of persons who come to reside in the United States, philosophical apparatus specially imported for any seminary of learning, all goods intended to be re-exported to a foreign port or place, in the same ship or vessel in which they shall be imported, and generally, all articles of the growth, product or manufactures of the United States.

Sec. 2. *And be it further enacted,* That an addition of ten per centum shall be made to the several rates of duties above specified and imposed, in respect to all goods, wares and merchandize, which, after the said last day of December next, shall be imported in ships or vessels not of the United States, except in the cases in which an additional duty is herein before specially laid on any goods, wares or merchandizes, which shall be imported in such ships or vessels.

Sec. 3. *And be it further enacted,* That all duties which shall be paid or secured to be paid by virtue of this act, shall be returned or discharged in respect to all such goods, wares or merchandize, whereupon they shall have been so paid, or secured to be paid, as within twelve calendar months after payment made or security given, shall be exported to any foreign port or place, except one per centum on the amount of the said duties, which shall be retained as an indemnification for whatever expence may have accrued concerning the same.

Sec. 4. *And be it further enacted,* That there shall be allowed and paid on dried and pickled fish, of the fisheries of the United States, and on other provisions salted within the said States, which after the said last day of December next shall be exported therefrom to any foreign port or place, in lieu of a drawback of the duty on the salt which shall have been expended thereupon, according to the following rates, namely, dried fish per quintal, ten cents, pickled fish and other salted provisions, per barrel, ten cents.

Sec. 5. *And be it further enacted,* That where duties by this act are imposed, or drawbacks allowed on any specific quantity of goods, wares and merchandize, the same shall be deemed to apply in proportion to any quantity, more or less, than such specific quantity.

Sec. 6. *And be it further enacted,* That all the duties which by virtue of the act intituled, "An act for laying a duty on goods, wares and merchandizes imported into the United States," accrued between the time specified in the said act for the commencement of the said duties, and the respective times when the collectors entered upon the duties of their respective offices in the several districts, be, and they are hereby remitted and discharged, and that in any case in which they may have been paid to the United States, restitution thereof shall be made.

Sec. 7. *And be it further enacted,* That the several duties imposed by this act shall continue to be collected and paid, until the debts and purposes, for which they are pledged and appropriated, shall be fully discharged. *Provided,* that nothing herein contained shall be construed to prevent the legislature of the United States from substituting other duties or taxes of equal value to any or all of the said duties and imposts.

FREDERICK AUGUSTUS MUHLENBERG,
Speaker of the House of Representatives.

JOHN ADAMS, *Vice-President of the United States, and President of the Senate.*

Approved, August the tenth, 1790.
GEORGE WASHINGTON, *President of the United States.*

SUPPLEMENT.

Printed by T. Davison, Whitefriars.

SUPPLEMENT.

No. I.

A Letter from an Officer of Rank in the Army, to one of his Majesty's Ministers of State respecting Louisiana.

SIR, C—— Street, May 21, 1794.

I BEG leave to submit to your able consideration a measure that might probably be accomplished without much difficulty, and would prove of infinite utility to several of the British colonies in the West Indies; tend greatly to secure against any danger from the United States the remaining British provinces in North America; and considerably extend the navigation and commerce of this country.

If all or any of these ends could be obtained, I hope the matter will not be deemed unworthy of the honour of your notice, although it be not suggested from a more respectable source.

What I allude to, sir, is this; *that on a peace and general arrangement of the present extensive troubles*, the cession of the island of New Orleans, with all, or a part of, West Florida, and as much of the territory bordering on the Missisippi as should be judged necessary, might be obtained by this country from the court of Spain; in which event the above-mentioned advantages would consequently follow.

In the present state of that country, all the West India

[E]

islands could be plentifully supplied from the Missisippi with every species of lumber, at cheaper price, lower expence of freight, and with less risk of capture in time of war, or in the navigation at all times, than from any other country whatsoever: besides which (now that the call must be greater than heretofore) it is to be observed, that lumber, in the provinces on the Atlantic, is daily becoming scarce, and is in some places exhausted: whereas, along the immense extent of the Missisippi and Missouri rivers, and the many great rivers that fall into them, that article is inexhaustible, and may almost be said to be indiminishable.

That country would also, in a little time, be able to supply the West Indies with abundance of many articles of provisions; particularly with rice, flour, all sorts of grain, roots, butter, cheese, &c. Louisiana would likewise supply vast numbers of horses fit for that climate, as the country abounds with them at this day, and they are multiplying rapidly. The herds of black cattle are still more numerous; but as every article intended for foreign consumption, from the American settlements on the Ohio, and the other rivers, discharging themselves into the Missisippi, can only be exported by the mouth of this latter river, they may in some degree be considered as the produce of Louisiana itself.

Besides the foregoing advantages which would result to the West India colonies from the nature of the produce and the proximity of the settlement, if it could be added to the British empire, the mother country would receive the greatest benefit.

When it is considered, that from the furthest distance up the Missouri river, whither our Indian traders from Canada at present resort, to the mouth of the Missisippi (an extent of above three thousand miles), there is an unfathomable and uninterrupted channel; and that both the banks are of a fertility surpassing the most exaggerated accounts of those of the Nile, and capable of yielding every production of both hemispheres; and when we further reflect on the many great rivers which discharge themselves into the Missisippi, particularly the Ohio, which is of itself navigable above twelve hundred miles, with several others falling into it, little less in appearance than the Ohio itself; and the neighbouring soil and climate offering every inducement to come and settle there, with no channel, as I have already observed, to export the produce by, except the Missisippi;—I say, sir, when all those circumstances are considered, there can hardly be a calculation formed of the *shipping* that will be necessary, in some short time hence, for the transport of the immense productions that will be sent down that river.

Of those, many would be found useful for our own manufactories; such as hemp, cotton, flax, tar, hides, tallow, wax, peltry, &c.; besides which, the present settlements in Louisiana yield great quantity of rice and indigo, with tobacco, of a quality not inferior to the best that is brought from the Brazils: nor does the silk-worm thrive in any country better than there. The vine too and olive tree flourish so well in Louisiana, that France found it necessary to prohibit early the cultivation of them. It should also be observed, that at New Orleans no expence would be required for establishing a colony; the country being already well settled with wealthy inhabitants, who neither want nor desire any king to render them flourishing, but a liberal government, such as every British colony enjoys.

The rapid progress lately made in the settling the banks of the Ohio, and the influx thereto of thousands annually from the states bordering on the Atlantic, will force the inhabitants of that district to open a communication with foreign markets, and to create a navy for themselves, unless they find purchasers for the spare produce of their settlements, or vessels to convey it to foreign markets, neither of which they meet with at present at New Orleans, the only port possible for them to have access to; for you are not, sir, to be told, that the jealous policy of Spain discourages rigorously every intercourse with that people: whereas, if New Orleans became a British colony, our merchants would buy, or our shipping convey to proper markets, every vendible article; and, in return, they could supply these upper settlements with British merchandize, by the river St. Lawrence, at a far more reasonable price than they could be afforded at, if procured by any other route.

If those conveniences were obtained, I have reason to think it is all these inland settlers desire; and in that event I have no doubt they would in time connect themselves with our government on any terms as we should propose or agree to, for they are in general composed of European emigrants, who, after serving out the term of their indenture, fix their residence there on account of the cheapness and fertility of the soil. Very great numbers of them sent a deputation some years ago to Canada, offering (if permitted) to remove within his majesty's limits; and they have not yet entered into any firm alliance with congress, nor would any thing induce them to unite with that government but the difficulty of getting sale for their produce, which will, if not removed, oblige them to seize upon New Orleans, and they will, in that case, invite American merchants to come and settle there, in order to furnish them with shipping; a measure which congress will gladly promote, unless they be anticipated by some other trading power, for it would soon employ more craft and seamen than half the ports of America do at this day.

Should the Americans thus once firmly possess themselves of that colony, it will be very difficult to dislodge them; and from the time they establish a footing in any port in the Gulph of Florida, the intercourse between the European nations and the West Indies *will be very insecure* indeed.

Exclusive of other advantages which would result to Britain from the possession of Louisiana, I can venture to affirm that it would conduce more than any other measure to the security of Canada (on which, of course, that of all the other British colonies depends), as it would not only render the extremity I have just mentioned unnecessary, but it could not fail besides to procure to Britain the commerce, and in time, perhaps, the alliance (if it would be accepted) of all the transmontane inhabitants, who, together with the southern Indians, would always be able to keep in awe the states bordering on the Atlantic; but without that the settlers on the Ohio are the most likely people to become the first invaders of that province, the loss of which must be followed by that of all his majesty's other possessions in North America, and involve in it consequences more alarming to the cod fishery and West India colonies than people are at this day aware of.

I hazard, sir, these opinions with the greater confidence from having a more perfect geographical and topographical knowledge of the countries in question, and a more intimate acquaintance with the character and sentiments of the leading men among their inhabitants, than perhaps fell to the lot of any other individual to acquire; having at various times resided among them, and having been many years ago employed by the late governor —— to make overtures to monsieur —— the late French governor of —— and to Don —— the first on the part of Spain, in order to sound how far it was possible, at that early period, to get New Orleans added to Florida. Confidential conversations and communications I had on that occasion with the former of those gentlemen confirmed me in an opinion I had previously entertained, that it would mutually benefit both countries if Louisiana and Canada were to belong to the same sovereignty: more especially as the rapidity of the current in the Missisippi, though so very favourable for carrying things down towards the sea, would yet, on the other hand, render the freight on heavy or bulky goods sent up against it so high, that they could be furnished from Canada at least two hundred per cent. cheaper.

I avoid, sir, making any remarks in the line of my own profession, knowing if those hints will be deemed worthy of so much attention, you can easily have an opinion on the *military* view of the measure, from men whose judgment ought deservedly to have greater weight than mine.

As to the doubt how far Spain could be prevailed upon to cede the territories I have mentioned, I am well aware that that government is to folly and absurdity fond of extensive territorial possessions, and consequently averse (though ever so unprofitable) from relinquishing the smallest part of them: yet if it should be properly represented to that court, that there is well-grounded cause to apprehend the Americans, inhabiting the borders of the Ohio, have a design upon Louisiana (of which I believe there can be no doubt), the cabinet of Madrid could not fail to see it would be wiser in Spain to put that colony into the possession of a nation on whose honour and good faith they could rely, than see so near to Mexico a banditti, of whose further encroachments they must be in perpetual dread.

By the cession of this colony his catholic majesty would not give up a single man of his natural-born subjects, there being none such in that province, except those in the king's employ; the inhabitants, whether cultivators of the soil, or employed in commerce, being French, Germans, and a few English.

Louisiana was ceded also in like manner, and for no known consideration, by France to Spain, the day preceding the signature of the articles of peace between England and France, in the year 1763; from that time it has caused much expence to Spain, and yielded little or nothing in return. The present inhabitants, who are to a man inimical to the Spanish government, desire nothing more ardently than to be received under that of Britain; in which, if their wish be not soon gratified, they will readily facilitate the conquest of it by the ***Americans:* nay it is astonishing, in consequence of the present existing troubles in France, that they have not attempted to expel the Spaniards as they did once before, and nothing can have prevented them but the strength and vigilance of the troops stationed there at present, aided perhaps by the principles of the leading men, who in general have been officers, and many in high rank, in the French king's service; and who, while they execrate the atrocities committed against their beloved sovereign's sacred person and life, would not take advantage of his avengers when endeavouring to punish the regicides, and restore his family.

If none of the forementioned considerations of sound policy, and which so nearly regard the security of her extensive possessions and commerce in that quarter, should incline Spain to adopt so wise a measure, as to cede Louisiana gratuitously to Britain, it is to be hoped the successes of his majesty's arms will leave at the disposal of government various objects from the conquests the nation shall have made, to offer to the court of Spain in lieu of it on the day of general peace.

Before I conclude it may not be amiss to remark, that Louisiana, though so easily attacked and taken, when in the hands of the Spaniards, would nevertheless be totally *hors d'insulte* if belonging to England, from the protection which could be afforded to it from Canada, and the assistance of the northern as well as southern Indian nations; who, from jealousy of the encroachments of the Americans, would cooperate with the English more heartily than they could be prevailed upon to do with any other people. I will repeat that at all events it behoves *every nation* in Europe, which has any concern with the West Indies, to *oppose* by every possible means the upstart and licentious states of America, from getting any footing in the Gulph of Florida,

* America has recently obtained the cession of Louisiana from Spain, through the medium of France. A.

otherwise they will have cause to repent it *when too late perhaps to remedy it.*

I had the honour several years ago to converse with my lord ——— on this subject, and his lordship even then saw clearly the advantage of getting Louisiana, but he did not think at the time (as we were in profound peace with all the world) that the cession of it from his catholic majesty was so accomplishable as I hope, from existing circumstances, it would be found at present.

If this measure, sir, could be effected under your auspices, the western part of the British empire would be no less beholden to your wise exertions, than the eastern is already universally allowed to be.

It is time, sir, that I beg pardon for the length of this letter and conclude. If the subject matter shall be found in any degree of that importance which I conceive, it will plead my excuse for the liberty I presume to take in addressing you, without having the honour of being known to you. Indeed, sir, a sense of that presumption would induce me to conceal my name, were it not that I wished my address should be known in case any further or more particular information on the subject in question might be wanted from me.

I have the honour to be, with the greatest respect,

Sir,

Your most obedient,

and most humble servant,

(Signed) ———

To ———.

No. II.

No. II.

(From the Daily Advertiser.)

CONDUCT OF THE COURT OF SPAIN.

The following communication we have received by post, which we readily insert in our paper, from the importance of the subject to which it relates.

To the Editor of the Daily Advertiser, &c.

SIR,

BEING an unfortunate sufferer to a very great extent by the seizure and confiscation of British ships and property in the Spanish ports, before and at the commencement of the late war with that country, and for which that court would not grant any relief, I send you a copy of the memorial presented to his majesty's government by the agent employed on the occasion, and a letter which was afterwards written by him on the same subject. It is a matter of astonishment and reget that no attention is given by government to the protection of the property of individuals thus situated, and seized before and at the commencement of a war. The stipulation, in most existing treaties, of six or twelve months for persons to retire with their property, &c. notwithstanding the breaking out of a war, is now entirely disregarded and defeated by the modern practice of slipping into hostilities by way of general reprisals. It is, however, to be hoped, that in future the interests of the subjects of this country, whenever so circumstanced, will not be again sacrificed, as they were at the close of the last war; and that the then administration, whoever may compose it, will recollect the spirited conduct of the marquis of Carmarthen, who, on the termination of the American war, or rather at the commencement of the subsequent peace, obtained from the old and magnanimous government of France compensation for the losses sustained by British subjects, from the seizure and confiscation of their ships and property which were in the French ports before and at the commencement of that war.

I am, &c.

Sunderland. X. Y.

MEMORIAL

To the Right Honourable Lord Hawkesbury, one of his Majesty's Principal Secretaries of State, &c.

The memorial of the owners of the British ships seized and detained in the several ports of Spain, previously to the commencement of the late war with that country,

Humbly sheweth,

THAT your memorialists, previously to the declaration of war on the part of this country against the crown of Spain, and in full faith of the then existing treaties of peace and commerce between the two countries, and of the security thereby afforded to the persons and property of the subjects of the respective countries, had sent a great number of vessels, the property of your memorialists, freighted with very valuable cargoes, to the different ports and harbours of Spain, for the purpose of disposing of their respective cargoes, in the accustomed way of commerce, to the subjects of that country.

That war was declared between the king of England and the king of Spain on the 9th day of November, 1796.

That some time before that event, and while the aforesaid treaties of alliance and commerce between this country and Spain were in full force, the government of Spain published a proclamation, bearing date in or about the month of August 1796, whereby it was ordained, that an embargo should be laid on all English ships in the ports and harbours of that country.

That your memorialists, and the masters or captains of the several ships or vessels belonging to your memorialists, at that time lying in the ports and harbours of Spain, entertaining no doubt of the safety of the ships and cargoes then under their care, and confiding in the protection afforded to persons and property similarly situated, not only by the law of nature and nations, but also by the stipulations of particular treaties, had taken no steps whereby they might be enabled to elude a sudden embargo, or to obviate the unfortunate consequence of so unlooked-for a measure.

That in consequence of the aforesaid proclamation, several vessels belonging to your memorialists, together with their respective cargoes, were immediately seized and detained in the various ports of Spain, and shortly after disposed of by order of the government of that country, whereby your memorialists have sustained great and most grievous inconvenience and loss.

That after the before-mentioned seizure and detention of the said vessels, and before their disposal, your memorialists caused many, though ineffectual, representations of the consequences thereof to be made to the government of Spain, and prayed that restitution of their property might be made to them, in pursuance of the terms of the treaties of amity and commerce then subsisting between the two countries.

That your memorialists humbly conceive the said detention and sale of their property to be directly against the meaning and intention of many treaties formerly made, and, as they presume, then in force between this country and Spain.

That by the 36th article of the treaty of peace, concluded between the late king Charles II. and the court of Spain, in the year 1667, it was provided, "that if it shall happen hereafter, that any difference fall out between the king of Great Britain and the king of Spain, whereby the mutual commerce and good correspondence may be endangered, the respective subjects and people of each party shall have notice thereof given them in time, that is to say, the space of six months, to transport their merchandize and effects, without giving them in that time any molestation or trouble, or retaining or embarking their goods, or persons."

That by the 18th article of the treaty of Utrecht it is provided, "that if the disputes which are composed should at any time be renewed between their said royal majesties, and break out into open war, the ships, merchandizes, and goods, both moveable and immoveable, of the subjects on both sides, which shall be found to be, and remain in the ports and dominions of the adverse party, shall not be confiscated, or suffer any damage, but the space of six months on the one part and on the other shall be granted to the said subjects of each of their said royal majesties, in order to their selling the aforesaid things, or any other of their effects, or carrying away and transporting the same from thence, whithersoever they please, without any molestation."

That in conformity to the said articles, and the reliance placed by your memorialists on the due observance of the terms thereof, the respective treaties in which they are contained then remaining in full force, and the principle thereof acknowledged, your memorialists presumed to hope they should have been restored to the full enjoyment of all their property so seized and detained in the ports of Spain, by virtue of the said proclamation. But it was at that time thought proper by the government of that country to pursue a contrary line of conduct; and the aforementioned ships, with their respective cargoes, belonging to your memorialists, were sold, as before stated, and no part of the produce thereof returned to your memorialists.

That your memorialists having thus suffered for many years under the deprivation of a very great and valuable part of their property, have no resource, but in the interference and mediation of your lordship; and they are rather emboldened to apply to your lordship on this occasion, not only by the natural justice of their claim to remuneration under the beforementioned circumstances, and on the ground of the aforesaid several treaties, but also by the express terms of the 14th article of the definitive treaty of peace just now signed between this country and France, conjointly with Spain and Holland.

That by the said 14th article of the definitive treaty it is expressly provided "that all the sequestrations laid on either side, on funds, revenues, and credits, of what nature soever they may be, belonging to any of the contracting powers, or to their citizens and subjects, shall be taken off immediately after the signature of the said definitive treaty." And it is also by the said article provided "that the decision of all claims among the individuals of the respective nations, for debts, property, estates, or rights, of any nature whatsoever, which should, according to received usages and the laws of nations, be preferred at the epoch of the peace, shall be referred to the competent tribunals; and that, in all those cases, speedy and complete justice shall be done in the countries wherein those claims shall be respectively preferred."

That your memorialists humbly conceive that no objection can be urged against the application of the universal principles of justice, or the spirit or letter of the aforementioned particular treaties to their case, as now laid before your lordship, on the ground of the want of precedent; for your memorialists beg leave to remind your lordship, that at the close of the American war a great number of owners of British vessels were in a situation exactly similar to that in which your memorialists at present unfortunately stand; their vessels, together with their cargoes, being in the French ports at the commencement of that war; and whilst there, seized, detained, condemned, and sold, by virtue of edicts or orders issued by the court of France for that purpose; and on the settlement of peace between the belligerent powers, the government of this country, on a representation made on the part of those British owners, was pleased to interfere, and obtained for them from the government of France the full value of the property that had been so condemned and sold. That under the aforesaid circumstances, your memorialists must suffer a very great and irreparable loss, unless the government of this country shall be pleased to exert itself on their behalf.

Your memorialists, therefore, most humbly pray your lordship to take their case into your lordship's consideration; and that your lordship will be pleased to interfere, on the part of his majesty's government, and to obtain for your memorialists such compensation for the beforementioned detention and sale of their property as shall be reasonable; or to procure for your memorialists such other relief, in respect of the matters before stated, as to your lordship's judgment and goodness shall seem meet.

And your lordship's memorialists, &c.

NAT. ATCHESON,
Agent.

MY LORD, Ely Place, 22d Dec. 1802.

Mr. Burdon, during the last sessions of parliament, had the honour to present to your lordship, on the part of the owners of several British ships which had been seized and detained in the several ports of Holland, France, and Spain, previously to the commencement of the late war with those countries, three memorials, praying your lordship's interference on the part of his majesty's government with those powers, for the purpose of obtaining from them some reasonable compensation for the loss and injury sustained by the memorialists, owing to the detention and sale of their property under the orders issued in regard thereto by those governments respectively; and the answer which your lordship was pleased to return to Mr. Burdon on the subject of those memorials having been communicated by him to the parties interested, they beg leave very respectfully to thank your lordship for the consideration you have had the goodness to bestow upon their case; but at the same time trust your lordship will permit them to express their apprehension, from the terms of your answer, that they may have failed to state the nature of their situation with sufficient accuracy, and that you will pardon the liberty which they have presumed to take in suggesting to your reconsideration such an explanation as they hope may induce your lordship to afford them that assistance and protection which, from the equity and justice of their case, they have been led humbly to request from the British government on their behalf.

Your lordship, as it appears to them, may have considered that the ships alluded to in the memorials were condemned by sentence of the courts of admiralty of the respective countries therein mentioned, for some cause originating with or after the declaration of war between the belligerent powers, which would subject them agreeably to the rule of the law of nations to the penalty of confiscation; whereas the property in question had in fact entered into, and was remaining at the respective times of the seizure thereof in the ports where it was seized in the innocent course of peaceful commerce, and with entire confidence on the part of the British owners, that all their rights therein were intitled to be held sacred and inviolable; a confidence in which they had the greater reason to rely inasmuch as if a difference of opinion should be entertained as to the general rule of law, applying to cases so circumstanced, when unrestrained by any conventional regulations, but which the memorialists scarcely think can prevail, consistently with justice and equity, still they were entitled expressly to protection in that respect under the faith of treaties in which it had been reciprocally contemplated and agreed between Great Britain and the several powers to whom those ports belonged; amongst other the provisions and stipulations therein contained, that in case of any war thereafter breaking out, six months should be allowed to their respective subjects for the removing of their merchandize and effects, or otherwise disposing of them as they should see fit; whereas even before any declaration of war, solemn or unsolemn, the said ships and cargoes in question were not only detained but sold as stated in the said memorials.

Under which circumstances it appears to the British owners interested in this unfortunate affair, and as they trust it will to your lordship, that in whatever form or by whatever tribunal their property was thus ordered to be disposed of, such a sentence cannot be supported as an adjudication duly passed upon the property of the subjects of powers becoming hostile under the circumstances and relations aforesaid, or by which the same can be considered as legally divested.

A very short examination of the dates of these transactions will establish the fact, that the orders of the respective powers of Holland, France, and Spain, by virtue of which the persons applying to your lordship on this occasion were deprived of their property, were made and issued, and carried into effect, far within the time allowed for the protection of property, in case of war, by the treaties to which they have taken the liberty to refer; and they look with additional confidence to the event of this application, from your lordship's intimate acquaintance with the law of nations, and the sound principles of natural justice. Humbly presuming to hope that your lordship will, upon reconsideration of their case, with that condescension and goodness which have always marked your lordship's conduct, be yet inclined to listen to their representation, and to procure them relief, according to the prayer of their memorials, or in such other way as it may seem most expedient to your lordship to be granted with reference to the losses they have respectively sustained. I am, my lord, with great respect, your lordship's most obedient and faithful servant,

NAT. ATCHESON,
Agent.

To the Right Honourable Lord Hawkesbury, &c. &c. &c.

No. III.

Observations on the Importance of a strict Adherence to the Navigation Laws of Great Britain; most respectfully inscribed to the Shipping Interest of Great Britain.

IT is the fate of Great Britain, a fate peculiarly her own, to depend upon her navy and her commerce for a continuance of the superiority she enjoys over the other nations of Europe. This truth has frequently influenced the deliberations of her legislators from an early period of her history; and to appreciate its influence, we have only to regard the unremitting attention that has been paid to the establishment and security of her maritime rights from the moment their value was felt up to the present hour, an hour in which those rights, as they have derived from various causes unprecedented importance, demand at our hands unprecedented care. This attention to the grand source of our wealth and glory has been rendered worthy of the wisdom that bestowed it; it has not evaporated in empty eulogiums, it has been embodied and concentrated in statutes enacted by successive parliaments, that have at length formed themselves into a system of navigation laws, which, if its operations are not counteracted by unforeseen circumstances, must continue to produce to this country an unfailing source of wealth and glory.

In its progress towards its present solidity, for the course of near five centuries, and amidst numberless subordinate regulations, it has been the undeviating aim of the wise framers of this system, to render *the commerce of the country* the medium of the *increase* of its *shipping*; and therefore, except where policy or necessity have compelled a contrary conduct, considerations of temporary advantages have sometimes been made to yield to the less dazzling, but more permanent, acquisition of naval power. To effect this salutary end, the various acts above alluded to have been framed and worded with great consideration and care, for the purpose of confining certain portions of our trade with foreign countries, and the whole of our coasting trade, to British-built ships alone, and to securing to such ships, commanded and three-fourths manned with British subjects, certain advantages, in which the vessels of foreigners could not, and ought not, to participate.

So early as the reign of Richard II., at a time when our shipping and commerce were in their infancy, the advantages, not to say the necessity, of such a system presented themselves so strongly to our ancestors, that in the fifth year of his reign an act of parliament was passed, by which it was ordained, that no merchandize should be shipped into or out of the realm but in British ships, on pain of forfeiture. This act was recognised, and its provisions enforced, by other acts of parliament in after times, during the reigns of Henry VII. and Henry VIII.; and in the reign of queen Elizabeth, an act of parliament passed, which, although in words it repealed the statute of Richard II., was in the same spirit, and calculated to produce similar effects. But in process of time, and as the country began to discern with more clearness the policy of regulations that naturally tended to awaken the industry and increase the wealth of its inhabitants, the desire to secure their observance, and extend their influence, became proportionably powerful, till at length, in the year 1651, an act was passed, which expressly prohibited all ships of foreign nations from trading with England, or with any English plantations; and no goods were suffered to be imported into England, or any of its dependencies, in any other than English bottoms, or in the ships of that European nation of which the merchandize imported was the genuine growth or manufacture.

The statute of the 12th Charles II. chap. 18. corroborates, if, after the experience we have had, any thing were wanting to corroborate, the wisdom of the principle in which the act of 1651, and the preceding navigation acts, were founded; for by this act, which was passed soon after the restoration, not only were the provisions of the act of 1651 continued (with some alterations as to the European trade), but a farther provision made, that the master and three-fourths of the mariners should also be English subjects, under forfeiture of the ship, and of all goods imported or exported therein.

During the succeeding reigns, up to the time of passing the 26th of his present majesty, commonly called lord Liverpool's act, the spirit of commerce continued to rise, and with it the concomitant conviction, that to continue and secure the advantages granted by preceding statutes to British-built ships and their owners, in the carrying on the commerce of the country, was the only method by which Great Britain could long remain in the possession of that proud pre-eminence which distinguishes her as a maritime nation; the act, therefore, of the seventh and eighth of William III., and others that cannot here be particularized, were all in various ways conducive to the confirmation of the exclusive rights of British owners, and the privileges of British-built ships.

Experience has shewn the correctness and importance of the views of those who from time to time have supported this system of navigation laws, which it is so much the interest of British ship-owners to uphold. The act of the 26th of his present majesty, and many other statutes, clearly demonstrate the anxiety of the country to guard this system, by a steady adherence to which we have been enabled, during the most arduous contest in which this country was ever engaged, to triumph over all the naval powers of Europe; and to the continuance of which alone we can look for the security and fruits of that triumph. "After this experience," says an * able writer on this system of navigation laws, "no one can doubt but that it is the real interest of Great Britain to give her principal attention to maritime affairs, to carry on her own trade in her own ships directly to all parts of the world, and to encourage her fisheries in every sea. From these sources she may always hope to obtain a naval force adequate to guard her shores from hostile invasion, and to secure her domestic felicity, both public and private, firm and unshaken as the foundations of the island."

On the other hand, should the wisdom and labours of successive ages be rendered unavailing *by the blindness and in-*

* *Vide* Reeves's History of Shipping, compiled for the Board of Trade.

difference of the present day—should these boasted laws of navigation, framed for the increase and the protection of British-built ships and British owners, have been enacted in vain—should *strangers* and *foreigners* be permitted to snatch from their hands the privileges which belong, and which have been solemnly assured by the country, to British owners alone—it will be a task not less difficult than it will be melancholy to calculate the mischiefs that must ensue to the maritime and the commercial interest of Britain.

It is with the deepest regret the shipping interest of this country observe, that the suspension of the navigation laws, during the last * two years, has already been attended with serious inconvenience and loss; and they fear the continuance of it, unless those laws are again speedily permitted to have their free and natural operation: and if by new regulations, or by any further relaxation of the present navigation laws, new and foreign competitors should be admitted to share in the advantages resulting from them, they apprehend that the maritime spirit of the country will decline—that the capital of British owners will lie unemployed, or be employed uselessly—while the shipping of Great Britain will lie rotting in her harbours, and her seamen emigrate to foreign countries in search of employment: it is therefore, particularly, at this time, the interest of Great Britain, and the duty of her government, to encourage her maritime pursuits. The events of the late war shew that many nations look with a jealous eye on the superiority we have gained by our carrying trade, and that they are ready to use every effort to participate in the benefits of our navigation, and to rival us, if possible, on our native element. To counteract these efforts with success, "we must not lose the recollection, that without an extensive naval commerce, carried on in British bottoms, we can neither rear nor retain our seamen, the grand support of our present preeminence; nor preserve our country from falling even below the level of surrounding nations."

Impressed with these sentiments, and in order more effectually to protect the shipping interest of Great Britain, and to prevent any infringement of the navigation laws, it is most seriously recommended to the owners of British ships to form *an association* for preserving those rights,

* These observations were written in 1801.

which the legislature has, in its wisdom, been pleased to confer on them exclusively; a measure which it must be regretted has been so long delayed, although earnestly recommended by many well-informed and disinterested persons, but which may yet, if embraced immediately, be the means of securing the privileges and the property of a most numerous and respectable body of British subjects---of preventing the undue advantages sought to be acquired by persons to whom the legislature has not intended to grant a benefit—and of keeping intire a body of laws peculiarly fitted to support and increase the commerce of the empire, the neglect of which will, it is to be feared, put it in the power of others, not merely to wrest from the owners of British ships the best produce of their industry, but to deprive them of the future means of exercising it, by excluding them from being the only carriers of British commerce.*

London, 6th November, 1801.

* The association of the owners of British ships, for the preservation of their rights, suggested at the close of this tract, was instituted at London in 1802, and it is worthy of observation, that they have on several occasions been highly applauded for their disinterestedness and public spirit, by persons of rank and literary talents. "The society has been recommended as likely to be productive of much good, by watching over one of the most important interests of the country, and by calling the attention of the legislature, and of the public, to any attempt that may be made to trench upon the principles or system of our navigation laws." Also, "The society is founded on very enlarged and liberal principles, and the vigilant wisdom with which it watches over the shipping interest of Great Britain is worthy of great praise."

No. IV.

No. IV.

PETITION PRESENTED IN 1801 TO THE BOARD OF TRADE, AGAINST THE SUSPENSION OF THE ACT OF NAVIGATION IN FAVOUR OF NEUTRAL SHIPS.

To the Lords of his Majesty's most Honourable Privy Council,

The humble petition of the several persons whose names are hereunto subscribed, being respectively ship-owners residing in the port of London, and interested in the Baltic and Hamburgh trade,

Sheweth,

THAT by an order of his majesty in council, bearing date the 21st day of May last, it is ordered, that it should be lawful from and after the date of the said order, and until six weeks after the commencement of the then next session of parliament, to import into any port of the United Kingdom, in foreign ships belonging to the subjects of any kingdom or state not then at war with his majesty, any hemp, flax, iron, tallow, masts, timber, square or otherwise deals, oak-staves, linen, isinglass, bristles, ashes, hides, mats, tar, pitch, linseed and rosin, upon payment of such duties (if any) as are or shall by law be payable upon such articles, when imported in any foreign-built ship. And it is thereby further ordered, that from and after the date of the said order, and until six weeks after the commencement of the then next session of parliament, it should be lawful to import in like manner any raw linen yarn upon payment of such duties (if any) as were or should be payable upon that article, when imported in a British-built ship, as by reference thereto will more fully appear; which order, your petitioners beg leave to state, is now highly prejudicial to the shipping interest of Great Britain, and of your petitioners in particular, as their ships have been usually engaged in the Baltic and Hamburgh trade, inasmuch as it not only places foreign ship-owners on a footing with British ship-owners, but gives them very great advantages, as they can navigate their vessels at one third of the expence incurred by British ship-owners in time of war.

Your petitioners also beg leave to state, that neutral ships are daily arriving in great numbers at all the ports in the Baltic, in order to bring into Great Britain and Ireland merchandize, &c. which would have been brought in British bottoms but for the order before recited; and that the trade to and from Hamburgh is at present almost wholly carried on in neutral vessels, to the manifest prejudice of your petitioners and the shipping interest of Great Britain, so that a very great number of British vessels are now unemployed from the circumstances before stated.

Your petitioners therefore pray your lordships will be pleased to take their case into your lordships immediate consideration, and either to * rescind the said order, or to grant them such other relief as to your lordships shall seem meet, in order that the shipping interest of Great Britain may not be deprived of those privileges and advantages which they had before the date of the said order.

And your petitioners will ever pray, &c.

* For some very interesting observations on the proceedings which took place on this petition, *vide Alley's* Vindication of lord Sheffield's Strictures, page 16 to 22.

No. V.

No. V.

Extract from the Minutes of the Proceedings of a General Meeting of Ship-Owners, held, by public Advertisement, at the George and Vulture Tavern, Cornhill, the 21st Day of April, 1802, to take into Consideration the intended Duties on the Tonnage of Ships, and the Effect which they may have on the Carrying Trade of Great Britain:

Thomas Rowcroft, Esq. in the Chair.

THE resolution of the House of Commons, that the several duties therein-mentioned should be imposed on the tonnage of ships, being read:—

Resolved, That it is the opinion of this meeting that the intended tax on the tonnage of shipping is impolitic, and, if carried into effect, will be injurious to the shipping interest of Great Britain, and ultimately tend to deprive this country of one of its greatest means of support.

Resolved, That the above resolution be transmitted to the ship-owners at the several out-ports, and that they be requested to co-operate with the ship-owners in London in such legal measures as they may think it necessary to adopt, in order to prevent the intended tax being carried into effect.

Resolved, That a Committee be appointed to carry the above resolutions into effect.

Resolved, That the chairman do write a letter to the Right Honourable the Chancellor of the Exchequer, requesting him to honour the Committee with an interview on the subject of these resolutions, before the third reading of the Export and Import Duty Bill.

(Signed) Thomas Rowcroft,
Chairman.

At a Meeting of the Committee of Ship-Owners, held the 28th Day of April, 1802, at Will's Coffee-house, Cornhill:

Mr. Hill in the Chair:

The sub-committee reported—That they had yesterday attended the Right Honourable the Chancellor of the Exchequer*, and that they were unable to convince him of the impolicy and injurious tendency of the intended tax on the tonnage of shipping.

Resolved, That a general meeting of ship-owners be convened on Thursday the sixth day of May next, at eleven o'clock in the forenoon, at the London Tavern, to receive the report of the committee, and to determine on such further measures which it may be adviseable to adopt respecting the tonnage duty, and *the present state of the shipping interest of Great Britain.*

(Signed) J. Hill, Chairman.

* The right honourable Henry Addington, afterwards lord Sidmouth.

No. VI.

No. VI.

Extracts from the Minutes of the Proceedings of the Society of Ship-Owners of Great Britain, since its Institution, 1802.

At a general meeting of ship-owners, held, by public advertisement, at the London Tavern, the 6th day of May, 1802, to receive the report of the committee appointed at the last general meeting, and to determine on such further measures which it might be advisable to adopt respecting *the present state* of the *shipping interest* of Great Britain:

Mr. Hill in the Chair:

The chairman reported the result of the interview of the committee with the Right Honourable the Chancellor of the Exchequer*, and that they had been unable to convince him of the impolicy and injurious tendency of the duty intended to be imposed on the tonnage of shipping.

Resolved, That it is the unanimous opinion of the ship-owners present at this meeting, that from the *present* state of Europe, there is every reason to apprehend the *shipping* of this country *will decline*, and that any tax on that species of property will be attended with the utmost danger to the state, by diminishing the great nursery of British seamen, and weakening that source of national defence.

Resolved, That it is the unanimous opinion of the ship-owners present at this meeting, that in order more effectually at this alarming crisis to promote and protect the shipping interest of Great Britain, and to endeavour *to prevent any further infringement of the navigation laws*, it is indispensably necessary to form and establish a society of ship-owners, with committees, to be annually chosen from amongst them in London and at the out-ports, who are from time to time to enter into and adopt such measures as shall be requisite for the preservation of the privileges, which the

* The Right Honourable Henry Addington.

legislature has in its wisdom conferred on the owners of British ships.

Resolved, That the minute to the above effect, signed by several ship-owners, and now produced and read, be subscribed by those present, and that a committee be appointed for the port of London for the year ensuing, viz. [Here follow the names of 47 persons of great respectability, who were the first committee for the port of London:] and that such committee do, without delay, prepare such rules and regulations which it may be proper to enter into for the purpose of carrying into effect the preceding resolution; but that such rules and regulations shall not have force, until the same have been confirmed at a general meeting to be held for that purpose. And that five of the said committee do constitute a quorum.

(Signed) J. Hill, Chairman.

At a meeting of the committee of ship-owners for the port of London, of the 20th May, 1802, at Wills' Coffee-house:

Mr. Hill in the Chair:

Resolved, That a person be employed to take an account of all the ships now on sale in the river Thames, with the names of the brokers or owners, and their burthen, age, and build, and the time such ships have been on sale; and that a letter be written to the out-ports to procure the like information of ships on sale there.

Resolved, That Mr. Akenhead, Mr. Dowson, Mr. Robinson, Mr. Tulloch, Mr. Moorsom, Mr. Curling, Mr. Keddey, and Mr. Brown, be appointed to make application to those owners or brokers in London who have ships for sale, and to ascertain from them how much they have declined in their demand or expectation of the price of such ships since the peace, and upon what their ideas of the difference of value are founded.

Resolved, That a statement be made, from different ships' accounts, of the actual rates of freight and expences during the late war, and also at the present time, to shew the inability of ship-owners to bear the tax on tonnage.

Resolved, That a statement be procured of the number of ships and their tonnage in the transport service on the 5th of October, 1801, and how many are in that service at the present time.

(Signed) J. HILL, Chairman.

At a meeting of the committee of ship-owners for the port of London, held at Wills' Coffee-house, 2d June, 1802:

Mr. GILLESPY in the Chair:

THE draft of the petition against the bill imposing duties on the tonnage of shipping, and on the depressed state of the shipping interest, according to the resolution of the former meeting of the committee, was read * and confirmed.

Resolved, That Mr. Lushington, one of the representatives in parliament for the city of London, be desired to present the said petition to the House of Commons; and that the other members for the said city and the borough of Southwark, and also for the out-ports, be requested to support the same; and that the secretary do communicate to those members this resolution, when Mr. Lushington has fixed the day for presenting the said Petition.

(Signed) T. GILLESPY, Chairman.

At a general meeting of ship-owners, held at the London Tavern, the 22d day of June, 1802, to receive the report of the committee for the port of London, and on other business:

Mr. HILL in the Chair:

THE petition to the honourable the House of Commons, for a repeal of the duties on tonnage, was read, and the several resolutions of the committee were confirmed.

Resolved, That the rules and regulations prepared by the

* See Parl. Debates in 8vo. Also Cobbet's Political Register, vols. 1, 2, *et seq.*

committee for "the society of ship-owners of Great Bri-"tain," and now read, be confirmed and printed for the use of the members, and that the same be transmitted to the ship-owners at the out-ports.

A letter addressed to the chairman, and signed by the principal ship-builders on the river Thames, was read, stating, "That in consequence of the final establish-"ment of peace, they had deemed it necessary to re-"duce the wages of workmen who were employed in "repairing ships, and that they had experienced very "considerable inconvenience in their endeavours to "carry the same into effect."

Resolved, That it is the opinion of this meeting, that the wages recently paid to workmen employed in repairing and building ships in the river Thames were exorbitant, and that the ship-owners present approve of a reduction being made in such wages by the ship-builders; and that it is their determination not to employ, independent of the ship-builders, any journeymen shipwrights, or others engaged in repairing and building of ships.

Resolved, That the thanks of this meeting be given to William Lushington, Esq. M. P. for the attention which he has invariably shewn to the interests of ship-owners, and in particular for his conduct and readiness in presenting their petition to Parliament for a repeal of the duty on tonnage.

(Signed) J. HILL, Chairman.

At a meeting of the committee of ship-owners for the port of London, held the 9th day of September, 1802, at Wills' Coffee-house, Cornhill:

Mr. HILL in the Chair:

THE secretary reported, That he had written to Mr. Wells, chairman of the committee of ship-builders, respecting the dispute with the shipwrights.

The committee then took into consideration the letter addressed to the secretary, respecting Mediterranean passes.

And also, a letter from James Smith, esq. master of the Trinity-house, Scarborough, respecting a claim made by the directors of Ramsgate Pier, for dues on ships returning *in ballast*; and on the construction recently given of an act of parliament respecting the admeasurement of ships, and the inconvenience resulting from it; and also a letter which appeared in the Hull Advertiser on the same subject: but the consideration of them, as well as of the termination of the differences between the ship-builders and their men, was adjourned until the next meeting of the committee.

(Signed) J. HILL, Chairman.

At a general meeting of ship-owners, held the first day of December, 1802, at the London Tavern, to receive the report of the committee of ship-owners for the port of London, respecting "the duty on "the tonnage of ships, and on oil and skins, the "produce of the British fisheries," and on other business of great importance to the shipping interest:

Mr. HILL in the Chair:

THE secretary reported from the committee for the port of London, that they had met regularly since its establishment on the second and fourth Thursday in each month to transact business, and that they had received several communications from the ship-owners in London and at the out-ports, on many important subjects relative to the general interest of shipping.

That the great object of the committee's attention had been the present depressed state of the shipping of the country, and towards endeavouring to obtain the repeal of the duty on the tonnage of ships, and on oil and skins, the produce of the British fisheries *.

The most important subjects which had come before the committee were the following, viz.

1st. The serious inconvenience many ship-owners had felt from being obliged to take out a licence, and give bond to the commissioners of his majesty's customs, from the particular construction and build of their ships. The subject was considered of so much consequence, that it had been re-

* The ship-owners at the following amongst other out-ports petitioned Parliament against the tonnage duty, viz. Sunderland, Bridlington, Wells, Whitby, Blythe, Hartley, Scarborough, South Shields, North Shields, Newcastle, Kirkaldie, Liverpool. See the Commons Journals for 1802 and 1803.

ferred to a sub-committee to take the same into their consideration, and to point out not only the several inconveniences resulting from the regulation, but the means by which they might be remedied without any injury whatever to the revenue, and to report the same to the committee, and which was at present under their consideration.

2dly. The next subject which had been submitted to the consideration of the committee was the claim recently set up by the directors of Ramsgate harbour, for payment of the harbour dues, *on colliers* returning *in ballast coastwise*, and from Guernsey or Jersey; and the committee had, at the request of the ship-owners at Sunderland and Scarborough, taken the opinion of a very eminent lawyer on the subject, and it appeared by that opinion the directors were not warranted by the act in demanding the harbour dues on colliers returning in ballast coastwise, or from Guernsey or Jersey as before stated*; and that the committee deemed it proper to intimate that several very serious facts had been communicated to them respecting the management of Ramsgate harbour and its revenue, which it was their intention at a proper time to take into their most serious consideration.

3dly. Another important subject which had been submitted to the committee was the present rates of pilotage from the Downs to Gravesend, and from thence to London; and as the several acts respecting the pilotage from the Downs and Orfordness to London *would shortly expire*, a sub-committee had been appointed to take the same into consideration, and to report to the committee what, in conjunction with the lord warden of the Cinque Ports, and the elder brethren of the Trinity-house, they may think will be most proper to be done in that respect †.

4thly. Another subject of the greatest magnitude to the ship-owners in the port of London, which had engaged the most serious and anxious attention of the committee, was the recent disputes between the ship-builders and their workmen; and as the termination of those disputes would be in the recollection of the ship-owners present, it was not requisite to go much into detail on the subject.

The committee having received a letter from Mr. Noakes, the secretary to the committee of ship-builders, stating that the differences with the workmen had been settled on the *precise* terms offered by the ship-builders, without stating

* See *post* for this case, and the opinion of the Court thereon.

† See *post* resolutions, and letter to Sir Charles Price on that subject.

what those terms were; the committee directed the secretary to write to Mr. Wells, the chairman of the committee of ship-builders, requesting him to inform the committee of ship-owners "the circumstances attending the conclusion of "the late negotiation with their workmen, and the principle upon which they had settled with them, with the "rate of wages it had been agreed the workmen were to receive per day," to which letter the committee regret to state no answer has been given; in consequence of which, at a special general meeting, held at the London Tavern on the 30th day of September last, some resolutions * were entered into, expressive of the disapprobation of the ship-owners of the motives which seem to have led to the conclusion of those disputes.

The committee were sorry to observe the conduct of the master shipwrights had been guided by so little attention to the shipping interest of the country, and eventually of their own, as to give way to the combinations of their workmen, who, previously to their late rise of wages, were capable of

* *Extract from the Minutes of the Proceedings of the Special General Meeting of the Ship-Owners in the Port of London of the 30th Day of September*, 1802.

"Resolved, That the ship-owners present at this meeting do highly disapprove of the manner in which the ship-builders have for some time past submitted to their workmen, who have lately committed acts of violence dangerous to the community, and destructive of those principles of subordination which ought always to be maintained between employers and their workmen; and they likewise observe with very great regret, the manner in which the recent disputes between the ship-builders and their men have terminated, by the masters treating with delegates from large bodies of their workmen, who it appears were combined together for illegal purposes.

"Resolved, That the ship-owners present at this meeting do likewise disapprove the sentiments expressed in a letter signed T. Noakes, who is secretary to the committee of ship-builders, and which was published in the Public Ledger, wherein it is stated, 'that the ship-builders, in justice to the ship-owners, had placed themselves in the situation of *mediators* between the two interested parties,' that is, *their* workmen and the *ship-owners*, who think it necessary to declare, that they conceive it to be the indispensable duty of the *ship-builders* to keep their men in due subordination, to prevent illegal combinations amongst them, and to exercise the right of employing and discharging such men as they may think proper; and that the ship-builders ought to prosecute with the utmost rigour of the law such of their men who may endeavour, by threats or acts of violence, to deter others from working and performing their duty who are so disposed; and in case the existing laws are inadequate to check in their origin such outrages, or to suppress them in their progress, the ship-builders owe it to the public, and it is a duty incumbent upon them, to apply to the legislature to remedy such serious and growing evils."

earning more money by six days' labour in the week than would maintain themselves and families in the necessaries of life befitting labouring men; and which consequently enabled them to waste a considerable portion of their time, and of their superfluous earnings, in attending clubs, and supporting combinations; the result of which is, they become masters of their employers, only work when and how they please, and make their families and themselves more dissipated and poor than they would be on wages suited to maintain them with frugality and industry; whilst, by enhancing the charges of building and repairing ships, they most materially injure the maritime interest of the country.

It therefore required the most grave attention and consideration of the legislature to remedy this serious and growing evil, and such legal restrictions ought to be obtained as would most effectually prevent similar combinations, and all contributions to maintain men in idleness, who will not work because they cannot obtain their own terms, should be made illegal.

5thly. The committee's most particular attention had been directed to ascertain the *real state* of the *shipping interest* of Great Britain at this most critical and trying juncture: and their inquiries had been made with the utmost impartiality and candour. Not satisfied with their own ideas on the subject, they had applied to those persons whose habits and situations in life were most likely to enable them to form true and unbiassed judgments on the subject; and it was with great regret the committee had to report, that the result of those inquiries too truly and fully corroborated and confirmed the opinion the committee had formed of the depressed state of the shipping of Great Britain.

In addition to the objects before stated, many other matters were incidentally submitted to the consideration of the committee, and disposed of, they hoped to the satisfaction of the parties. The committee had not been unmindful of the peculiar situation of many ship-owners, whose masters had *inadvertently* lost or mislaid their Mediterranean passes; and the committee flattered themselves, that the *shipping interest* of the country will be most materially benefited by the *permanent establishment* of the society.

That the committee ventured most earnestly to recommend *a strict adherence to the spirit of the navigation laws of the kingdom*, as the privileges which had been of late years allowed to *foreign bottoms* in consequence of the suspension of those laws, had been attended with very injurious consequences to the maritime interest of the country; and they most strongly deprecated any attempt or endeavour to relax those wholesome and beneficial maritime regulations, which had so conspicuously and effectually contributed to the greatness and power of the country; especially at a time when all the *other maritime nations* of the world viewed with an envious and jealous eye the superiority we had gained by our *carrying trade*, and who were at this time most sedulously using every effort to participate in the benefits of our navigation, and to rival us, if possible, on our natural element.

The chairman then reported the result of the second interview of the committee with the right honourable the Chancellor of the Exchequer, and stated, that they had been unable to convince him of the impolicy and injurious tendency of the duty on the tonnage of ships, and on oil and skins, the produce of the British fisheries, and consequently of the urgent necessity of repealing the same.

Resolved unanimously, That the committee be instructed to wait on the right honourable the lord mayor *, and to request his lordship to present to the honourable the House of Commons the petition of the ship-owners in the port of London, for the repeal of the duty on the tonnage of ships, and on oil and skins, the produce of the British fisheries.

Resolved unanimously, That the committee be instructed to request the other members of parliament for the city of London, the members of parliament for the borough of Southwark, and for the counties of Middlesex and Surry, to attend in the House of Commons to support the petition, when presented by the right honourable the lord mayor.

Resolved unanimously, That it be recommended to the committee, previous to the petition being presented by the right honourable the lord mayor to the House of Commons, to wait upon not only the several members of parliament for the out-ports, who have received petitions from their constituents for the repeal of the tonnage duty, but likewise upon those members who have been requested to support the application for the same.

* Sir Charles Price, Bart.

Resolved unanimously, That the thanks of the ship-owners present at this meeting be given to the committee for the port of London, for their constant and indefatigable attention to the several important matters relative to the shipping interest which have been submitted to their consideration.

Resolved unanimously, That the thanks of the ship-owners present at this meeting be given to the chairman, for his unwearied assiduity and attention to the general interest of ship-owners.

(Signed) J. HILL, Chairman.

At a numerous meeting of ship-owners, convened by public advertisement, and held the first day of February, 1803, at the London Tavern, to take into consideration several matters of great importance to the shipping interest:

Mr. HILL in the Chair:

THE secretary reported—That since the last general meeting the committee had been anxiously engaged in obtaining documents to establish the correctness of the statements they had previously made, respecting the present state of the shipping interest of Great Britain, and that it appeared by the documents received by the committee, that the opinion they had formed on that subject was completely confirmed.

That the committee, in order to obtain the most correct and certain information of the present state of the shipping in the port of London, had applied to the several ship-builders on the river Thames, and it appeared by their letters annexed*, that only two ships had been built in the river Thames, for the *merchants' service*, since the 5th of October, 1801; namely, the Pacific of 307 tons burthen, for the South-Sea trade; and another of 600 tons, now building on speculation: and that it also appeared, that no other ships had been contracted to be built in the river Thames for the *merchants' service* since the 5th October, 1801.

That the committee, with a view to ascertain the real de-

* Appendix to this Report of the Committee, No. 1.

preciation in the value of shipping since the late peace, had not only reviewed with great care and attention the opinions of the several respectable brokers * who had been applied to on the subject, but they had conversed with almost every person in town, who had been in any way concerned in the sale of ships since that period; and the committee are satisfied that their opinion on that subject also stands confirmed on the most indubitable testimony, and that the value of shipping has decreased at least one-third since the peace.

That the committee had likewise, after great labour, made several comparative statements of the expences incurred in the outfit of ships between the two years immediately succeeding the American war, and the last and present year; and it appears from documents of *actual* disbursements †, that provisions of all kinds had, on an average, advanced about £89 per cent; that materials and stores of all sorts had advanced in like manner about £84 per cent; and that seamen's wages had, on an average of the different classes of seamen, advanced about £44 per cent; whilst the rate of freights had only on an average advanced about £20 per cent: and that the committee are convinced, whenever an investigation shall take place on this subject, that these statements will be found to be moderate and just: and it also appeared that since the year 1783, there had been an increase ‡ of the duties on the importation of naval stores of above £50 per cent.

That the committee had also obtained statements of the actual expenditure and earnings of ships in different trades, and it was with great concern the committee had to report, that at present ships in general were navigated to little or no profit, and many of them to actual loss.

That the committee thought it necessary to intimate that it appeared by the letters received by the secretary from *several* of the out-ports, that ship-building at such ports was not in a more flourishing state than in the port of London, and that the owners at the out-ports were deeply impressed with the same sentiments and opinions with the committee of the present depressed state of the shipping interest in general.

That the committee considered it to be their duty thus publicly to declare, that their investigations had been con-

* Appendix to this Report, No. 2. and 3. † Ibid, No. 4. ‡ Ibid, No. 5.

ducted with the greatest fairness, candour, and impartiality, and had not been in any one instance whatever influenced by private views or party feeling; that they felt no hesitation in stating their confidence, that the public will attribute their conduct on this occasion to the sources from which it sprung; and that such confidence they had a right to entertain, as they were conscious of no other motives than a due sense of justice to their country and to themselves, a high sentiment of the national importance of the shipping interest of Great Britain, and the recollection that to it alone were owing the glory and greatness of the British empire.

Extracted from the minutes—

By order,

NAT. ATCHESON,

Secretary.

APPENDIX TO THE ABOVE REPORT.

No. I.

LETTERS

FROM THE SHIP-BUILDERS WITHIN THE PORT OF LONDON.

SIR, Northfleet, 27th December, 1802.

PLEASE to acquaint your committee, that I have built and launched since the 5th of October, 1801, the East India ship David Scott, burthen 1276 tons, contracted for 23d of July, 1800, launched 7th November, 1801: the East India ship

Perseverance, burthen 1271 tons, contracted for 13th of November, 1800, and launched December 5th, 1801: the East India ship Earl Camden, burthen 1271 tons, contracted for 22d of July, 1801, launched October 27th, 1802. An East India ship to be launched next January; burthen about 800 tons; contracted for November 21st, 1801. In answer to your second question, I did not commence business till the beginning of the year 1788.

I am, Sir,

Your obedient Servant,

THOMAS PITCHER.

To Nat. Atcheson, Esq. Secretary to the Society of Ship-Owners of Great Britain.

SIR,

In reply to yours of the 24th instant, we beg to annex a statement of ships built by us about the periods you mention, and also to inform you that we are *not* now building, nor have we contracted to build, *any merchant vessel*, except two East-Indiamen, since the commencement of the peace.

We are, Sir,

Your most obedient humble Servants,

RANDALL and BRENT.

Rotherhithe, December 27th, 1802.

To NAT. ATCHESON, Esq. &c. &c.

Ships built by Messrs. Randall and Co.	Trade.	Burthen in Tons.	Contracted for.	Launched.
General Goddard	East India	758	March, 1781	Jan. 30, 1782
Duke of Montrose	Ditto	755	Jan. 28, 1784	Nov. 27, 1784
Queen	Ditto	799	Nov. 1784	Nov. 3, 1785
Henry	West India	384	April 7, 1782	Oct. 9, 1782
John and Ann	Ditto	417	built on speculation	Nov. 21, 1783
Hibberts	Ditto	389	June 11, 1783	June 5, 1784
Grenada Packet	Ditto	273	May 7, 1784	Oct. 2, 1784
Culloden	74 Guns	1655	June 30, 1779	June 16, 1783
Leda	36 Guns	871	Dec. 24, 1779	Dec. 12, 1783
Expedition	44 Guns	896	June 5, 1782	Oct. 29, 1784
Defiance	74 Guns	1612	June 30, 1779	Dec. 10, 1783
Ramillies	74 Guns	1652	June, 1782	July 11, 1785
Audacious	74 Guns	1604	June, 1782	July 21, 1785

1801.

Simon and Bella	West India	300	Aug. 1801	Sept. 16, 1802
Elphinstone	East India	1276	July 29, 1801	Nov. 25, 1802
	Ditto	818	June 12, 1801	
Caermarthen	Ditto	544	Oct. 4, 1801	Nov. 25, 1802
	Ditto	544	Oct. 4, 1801	
Illustrious	74 Guns	1729	Jan. 27, 1800	Now building

SIR, Deptford, 28th December, 1802.

AGREEABLE to your request, I herewith hand you annexed the statement of ships contracted for by me during the first and second years of the peace, after the American war. And I also acquaint you that *I have neither contracted for, nor built,* any *merchant ship,* since the fifth of October, 1801.

I am, Sir,

Your most obedient Servant,

JOHN DUDMAN.

To NAT. ATCHESON, Esq. &c. &c.

SHIPS built by Mr. JOHN DUDMAN, at Grove-street, Deptford.

Name.	Captain.	Tonnage	Date of contract.	When launched.	Service.
Portland Packet	S. Spargo	200	20th July, 1782	2d June, 1783	Post office
Brooke . .	S. Oliver	329	21st Jan. 1784	16th Sept. 1784	Antigua
Lansdown (built on speculation)	. . .	571	Nov. 1782	5th Sept. 1785	Sold to John Clements, Esq. for an extra East Indiaman
Amelia . .	A. Caldeleugh	280	1st May, 1785	19th Dec. 1785	Carolina
New Adventure (built on speculation)	. . .	227	Dec. 1784	20th March, 1786	Sold for the Greenland fishery.
Ranger . .	A. Petticrew	358	27th Sept. 1785	15th July, 1786	Jamaica
William and Elizabeth	T. Archdeacon	342	1st Oct. 1785	7th Nov. 1786	Jamaica

---

SIR, Rotherhithe, 28th December, 1802.

IN compliance with the request of the committee of shipowners for the port of London, I beg leave to state as follows, for their information, viz.

SHIPS built by the late PETER MESTAER, between the 16th of April, 1783, and the 31st of December, 1785, for the *merchants' service*, being the two years after peace with America.

The St. Carlos	built in 1784	. 230 tons	. New York trade	contracted for after the peace.
Thames .	built in 1785	. 221 tons	. Oporto trade	
Simon Taylor	Ditto	. 449 tons	. West India trade	
Douglas . .	Ditto	. 254 tons	. New York trade	
Queen . .	Ditto	. 232 tons	. Oporto trade	

I have built *one* ship for the *merchant service*, since the 5th of October, 1801, contracted for in February, 1802, viz.

The Pacific . . . . . 307 tons . South Sea trade

And I am now building a ship of 600 tons burthen *on speculation*, adapted for an extra Indiaman, or a West Indiaman.

I am, Sir,

Your obedient humble Servant,

PETER EVERITT MESTAER.

To NAT. ATCHESON, Esq. &c. &c

GENTLEMEN,

IN answer to your letter of the 24th instant, we have to inform you we have contracted for *no other ships* but those intended for the East India Company's service, since the 5th October, 1801.

We are, Gentlemen,

Your obedient humble Servants,

PERRYS, WELLS, and GREEN

29th December, 1802.

To the Committee of Ship-owners for the Port of London.

GENTLEMEN, Limehouse, Dec. 29th, 1802.

AGREEABLE to your request, I inform you I have *not* built any ships for the *Merchants Service* since 5th October, 1801; neither have I any ships building or contracted for at present.

I am,
Gentlemen,
Your obedient humble Servant,
ALMON HILL.

To the Committee of Ship-Owners for the Port of London.

GENTLEMEN,

IN answer to yours of the 24th inst. we give annexed the number and names of the ships we have built since the 5th October 1801, with their tonnage, and the service for which they are intended; also the number of ships which we built for the Merchants Service in the first and second year after the American war, the service they were employed in, and the time of their being contracted for, and launched.

We are,
Gentlemen,
Your most obedient Servants,
FRANCIS BARNARD, Sons, and ROBERTS.

Deptford, December 29, 1802.

MERCHANT SHIPS launched since the last Peace in 1801.

	Tons.		
Baring	818	East-India Trade	Contracted for 1800. Launched in 1801.
Bensley Hoy	132	East-India Company	Contracted . 1801. Launched . 1802.
Warren Hastings	1260	East-India Trade	Contracted . 1801. Launched . 1802.
Lord Castlereagh	812	East-India Trade	Contracted . 1801. Launched . 1802.

No Merchants ships contracted for *at this time.*

[K]

MERCHANTS SHIPS contracted for and launched in the two years after the American war.

	Tons.			
Rockingham .	800 East-India Trade	Contracted . 1784. Launched . 1785.
Juno .	350 West-India Trade	Contracted . 1785. Launched . 1785.
Integrity Hoy .	45 Employed in the River	Contracted . 1785. Launched . 1785.

To the Committee of Ship-Owners for the Port of London.

SIR,

In reply to your letter of the 24th inst. I acquaint you I have *not*, since the year 1800, built *one* ship or vessel, nor is there at present any appearance of application to contract for any; and I am sorry to add, very little probability of filling our docks with ships *for repair* the next spring of the year.

At this juncture I really do not know of any ship or vessel building in the river *Thames*, except ships of war, and those for the honourable East India Company Service; save one small vessel at Messrs. Brents, Greenland-Dock.

I read in the Public Ledger ships offered for sale which are now building in the out-ports, which they cannot get rid of. At the conclusion of the American war many were built, and old work brisk.

I am, Sir, respectfully,

Your obedient Servant,

JOS. YOUNG.

Rotherhithe, 31st Dec. 1802.

To Nat. Atcheson, Esq. &c. &c.

No. II.

STATEMENT of the Depreciation in the Value of Ships since the 5th October, 1801, as reported by some of the most respectable Ship-Brokers in the City of London, and classed according to their several Opinions, as expressed in their Letters in answer to the Enquiries of the Committee of Ship-owners for the Port of London.

Brokers.	Depreciation per Cent in 1st Class.			Do. in 2d Class.			Do. in 3d Class.			Do. in 4th Class.			Average Depreciation per Cent on the Whole.		
	l.	*s.*	*d.*	*l.*	*s.*	*d.*	*l.*	*s.*	*d.*	*l.*	*s.*	*d.*	*l.*	*s.*	*d.*
William Beatson -	12	10	0	27	10	0	50	0	0	-	-		30	0	0
John Blackett -	-	-		30	0	0	40	0	0	62	0	0	44	3	4
Joseph Dowson and Son	12	10	0	30	0	0	40	0	0	-	-		27	10	0
James Duncan -	-	-		33	6	8	50	0	0	-	-		41	13	4
Elyard, Price & Haslope	-	-		25	0	0	30	0	0	-	-		27	10	0
Hopkins and Gray -	-	-		30	0	0	40	0	0	-	-		35	0	0
Thomas Powditch -	-	-		33	6	8	50	0	0	-	-		41	13	4
John Tulloch - -	25	0	0	30	0	0	40	0	0	50	0	0	35	0	0
Waltham and Lloyd	10	0	0	30	0	0	50	0	0	-	-		30	0	0

The Depreciation upon the Average of the above Statement is - - } £34 14 5 per Cent

No. III.

STATEMENT of the War and Peace Prices of sundry Ships, ascertained by actual Sales in each Period.

Ships.	Owners.	Port.	Tons prReg.	War Price or Cost.	Peace Price.
Ranger -	Jas. Dunning	Sunderland	210	£ 3200	2000
Nancy -	Wm. Thompson	London	302	3800	2200
Minerva -	Thos. Nicholson	Sunderland	368	5800	4000
Alfred - -	Ditto	Ditto	312	5500	4400
Castle Douglas	Douglas & Shaw	London		2450	1500
Thomas -	Dan. M'Carthy	Ditto	360	1800	900
Good Intent	Robt. Thompson	Shields	277	3100	2550
Anatolia -	Marshall and Co.	London	175	2000	1580
Henry - -	Thos. Rowe	Ditto	251	3351	2600
Fame - -	Wm. Corse -	Newcastle	240	2650	1800
Good Intent	- - - -	London	208	3800	2150
Guardian -	Thelluson -	Ditto	286	4000	1810
Dart - -	Benson and Co.	Ditto	120	2000	1250
Bellona -	Blackett -	Ditto	369	5300	2700
Julius Cæsar	Slegg - -	Ditto	420	5000	2600
Union - -	Blackett -	Ditto	340	3600	1800
Jamaica Planter	Ditto -	Ditto	350	3200	1700
		Decrease in Value £38 per Cent.			

By this statement of the actual sales of the above ships, the average depreciation in their value is about £38 per cent. since the peace, and in the months of May and June, 1802, there were offered for sale within the port of London 152 ships, amounting in the aggregate to 40,190 tons. For the names and tonnage of these ships, vide Appendix to lord Sheffield's Strictures. Edition, 1806.

No. IV.

STATEMENT of the Prices of Ship's Provisions, Materials, and Wages, in the Years 1783 and 1784, the two first Years of the Peace after the American War, compared with the Prices of those Articles in the Year 1802.

	Prices in 1783.	Prices in 1784.	Prices in 1802.	Advance on each article per cent, since 1783.
PROVISIONS.	*l. s. d.*	*l. s. d.*	*l. s. d.*	*l. s. d.*
Fresh beef, per cwt. - -	1 7 0	1 6 0	2 16 0	107 8 2 per cent
Ship bread, ditto - -	0 13 0	0 0 0	1 1 0	61 10 9 ——
Flour, per sack - -	2 0 0	0 0 0	3 0 0	50 0 0 ——
Peas, per bushel - -	0 5 6	0 0 0	0 10 0	81 16 5 ——
Beer, per barrel - -	0 7 4	0 0 0	0 13 0	75 5 5 ——
Salt beef, per tierce -	3 10 0	3 5 0	8 8 0	140 0 0 ——
Salt pork, per barrel -	2 10 0	2 7 6	5 5 0	110 0 0 ——
				Average advance on provisions *l. s. d.* 89 8 8
MATERIALS, STORES, &c.				
Rope, per cwt. - -	1 8 0	1 7 0	3 7 0	125 0 0 per cent
Masts, per load, fit for an average-sized ship -	7 10 0	0 0 0	16 0 0	113 6 8 ——
Sails, made up of No. 1, canvas per yard - -	0 1 6	0 0 0	0 2 1	38 17 9 ——
English oak timber, per load	2 15 0	0 0 0	5 0 0	81 16 4 ——
Quebec ditto ditto -	4 0 0	0 0 0	8 0 0	100 0 0 ——
Builder's price in the river, per ton measurement -	9 0 0	0 0 0	13 10 0	50 0 0 ——
				Average advance on materials, stores, &c *l. s. d.* 84 16 9
SEAMEN'S WAGES.				
Mates and carpenters, to the West Indies, per month	3 10 0	0 0 0	5 0 0	42 17 2 per cent
Seamen ditto ditto	1 7 0	0 0 0	2 0 0	48 2 11 ——
Ditto Mediterranean ditto	1 7 0	0 0 0	2 0 0	48 2 11 ——
Ditto Baltic ditto	1 15 0	0 0 0	2 10 0	42 17 2 ——
Shipwright's wages per day	0 3 6	0 0 0	0 5 0	42 17 2 ——
Caulker's ditto ditto	0 4 0	0 0 0	0 5 7½	40 12 7 ——
				Average advance on seamen's wages *l. s. d.* 44 4 11

No. V.—STATEMENT of the Increase of the Duties on the Importation of Naval Stores, since the Year 1783.

Article		1783. *l. s. d.*	Branches.	*l. s. d.*	1802.—Total. *l. s. d.*		*l. s. d.*	
Hemp	per ton	3 13 4	Customs	4 3 0				
			Importation duty	1 3 2	5 6 2	Increase	44 15 $5\frac{1}{2}$	per cent.
Flax	per ton	free	- - -	- - -	free			
Iron	per ton	2 16 2	Customs	3 4 $7\frac{3}{10}$				
			Importation duty	0 13 0	3 17 $7\frac{3}{10}$	Increase	38 2 $10\frac{18}{20}$	per cent.
Tar	per last of 12 barrels	0 12 $4\frac{1}{2}$	Customs	0 10 $3\frac{4}{20}$				
			Importation duty	0 2 11	0 13 $2\frac{4}{20}$	Increase	6 10 $7\frac{14}{20}$	per cent.
Pitch	per last of 12 barrels	0 12 5	Customs	0 13 $7\frac{18}{20}$				
			Importation duty	0 3 8	0 17 $3\frac{18}{20}$	Increase	39 10 $7\frac{5}{20}$	per cent.
Rosin	per ton	2 5 0	Customs	2 9 6				
			Importation duty	0 6 8	2 16 2	Increase	24 16 $3\frac{1}{8}$	per cent.
Cordage	per ton	8 10 0	Customs	9 7 0				
			Importation duty	1 6 0	10 13 0	Increase	25 5 $10\frac{1}{9}$	per cent.
Masts (above 12 inches) per load		0 6 8	Customs	0 14 8				
			Importation duty	0 7 7	1 2 3	Increase	233 15 0	per cent.
Deals, of 8 to 20 feet length, not exceeding $3\frac{1}{4}$ inches thickness, per hundred		2 13 0	Customs	5 16 $8\frac{8}{20}$				
			Importation duty	0 11 3	6 7 $11\frac{8}{20}$	Increase	141 8 $3\frac{12}{20}$	per cent.
Fir timber	per load	0 6 8	Customs	0 14 8				
			Importation duty	0 2 2	0 16 10	Increase	152 10 0	per cent.
Oak plank	2 inches thick and upwards	0 19 10	Customs	1 9 $1\frac{16}{20}$				
			Importation duty	0 6 8	1 15 $9\frac{16}{20}$	Increase	88 11 $9\frac{18}{20}$	per cent.
Turpentine common, per cwt.		0 2 3	Customs	0 2 $5\frac{14}{20}$				
			Importation duty	0 0 $2\frac{4}{20}$	0 2 $7\frac{14}{20}$	Increase	18 2 $11\frac{1}{2}$	per cent.
		12 17 $8\frac{1}{2}$			34 8 $10\frac{14}{20}$			

At a meeting of the committee of ship-owners for the port of London, held the 7th April 1803, at Will's Coffee-house:

Mr. Dowson in the Chair:

The secretary read the report of the sub-committee on the licences and bonds required by the commissioners of the customs, under the revenue acts, in consequence of the construction or build of certain ships.

Resolved, That the said report be agreed to, and that a memorial be presented to the board of trade on the subject.

(Signed) J. Dowson, Chairman.

MEMORIAL.

To the Right Honourable the Lords of the Committee of his Majesty's Privy Council, appointed for the Consideration of all Matters relating to Trade and Foreign Plantations.

The Memorial of the Owners of British Ships, who have been obliged to take out Licences and give Bonds, in consequence of the particular Build and Construction of their Ships,

Humbly sheweth,

That by a certain act of parliament made and passed in the 13th year of the reign of his present majesty, for the better ascertaining the tonnage and burthen of ships and vessels importing and exporting goods into and from this kingdom, or hovering upon the coasts thereof, it is enacted, that the rule for admeasuring such ships or vessels, the tonnage and burthen whereof should be necessary to be ascertained and known by any act or acts of parliament made, or thereafter to be made, concerning the revenues of customs, excise, or salt duty, should be as follows; (that is to say) that the length should be taken on a strait line along the rabbit of the keel of the ship, from the back of the main-stern-post to a perpendicular line from the fore-part of the main-stem under the bowsprit, from which subtracting three-fifths of the breadth, the remainder should be esteemed the just length of the keel; and to find the tonnage and breadth should be taken from the outside of the outside planks in the broadest part of the ship, be it either above or below the main-wales, exclusive of all manner of doubling planks that may be wrought upon the sides of the ship, then multiplying the length of the keel by the breadth so taken, and that product by half the breadth, and dividing the whole by ninety-four, the quotient should be deemed the true contents of the tonnage.

That by another act of parliament made and passed in the 26th year of the reign of his said present majesty, it is enacted, that in cases where it may be necessary to ascertain the tonnage of any such ships or vessels when afloat, the following method should be observed; (viz.) drop a plumb-line over the stern of the ship, and measure the distance between such line and the after-part of the stern-posts, at the load water-mark; then measure from the top of the said plumb-line in a parallel direction with the water to a particular point, immediately over the load water-mark at the fore-part of the main-stem, subtracting from such measurement the above distance, the remainder will be the ship's extreme length, from which is to be deducted three inches for every foot of the load draft of water for the rake abaft, and also three-fifths for the ship's breadth for the rake forward, the remainder shall be esteemed the just length of the keel to find the tonnage; and then the said act directs, that the breadth of the ship shall be taken, and the contents of the tonnage ascertained, in the same manner as in the aforementioned act of the 13th of his majesty's reign is directed.

That by certain acts of parliament passed in the 24th, 27th, 28th, 34th, 36th, 38th, 39th, and 40th, years of his said present majesty's reign, certain ships, vessels, and boats, therein mentioned and described, are in certain cases subject to forfeiture, unless the owners thereof shall have a licence, as therein described and directed, for navigating the same, from the admiralty, or some person duly authorised by the lords commissioners of the admiralty to grant the same.

That by the said acts, particularly by the acts of the 24th, 39th, and 40th years of the present king, it is, amongst other things, enacted, that such licence, when so taken out, shall nevertheless be void and of no effect, unless the owner and owners of such ships, vessels, or boats, as therein mentioned, shall also give sufficient security by bond to his majesty, his heirs and successors, in double the value of such ship or vessel, to be approved of by and to the satisfaction of such collector, comptroller, or other proper officer of the customs, as therein mentioned; with condition that such ship or vessel shall not be employed in the importation or exportation of tea, foreign spirituous liquors, or other prohibited goods, and that such ship, vessel, or boat, shall not be used or employed in hovering within the limits of any of the ports of this kingdom, or within four leagues of any coast thereof, or in any other manner, or in any trade or employment, whatsoever, contrary to law.

That for a considerable length of time past, until very lately, it had not been the practice to enforce the above acts of parliament beyond what your memorialists humbly conceive and submit to be the true spirit and meaning of them; and consequently the general body of ship-owners were not considered to be within the intent of those acts, and were free from the grievances which the misapplication of those acts was calculated to produce to the fair trader.

That about two years since certain regulations were made by his majesty's commissioners of the customs; whereby it was declared that the owners of ships of a certain description, that is to say, '*Every ship where the length exceeds three feet and a half to one foot in breadth,*' and which includes nearly all the ships employed in the carrying trade of the country, should be obliged not only to take out a licence from the lords commissioners of the admiralty for navigating and trading with such ships, but also to enter into a bond to his majesty, his heirs and successors, in double and sometimes treble the value of such ship or vessel:—" That such ship or vessel shall not be employed in the importation or landing of any tea, or foreign spirituous liquors, or any prohibited or other goods, contrary to the true intent and meaning of any act of parliament which now is or hereafter may be enforced, or in the exportation of any goods which are or may be prohibited to be exported from this kingdom, or in the re-landing of any goods whatsoever contrary to law, which are entered outwards for exportation for any drawback or bounty, or which are or may be prohibited to be used or worn in Great Britain; that such ship or vessel shall not be found at anchor, or hovering within the said limits or distance, contrary to the true intent and meaning of the thereinbefore

[L]

recited act passed in the 24th year of the reign of his present majesty; that such ship or vessel shall not be found within the distances and situations particularly described and set forth in the thereinbefore recited act passed in the 34th year of the reign of his present majesty, contrary to the provisions and directions of the said act; that such ship or vessel shall not be employed or be found or discovered to have been, out of the limits within which the said ship or vessel is licensed to navigate or trade, contrary to the directions and provisions of the before recited act passed in the 27th year of the reign of his present majesty; that such ship or vessel shall not be engaged for, or used in, any trade or employment whatsoever, other than that described and set forth in the licence for such ship or vessel, contrary to the thereinbefore-recited act passed in the 38th year of the reign of his present majesty; and further, that such ship or vessel shall not be used or employed in any other way or manner whatever contrary to the law in force relating to the revenue of customs on and immediately before the passing of the said thereinbefore recited act made in the 39th and 40th years of the reign of his present majesty; and that the licence granted for the said ship or vessel shall, in case the said ship or vessel shall be lost, broken up, sold, or otherwise disposed of, be delivered up to the collector of the customs for the time being, or his deputy, at the port therein mentioned, within the space of three months from the time such ship or vessel shall be lost, broken up, or otherwise disposed of."

That the owners of the description of ships comprised in the above-mentioned regulation made by the commissioners of the customs have never before the making thereof been in any manner called upon or obliged to take out licences from the admiralty, or enter into any such bond or security, as before stated.

That after a very careful perusal of the several acts of parliament referred to in the margin of the printed forms of the said bonds, it is evident that the regulations therein contained were not meant by the legislature to be applied to the merchants' ships, as built and used by the general body of British ship-owners; and that it does not appear to your memorialists that any authority is thereby vested in the commissioners of the customs to compel the owners of such ships to take out licences from the lords of the admiralty, or to enter into any such bond or security as aforementioned;

and that therefore, in their opinion, the said commissioners of the customs have exceeded the bounds of their authority in so doing, by a misconception of the said act of the 13th year of his present majesty.

That some of your memorialists, under this conception, and feeling themselves highly aggrieved by the afore-mentioned regulation, have made applications in the usual form to the said commissioners of the customs, requesting they would shew to your memorialists under what act or acts of parliament in particular they claimed the power to make and enforce such regulation; but which the said commissioners have declined to do, merely answering, "they acted according to law."

That it appears to your memorialists to be clear, that the said acts of parliament were never meant to apply to that description of ships hereinbefore particularly mentioned and described; inasmuch as they submit to your lordships, that should the said acts be so construed to apply, it would become impossible, under the restraints they impose, for any man to employ his property in shipping concerns, or, indeed, for the commerce of the country with other nations to be carried on with that spirit of enterprize which has hitherto been its distinguished characteristic.

That amongst the unexampled, and, your memorialists venture to add, the undeserved hardships such a construction of these acts of parliament must inevitably inflict upon a numerous and useful body of men, your memorialists cannot forbear on the present occasion to point out to your lordships, that thereby the most respectable ship-owners are put into the same perilous situation with the most notorious smugglers; since it is in the power not only of the master of such ship, with whom it is impossible for an owner at all times to avoid having differences, but of any of the crew, to bring upon the owner by acts committed without his consent, but even without his knowledge, and beyond his power to prevent, and by information afterwards given thereof, the heavy penalties contained in the said acts, and the forfeiture of the said bonds.

That by the said acts all ships, liable to have licence or not, which are found upon the coast, or within four leagues thereof, or within the limits of any of the ports within this kingdom, or that shall be discovered to have been within the said limits or distance, and not proceeding on her voyage, wind and weather permitting, having on board in any vessel or cask which shall not contain sixty gallons at the least, any greater quantity of brandy or other spirituous liquors than two gallons for each seaman, or having on board six pounds weight of tea or twenty pounds weight of coffee, or any goods whatever liable to forfeiture, shall be forfeited.

That in cases where a merchant ship has had a quick passage, or when the crew consists of twenty men or any greater number, and in many other similar cases, it will be difficult, if not impossible, to avoid having on board such ship a larger quantity of tea and coffee than the amount of the small allowance pointed out by the said act; and, at all events, it will be utterly out of the power of any ship-owner to prevent the forfeiture imposed by the said act of parliament and bond, if the master of the ship or any of the crew think proper to commit any act against the provisions of the said acts of parliament and the condition of the said bond.

That by the terms of the said licences the trade or employment in which any ship or vessel so licensed shall be engaged is directed to be specified, and the limits of the navigation and trade of such ship or vessel described.

That it also appears that *the vessels particularly intended* by the legislature to be *included* within the intent and meaning of the several acts set forth in the margin of the said bonds *do not come within* the last-mentioned regulation of the said commissioners of the customs.

That it is provided by the aforesaid acts, and by the condition of the said bond as above stated, that the licence granted for any ship or vessel shall, in case such ship or vessel be lost, broken up, sold, or otherwise disposed of, be delivered up to the collector of the customs for the time being, or his deputy, at the port therein to be specified, within the space of three calendar months from the time such ship or vessel shall be lost, broken up, sold, or otherwise disposed of; and if this be not done, the owner of such ship or vessel becomes liable to the heavy penalties and forfeitures inflicted by the said acts and bond.

That such licence is never in the possession of the owner of the ship, but is usually on board and in the possession of the master, and must therefore, in case such ship be lost, be lost also; or may be wilfully secreted or destroyed, or accidentally mislaid, by the master, for whose culpability, negligence, or misfortune, the owner alone is, by the condition of the said bond, rendered liable.

That by these and many other means too numerous and complicated to lay before your lordships within the limits of this memorial, oppressions heretofore unknown, and which, as your memorialists submit, were not meant by the legislature in passing the aforementioned acts of parliament, are imposed on British ship-owners, and a responsibility on their parts created, not only alarming and dreadful in its operation, but of a nature new, and, as they submit, irreconcilable with every principle of policy and justice.

That your memorialists beg leave to declare to your lordships, that they are convinced ship-owners have no wish to shrink from their fair share of the public burthens, or from a perfect obedience to the laws of the land; that in particular they have ever been and are anxious to be considered as continuing to be observant of, and willing to support to the utmost of their power, the revenue laws of their country; and that their only aim is to be free from a liability for the acts of others, over whom, in respect of those acts, they have no power, and who may have many temptations, while free from all hazards themselves, to involve persons, in the situation of your memorialists, in disgrace and ruin.

That if the said commissioners of the customs are at liberty to enforce the observance of the aforementioned regulation, no alternative will be left to the owners of British shipping but to submit to a liability at which every thinking man must tremble, or to withdraw his capital from a pursuit fair and honourable to himself and highly useful to his country; a measure which, in many cases, cannot be adopted without infinite injury to both.

That the said acts of parliament of the 13th and 26th of his present majesty have directed the method to be used in all cases whatever for the admeasurement of ships, and which your memorialists humbly submit to your lordships, if adhered to, will prevent the ships before described coming within the said regulation of the commissioners of the customs, and a strict adherence to which would, in the apprehension of your memorialists, produce no injury to the revenue.

That your memorialists are ready to give every security that can be reasonably required of them, either in the nature of bonds, separate from those of the masters of their respective ships, or in any mode that shall be thought adviseable, for the due observance of the revenue laws, so far as they personally and individually are concerned in the observance thereof, and for their own personal and individual acts; but they trust they shall not be compelled to enter into obligations, the performance of which does not depend in any measure on themselves.

Your memorialists therefore humbly hope your lordships will be pleased to take the preceding circumstances into your lordships' consideration, and to direct that the commissioners of the customs may desist from enforcing their aforementioned regulation in future, and that the same be discontinued, and that all bonds and securities given by any of the owners of such British ships, in pursuance thereof, be delivered to the respective persons who have executed the same, to be cancelled; or that your lordships will be pleased to make such order in the case as to your lordships shall seem meet.

And your memorialists, &c. &c.

THE FORM OF THE BOND REFERRED TO.

KNOW all men by these presents, that we

are held and firmly bound unto our sovereign lord George the Third, by the grace of God, of the united kingdom of Great Britain and Ireland king, defender of the faith, in the sum of pounds, of good and lawful money of Great Britain, to be paid to our said lord the king, his heirs or successors: to which payment, well and truly to be made, we bind ourselves, and every of us, jointly and severally, for and in the whole, our heirs, executors, and administrators, and every of them, firmly by these presents. Sealed with our seals. Dated this day of in the year of the reign of his said majesty, and in the year of our Lord one thousand eight hundred and

WHEREAS, by certain acts of parliament passed in the twenty-fourth, twenty-seventh, twenty-eighth, thirty-fourth, thirty-sixth, and thirty-eighth years of the reign of his present majesty, certain ships, vessels, and boats, therein particularly described, are, in certain cases, subject to forfeiture, unless the owners thereof shall have a licence, as therein described and directed, for navigating the same from the lord high admiral of Great Britain or commissioners of the admiralty for the time being, or any person authorized by them to grant the same. And whereas the owner of every ship, vessel, or boat, so licensed, is required to give certain security, as in the said acts directed, before such ship, vessel, or boat, proceeds to sea, or sails out of any port, harbour, or creek, in this kingdom.

And whereas, by an act passed in the thirty-ninth and fortieth years of the reign of his present majesty, for (amongst other things) extending bonds given on licensing ships, vessels, or boats, to all cases wherein ships, vessels, or boats may be liable to forfeiture, the terms and conditions of such security are directed to be extended and taken in manner hereinafter mentioned. And whereas, owner of the called of of the length of of the breadth of and the depth of being a within the meaning of the said in part recited acts, hath this day produced a licence for the same under the hands of the commissioners for executing the office of lord high admiral of Great Britain, and seal of the office of the admiralty, to the purport and effect mentioned and contained in the said hereinbefore recited acts of parliament.

Now the condition of this obligation is such, that if the aforesaid shall not be employed in the importation or landing of any tea, or foreign spirituous liquors, or any prohibited or other goods, contrary to the true intent and meaning of any act of parliament which now is or hereafter may be in force, or in the exportation of any goods which are or may be prohibited to be exported from this kingdom, or in the re-landing of any goods whatsoever, contrary to law, which are entered outwards for exportation for any drawback or bounty, or which are or may be prohibited to be used or worn in Great Britain. And if the said shall not be found at anchor, or hovering within the limits of any of the ports of this kingdom, or within four leagues of the coast thereof, nor discovered to have been within the said limits or distance, contrary to the true intent or meaning of the hereinbefore recited act passed in the 24th year of the reign of his present majesty. And if the said shall not be found within the distances and situations particularly described and set forth in the hereinbefore recited act passed in the 34th year of the reign of his present majesty, contrary to the directions and provisions of the said act. And also if the said shall not be employed, or be found, or discovered to have been, out of the limits within which the said is *licensed to navigate or trade*, contrary to the directions and provisions of the before recited act passed in the 27th year of the reign of his present majesty. And if the said shall not be engaged for, or used in, any trade or employment whatever, *other than that described and set forth in the licence* for such , contrary to the before recited act passed in the 38th year of the reign of his present majesty. And further, if the said shall not be used or employed in any other way or manner whatever, contrary to the laws in force relating to the revenue of customs, on and immediately before the passing of the said before recited act made in the 39th and 40th years of the reign of his present majesty. And if the licence granted for the said shall, in case the said shall be lost, broken up, sold, or otherwise disposed of, be delivered up to the collector of the customs for the time being, or his deputy, at the port of within the space of three calendar months from the time such shall be lost, broken up, sold, or otherwise disposed of, then the above-written obligation to be void, otherwise to be and remain in full force and virtue.

Sealed and delivered (being first duly stamped) in the presence of L. S.

LETTER FROM SIR STEPHEN COTTERELL.

Office of the Committee of Privy Council for Trade, Whitehall, July 18, 1802.

SIR,

THE memorial transmitted by you on the 5th of May last, on behalf of the owners of British ships who have been obliged to take out licences and give bonds in consequence of the particular construction of their ships, having been referred to the commissioners of his majesty's customs by the direction of the lords of the committee for trade; and their lordships having received the report of the said commissioners thereupon, by which it appears that, in consequence of doubts having been entertained at a former period, the case had been submitted to his majesty's law officers, who were of opinion, that every vessel which comes within the descriptions in the several acts relating to this subject does require to have licences, I am directed to acquaint you, that the prayer of the said memorial cannot be complied with. I am, sir,

Your most obedient humble servant,

(Signed) STEPH. COTTERELL.

To NAT. ATCHESON, Esq. &c. &c.

At a general meeting of ship-owners held the 26th April, 1803, at the London Tavern, to take into consideration *the present very critical state of the shipping interest:*

P. KENNION, Esq. in the Chair:

Resolved unanimously, THAT the ship-owners present at this meeting are confirmed in their opinion of the injurious operation of the tax on the tonnage of shipping, and that it is the most impolitic and ruinous principle of taxation that could have been adopted in a maritime country; and as the uniform system of the legislature of Great Britain had previously been for centuries to encourage, by every facility in its power, the maritime interest of the nation: the ship-owners present at this meeting rely with confidence on the justice of the legislature, and they trust it will not continue a tax, the effect of which will most inevitably tend, not only to decrease the carrying trade of the country, but very materially injure its commerce and manufacturers.

Resolved unanimously, That the thanks of the ship-owners present at this meeting be given to the right honourable the lord mayor *, for his great attention to the shipping

* Sir Charles Price, Bart.

[M]

interest, and that his lordship be requested to procure the * petition from the ship-owners of the port of London, for the repeal of the tonnage duty, to be taken into consideration previous to the discussion of that part of the intended consolidated act which relates to the duty on the tonnage of ships.

Resolved, That the preceding resolutions be transmitted to the lord mayor by the secretary.

(Signed) P. KENNION, Chairman.

At a meeting of the committee of ship-owners for the port of London, held the 5th May, 1803, at Wills' Coffee-house:

Mr. HILL in the Chair:

RAMSGATE HARBOUR DUES.

THE secretary read a letter from Sunderland on this subject, dated 9th April, 1803:

Resolved, That as it is to ascertain the liability of the ships in the coal trade to pay the Ramsgate harbour dues when returning in ballast, the committee are of opinion, that the committee at Sunderland are *warranted in adopting* the suggestion in the letter of Rowland Burdon, Esq. M.P. to them, and in taking measures to ascertain by law the point in question, and that the secretary be desired to lay the case again before Mr. Wood for his further consideration.

Resolved, That the secretary be instructed to put up a notice at Lloyd's to the following effect:

Mediterranean Passes.

Ship-owners who have experienced any inconvenience, or sustained any injury, from having *inadvertently* lost or mislaid the Mediterranean passes of their respective ships, are requested to transmit statements of their several cases to Mr. Atcheson, secretary to the committee of ship-owners for the port of London.

5th May, 1803.

(Signed) J. HILL, Chairman.

* Vide Parliamentary Debates; also, Cobbet's Political Register, vols. 1, and 2; also, Journals of the House of Commons, 1803.

At a meeting of the committee of ship-owners for the port of London, held the 19th day of May, 1803, at Wills' Coffee-house:

JAMES PYCROFT, Esq. in the Chair:

THE secretary read the resolutions of the House of Commons, as stated in the votes, respecting the dock dues in the port of London.

Resolved, That the secretary be requested to wait on the lord mayor and Mr. Vansittart, and to endeavour to obtain an exemption for ships entering inwards and outwards *in ballast* from the payment of the dock or canal dues.

Resolved unanimously, That the right honourable the lord mayor be desired to wait on the right honourable the chancellor of the exchequer, and to request that the duties on the tonnage of shipping may be separated from the consolidated bill now pending in parliament, and also to inform Mr. Addington, that *from the peculiar situation of the country*, the ship-owners of the port of London forbear to press their application to parliament, and submit to the continuance of the duty on the tonnage of shipping under proper modifications, but expressly on condition that the said duties on tonnage *shall cease at the end of the present war.*

(Signed) J. PYCROFT, Chairman.

At a meeting of the committee of ship-owners for the port of London, held the 16th June, 1803, at Wills' Coffee-house:

Mr. HILL in the Chair:

Resolved, THAT the chairman be requested to wait on the right honourable the lord mayor, and to desire that he will endeavour to prevail on his majesty's ministers to delay the bill for *the suspension of the Navigation Act*, until the ship-owners have had an opportunity of seeing it; and also to request some explanation relative to the increase duties on tonnage; and in case no relief can be obtained in that respect, that the lord mayor be desired to use his endeavours to obtain that both the former and the intended further duties on tonnage *shall cease with the war.*

(Signed) J. HILL, Chairman.

At a meeting of the committee of ship-owners for the port of London, held the 6th June, 1805:

Mr. BLACKETT in the Chair:

Resolved, THAT it is highly expedient that this committee should cause an inquiry to be made of the increase of fees and other charges imposed on ships and goods in the port of London not granted by the legislature, from 1785 to 1805, both inclusive.

(Signed) J. BLACKETT, Chairman.

At a meeting of the committee of ship-owners for the port of London, held the 1st November, 1803:

ROBERT CURLING, Esq. in the Chair:

Resolved, THAT the secretary be requested to apply to Mr. Marsham for copies of all the orders made and published by the directors of the West-India dock company, in order that the ship-owners in the West-India trade may be apprised of them, and give the necessary instructions to their respective masters.

(Signed) ROBERT CURLING, Chairman.

At a general meeting of the society of ship-owners of Great Britain, held at the London Tavern, on Thursday, the 22d day of March, 1804:

ROBERT CURLING, Esq. in the Chair:

THE secretary read the report of the committee, stating, "that the committee deemed it necessary to request the attention of the meeting to the several objects which had been noticed by them since their appointment.

"The society, it was to be observed, was instituted in 1802, in consequence of the depreciated state of the shipping interest, and the various inconveniences to which ship-owners were then liable. Their first and most important object had been to endeavour to convince the king's ministers of the impolicy of imposing any direct tax on shipping: and they are satisfied, that in case an investigation into the actual state of the navigation of the country had taken place, and which was so earnestly desired by them, much of the distress which is continued to be felt by the shipping interest would have been avoided; their statements would have been found correct, and not fallacious or exaggerated, as they were so industriously represented to be; and the country would not at the present time have had to regret the injurious operation of the application of so new a principle of taxation in a maritime country, *the continued suspension of the Navigation Act*, and the emigration of many brave native seamen, who are either now in the employment of America, or in the service of the enemy. This object the committee had not been able completely to attain: they, however, hope, that the *frequent recurrence to these points*, and the repeated intimations which have been given to many of the members of the legislature on the subject, will occasion, at no distant day, a *parliamentary* inquiry into *the actual state of the navigation* of Great Britain. The committee forbear at present commenting further on these most important objects to the country, or to expatiate more fully on the present depressed state of the shipping interest and the causes which have occasioned it; they are too obvious to need enumeration, and the ultimate ruinous consequences to be expected from them can only be averted by *a strict adherence* to the provisions of the Navigation Act, which our ancestors considered so essentially requisite to the glory and welfare of the empire, and by affording to British ship-owners such facilities as will at least enable them to navigate their ships upon an equal footing with foreigners.

"The other subjects which had come before the committee were the following, viz.

1st. The serious inconvenience many ship-owners have felt, and still continue to feel, from being obliged to take out licences and give bonds to the commissioners of his majesty's customs, from the particular construction and build of their ships. The subject was considered of so much consequence, that it had been referred to a sub-committee to take the same into their consideration, and point out not only the several inconveniences resulting from the regulation, but the means by which they might be remedied, without any injury whatever to the revenue; and to report the same to the committee: accordingly a memorial had been presented to the lords committee of trade on the subject; but the committee are sorry to observe, that their lordships have refused to make any alteration in the regulations of the commissioners of the customs.

2dly. The next subject which had been submitted to the consideration of the committee, was the claim recently set up by the trustees of Ramsgate harbour for payment of the harbour dues *on colliers* returning *in ballast* coastwise, and from Guernsey or Jersey: and the committee had, at the request of the ship-owners at Sunderland and Scarborough, taken the opinion of a very eminent lawyer on the subject; and it appeared by that opinion, that the trustees were not warranted by the act in demanding the harbour dues on colliers returning *in ballast* coastwise, or from Guernsey or Jersey, as before stated. In consequence of that opinion, a case had been by consent submitted to the consideration of two of the judges, and which remained for a second argument *.

* *Ramsgate Harbour Act.*

Case respecting colliers returning in ballast being liable to the duties imposed by this act:

In the court of Pleas at Durham:

Sanderson and others, Plaintiffs; and Scarth, Defendant.

This cause being an action of assumpsit for money had and received by the defendant for the use of the plaintiffs, came on to be tried at the last Durham assizes, before Mr. Baron Thompson, when a verdict, by consent, was taken by the plaintiff, subject to the opinion of the court on the following case, viz.

That, in pursuance of an act passed in the 32d year of the reign of his present majesty, entitled, An Act for the Maintenance and Improvement of the Harbour of Ramsgate, in the county of Kent; and for cleansing, amending, and preserving the Haven of Sandwich, in the same county, the trustees for carrying the said act into execution did settle and impose the several rates and duties hereinafter mentioned, to commence and become payable from and after *the 25th day of June*, 1792, inclusive, (that is to say) the rate and duty of 3d. per ton to be paid by the master or owner of every ship, vessel, or crayer, of the burthen of twenty tons or upwards, and not exceeding the burthen of 300 tons, whether the same be laden *or in ballast*, passing from, to, or by Ramsgate, whether on the east or west side of the Goodwin Sands, or otherwise, passing by or coming into the harbour there, (other than and except ships laden with coals, grindstones, or purbeck, Portland or other stones, not having a receipt testifying his payment before, or on that voyage:) and for every ship, vessel, or crayer, which shall exceed the burthen of three hundred tons, the rate or duty of one penny for each ton of such ship, except ships laden with coals, grindstone, purbeck, Portland or other stones; and for every chaldron of coals, or ton of grindstones, purbeck, Portland or other stones, a rate of three halfpence to be paid in such manner, and so often, as in the said act in those respects mentioned.—*By which said act it is enacted, that the said duties shall be paid every time such ship, vessel, or crayer, shall sail from, arrive or come into,*

3dly. Another important subject which had been submitted to the committee, was the *rates of pilotage* from the

harbour, at or pass by Ramsgate as aforesaid; except as thereinafter is mentioned: and by which said act it is declared, that no coasting vessel or fisherman shall pay the duty charged by the said act oftener than once in every one year; nor shall any collier returning in ballast from the French or Flemish coast, producing a certificate of having paid the duty on her outward bound voyage for her cargo of coals, be liable to the payment of any such duty for her inward bound voyage. And which said rates and duties were forthwith duly published in manner directed by the said act, and still remain in full force and unaltered.

That the plaintiffs were and are owners of the ship Violet, being a ship of the burthen of 166 tons, employed in carrying coals from Sunderland and other ports of England, to other ports of England, and returning immediately *in ballast* to her port of loading. That the said ship, early in the present year, sailed with a cargo of coals from Sunderland to Portsmouth, and delivered the same there; and the master of the said ship paid there, on his *outward* bound voyage, the Ramsgate harbour duties of three halfpence per chaldron on the said ship's cargo of coals, pursuant to the said act. That the said ship after delivering her said cargo of coals at Portsmouth returned immediately *in ballast* to Sunderland; and the master there paid on his homeward bound voyage the Ramsgate harbour duty of threepence *per ton on the burthen of* the said ship.

That afterwards, in the month of April last, the said ship sailed *again* with another cargo of coals from Sunderland to Portsmouth, and delivered the same there, and the master *again* paid there, on his last-mentioned *outward bound* voyage, the Ramsgate harbour duties of three halfpence per chaldron on the ship's last-mentioned cargo of coals.

That the said ship having delivered the said last-mentioned cargo of coals at Portsmouth aforesaid, returned to Sunderland aforesaid *in ballast*; and on the arrival there, the defendant being the *collector* duly appointed of the *Ramsgate harbour dues* payable at the port of Sunderland, demanded of the plaintiff the sum of 2*l.* 1*s.* 6*d.* for the Ramsgate harbour duty of threepence per ton for the last-mentioned *homeward bound* voyage of the said ship; and which sum of 2*l.* 1*s.* 6*d.* the plaintiffs paid to the defendant under protest against its being legally payable, and without prejudice to their right to recover it back: for this payment, the following receipt was given by the deputy collector of the said duties to the master of the said ship.

Port of Sunderland,
Receipt, No. 78. Ramsgate Harbour Duty.

Received the 11th day of June, 1803, of Captain William Mackie, master of the Violet, registered at Sunderland, of the burthen of 166 tons, bound from Portsmouth to Sunderland, the sum of 2*l.* 1*s.* 6*d.* for the duty of threepence per ton payable for the *voyage home*, to the trustees for the maintenance and improvement of the harbour of Ramsgate, by virtue of an act of parliament made in the 32d year of the reign of his majesty king George the Third.

C. S. Hill, for the Collector.

The question reserved for the opinion of the court is, whether the plaintiffs are entitled to recover?

(Signed) John Richardson, for Plaintiffs.
Robert Ward, for Defendants.

Certificate.

Downs to Gravesend, and from thence to London: and as the several acts respecting the pilotage from the Downs and Orfordness to London will shortly expire, a sub-committee had been appointed to take the same into consideration, and to report to the committee what, in conjunction with the lord warden of the Cinque Ports and the elder brethren of the Trinity-house, they may think will be most proper to be done in that respect *.

4thly. Another subject of the greatest magnitude to the ship-owners in the port of London, which had engaged the most serious and anxious attention of the committee, was the disputes in the autumn of 1802, between the ship-builders and their workmen; and in consequence of the manner in which those differences had been adjusted by the builders who had applied to the committee on the subject, the society had at a general meeting entered into some resolutions expressive of their disapprobation of the motives of the ship-

Certificate.

Sanderson and others, Plaintiffs; and Scarth, Defendant.

A verdict having been taken for the plaintiffs on the trial of this cause at the last Durham assizes, subject to the opinion of the court upon a case then reserved, and that case having been since argued before us by counsel on both sides, we are of opinion that the plaintiffs are entitled to recover according to such verdict; and do hereby order, that the plaintiffs be at liberty to enter up judgment thereon.—Dated the 28th June, 1804.

A. Thomson.
A. Chambre.

Counsel for the plaintiffs—Mr. Serjeant Cockell, Mr. Wood, Mr. Topping, and Mr. J. Richardson.
Solicitor—Mr. Atcheson.
Counsel for the defendants—Mr. Park, Mr. ——, and Mr. R. Ward.
Solicitors—Messrs. Wadeson and Co.

Copy of the Resolutions of the Board of Directors of Ramsgate Harbour, the 27th July, 1804.

Read a letter from Mr. Atcheson to the solicitor of this trust, on behalf of the ship-owners, for repayment of monies collected for duties on colliers passing the harbour *in ballast*, and for an account of the monies so received.

The secretary stated, that as the tonnage duties imposed on vessels are payable, whether laden or in ballast, it was not requisite to distinguish whether the duties on tonnage were collected for colliers or other vessels, and that no correct account can be made out.

Resolved, That the ship-owners be requested to send in an account of the sums claimed to be *repaid* to them, and to produce the receipts to the secretary. (Signed) Thos. Pritzler,

* See *post* extract from minutes of 26th Sept. 1805.

builders which appeared to them to have led to the conclusion of those disputes.

5thly. The committee had, during the last session of parliament, deemed it expedient, from motives of public duty, to oppose the duties which were attempted by the Bell Rock Light-house Bill to be imposed on *all* ships *passing the line of the latitude of Bell Rock*, on which a light-house was proposed to be erected, so far as such duties would have affected *the Baltic trade;* and it appears that the duties which were to have been so charged would have produced upwards of 10,000*l.* per annum to that light-house, but for the timely interference of this committee *.

6thly. The committee had likewise obtained in the last session of parliament an exemption from the payment of the duties (usually called dock dues) imposed on all ships entering inwards or clearing outwards from the port of London *in ballast*, by the Act for the Improvement of the Port of London, which, *with the fees*, &c. amounted to upwards of 4000*l*. per annum.

"In addition to the objects before stated, many other matters had been incidentally submitted to the consideration of the committee, who had not been unmindful either of the peculiar situation of many ship-owners, whose masters had inadvertently lost or mislaid their Mediterranean passes; or the many inconveniences which had arisen from several of the regulations adopted at the West-India docks, but which, from the explanations recently given by the directors, they were led to believe will be in future avoided.

* Vide 46 Geo. 3. c. —, which is founded on the following resolutions of the House of Commons on the 27th June, 1806:

1. That it would be of great benefit to the trade and navigation of this kingdom if a light-house was erected on the Bell or Cape Rock, lying on the east coast of Scotland, near the entrance of the Firths of Forth and Tay.

2. That every ship or decked vessel of the united kingdom of Great Britain and Ireland, navigated according to law, which shall sail to or from any port or place on the east coast of Scotland, between Peterhead on the north, and Berwick-upon-Tweed on the South, inclusive; and whether the said ship or vessel shall be outward or homeward bound, or on a foreign voyage, or sailing coastwise; as also, all ships and vessels as above described, which shall sail within a line drawn from Peterhead on the north, to the said port of Berwick on the south, both inclusive, shall be charged with and pay to the commissioners of northern light-houses towards erecting and maintaining the said light-house, a sum not exceeding one penny halfpenny for every ton of such ship or vessel; and every foreign ship or decked vessel sailing as aforesaid shall be charged with, and pay a sum not exceeding three pence, for every ton thereof.

"The committee flattered themselves, that the shipping interest of the country will be most materially benefited by the *permanent* establishment of the society; its *principal* object being to give effect to the *old maritime principles* of the country, and *the establishments* which have *arisen out of them*. The committee have not thought it necessary to notice particularly the various papers and documents which they had printed relative to the tonnage duty; but beg leave to refer to them, and *again* to declare, "that their investigation of the several subjects which had been submitted to their consideration since the establishment of the society had been conducted with the greatest impartiality, and that they had not been on any occasion influenced by private views or party feeling; and that their anxiety to give permanency to the establishment of the society arises from no other motive than a due sense of justice to their country and to themselves—a high sentiment of the national importance of the shipping interest, and the remembrance that to it is to be attributed the glory and greatness of the British empire."

Resolved unanimously, That the report of the committee be confirmed.

The secretary then reported, That he had received from lord Sheffield, for the chairman, a copy of his lordship's "Strictures on the Necessity of inviolably maintaining the Navigation and Colonial System of Great Britain."

Resolved unanimously, That the thanks of the society be given to lord Sheffield, for his important observations on the "Necessity of inviolably maintaining the Navigation and Colonial System of Great Britain;" and that the secretary do communicate this resolution to his lordship.

(Signed) R. Curling, Chairman.

At a meeting of the committee of ship-owners for the port of London, held the 19th April, 1804:

Mr. Akenhead in the Chair:

The secretary read the several papers presented by Mr. Chapman, relative to the suspension of the Act of Navigation.

Resolved unanimously, That a petition be presented to parliament against any further suspension of the Act of

Navigation, and praying that the same may, in future, be strictly enforced.

(Signed) J. AKENHEAD, Chairman.

At a meeting of the committee of ship-owners for the port of London, held the 10th May, 1804:

Mr. W. CURLING in the Chair:

THE secretary read the petitions to parliament against the further suspension of the Act of Navigation *.

Resolved unanimously, That the right honourable John lord Sheffield be requested to present the petition to the House of Lords.

Resolved unanimously, That Sir Charles Price, Bart. be requested to present the petition to the House of Commons.

(Signed) W. CURLING, Chairman.

At a general meeting of the society of ship-owners of Great Britain, held at the London Tavern, on Thursday, the 7th day of June, 1804:

THOMAS HORNCASTLE, Esq. in the Chair:

THE secretary then read the votes of the honourable the House of Commons for Thursday the 31st of May last, setting forth *only part* of the petition from the ship-owners of the port of London, respecting the suspension of the Navigation Act.

Resolved unanimously, That the whole of the petition presented to the honourable the House of Commons from the ship-owners at this port respecting the suspension of the Navigation Act be inserted in two of the Daily Papers, in order that the country may be acquainted with the merits of the said petition, and of the *ruinous consequences* resulting from the *continued suspension* of the Navigation Act.

Resolved unanimously, That the thanks of this society be given to lord Sheffield, for presenting the petition of the

* *Vide* Collection of Debates on the American Intercourse Bill, &c. Edition, 1806.

ship-owners of this port to the right honourable the House of Lords, respecting the suspension of the Navigation Act.

Resolved unanimously, That the thanks of this society be given to * Harvey Christian Coombe, Esq. alderman, and one of the representatives in parliament for the city of London, for presenting to the honourable House of Commons the petition of the ship-owners of this port on the same subject.

Resolved unanimously, That the thanks of this society be given to the honourable Henry Lascelles, for presenting to the honourable the House of Commons the petition of the ship-owners at the port of Scarborough, on the same subject.

Resolved unanimously, That the thanks of this society be given to Sir William Heathcote, Bart. for presenting to the honourable the House of Commons the petition of the ship-owners at the port of Portsmouth, on the same subject.

Resolved unanimously, That the thanks of this society be given to Sir Ralph Milbanke, Bart. for presenting to the honourable the House of Commons the petition of the ship-owners of the port of Sunderland, on the same subject.

Resolved unanimously, That the thanks of this society be given to John Staniforth, Esq. M. P. for his attention to the committee of ship-owners for the port of London.

The treasurer's accounts for the last year were then presented, read, and approved.

Resolved unanimously, That the thanks of this society be given to the treasurer, Mr. Isaac Robinson, for his strict attention to the duties of his office, and to the general interests of the society for the last two years.

Resolved unanimously, That the thanks of this society be given to the secretary, Mr. Atcheson, for his active and indefatigable exertions in support of the shipping interest of the country, and for his unremitting attention to the business of this society.

Resolved unanimously, That the thanks of this meeting be given to Mr. Horncastle, for his attention and impartial conduct of the chair.

(Signed) Thomas Horncastle, Chairman.

* Mr. Coombe presented this petition, in the absence of Sir Charles Price from indisposition.

At a meeting of the general committee of ship-owners for the port of London, at Wills' Coffee-house, the 28th day of February, 1805, convened to take into consideration the propriety of presenting a memorial to the right honourable the lords of the committee of council for the affairs of trade and foreign plantations, on the present alarming state of the shipping interest of Great Britain, in consequence of the result of a recent interview with that board on the subject:

ROBERT CURLING, Esq. in the Chair:

Resolved unanimously, THAT as it appears necessary that the inconveniences and depression complained of by the shipping interest should be distinctly stated in a memorial to the * board of trade, according to the suggestion of that board—that the secretary be instructed to write a circular letter to the ship-owners at the out-ports, requesting their co-operation, and at the same time to recommend to them the expediency of previously establishing a fund for defraying the expences attending the investigation of so im-

* At this period his grace the duke of *Montrose* was president, and the right honourable *George Rose* vice president of the board of trade. See extract from minutes *post*, June 19, 1806.

" Resolved unanimously, That it is the opinion of this committee that it is now more than ever important that the exertions which were begun by this committee in 1801, and continued in the years 1802 and 1803, to obtain attention to the interests of British shipping, should be renewed with increased activity, as the *good effect* of the measures adopted in Mr. Pitt's *last* administration in 1804, for gradually regaining the inestimable advantages this country must at all times derive from the Navigation Act when enforced, began to be manifested; and if those measures had been followed up, with others dictated by wisdom, which there is good reason to believe was intended, the carrying trade between America and the West Indies would soon have been restored to British ship-owners."

See also Extract of 31st July, 1806.

" Resolved unanimously, That the thanks of this meeting be given to the right honourable George Rose, the right honourable sir Wm. Grant, the right honourable sir Wm. Scott, lord Castlereagh, the right honourable George Canning, the honourable Spencer Perceval, Mr. Staniforth, and the several other members of the House of Commons, who have expressed their decided opinion, formed on the fullest and coolest reflection, against any further departure from the navigation and colonial system of Great Britain, relaxed partially and temporarily in the late war, for reasons, whether justifiable or otherwise, not necessary now to be entered on, but which system the experience of the *late* government had induced them to adopt measures for *completely restoring*, and which, *in part, had been effected*."

portant a subject; and also, to desire the ship-owners at the out-ports, in their communications to the secretary on this subject, to state specifically the inconveniences experienced at their respective ports.

Resolved unanimously, That a sub-committee consisting of Mr. Curling, Mr. Thomas Brown, Mr. George Brown, Mr. Thomas Horncastle, Mr. John Akenhead, Mr. John Blacket, Mr. Joseph Dowson, Mr. William Curling, Mr. Old, Mr. Robert Chapman, Mr. Jackson, and Mr. Williams (and any three of them to be a quorum), be appointed to prepare a memorial to the right hon. the lords of the committee of council for the affairs of trade and foreign plantations, on the present alarming state of the shipping interest of Great Britain; and to state therein, that they are ready to substantiate the same by evidence whenever required, and that such sub-committee *be an open committee.*

Resolved unanimously, That the sub-committee do meet on Tuesday and Thursday in each week, at one o'clock *precisely*, at the secretary's office, in Austin Friars, until the memorial and statements in the support of it are prepared; and that these resolutions be sent to the members of the general committee, and to the ship-owners at the out-ports.

(Signed) ROBERT CURLING, Chairman.

At a meeting of the general committee of ship-owners for the port of London, held at Wills' Coffee-house, Cornhill, the 22d day of May, 1805:

RALPH KEDDEY, Esq. in the Chair:

THE secretary stated, that he had received two letters from Ambrose Weston, Esq. solicitor to the corporation of the Trinity-house, of Deptford Strond, on the subject of the * Lastage and Ballast Bill then before parliament:—and the same were read, and also several clauses of the said bill, and the rates proposed, not only to be levied for ballast on ships in the West-India and London docks, but also on ships in the river Thames.

* *Vide* Stat. 45 Geo. 3, c. 98. passed June, 1805—which continues the *former* rates for ballast delivered in the *River*, and contains some new regulations respecting the delivery of ballast in the East and West India and London docks, and at the chalk wharfs below Woolwich.

Resolved unanimously, That from the *present serious depression* of British shipping, and from the enormous increase of charges on ships frequenting the port of London—it is the opinion of this committee, that they cannot, consistent with the duty they owe to the ship-owners of the country, and with a due regard to their own interest, agree to any proposition to raise, at this time, the price of ballast within the port of London, especially as no actual necessity has yet been shewn to justify or warrant such a measure; and that a petition be presented to parliament against the same.

Resolved, That the secretary be instructed to transmit the preceding resolution to Ambrose Weston, Esq. solicitor to the corporation of the Trinity-house of Deptford Strond.

(Signed) RALPH KEDDEY, Chairman.

PETITION AGAINST BALLAST BILL.

To the Honourable the Commons of the United Kingdom of Great Britain and Ireland, in Parliament assembled.

The humble petition of the several persons whose names are hereunder written, being owners of or otherwise interested in British ships and vessels frequenting and trading to the port of London,

Sheweth,

THAT a bill is now pending in this honourable house "To repeal two acts passed in the sixth and thirty-second years of his late majesty, for the regulation of Lastage and Ballastage in the River Thames, and to make more effectual regulations thereto." That the said bill contains certain clauses, imposing additional duties on the owners of all British ships frequenting the port of London, for such ballast as they may have occasion to take on board their respective ships, whether it consists of the soil of the river Thames, or any other article which they may take on board, as such; which additional duties, if passed into a law, will not only be injurious to your petitioners and the other owners of ships and vessels frequenting the port of London, but will be highly prejudicial to the public.

That it is with great concern your petitioners have *still to lament* the serious *depression* of the shipping interest of the country, especially the shipping engaged in the coal trade, and which, instead of being subjected to any further additional local or public burthen, your petitioners most humbly submit, requires aid and relief.

That the clauses in the said bill which relate to the delivery of ballast for ships in the West-India and London docks, will prove extremely inconvenient and injurious to your petitioners and the other owners of ships engaged in the West-India trade.

That the provisions, restrictions, and regulations contained in the said bill, if passed into a law, would create great delay in the dispatch of ships trading to the port of London, especially colliers, and would be attended with great expence to your petitioners; and the said bill contains several other clauses and provisions which, if passed into a law, would likewise be very injurious to your petitioners.

Your petitioners therefore humbly pray that they may be heard by counsel against so much of the said bill as affects them, and that the said bill may not pass into a law as it now stands; and that your petitioners may have such other relief in the premises as to this honourable house shall seem meet,

And your petitioners shall ever pray, &c.

At a meeting of the committee of ship-owners of the port of London, at Wills' Coffee-house, 5th Sept. 1805:

Mr. AKENHEAD in the Chair:

IT having been stated that several *boats* belonging to *merchant* ships in the river Thames had been seized and condemned under the 34th Geo. 3, chap. 50, and other revenue acts,

Resolved, That a memorial be presented to the lords commissioners of the treasury, stating the preceding circumstances, and praying that all boats belonging to *merchant ships* shall be exempted from the operation of those acts, and that the owners shall not be compelled to take out licences for such boats in future.

(Signed) J. AKENHEAD, Chairman.

At a general meeting of the society of ship-owners of Great Britain, held at the London Tavern, this 8th day of August, 1805:

RALPH KEDDEY, Esq. in the Chair:

THE secretary read the following Note from Sir Charles Price, Bart. and also the letter addressed to him by the right honourable George Rose, on the intended Pilotage Bill.

To Nat. Atcheson, Esq.

Sir Charles Price presents his compliments to Mr. Atcheson, and herewith sends him a bill intended to be brought into parliament for the better regulation of pilots, with a letter he received from Mr. Rose. Mr. Atcheson will lay the same before the ship-owners, &c. and acquaint them Sir Charles will have pleasure in receiving their opinions.

Bedford-square, 27th July, 1805.

To Sir Charles Price, Bart.

SIR,

I transmit you herewith a printed copy of "A Bill for the better Regulation of Pilots and Pilotage of Vessels navigating the British Seas," which I had the honour of introducing into the House of Commons in the last session of parliament: I did not attempt to have it further proceeded in than going through a committee to have the blanks filled up, as I was aware that the importance of the subject, and the difficulties likely to attend any satisfactory measure respecting it, rendered it highly desirable, not only that full time should be allowed for receiving and considering objections to the bill, but that it was requisite to make the most extensive communications, in the hope of receiving useful suggestions for the improvement of it. At present the scope of the bill comprehends only the British channel, and from the South Foreland to the Thames, except in clause A, page 4, requiring the transmission of the names of *all* pilots to the custom-house, which was necessary that it may be known how to address them quarantine orders. If, however, the merchants, ship-owners, &c. shall be desirous

[O]

of having other provisions of the bill extended to the North Sea, St. George's Channel, or the Bristol Channel, and any intimation is made of that to me during the recess, I will take care that such proposition shall be attentively considered by competent judges before a new bill is proposed in the next session, and you will, of course, have an opportunity of seeing, that in any event due attention is paid to it: I trust you will have the goodness to excuse my giving you this trouble on a subject deeply interesting to the country, not only as respecting very valuable property, but still more so, as affecting the lives of the people, both as to protection from shipwreck, and from infectious disorders. My object in doing this is to give you an opportunity of making a communication to some of your constituents on the matter, if you shall think it right to do so.

I am, Sir,

Your most obedient servant,

Old Palace-yard, July 22, 1805. (Signed) Geo. Rose.

Resolved, That the intended Pilotage Bill be submitted to a committee of the following persons; and they are requested to report thereon at the next meeting, on the second Thursday in September next, viz.

Mr. Akenhead, Mr. Blackett, Mr. Galilee,
Mr. Robinson, Mr. Dowson, and Mr. Horncastle.

Resolved unanimously, That the thanks of this meeting be given to the right honourable George Rose, for his obliging communication to Sir Charles Price, Bart. on the intended Pilotage Bill*, and also for his great attention to the general interest of British ship-owners; and that the secretary do communicate the same to Mr. Rose.

Resolved unanimously, That the thanks of this meeting be given to Sir Charles Price, Bart. for his obliging communication of Mr. Rose's letter on the intended Pilotage Bill, and for his great attention to the interest of British ship-owners.

Resolved, That the paper on crimpage be referred to the sub-committee on the Pilotage Bill.

(Signed) R. Keddey, Chairman.

* *Vide post*, page cx.

At a meeting of the committee of ship-owners of the port of London, at Wills' Coffee-house, 12th September, 1805:

Mr. William Curling in the Chair:

Resolved, That an application be made to the honourable the directors of the West-India dock company, requesting that they will permit the new buildings on the south side of the docks to be used for warehousing sugars, as it will afford greater dispatch in the discharge of the homeward-bound ships, and avoid the delay and inconvenience which will otherwise take place.

Resolved, That the secretary do transmit the above resolution to Mr. Marsham, requesting him to lay the same before the directors.

The secretary read the draft memorial to the lords commissioners of the treasury respecting the *seizure of the boats* belonging to ships in the *merchants'* service, viz.

To the Right Hon. the Lords Commissioners of his Majesty's Treasury.

The memorial of the committee of ship-owners for the port of London, in behalf of themselves and other owners of British ships,

Humbly sheweth,

That by certain acts of parliament respectively passed in the 24th, 27th, 28th, and 34th years of his present majesty's reign, *certain boats* therein mentioned and described are in certain cases subject to seizure and forfeiture, unless such boats shall be built and constructed upon the plan and be of the dimensions particularly set forth in the same acts; (that is to say) " unless such boats shall have planks of three quarters of an inch thick, and her timbers one inch and a half square, and not more than nine inches from timber to timber."

That by the said acts, it is among other things enacted, " That if any cutter, lugger, shallop, wherry, smack, yawl, or boat, belonging in the whole or in part to any of his majesty's subjects, shall be found or discovered to have been within the limits of any of the ports of this kingdom, or within the distance of four leagues, or within the distance in the said act particularly described, having on board any arms or ammunition whatever, except by licence from the lord high admiral or the commissioners of the admiralty for the time being as thereinafter mentioned; every such cutter, lugger, shallop, wherry, smack, yawl, or boat shall be forfeited, together with all the goods (if any) which shall be laden therein, and all her guns, tackle, and furniture, and the same shall and may be seized by any officer or officers of the custom or excise: Provided always, That this act shall not extend, or be construed to extend, to any ship or vessel on a voyage from any part of America, or the East or West Indies, or Africa, or the Mediterranean, so as to subject the same to forfeiture for having spirits, tea, coffee, or tobacco or snuff on board; nor to forfeit any cutter, lugger, shallop, wherry, smack, yawl, or boat belonging to or employed in the service of his majesty's navy, victualling-office, ordnance, customs, excise, or post-office, *nor to any such vessel* as aforesaid, or lighter, which shall be used solely on any rivers, canals, or inland navigations, *nor to any cutter, lugger, shallop, wherry, smack, yawl, or boat whatever*, the owner of which shall have a licence from the lord high admiral of Great Britain, or the commissioners of the admiralty for the time being, or any person authorised by them to grant the same, such licence *being obtained and entered* agreeable to the recited act of the twenty-fourth year of his present majesty, and *being actually on board such* cutter, lugger, shallop, wherry, smack, yawl, or boat at the time of her being detained or examined by any officer or officers of the customs or excise, and produced to him or them on demand *during* such detention or examination, nor to subject to forfeiture any ship or vessel for having arms or ammunition on board which shall have been regularly entered and cleared at any custom-house in any of his majesty's dominions as mercandize, or for the use of his majesty's stores or garrisons, and which shall be regularly stowed in the hold of such ship or vessel; nor to forfeit any cutter, lugger, shallop, wherry, smack, yawl, or boat which shall *bonâ fide* be wholly and solely employed in the cod, herring, mackarel, or other fisheries carried on from Great Britain, and shall have on board a sufficient quantity of hooks and lines, or nets, for properly carrying on the said fisheries respectively, and shall clear out at some port in Great Britain for such fisheries respectively."

That in consequence of the said acts, or some of them, many boats belonging to the ships of your petitioners, and other British ship-owners engaged in the merchants' service, have been seized by the officers of his majesty's customs, for being constructed otherwise than according to the regulations mentioned in the said acts.

That your memorialists have, in consequence of the operation of the said acts, been put to very great and serious inconveniences and expences by the seizure of their boats, which, if constructed according to the direction of the said act, would not be of any service to the crews of merchants' ships, who require boats built according to the construction of the boats of your petitioners, which have been seized as before stated.

That if they were built in any other manner, they would not answer the general purposes in the merchants' service for which they are used.

That when a licence is obtained under these acts, it does not afford protection from seizure, unless it is actually kept on board the said open boats which are employed in the general service of the ships to which they belong, and not in any other manner; and it is not usual to keep any person on board of these open boats, unless when so employed; it is therefore both inconvenient and unsafe to leave such licences in those boats.

Your memorialists, therefore, humbly hope your lordships will be pleased to take the preceding circumstances into your lordships' consideration, and to direct that the boats belonging to ships in the merchants' service, *not* being armed, may be exempt from the operation of the beforementioned acts, and not be liable to seizure from not being constructed according to the provisions of the said acts, and that the owners thereof shall not be compellable to take out licences for such boats in future; or that your lordships will be pleased to make such order in the case as to your lordships shall seem meet.

And your memorialists will ever pray.

Resolved, That the said petition be agreed to, and * transmitted by the secretary to the secretaries of the treasury.

(Signed) W. Curling, Chairman.

* Presented in Sept. 1805, and referred to the commissioners of the customs to report thereon.

At a meeting of the committee of ship-owners for the port of London, at Wills' Coffee-house, 26th of September, 1805:

Mr. GALILEE in the Chair:

THE secretary read the Pilotage Bill, which was gone through clause by clause; and some alterations being made therein, he was ordered to write to Sir Charles Price thereon.

(Signed) S. GALILEE, Chairman.

Letter to Sir Charles Price, Bart. in pursuance of the preceding Resolution.

DEAR SIR, *Austin Friars*, 31*st Dec.* 1805.

I HAVE to apologize for not having transmitted to you earlier the sentiments of the committee of ship-owners of the port of London on the Bill for the better Regulation of Pilots, &c. but my absence from town prevented me. The committee instruct me to request you to communicate to Mr. Rose the very high sense they entertain of his attention to the interest of British ship-owners, and they flatter themselves, that, under the auspices of the present administration, they may look forward to an amelioration of the very great charges and expences imposed upon them in the port of London.

With respect to the *Pilotage Bill*, they approve of its principle; but they beg leave to suggest to you, for the consideration of Mr. Rose, some few alterations in it which are marked in the margin of the printed copy of the bill inclosed: if, contrary to their expectations, there should be any objections to the alterations proposed, the committee hope they will be afforded an opportunity of being heard in support of them, previous to the bill being resumed in the house, as they are very desirous of avoiding even the appearance of any opposition to the measure.

I am likewise directed to desire you will inform Mr. Rose of a very serious inconvenience which has often been felt by the owners of British ships frequenting the port of London: I mean in those instances where their ships have sustained damage in the *river* Thames, by *foreign* vessels running foul of them: as the court of admiralty has not any jurisdiction in such cases, they are therefore left without any remedy whatever if the foreign ship proceeds to sea; and in case she does not, their only redress is an action at law against the captain of the foreign vessel, who may be, perhaps, not possessed of any property whatever; and then he may leave the kingdom before final judgment can be obtained in the action which may be brought against him.

In an instance which recently occurred, where a ship, coal laden, was run down and entirely lost opposite Purfleet; the owner of the collier, and who was the master, applied to his proctor on the occasion, who obtained a warrant to detain the foreign ship, which he did; but, on bail being put in, in order to release her, it was found the court of admiralty had no jurisdiction, the accident not having happened on the *high seas*. The suit in that court was therefore abandoned, and an application (founded upon an affidavit, stating the facts of the case, and that the accident arose solely from the improper conduct of the master of the *foreign* ship, and that he was about to leave the kingdom) was made to Mr. Justice ——— for a special order to hold the master of the foreign ship to bail for the value of the collier and cargo, about 2500*l.*, and which, after great consideration, and seemingly much hesitation, his lordship consented to; but then, only to hold him to bail for 1000*l.* * Under these circumstances, it has been thought by several well-informed persons, that if the jurisdiction of the court of admiralty could be extended to embrace accidents like these, which occur very frequently in the *river Thames*, from the great number of foreign ships using the port of London, it will be a public benefit, confining the jurisdiction of that court, in that respect, to the case of *foreign* vessels.

You will therefore, Sir, particularly oblige, by mentioning this suggestion to Mr. Rose, as it is thought a clause to that effect may, with propriety, subject to the approbation of Sir William Scott, be introduced into the *Pilotage* Bill.

I am, dear Sir,

Your obliged and faithful servant,

(Signed) NAT. ATCHESON.

To Sir Charles Price, Bart.
&c. &c.

* In the case referred to, the owner of the collier recovered the value of his ship and cargo, but the bail only paid the 1000*l.* and costs, the captain of the *foreign* vessel having left the kingdom; and the plaintiff has been obliged to send an authority abroad to sue him for the remainder of the damages.

At a meeting of the committee of ship-owners for the port of London, held at Wills' Coffee-house, this 31st day of October, 1805:

Mr. Akenhead in the Chair:

The secretary read the report from the town-clerk of the city of London, respecting the harbour masters regulations.

A Common Council holden in the Chamber of Guildhall of the City of London, on Friday the 25th Day of Oct. 1805.

Perchard, Mayor.

The committee for improving the port of London did this day deliver into this court a report in writing, under their hands, relative to the petition of the ship-owners in respect to the bye laws for regulating the port of London, which was read in these words:

To the right hon. the lord mayor, aldermen, and commons of the city of London, in common council assembled:

We, whose names are hereunto subscribed, your committee appointed to carry into execution the several acts of parliament for rendering more commodious, and for better regulating the port of London, to whom it was referred on the 22d day of February last, to take into consideration the petition of the committee of ship-owners and others, in relation to the proposed bye laws for regulating the said port, and to report our opinion thereon, do certify, that, in pursuance of such reference, we have been attended by the said committee of ship-owners, with Mr. Nathaniel Atcheson, their attorney, who were heard in support of the allegations contained in their petition, and suggested, in writing, sundry alterations to be made in the said bye laws, which we took into our serious consideration and referred to Mr. Solicitor, and Mr. Mathias Lucas, one of our members, together with the said Mr. Atcheson, to take into their further consideration, and to arrange such bye laws as should appear to embrace all the objects of your committee, and the said committee of ship-owners; and they having prepared the said bye laws, submitted them to our consideration, and we approving thereof, have annexed them to this our report for the consideration of this honourable court: and, at the same time, beg leave to suggest other alterations and additions to be made in the said bye laws, which we have also hereunto annexed, and are of opinion they should be engrafted and incorporated with the bye laws now before this honourable court for consideration, all which we submit, this 17th day of October, 1805.

J. Rowlatt
Samuel Goodbehere
E. Colebatch
Nathaniel Davies
Thomas Skinner
S. Wadd
William Rawlins
W. Box
James Birt.

And a motion being made, and question put, that the whole of the bye laws for regulating the port of London be reprinted with the proposed alterations and additions in the report from the committee this day, and the alterations made by this court on the 7th day of February last; and that a copy thereof be sent to every member of this court, and the same was resolved in the affirmative, and ordered accordingly *. WOODTHORPE.

Wm. Jones, Clerk, Co. Co.

Resolved, That the subject of making ships *in ballast* clear at the custom-house, before they can receive their sailing instructions, under the Convoy Act, be taken into consideration at the next meeting of the committee.

(Signed) J. AKENHEAD, Chairman.

At a meeting of the committee of ship-owners for the port of London, held at Wills' Coffee-house, this 23d January, 1806:

Mr. WILLIAM CURLING in the Chair:

THE secretary read the report of the sub-committee respecting ships *in ballast* being obliged to *clear out* before they could obtain their instructions to sail with convoy.

* At a *subsequent* court of common council, *certain regulations*, such as striking topmasts, &c. which had been omitted by agreement, were restored without any notice to, or concurrence of, the committee of ship-owners.

[P]

Resolved, That the report be approved of, and that a letter be written on the subject to the board of trade by the secretary.

(Signed) W. CURLING, Chairman.

Letter addressed to the Board of Trade in pursuance of the above Resolution.

To the right honourable the lords of the committee of his majesty's privy council for the affairs of trade and plantations.

MY LORDS,

I AM directed by the committee of ship-owners for the port of London, to represent to your lordships a very serious inconvenience and expence to which the owners of ships frequenting that port are subject to, from the officers of his majesty's customs *now* requiring all ships *outward* bound, *in ballast*, to clear at the custom-house; in consequence of which, they are obliged to pay *the fees* demanded by the officers of the customs for *such clearances*.

I am likewise instructed to state to your lordships, that it appears to the committee, that at different periods since the year 1787, attempts have been made by the officers of the customs to oblige ships, sailing from the port of London *in ballast*, to clear out *in form*; but the ship-owners considering the law did not compel them to clear their ships under such circumstances, did effectually resist such attempts, and in doing which, they certainly were justified under the act of 24 Geo. 3, ch. 47, sect. 24, commonly called the Smuggling Act, which recites, " That from and after the 1st of Oct. " 1784, the master of every ship or vessel arriving at any " port, harbour, or creek, or going out from any port, har- " bour, or creek in this kingdom, *in ballast*, shall, if called " upon by the collector or comptroller, or other proper " officer of the customs, make a just and true report of such " ship or vessel, both inwards and outwards, and answer, " upon oath, to such questions relative to the voyage and " navigation of the vessel as shall be put to him by the col- " lector, comptroller, or other proper officer of the customs " where he shall arrive, or from whence he shall depart, " under the penalty of forfeitjng 100*l.* for every neglect, " omission, or refusal so to do, which oath the said collector "or other proper officer is, and are hereby authorised and "required to administer, provided always, that *no* master or "other person having the charge or command of any ship or "vessel *in ballast*, making report as above required, shall, in "respect thereof, *be liable* to the payment *of any fees*, "other than such, as such ship or vessel was subject to pay "*previous* to the passing of this act."

That, notwithstanding the act before recited, and although it *never was customary*, previous thereto, for ships *in ballast* to *clear outwards;* and although it could not have been the intention of the legislature, in passing the *last Convoy* Act, to subject the owners of ships proceeding to sea *in ballast* to such inconvenience and expence; yet the officers of the customs construe the fifth section of that statute, being the 43 Geo. 3. ch. 57, which directs, "That they shall not permit vessels to be cleared out until the master has given "bond not to sail without convoy, and not to separate from "it," as compulsory on the owners of *all* ships *in ballast*, or otherwise, to undergo generally, and in all cases, the *regular forms of clearing outwards* in all its branches; but the committee of ship-owners humbly presume this clause was not intended to apply to ships *in ballast*, nor does it, as they are advised, in any manner affect them, and such, it is conceived, is the opinion of the law officers of the customs; for there is no instance of any legal process being instituted by the crown to enforce such a regulation; and therefore, an application, it is understood, was made to the lords commissioners of the admiralty on the subject of the bond required by the last-mentioned act, who have directed the *commanders* of convoys to *refuse sailing instructions* to the masters of ships *in ballast*, which shall not have been *previously cleared* at the custom-house, which direction is now strictly enforced by the commanders of convoys, and is attended with great inconvenience, delay, and expence to the owners of such ships, and in particular, ships bound to *the Baltic*, without securing, more effectually, a strict performance of the regulations of the Convoy Act, or producing any benefit to his majesty's revenue, further than in the payment of the *stamp duty* imposed on the bonds directed to be given by that statute.

The committee humbly hope your lordships will take these circumstances into consideration, and to afford them relief from so *unnecessary*, and, indeed, vexatious a regulation, and which subjects them to an expence of between 4*l.* and 5*l.* on *each* voyage; but if your lordships are of opinion that some regulation should prevail in this respect, they trust your lordships will excuse them from presuming to intimate, that they apprehend the object of the legislature in passing the *Convoy* Act will be fully answered, if an officer of the customs is appointed to take the convoy bond *only* from the masters of ships *in ballast*, and to charge them with the *stamp* duty thereon, and a *reasonable fee* for filling it up, without obliging them to pay *all the other fees and expences* attached to *regular clearances* at the custom-house, which they are now obliged to pay as before stated.

The committee flatter themselves your lordships will excuse this intrusion upon your lordships' attention; but they are compelled to apply to your lordships at this time for relief, not only from the circumstances before stated, but likewise from the very enormous charges and expences which are now imposed upon the trade and shipping of the port of London.

I am, my lords,
With great respect,
Your lordships'
Most obedient and faithful servant,

Austin Friars, March 1, 1806. NAT. ATCHESON, Sec.

At a meeting of the committee of ship-owners for the port of London, held at Wills' Coffee-house, this 13th March, 1806:

Mr. WILLIAM CURLING in the Chair:

Resolved, THAT a letter be addressed to the right hon. the board of trade, on the subject of the *condemnation* and *sales* of *British* ships in the *British West-India* colonies, and requesting that such regulations may be adopted which will *prohibit* such fraudulent condemnations and sales in future.

(Signed) WILLIAM CURLING, Chairman.

Letter addressed to the Board of Trade in pursuance of the preceding Resolution.

To the right honourable the lords of the committee of his majesty's privy council for the affairs of trade and plantation.

My Lords,

I am instructed by the committee of ship-owners for the port of London to communicate to your lordships a very serious and growing evil, which has, within these few years past, prevailed in his majesty's West-India colonies, and which, from recent information received from thence, induces the committee not to hesitate any longer in requesting your lordships' early attention to the subject.

The committee regret to state to your lordships, that *fraudulent* transfers of British ships have become very frequent in the West-India islands, by the collusion of the masters of them, with persons residing there, without the privity or knowledge of the owners in the mother country. The manner in which such transfers are made is as follows:

The master states that the ship is not seaworthy, or has sustained so much damage on her passage out, as not to render her fit to return to England with West-India produce: he accordingly presents a petition to the judge of the vice admiralty court of the island where his vessel may be lying, stating the above, or similar circumstances, and praying the judge to order a survey, which is, of course, directed to be made: the master then, with other persons who are connected with him, either return that the ship is unworthy of any repair whatsoever, or that such repairs cannot be made in the island where the ship is, or that the repairs to be made will amount to more than the value of the ship, or what afterwards would arise from a sale of her.

Upon this certificate of survey being returned to the judge of the vice admiralty court, he condemns the ship, and directs her to be sold for the benefit of the owners, underwriters, and others concerned, and that the masters, officers, and crew, shall have no further claim on the owners from the day of the sale. The ship is then put up to sale, and sold for a very inconsiderable sum of money—very often far below one fourth part of her real value.

The master then sends to England to his owners a protest, with an office copy of the proceedings in the vice admiralty court, directing the sale, &c. in order that his owners, if insured, may recover the loss they sustain by the sale of the ship from the underwriters; but, in some instances, the ships have arrived in England with cargoes from the colonies under the direction of the new masters appointed by the purchasers, even *before* those documents have been received by the original owners.

The purchaser of the ship, immediately after the sale, applies to the officers of his majesty's customs, in the island where the ship is condemned, for a new register for the ship, which is granted by them, *although there is no transfer or assignment of the interest of the original owners, by bill of sale, or otherwise;* the condemnation of the judge of the vice admiralty court, as before stated, being deemed *by them* sufficient, notwithstanding the provision of the Register Acts. (See 34 Geo. 3. c. 68, sect. 20, &c.)

I beg leave, for the information of your lordships, to annex * a copy of the plantation register lately granted at for the ship , of , under circumstances similar to those before stated. That ship, perfectly seaworthy, sailed from London in March, 1805, chartered by Messrs. . She arrived in the island of , in June following, delivered her outward cargo in good order and condition; but the ship, having sprung a leak, made some water in her passage, which obliged the captain to have, occasionally, one pump going. On his arrival at he petitioned for a survey, the ship then being in bay, which was ordered by the judge of the vice admiralty court of the island. Accordingly, two or three persons connected with the master went from port to the ship, and made a very partial survey of her, a considerable part of the outward cargo being then on board.

They then certified to the judge, "that the ship was not "fit to take in a cargo for England, and that she was, in fact, "not seaworthy; and that to repair her in the islands would "cost 17,570 dollars; and after that, the ship would not be "worth more than 2500*l.* in England in time of war; and "in time of peace, should it take place, she would not be "worth more than 1600*l.* sterling. They then state, that "the ship might proceed with safety to , or any "other port in those seas; but doubted much, whether the

* It is not considered necessary to set forth this certificate of registry, which was annexed to the original letter.

"insurance would be good after the ship had left that "island."

The judge, upon this certificate, condemned the ship, which was valued by the owners in England at 2600*l.* She was then put up to sale at , though then lying in bay at some distance, and sold only for 898 *l.* currency, at 200 per cent. The master then sent his owners an account of it, after deducting therefrom the expences of survey, sale, agents, commission, &c. leaving only a balance due to them of 41 *l.* 4*s.* 8*d.* currency, or about 20*l.* *sterling.*

The new purchaser soon after brought the ship from bay to port , obtained the *register annexed*, and then went in her to (another island), and during a beating passage of six days the ship made no water. At the purchaser had a survey upon the ship, having previously had her caulked; and the surveyors certified, that her planks were sound, &c. that she was seaworthy, and fit to take in a cargo of West-India produce. It appears that the purchaser expended only about 300*l.* sterling in the caulking, and in the necessary outfit of the ship at for the voyage to England, where she has since arrived, after a very boisterous passage, in the West-India docks at Blackwall with a full cargo; and the original owners, under the opinion of , intend to proceed at law to recover possession of her and freight.

In all the cases of this description which have come to the knowledge of the committee, they appear to have originated with a view to defraud the original owners and underwriters; and as the vice admiralty courts of the West-India islands have no civil jurisdiction in these matters, the condemnations and sales have been held to be illegal and void.—See Hayman *v.* Moulton and others, Espinasse's N. P. Reports, vol. 5, page 65 *.

Under these circumstances, and as information has been recently received of several British ships having been condemned in like manner in Antigua and other places, the committee are induced to solicit your lordships' attention to this subject, in order that such fraudulent practices may be prevented in future. The committee do not venture to point

* See also the case of Andrews *v.* Murray, tried before lord Ellenborough at Guildhall Sittings after Trinity Term, 1806, wherein it was decided that these kind of sales were illegal.

out to your lordships what may be proper to be done in that respect, relying confidently on your lordships' wisdom speedily to adopt such regulations as will secure British ship-owners and underwriters from such attempts to defraud and injure them in future.

I am also directed by the committee to communicate to your lordships the information they are in possession of, respecting many of the cases before referred to, and to wait upon your lordships whenever you will please to condescend to appoint a time for that purpose.

I am, my Lord,

With great respect,

Your Lordships'

Most obedient faithful servant,

(Signed) NAT. ATCHESON, Sec.

Extract from the Report of the Commissioners of the Customs, of 21st May, 1806, on the above Application to the Board of Trade, transmitted to Mr. Atcheson, by the Direction of Lord Auckland.

"THAT with respect to the frauds stated to be committed in the plantations, in the transfer of the property of British ships, to the prejudice of the owners residing in England, by the collusion of the masters, who, under pretence of such ships not being seaworthy, obtain the condemnation thereof in the vice admiralty courts in the West Indies, the same do not come within the cognizance of this board.

"That considering, however, the granting of *new* certificates of registry for such ships (as appears to have been done by our officers at , in the case of the ship, , mentioned in the petition), a question of much general importance; we have taken the opinions of the practical officers here, and of the three solicitors to the board, thereon.

"That it appears from the opinions thus taken, that the officers of this revenue in the West Indies are *not* required to have regard to the *validity* of the *decrees* of the vice admiralty courts; but that on such decrees being produced, they cannot *safely* refuse to grant *new* certificates of registry to the purchasers of vessels sold in virtue thereof*, *on all the requisites of law being complied with;* for if such decree should be void, the new registers, it is stated, would convey no title, but the property of the ships remain in the general owners."

At a meeting of the committee of ship-owners for the port of London, held this 15th day of April, 1806, at the London Tavern, to take into consideration such measures as may be legally adopted to prevent any *further suspension* of the Navigation Laws of Great Britain; and, in particular, the bill intended to be brought into parliament, to authorise the governors of the British West-India islands to suspend the same in favour of *American* bottoms whenever they think proper, *during war*, and on other special affairs:

ROBERT CURLING, Esq. in the Chair:

Resolved unanimously, THAT it is the opinion of this committee, that it will be highly injurious to the shipping interest of Great Britain and Ireland to authorise, by act of parliament, the governors of the British West-India islands to *suspend*, at their discretion, the navigation laws of the country, and to admit American vessels to trade with the colonies *contrary* to the provisions of those statutes.

Resolved unanimously, That it is the opinion of this committee, that *no necessity exists* for investing the governors of the British West-India islands in future with authority to *suspend*, at their discretion, the navigation laws of Great Britain, in favour of American or other neutral vessels; and that to introduce such *a principle into an act of indemnity* is *novel* and *dangerous*, as it will inevitably tend to establish a system highly injurious to the maritime interest of the country, and lessen that responsibility, which otherwise

* N. B. It is proper to observe, that none of the formalities of the law, as required by the Register Acts, are complied with. The plantation register is granted on the production of the decree of the vice courts of admiralty, although, on the face of such decree, it appears that the cause of condemnation is not within the jurisdiction of those courts, which are prize courts only, and have no civil jurisdiction whatever.

[Q]

would attach upon those persons who may advise any infringement of the provisions of those statutes *.

Resolved unanimously, That it is the opinion of this committee, that the *frequent recent suspensions* of the navigation laws of the country have been highly injurious to its shipping interest, which is not in so flourishing a state, or so adequately or profitably employed, as it would have been, had not such facilities been afforded to neutral vessels by the frequent suspension of the Navigation Acts.

Resolved unanimously, That a † petition be presented to both houses of parliament, humbly praying, that the provisions of the Navigation Acts may be strictly enforced in future; and also, that *an inquiry may be made into the actual state of the shipping and navigation of Great Britain and Ireland*; and also, as to the expediency of altering or revising the *alien and other duties*, so as to place *British* ships on an *equal footing* with *foreign* vessels, in order to lessen those evils which have resulted from the great increased foreign competition British ship-owners have had, unfortunately for the general interest of this country, to contend with.

Resolved unanimously, That a sub-committee be appointed to prepare such petition, and that the same be submitted to the consideration of this committee at their next meeting, to be held at this place, on Monday next, at one o'clock precisely.

Resolved unanimously, That the preceding resolutions be inserted in the Morning and Evening Newspapers, and transmitted to the ship-owners at the out-ports.

Resolved unanimously, That the thanks of this meeting be given to the chairman, for his attention to the general interest of British ship-owners; and, in particular, for his conduct on this occasion.

(Signed) ROB. CURLING, Chairman.

At a meeting of the committee of ship-owners for the port of London, held at the London Tavern, this 26th April, 1806:

R. CURLING, Esq. in the Chair:

Resolved, THAT the secretary do write to the out-ports

* The *Indemnity* Bill referred to passed in April, 1806, but did not contain any prospective clause, as was apprehended.

† *Vide* Parliamentary Debates on the American Intercourse Bill, &c. in 8vo. Edition 1806, which contain the several petitions presented to the legislature on this subject, and also all the official papers relating to it, with many other important documents.

for an account of the ships now building there, and also in the river Thames, and whether they are building on contract or speculation, and when they were first laid down.

(Signed) R. Curling, Chairman.

1st, *An Account of the State of Ship-building for the Merchants Service within the Port of London, in May,* 1806.

The following circular letter was written to the several ship-builders in the river Thames, by order of the committee of ship-owners for the port of London, in order to ascertain the state of ship-building within that port.

GENTLEMEN, Austin Friars, 26th April, 1806.

The committee of ship-owners for the port of London will be greatly obliged to you to inform me the number and the tonnage of the ships built at your yards since December, 1802, distinguishing each year; and whether the ships were for the East India Company's service or the merchants' service in general. Your early answer will be esteemed, as the committee are particularly anxious to ascertain, correctly, the present state of ship-building in Great Britain.

I am, &c. &c.

(Signed) Nat. Atcheson, Secretary.

To Messrs. Perry, Wells, and Co. Blackwall.
Messrs. Brent, Rotherhithe.
Thomas Pitcher, Esq. Northfleet.
P. E. Mestaer, Esq. Rotherhithe.
John Dudman, Esq. Deptford.
Messrs. Barnard and Co. Deptford.
Messrs. Woolcombe and Co. Rotherhithe.
Messrs. Curling and Co. Limehouse.
Almon Hill, Esq. Limehouse.
John Ayles, Esq. Wapping.
Messrs. Tibbits, Hitchcock, and Co. Limehouse.
Joshua Young, Esq. Rotherhithe.
Messrs. Fletcher, Shadwell.
E. Thompson, Esq. Rotherhithe.

SIR, Rotherhithe, April 28, 1806.

In answer to the request of the committee signified to us by your letter of the 26th instant, we inform you we have *not* built any ships or vessels whatever subsequent to the month of December, 1802.

We are, Sir,

Your humble Servants,

To Nat. Atcheson, Esq. &c. W. Woolcombe and Son.

SIR, Rotherhithe, 28th April, 1806.

In answer to yours of the 26th instant, I acquaint you that the following ships have been built by me since December, 1802, viz.

Names.	Tons.	When launched.	Service.
Prince of Wales	820	Feb. 8, 1803	East India.
Thames	374	Dec. 14, 1803	South Seas, but now a sloop of war.
Lord Keith	600	May 12, 1804	East India.
New Ship	409	Now building	West India.
New Schooner	60	Now building	Sugar droger.

I am, Sir,

Your obedient humble Servant,

(For P. E. Mestaer),

To Nat. Atcheson, Esq. &c. Corn. Trufitt.

SIR, Deptford Green, April 28, 1806.

In answer to yours of the 26th instant, requesting to know the number and tonnage of ships built by us since the year 1802, for the information of the ship-owners of the port of London, we have inclosed every description of ships and vessels launched by us from that time.

For Government.

Repulse,	74 guns,	$1726\frac{6}{94}$ tons,	launched	July 21, 1803.
Harrier,	18 guns,	$383\frac{16}{94}$ tons,	ditto	ditto 1804.
Elk,	18 guns,	$382\frac{11}{94}$ tons,	ditto	July 22, 1804.

For the East India Company.

Grant, Smith,	Hoys,	128 tons,	launched	Oct. 28, 1805.
Cotton,	ditto,	129 tons,	ditto	Jan. 6, 1806.

For Merchants.

Ida West Indiaman,	$465\frac{39}{94}$ tons,	launched	Sept. 20, 1804.
Metcalf East Indiaman,	$819\frac{6}{94}$ tons,	ditto	Nov. 19, 1804.
Phœnix ditto, -	$818\frac{84}{94}$ tons,	ditto	Dec. 3, 1804.
William Pitt, ditto	$819\frac{23}{94}$ tons,	ditto	March 30, 1805.

Now under contract with government for building the Marlborough, of 74 guns, which stands in a state to season; we have no contract at this time for building any merchant ships. We hope the above account will meet your approbation, and we shall be happy, at all times, to give the society every information in our power.

We are your most obedient Servants,

FRANCES BARNARD, SON, and ROBERTS.

To Nat. Atcheson, Esq. &c.

SIR, Limehouse, 28th April, 1806.

IN answer to your favour of the 26th instant, we beg leave to inform you we have *not* built any ship during the time mentioned in your letter.

We remain, Sir,

Your most humble Servants,

TIBBUT, HITCHCOCK, and BATSON.

To Nat. Atcheson, Esq. &c.

SIR, Limehouse, April 29, 1806.

IN reply to yours of the 26th instant, we have to inform you that since the period alluded to *not* any ship or vessel has been built in any of our premises.

We remain, Sir,

Your obedient Servants,

To Nat. Atcheson, Esq. &c. CURLING, COX, and Co.

SIR, Limehouse, near West India Docks, April 30, 1806.

IN answer to yours of the 24th instant, requesting to be

informed the number and tonnage of ships built by me, in my yard, since December, 1802, please to inform the committee of ship-owners, I have *not* built any ships since the above period.

I am, Sir,
Your humble Servant,
To Nat. Atcheson, Esq. &c. ALMON HILL.

SIR, Globe-yard, Rotherhithe, 2d May, 1806.

IN reply to your favour of yesterday, I beg leave to inform you that, during the period you mention, there has *not* been any ships built in my premises.

I am, Sir,
Your most obedient Servant,
To Nat. Atcheson, Esq. &c. E. THOMPSON.

SIR, Grove-street, Deptford, May 3, 1806.

THE inclosed is a statement of the merchant ships built in my yard since the 1st of December, 1802.

Ships Name.	*Captains Name.*	*Tonnage.*	*Date of Contract.*	*Date when launched.*	*Service.*
Cumberland	Wm. Ward Farrer	1257	24 June, 1801	11 Dec. 1802	East India.
Lord Melville	Charles Lennox	818	8 Oct. 1801	9 March, 1803	Do.
Surry	John Cumberlege	819	5 Jan. 1803	3 Nov. 1804	Do.
Jane, Dutchess of Gordon	John Cameron	820	15 Jan. 1803	14 Jan. 1235	Do.
Streatham	John Dale	819	5 Feb. 1803	13 April, 1805	Do.
George Hibbert	Wm. Thompson	316	22 Aug. 1803	3 Oct. 1803	Jamaica.

I am, Sir,
Your most obedient Servant,
To Nat. Atcheson, Esq. &c. JOHN DUDMAN.

SIR, New Crane Dock, Wapping Wall, May 3, 1806.

IN reply to yours, I am desired by Mr. John Ayles to inform you, a ship named the Collingwood, of 256 tons, was built by him at Gun Dock, Wapping, and launched on the 9th of November last, and is now bound on a voyage to Trinidad. It was the only one built by him, and he has no other at present on the stocks.

I am, Sir, for Mr. John Ayles,
Your obedient Servant,
To Nat. Atcheson, Esq. &c. R. H. WESTON.

SIR, Rotherhithe, May 3, 1806.

IN answer to your letter of yesterday, we beg leave to inform you we have launched from our yards, since December, 1802, the under-mentioned ships.

1803.		*Tons.*	
Jan. 8,	Lady Castlereagh -	818	- for the E. I. Company.
8,	Union - -	544	- for ditto.
Feb. 26,	Diligence -	103	- for ditto.
May 20,	Nautilus yacht -	40	- for Earl Dysart.

We are, Sir,
Your obedient Servants,
To Nat. Atcheson, Esq. &c. S. and D. BRENT.
See post.

SIR, Northfleet, May 4, 1806.

BEING from home some days prevented me answering yours of the first instant before:—

Ships built at Northfleet since December, 1802.

East India ship, Ceylon, burden 800 tons, launched Feb. 15, 1803.

East India ship, Devonshire, burden 800 tons, launched Dec. 18, 1804.

I am, Sir,
Your obedient humble Servant,
To Nat. Atcheson, Esq. &c. THOMAS PITCHER.

SIR, Rotherhithe, May 1, 1806.

WE acknowledge the favour of receiving your note, and in reply thereto acquaint you that our *three* building slips have been *unemployed* these several years past; and that we have not constructed a ship of any description whatever, or even been applied to for that purpose.

We remain yours, respectfully,
To Nat. Atcheson, Esq. &c. YOUNG and WALLIS.

SIR, Blackwall, May 1, 1806.

WE beg leave to inclose you the information you applied to us for respecting the number of ships built by us. And are, Sir, respectfully,
Your obedient Servants,
PERRY, WELLS, and GREEN.

	Tonnage.	Service.	
2 Ballast lighters	- - -	Trinity House.	
3 Fir brigantines	382 each	- Government.	
1 Mortar boat	- - - -	Do.	
1 New East Indiaman	1257	- - - -	launched in Feb. 1803.
1 Do. Do.	818	- - - -	Do. in January.
1 74 gun ship	- 1729	- Government	- launched in Aug. 1803.
Building.			
3 74 gun ships	- 1729 each	- Government	
1 East Indiaman	- 1257.		

To Nat. Atcheson, Esq.

SIR, 12th May, 1806, *Vide ante.*

In answer to your note of this day, I have to inform you that the only ships we have *now* building are, the York, 74—and, *rebuilding*, one of 450 tons, which had been put up at Weymouth, but only about half finished there.

I am, Sir,

Your most obedient Servant,

To Nat. Atcheson, Esq. Dan. Brent.

Abstract

ABSTRACT

OF

Ships built in the River Thames since Dec. 1802, *and of those building in May*, 1806.

Ship-builders within the port of London.	Ships King's service.	Ships. East India Company's service.	Ships. Merchants service.	Ships. Fisheries.	Small vessels.
Messrs. Woolcombe					
P. E. Mestaer, Esq.	. .	2	1	1	1 Sugar Droger.
Mess. Barnard and Co.	3	3	1	. .	2 Hoys, E. Ind. Comp. service.
Mess. Tibbut and Co.					
Mess. Curling and Co.					
Almon Hill, Esq. .					
E. Thompson, Esq. .					
John Dudman, Esq.	. .	5	1		
John Ayles, Esq. .	. .	. . .	1		
Mess. Brent . . .	1	2	1*	. .	1 Hoy, E. I. C. 1 Pleasure yacht
Mess. Perry, Wells, and Green . .	7	3	. . .	. .	2 Bal. lighters 1 Mortar boat.
Thomas Pitcher, Esq.	. .	2			
Mess. Fletcher . .					
Mess. Young & Wallis					
Total ships and vessels built on the river Thames since Dec. 1802, and which are now building . .	11	17	5	1	8

* This ship is rebuilding. See Letter, page cxxviii.

A correct Statement of the Ships *broomed* and for Sale within the Port of London in May, 1806; distinguishing new Ships never employed, from those Ships which have been at Sea.

	Ships' Names.	Masters.	Owners or Brokers.	Tons.	
	Ebenezer	Breem	No Bfoker	77	
	Jupiter	———	Berthon	341	
	Linen Hall	———	St. Barbe and Co.	140	
	Four Friends	———	Lyall	152	
	Ceres	———	Ditto	70	
	William	———	Breed and Co. (Griffin Wharf)	157	
	Attempt	———	Captain	89	
	Trafalgar	Latterman	Captain	175	New.
	Rover	———	Taylor and Fry	135	
10	Alice	———	Campbell and Geddes	300	
	Prize	———	Cole	60	
	Lord Nelson	Mucket	Captain	65	
	Resolution	———	Edwards	86	
	Industry	———	Robertson, 14, Austin Friars	250	
	Alert	———	Way and Scott	128	
	Fanny	———	Hay	150	
	Adeona	———	Drinkald	190	
	Cameleon	———	Urquhart and Hope	157	
	Active	———	Beatson	157	
20	Catherine and Eliza	———	Ditto	138	
	Orion	———	Ditto	197	
	Experiment	———	Mestears	150	
	Blackett	———	Whitelock	414	
	Spy	———	St. Barbe and Green	269	
	Unicorn	———	———	300	
	Atlas	———	Mestears	560	
	Name unknown	———	———	250	
	Harriett	Coffin	Mather	230	
	Lord Duncan	———	Havelock	935	
30	Walker	———	Hardy	335	
	Name unknown	———	———	120	
	Hero	Hardy	Ayles	267	
	Jesse	Atkins	Captain	140	
	Recovery	Lyne	Rowcroft	468	
	Name unknown	———	———	100	
	William	Haslewood	Captain	100	
	Young Regulus	Lusk	Drinkald	124	
	Friends	Toby	L. Williams	196	
	Sisters	Heartly	Rowcroft	315	
40	Economy	Smith	Lushington	192	
40	Carried over		Carried over	8680	

	Ships' Names.	Masters.	Owners or Brokers.	Tons.	
40	Brought up		Brought up	8680	
	Eliza	—	Anderson	150	
	Ploughman	Hill	Todd	165	New.
	Intrinsic	Storey	Fairless	411	New.
	Brilliant	Ellington	Wake	242	New.
	Halcyon	Turnbull	Ditto	160	New
	Supply	Hall	Captain	212	
	Supply	—	Faith	218	
	Malta	Brown	Gillespy	361	New.
	Pomona	Hurry	Captain	365	
50	Ocean	—	Smith, St. Barbe and Co.	481	
	Albion	—	Hurry and Co.	365	
	Marlborough	—	Smith, St. Barbe and Co.	415	New.
	London	—	Ditto	279	
	Force	—	Young and Wallis	169	
	Jane	—	Geo. Ioad	250	
	Lion	—	Ditto	190	
	Active	—	Mestears	496	
	Favourite	—	E. Thompson	230	
	Lord Collingwood	—	Wayte	188	New.
60	Lord Collingwood	—	Bulmer	479	New.
	Reliance	—	Phyn and Co.	291	
	British Volunteer	—	Thompson	145	
	Somerset	Earl	Captain	146	
	Adventure	—	Beatson	90	
	Royal Sovereign	—	Graham	350	
	Flora	—	Ditto	150	
	Catherine	—	Ditto	190	
	Cupido	—	Ditto	180	
	Hyega	—	Ditto	168	
70	Maria	—	Ditto	270	
	Elsego	—	Apsey and Co.	180	
	Swan	—	Ditto	107	
	Courier	—	Ditto	71	
	Eliza	—	Dartnell and Co.	268	
	Mercurius	—	—	230	
	Hercules	—	Dowson and Co.	270	
	Asphilon	—	Addison	367	
77	Total.		Total	17969	

London, 12th May, 1806.

We certify the above statement to be correct,

JOHN CHEAP. } Surveyors for
A. PASSMORE. } Lloyds.

N. B. It is believed there are many other ships at present for sale in the port of London which are not *broomed.*

2d. An Account of the State of Ship-building at the several Ports of Great Britain after-mentioned in April and May, 1806.

Circular letter addressed to persons resident at the outports, viz.

SIR, Austin Friars, April 26, 1806.

THE committee of ship-owners for the port of London will be very much obliged to you to inform me the number of ships and vessels, and their tonnage, *now* building at your port, and whether they are building on contract or speculation, and when they were first laid down.

Your early answer will be greatly esteemed, as the committee are desirous of ascertaining, *correctly*, the present state of ship-building in Great-Britain.

I am, Sir,

Your obedient Servant,

To —— NAT. ATCHESON.

SIR, Wells, April 28, 1806.

WE received your letter of the 26th, and, upon enquiry, we find there is one ship building, 140 tons register, laid down in September last upon speculation, but is now sold.

We remain,

Your most obedient Servants,

To Nat. Atcheson, Esq. &c. JOHN BLOOM and SON.

SIR, Chepstow, April 28, 1806.

IN answer to your letter of the 26th instant, we have a new brig, about 190 tons, launched a few months ago, *now to dispose of:* we have also, *on the stocks*, a ship of about 300 tons, carpenter's admeasurement, *not* yet sold. Messrs. Buckle and Co. have a ship ready to launch of about 170 tons, *to sell;* and these are all the vessels building in this port.

We are, Sir,

Your most obedient Servants,

BOWSHER, HODGES, and WATKINS.

To Nat. Atcheson, Esq. &c.

SIR, Stockton, April 28, 1806.

In compliance with your request, I have to inform you there is only *one* vessel building here at present, and by contract, her admeasurement about 180 tons, register tonnage.

I am, dear Sir,
Your obedient Servant,
To Nat. Atcheson, Esq. &c. ROWLAND WEBSTER.

SIR, Lynn, April 28, 1806.

Your last letter of the 26th, which I received last post, I take the earliest opportunity of replying to; and I beg to assure you and the gentlemen of the committee of ship-owners, that I shall always, with great pleasure, procure them any information they may wish for at this port.

We have in Lynn *three* ship-yards, one (belonging to Messrs. Brinley) has been employed entirely in building different vessels *for government*, for the last six or seven years.

The *second* belongs to Mr. Jos. Wales, who has *not* been able to sell to his mind the last six vessels he has built, so has kept them employed himself. The last was launched in November last, and *at present* he has *nothing* building, nor do I hear that he has any intention of laying down another ship.

The *third* yard belongs to Mr. Mark Watson; he has building a ship of about 300 tons measurement, *which has been in hand near four years*, and the hull not nearly completed yet. She is *not* sold, and the builder must lose a great deal of money by her. Mr. Watson has also begun a small vessel, of about 120 tons, for his son-in-law, but he only works on her when his men are not employed *on old work*. She has been laid down three months, but has merely the ram up and half a dozen floor timbers across. In short, there are only *two* ships *now building here*, and *neither of them sold*. Nothing can be more deplorable than is the present state of our shipping at this port. A man who goes in his own vessel may contrive, with his wages and a few boys, to make all ends meet; but a ship-owner (merely so) *cannot* get a penny.

I am, Sir,
Your most obedient Servant,
To Nat. Atcheson, Esq. &c. LIONEL SELF.

SIR — Lancaster, April 29, 1806.

Agreeably to your letter of the 26th instant, I inform you of the number of ships and vessels, their tonnage, &c. *now* building at this port.

		Tons register.		Laid down.	
1 Ship	-	450	-	Jan. 1806	Speculation.
1	-	310	-	Ditto	
1	-	280	-	April 1806	
1	-	100	-	Oct. 1805	Contract.
1	-	65	-	Dec. 1805	
1	-	58	-	Feb. 1806	

A change in the board of trade here being about to take place, your next communication, addressed to the worshipful the mayor, will meet due attention.

I am, Sir,

Your obedient Servant,

To Nat. Atcheson, Esq. &c. — John Dennison,

President of the board of trade.

SIR, — Scarborough, April 29, 1806.

Yours of the 26th instant I duly received, requesting to be informed of the number of ships and vessels, and their tonnage, *now* building at Scarborough, and whether they are building on contract or on speculation, and when they were first laid down.

Ship-builder.		Laid down.	Tons measurement.	On Speculation.
Mr. Tindal	1 Ship	Nov. 1804	140	Finished.
Ditto	1	June 1805	120	
Ditto	1	Oct. 1805	380	Not finished.
Mr. Hewit	1	May 1803	300	Ditto.
Ditto	1	Aug. 1805	112	
Mr. Dale	1	June 1805	110	Ditto.
Mr. Newham	1	Oct. 1803	105	Finished.
Ditto	1	Aug. 1805	215	Not finished.
Mr. Wharton	1	Oct, 1804	210	Ditto.

The above nine ships are all for sale.

I am, Sir,

Your most obedient Servant,

To Nat. Atcheson, Esq. &c. — Benjamin Fowler.

SIR, Boston, April 28, 1806.

In answer to your letter of the 26th instant, here are only *two* vessels building in this place, and *both on speculation*; one is 90 tons register, and the other 80 tons register: the first has been laid down about two weeks, and the other four weeks.

We are respectfully, Sir,

Your obedient Servants,

S. Bernard and Sons.

To Nat. Atcheson, Esq. &c. Per Sam. Bernard, Jun.

SIR, Bristol, April 30, 1806.

In answer to your enquiry of the 26th instant, the under, we hope, will be sufficient. If you want any other information we shall feel pleasure in communicating it; being, very respectfully,

Your most humble Servants,

Thomas and Jos. Hellicar.

One ship, about 560 tons, on speculation, by Hillhouse, Son, and Co. laid down six months.

One ditto, 450 tons, on contract, by Sid. Teast, laid down one month.

One ditto, 450 tons, on contract, by James Brice and Co. laid down twelve months.

One brig, 175 tons, on speculation, by ditto, laid down twelve months.

To Nat. Atcheson, Esq. &c.

SIR, Leith, April 30, 1806.

We beg leave to reply to your favour of the 26th instant, and to annex note of ships building at our port, with their respective dates when laid down.

We are, with respect, Sir,

Your obedient Servants,

John Watson and Co.

For John Watson, Jun.

Messrs. Menzies and Goalan are building, *on speculation*, a ship of 300 tons; measurement that was laid down in March, 1805.

Messrs. Strachan and Gaven are building, *on speculation*, a vessel of 220 tons; measurement that was laid down in April, 1805.

Mr. Alexander Hill is building, *on speculation*, a vessel of 145 tons; measurement that was laid down in June, 1805.

Messrs. Morton and Burns are building a vessel, *upon contract*, of 70 tons; measurement that was laid down in March, 1806.

To Nat. Atcheson, Esq. &c.

RESPECTED FRIEND, North Shields, 2d of 5th Month—May, 1806.

I WAS duly favoured with thy printed letter of the 26th ult. and have made the necessary enquiry; the result as follows:

Ships building at North Shields.

T. Hearn, one ship, 260 tons, laid down 12 months since, seven-eighths built, on speculation.

E. Hurry, one ship, 250 tons, one half built, ditto.

At South Shields.

T. Swan and Co. one ship, 300 tons, laid down two years since, one eighth built, *on speculation.*

N. Fairless, one ship, 300 tons, laid down 12 months, one half built, *ditto.*

J. Craister, one ship, 263 tons, ready to launch, *recently sold*, ditto.

Ditto -	1 ship	146 tons	- ¾ built		on spec.
J. Laing - -	1	132	- ¼ ditto	-	ditto.
Blackburn and Ware	1	350	- ⅓ ditto	-	ditto.
Nicholson and Horn	1	370	- ¼ ditto	-	ditto.
Ditto - -	1	128	- ⅔ ditto	-	ditto.
Ditto - -	1	370	*launched, but not sold* do.		
Ditto - -	1	138	*launched, but not sold* do.		

Ships building between Shields and Newcastle.

E. Hurry, Howden, a small vessel, 140 tons, on speculation.

J. Lessley, the stern and half a keel laid six months since, ditto.

H. Wright, one ship, 340 tons, lower harpins up twelve months, ditto.

Ditto, one ship, 120 tons, *nearly* ready to launch, ditto.

William Carse, one ship, 290 tons, framed, laid down last November, ditto.

William Hawkes, one ship, 200 tons, framed, on contract.

Gothard, one ship, 137 tons, *ready to launch*, ditto.

Ditto, one ship, 360 tons, laid down two years since, one-fourth built, on speculation.

All the ships building *on speculation* are so done to *employ* the builders' *apprentices*, and to keep a *few men in reserve* for the purpose of *repairing ships*. From the best information I can get, the builders lose, on an average, 10*l.* per cent. at least, by such speculations; the following memorandum was given me this morning by Nich. Fairless:—

"I am a ship-builder at South Shields, in the county of Durham, and have upon hands *three* ships, which, at prime cost, without any profit included to the builder, cost me 14,700*l.*; they are of the first quality, and I have offered them for sale 10 per cent. *below prime cost, but have not been able to sell them.*"

There are four frigates or sloops, a gun-brig, and two schooners building on this river for government, on which are employed about 400 shipwrights, *who*, but for this employment, *would have been turned adrift.* Any further services which the committee of ship-owners think that I can render them they may command.

I am, respectfully,
Thy assured Friend,
HENRY TAYLOR.

P. S. I omitted in its place to mention a small vessel building by R. Bulmer and Co. about 180 tons, doubtless on speculation; also omitted a small vessel building by Mr. Charlton, of 89 tons, on speculation, laid down 1805.

To Nat. Atcheson, Esq. &c.

Ships building at Sunderland.

The following statement was transmitted to Mr. Atcheson by Michael Longridge, Esq. of Sunderland, and received the 5th of May, 1806.

Ship-builders.	Ships.	Tons.	When begun.	
Mr. Brown -	1 -	134 -	1805, June 3	speculation.

[S]

Mr. Wake -	1 - 120 -	1806, March 27	do.
Mr. Whinnem -	2 - 220	1805, Dec. 7 -	do.
		1806, March 13	do.
Mr. Hall -	1 - 120 -	1806, March 5	do.
Mr. Laing -	2 - 360	1805, Sept. 21	do.
		—— Sept. 28	do.
Mr. Booth -	1 - 210 -	1806, May 15	do.
Mr. Nicholson -	1 - 160 -	1806, Feb. 22	do.
Mr. Scurfield -	1 - 119 -	1805, Sept. 22	since sold.
Mr. Maling -	2 - 280	1805, Aug. 26	do.
		1806, Jan. 22	do.
Mr. Burn - -	2 - 350	1805, Sept. 23	speculation.
		1806, Feb. 14	do.
Mess. Raffield & Co.	2 - 220	1805, Nov. 2	do.
		—— Dec. 1	do.
Mr. William Potts	1 - 100 -	1806, Feb. 20	do.
Mr. Edward Potts	1 - 100 -	1806, April 18	do.
Mr. R. Reay -	1 - 130 -	1805, Nov. 27	do.
Mr. Crowe -	1 - 100 -	1806, March 10	do.
Mr. T. Brown -	1 - 100 -	1805, Sept. 29	do.
Mr. Howard -	3 - 380	1805, July 1	do.
		1806, Jan. 4	do.
		—— April 17	since sold.
Mr. Robson -	1 - 100 -	1805, June 5	speculation.

To Nat. Atcheson, Esq. &c.

SIR, Kirkaldy, May 2, 1806.

I RECEIVED your favour of the 26th ult. and, agreeable to your desire, I annex a note of the *few* ships building within this port. *The ship-owners here have suffered much for several years back.* The high price of wages, and every article connected with shipping, added to the *great number of foreigners* employed in the *carrying trade*, have reduced the business so low that *there is no return got for the capital employed.*

Since the commencement of the present war, government has taken up one-fifth of the tonnage belonging to this port for the transport-service: were it not for this circumstance our owners would be in the greatest distress; many of their ships *being at present laid up* by the walls, *having no prospect of employ for them.*

Ships building.

One vessel,	100 tons,	on speculation,	six months laid on.
	100	do.	twelve do.
	130	contract,	four do.

I am, Sir,
Your most obedient Servant,
To Nat. Atcheson, Esq. &c. JOHN SPITTAL.

DEAR SIR, Chamber of Commerce, Portsmouth, May 6, 1806.

I HAVE made enquiry, and do *not* learn that there is a single *merchant* vessel building at *any* of the yards *within the Isle of Wight,* either on contract or speculation.

I am, dear Sir,
Your most humble Servant,
To Nat. Atcheson, Esq. &c. THOMAS HEATHER.

SIR, Harwich, May 6, 1806.

YOUR favour of yesterday's date is before me, acquainting me with the request of the committee of ship-owners to be informed what ships may be building at this port. In answer, I have to mention that *no* ships or vessels of any description *are at present building at Harwich;* but at Manningtree (twelve miles distant up the river Stow), and called in this port, a sloop of war, contracted for with the navy board in November last, is now framing.

I am, Sir,
Your very humble Servant,
To Isaac Robinson, Esq. London. J. GRAHAM.

DEAR SIR, Whitehaven, May 5, 1806.

IN answer to the inquiry of your letter of the 26th ult. there are building at this port,

1 Ship, about 400 tons; keel laid down four months; on contract.

1 do. 200 tons; keel laid down one month; speculation.

1 do. 100 do. three months; do.

1 do. 400 do. timber converting; keel *not* laid down; on speculation.

I am, Sir,

Your obedient Servant,

To Nat. Atcheson, Esq. &c. JOHN STEWARD.

A List of Ships building at Blyth, May 5, 1806.

When laid down.		Tons burthen.	
Nov. 1802	-	332	- built on speculation; *has been finished* upwards of two years, and *not* yet sold.
Aug. 1804	-	130	- built on speculation; *has been finished* twelve months, and *unsold* yet.
July, 1805	-	135	- *building* on speculation; } unsold.
July, 1805	-	106	- do. } unsold.
Oct. 1805	-	235	- do. } unsold.
Jan. 1806	-	122	- *building* on contract, and nearly finished.

SIR,

I RECEIVED your letter of the 26th ult. and, agreeable to your request, send you above the number of ships building in this port.

I am, Sir,

Your obedient Servant,

To Nat. Atcheson, Esq. &c. JOHN CLARK.

SIR, Bridgewater, May 7, 1806.

YOURS of the 26th ult, I have before me, and herewith furnish you with your request: here are two new vessels building; one by Mr. Williams, East, the water register, about 60 tons, has been two years building, or thereabouts; the other is my own, and building the western side, is nearly finished, registers 125 tons, or thereabouts, and is *on speculation;* was laid down the 1st June, 1805.

N.B. Mr. Williams' is *contracted for.*

I am, Sir,

Your very humble Servant,

To Nat. Atcheson, Esq. &c. WM. LOWTHER.

DEAR SIR, Dartmouth, May 8, 1806.

IN reply to yours, for the information of the society, there are two vessels *now lying on hand*, *launched* some time since; say one about 150, the other 120, tons: one laid down about twelve months since by Mr. William Newman, about 140 tons, on speculation: a sloop, 60 tons, nearly finished, on contract: one laid down by Mr. Leathy, about two months since, on contract, 110 tons.

I remain, very sincerely,

Your humble Servant,

To Mr. John Sparke, London. R. HUTCHINGS.

DEAR SIR, Topsham, May 8, 1806.

IN reply to your favour, I beg to inform you there is *not* a merchant vessel *now* building, either by contract or speculation, in our port. At Teignmouth (about fourteen miles west), I believe two or three, about 100 or 130 tons each. At *Dartmouth*, I believe *none*, nor at *Plymouth*, only a small fishing sloop or two.

I am, at command,

Your most obedient, very humble Servant,

To Robert Curling, Esq. London. ROB. DAVY.

SIR, Yarmouth, May 9, 1806.

I WAS in due course favoured with your letter of the 5th instant, and on the other side I send you the number of ships and vessels building at this place. There are six men of war building here for government; three by Messrs. Stone and Custance, and three by Mr. John Preston, which I *have not noticed* in the statement.

Ship-builders at Yarmouth.	Vessels.	Tons.		
Mr. Jacob Preston	1	300	speculation	8 months.
Isaac Preston	2	120	do.	6
John Preston	2	100	do.	just laid down.
Nathaniel Palmer	2	80	do.	3 months.
Mess. Stone & Custance	1	120	do.	3 months.
Mr. Crone	1	80	do.	just laid down.

Mr. Chamberlain	1	80	speculation	3 months.
John L. Douglas	1	110	on contract	3 months.
Lovewell	none.			

I am, respectfully, Sir,

Your very obedient Servant,

To Nat. Atcheson, Esq. &c. SAM. PAGET, jun.

State of Ship-building at Teignmouth Within, and the Harbour of Teignmouth in the Port of Exeter.

Mr. John Stevens' yard—1 brig, 170 tons: 1 sloop, 60 tons; *contract;* laid down, brig 1805, sloop 1804.

Thomas Sutton's yard—1 frigate, 2 schooners, for *government account.*

John Heath's yard—1 frigate, for *government account.*

Do.—1 brig, 160 tons, on speculation; laid down 1804.

William Curtis's yard—1 do. 120 tons, on speculation; laid down 1806.

John Tucker's yard—none at present.

William Rundle's yard—1 ship, 170 tons, *on contract,* 1805, *just launched.*

To Nat. Atcheson, Esq. &c. JOHN SPARK.

SIR, Bideford, May 10, 1806.

YOUR letter of the 26th ultimo, directed to us at Barnstaple, came safe to hand, and we are sorry that it has not been in our power till now to forward you an accurate list of the vessels building within our bar. It will at all times give us pleasure to render our best assistance in all undertakings for the public good; and we beg that you will at all times freely command,

Sir,

Your most obedient humble Servants,

To Nat. Atcheson, Esq. &c. JOHN WILLCOCK and SON.

List of Ships inclosed in the above Letter.

	For Government Service.	Tons	Merchants Service and Coasting Trade.	Tons	Contract or Speculation.	When laid down.
Bideford -	1 Fire ship -	422	1 Sloop -	45	Contract	March, 1806
	1 Gun brig -	382	1 Brig - -	108	do.	Nov. 1805
	1 Sloop of-war	422	do. - -	83	do.	do.
	....	....	1 Sloop -	51	do.	Jan. 1806
	....	....	1 Brig - -	80	Speculation	Feb. 1805
	....	....	1 do. - -	140	Contract	do.
	....	....	1 do. - -	120	do.	March, 1806
Appledore -	1 Frigate - -	885	1 do. - -	160	do.	Sept. 1804
	....	....	1 Sloop -	24	Speculation	Jan. 1806
	....	....	1 do. - -	60	Contract.	May, 1805
	....	....	1 do. - -	70	do.	June, 1805
	....	....	1 do. - -	90	do.	Jan. 1806
Barnstaple -	....	....	1 Brig - -	130	do.	March, 1806
	1 Gun brig -	260	1 do. - -	85	do.	April, 1806
Cleavehouses	1 Frigate - -	520	1 Cutter -	30	Speculation	March, 1806
	1 do. - -	520	1 Sloop -	46	do.	April, 1806
	1 Sloop of war	422	....	....	....	....

DEAR SIR, Hull, May 11, 1806.

YOURS I duly received, and immediately waited on the ship-builders of this place; and on the other side you have the number of ships building, and already built, on speculation. The shipping interest of this port is *very much on the decline*—if any are either lost or taken, *the owners do not wish to replace them*, on account of every thing being so heavy on the shipping interest.—I have three ships, and if any thing should happen to any of them, *I will not replace them.*

Ship-builders, &c.

Mr. J. Shepherd has *two* on his own account, which have been advertised *six months* and upwards, and *cannot be sold.*—Mr. P. Atkinson has *several* from 105 to 215 tons; wishes to decline business, as from what ships he has built, they cannot be sold, there being no demand.—Hall and Richardson are now building *one for sale.*—R. Gleadow has *one* on the stocks *on speculation*, 275 tons.—Westerdale and Barnes one, twelvemonths on stocks, just sold to Liverpool, 265 tons.—Mr. Wm. Gibson is building *one for sale*, 268 tons.—

Mr. T. Stevenson, *just left* Paghill, not being able to get a contract. *Several small builders have declined business on account of no demand.*—One ship now, all timbered, at Grovehill, and has been two years on the stocks, and cannot be sold, 140 tons.—Mr. Foster, of Selby, one vessel just launched, 150 tons, for sale.—Mr. Smith, of Gainsbro', two for sale; I don't hear of any contract in this port, or up these rivers. Many more ships were built when shipping interest was flourishing.—*Ships building here for the merchant service are all on speculation, and no demand.*—Any further information that I can give, shall be happy in so doing; as amendment for the shipping interest is very much wanted.

I am, dear Sir,

Your humble Servant,

To Mr. John Sparke, London. MICH. ANDREWS.

SIR, Aberdeen, May 10, 1806.

YOUR favour of the 26th of April was received, and in answer to it, the ship-building trade, not only at this port, but at *Montrose, Peterhead,* and the *other neighbouring ports,* has very much decreased of late; so much so that, from the years 1798 to 1801, we had never less than from twelve to fifteen vessels *always on the stocks* at one time; and their tonnage from 80 to as large as 370 tons register; and they were *generally contracted for* as soon as they were begun to be built: whereas at present we have seldom more than from four to seven building at one time, and their tonnage from 80 to 160 tons register. The two last that were launched were not sold until several months after they were ready to launch, and then at very low prices; and, *were it not to keep the men employed* that the master ship-builders *require for old work,* we suppose the building trade could not be carried on at the present prices of timber and wages, contrasted with the price per ton when finished; this we can safely assert, as having a large connection in shipping ourselves, we are necessitated to keep a building yard for our own private use, *which we find very unproductive.*—If the committee want any other information in our power, we shall be happy to give it.

We are, with respect, Sir,

Your obedient humble Servants,

To Nat. Atcheson, Esq. ROB. GIBBON and SON.

DEAR SIR, Weymouth, May 13, 1806.

YOUR favour of 26th April would have had a more prompt answer, but I was unfortunately from home when it arrived, and did not return till Saturday last, since which I have made enquiry respecting vessels *now* building here, and find there are on the stocks,

One brig of 143 tons, laid down April 1803, nearly finished.

One sloop of 55 tons, laid down March 1805, about half ditto.

One ditto of 61 tons, laid down April 1805, nearly ditto.

One brig of 203 tons, laid down April 1805, about a quarter ditto.

All building on speculation.

If I can render the society of ship-owners, or yourself, any further service in this or any other respect, I shall be happy in so doing.

I am, Sir,

Your obedient Servant,

To Nat. Atcheson, Esq. &c. EDMUND HENNING.

Ships building at Whitby.

Whitby, May 12, 1806.

When laid down.	Ship-builders.	Ships.	Tons.
April 19, 1806	Mess. Fishburn and Broderick	1	about 400
24	do.	1	do. 140
May 9	do.	1	do. 300
Oct. 1804	Mess. Longburne	1	do. 120
	Mr. Thomas Barrick, not any building at present		
	A vessel laid in the dock, 123 tons.		
May 1805	Mr. John Barry	1	about 385
April 4, 1806	Mess. Holt and Richardson	1	do. 120
Dec. 1805	Mess. Iskdale and Co.	1	do. 211
April 19, 1806	do.	1	do. 190
	Ships	8	1866

All building on speculation.

(Signed) JOHN BARRY.

[T]

SIR, Arbroath, May 12, 1806.

I was favoured with yours of the 7th current: in answer to which, there are at this port only two small vessels building just now; the one is a sloop, upon contract, and was laid down about the 20th December last, measuring fifty-six tons, capenters' tonnage; and the other is a brig, upon speculation, which was laid down about the 15th Feb. last, and will measure about 138 tons.

I am, Sir,

Your most obedient Servant,

To Nat. Atcheson, Esq. &c. JOHN CHRISTIE.

DEAR SIR, Bo-Ness, May 12, 1806.

YOUR favours of the 7th instant came duly to hand, and observe the contents. I am building a ship by *contract* of about 330 tons register; she was laid down the 1st of March last: one of sixty-four tons register, laid down in the month of February: and my neighbour, Mr. Smart, is building one of thirty tons register, laid down last month.

I am, dear Sir,

Your most obedient Servant,

To Nat. Atcheson, Esq. &c. GEORGE HART.

SIR, Hull, May 17, 1806.

YOUR letter, addressed to me at Kingston port, under date of 7th of May instant, I have had sent me here, being the place of my residence. I have for the last four or five years persevered in building ships, vainly hoping that the value of shipping would grow better, first one year and then a second year, and so on until I found by experience, and to my very great loss, that my ships kept increasing in my hands, without being able to sell any; it being my plan to build the ships and to sell them: instead of which, I have now on my hands twelve ships from 120 to 610 tons register measurement; and, with the exception of three, which are in the employ of government, are *all doing nothing;* and I conceived it is more to my interest *to let them remain unemployed* than to employ them at the *current* freights, which

I know will sink more money; for I do not know any *one single employ* that a ship can pay her way: and as a proof of it, there are no buyers. My property in shipping is not less than 60,000*l.*; and if I wanted to raise one-sixtieth part of the money, *that property would not produce it*, unless it was sold for about half its cost: however, such is the very great depression, and although I can build ships at Kingston port cheaper than any man in Britain, having my people at the very moderate wages of 4*s.* 5*s.* 7*s.* and up to 8*s.* and 10*s.* per week, they finding themselves with meat and every other necessary, that I have resolved to give up building any more ships, and have offered to give up the indentures to all my apprentices, being eighteen in number, and none at higher wages than 8*s.* per week, being a set of as fine stout young fellows as are in Britain, few of them stand less than five feet ten inches high, rather than continue a business that yields no profit. I ought to mention to you that I have *no rent* to pay for all the ground I occupy to lay my timber upon, and where I build my ships; yet under all these favourable circumstances I now see it is prudent to give it up, and I have already ordered my builder there to take down all my sheds and other conveniences, and sell the materials for what they will fetch. I think a stronger proof cannot be given that ship-building, if you are to keep or employ them, is a bad trade. I beg leave to observe that I don't do this, that is, give up this once profitable trade, because I want money, but, on the contrary, because it is a *ruinous* trade. I have built six ships at my yard within the last four years, *all on speculation;* not one was contracted for; and only one since sold: the last of these vessels is now on the stocks; that as well as the other four remain in my hands. The six measured 1650 tons: one is 613 tons, two of 294 tons each, and two of about 130 tons, and one of 190 tons; also a sloop of 70 tons. If any further information is wanted from me I will readily communicate it. In this port not one vessel is building on contract, except two or three sloops of war.

I am, respectfully,

Your most obedient Servant,

To Nat. Atcheson, Esq. W. OSBOURNE.

SIR, Bridlington, May 19, 1806.

IN reply to your letter of the 13th instant, I have to say,

there is one vessel building here by Mr. Francis Ellis, the builder, admeasures about 175 tons, not contracted for. I should feel a pleasure at any time in rendering you any information on any subject of that kind.

Believe me, dear Sir,

Your obedient humble servant,

THOMAS LAMPLOUGH.

N. B. Suppose the above vessel may be ready for launching in six months, but that depends upon old work.

To Tho. Horncastle, Esq. &c. &c.

DEAR SIR, Hull, May 20, 1806.

YOUR favour of the 13th instant I received on Sunday, and that of the 17th in due course, with two copies of the state of the shipping interest, one of which I delivered to Mr. Andrew, agreeable to your desire. We went this morning to the different ship-yards at this place, and at foot you have the result of our enquiry, which hope will prove satisfactory to the committee, *to whom the ship-owners of Great Britain are much obliged for the trouble they have and are taking:* the ship-builders here complain very much of the stagnation in their business. I shall be glad to render the committee any service in my power, and remain,

Dear Sir,

Your obedient Servant,

WM. HORNCASTLE.

Peter Atkinson and Co. one ship, 215 tons, laid down three months since on speculation, nearly planked.

Ditto, 175 tons, launched about four months, and called the Trafalgar, now in London, for sale.

Ditto, lighter, 20 tons, launched six months, remains unsold.

Ditto, brig, 104 tons, launched one month, sold yesterday, and called the Mary.

William Gibson, one frigate, about 1050 tons, nearly framed.

Ditto, 268 tons, just laid down on speculation, to keep his men together for old work.

Robert Gleadow, one ship, 270 tons, laid down fourteen

months, on speculation, since sold, and will launch the beginning of June.

Hall and Richardson, one ship, 190 tons, laid down about a month, framed, and wales about.

Shepherd, a brig, 149 tons, launched eighteen months, was twelve months building, and remains on hand unsold.

Ditto, one ship, 210 tons, laid down last August, on speculation, and ready for launching, unsold.

Ditto, a market boat, 36 tons, contracted, one month laid down, timbered.

Westerdale and Barnes, one ship, 266 tons, laid down fifteen months since on speculation, and sold about a month ago, expect to launch this evening.

At Stockwith.

Walton, one ship, 190 tons, laid down eight months, on speculation, ready to launch.

Ditto, 220 tons, on speculation, wales about.

Titterton, one ship, 150 tons, laid down twelve months, speculation, planked.

Gainsborough.

Smith, one ship, 350 tons, three months, ditto, framed.

Paghill and Paul.

Stevenson, a frigate, in frame for seasoning.

At Thorne.

John Foster, two vessels, contracted for lately, but do not know the dimensions, or what state they are in.

To Tho. Horncastle, Esq.

SIR, Chester, May 20, 1806.

I RECEIVED yours of the 13th instant, and now send you, annexed, the number of vessels, with the tonnage, &c. that are building at this place.

I remain,

Your humble Servant,

JOHN TROUGHTON.

Messrs. Corson, Forbes, Cortney, and Co. have four vessels building, the whole register tonnage about 1500 tons, all none on contract; discharged several men—advertized the premises to let, but has had no offer to take it—he will also take no apprentices.

Mr. Shepherd launched a vessel of 149 tons, 18 months since, and has one of 210 tons ready, they have been advertized for sale many months; will be glad to sell for 150 and 200 each less than they cost to quit them; has no contract, nor has had any near these two years; made a contract for one of 360 about four months ago, but the party contracting with him threw up the contract, and would not build. These vessels are built for no other motive than to keep his apprentices and men employed; he means to discharge his men, and will take no apprentices.

Mr. Gibson is building a frigate for government, and has just laid down a vessel of 250 tons on the same speculation as the other; has not built a vessel these four years on contract—has not taken any apprentice for the last six months, and will not take an apprentice; he also must discharge some of his people.

Hall and Richardson have a vessel of 140 tons just laid down, building on the same principles as the rest, have no contract, nor have built more than one by contract for the last two years: they also must discharge some men, not having employment for them, and will take no apprentices.

Mr. Gleadow has a vessel of 270 tons nearly finished, was laid down for his own account; since sold at a loss, has no contract, nor expects any; he is careless what becomes of his people, as he has little or no employment for them.

Mr. Stevenson has a frigate for government, but has no other contract; and rather than build on his own account he has let his men go, and is now doing nothing, as the frigate is seasoning in her timbers by his agreement, so that a stroke of his hammer is not heard in his yard; in short, all the yards in this place look more like deserted villages than ship-yards.

N. B. Mr. Stevenson does not live here, but as he is building within four miles of this place, I thought it right to include his statement with the other six builders, whose yards are the only ones in Hull.

To Nat. Atcheson, Esq. &c.

SIR, Peterhead, May 20, 1806.

IN answer to your letter of the 7th instant, there are only at present two small sloops of 70 tons each building at this place, which are not contracted for: they have been on the stocks for three months.

I am, Sir,

Your most obedient Servant,

To Nat. Atcheson, Esq. &c. JAMES HUTCHISON.

SIR, Port Glasgow, May 25, 1806.

AT the request of captain George Brown of London, I beg leave to hand you prefixed, for the information of the committee of ship-owners for the port of London, a list of ships and vessels building at present in the river Clyde.

I am, Sir, respectfully,

Your most obedient Servant,

RICHARD BROWN.

List of Ships and Vessels building on the River Clyde, May 25, 1806.

	Tons
By John Scott and Sons, on contract, laid down in Jan. last for the West-India trade, two ships of 400 tons each - - - - - - -	800
By the same, on speculation, a vessel of 120 tons, for the coasting trade - - - - -	120
By Francis Morgan, on speculation, a vessel of 100 tons, for the coasting trade - - - - -	100
By Steel and Carsewell, on speculation, a vessel of 70 tons, for the coasting trade - - - -	70
By John Martin, on speculation, a vessel of 120 tons, for the coasting trade - - - - -	120
To Nat. Atcheson, Esq. &c. Tons -	1210

Liverpool, June, 1806.

ALL the ships building in Liverpool were begun on speculation, and are as follows:

[U]

By Humble and Co. begun March, 1804 - 390 tons, nearly finished.
By Bulawin and Co. March, 1805 - 267 tons, nearly finished.
By Smalshaw - Jan. 1806 - 260 tons, one-fourth built.
By J. P. Hind - 1803 - 165 tons, a brig ready for launching.
By J. and I. Fisher - Dec. 1805 - 160 tons, about one-fourth built.

SIR, Dundee, June 2, 1806.

AGREEABLE to the desire of Mr. George Syme of London, I have noted below the number of ships building at this port, with the other information you require.

And am, Sir,

Your most obedient humble Servant,

To Nat. Atcheson, Esq. &c. ALEX. BALFOUR.

Vessels on the Stocks at Dundee, June 3, 1806. -

1 Brig	-	105 tons register	for sale.
1 -	-	140	
1 -	-	170 - -	on contract.
3		415	

ABSTRACT.

An Account of the Number of Ships and Vessels of all Sizes which were building for the Merchants Service and Coasting Trade, at the *undermentioned* Ports in Great Britain, in April and May, 1806; and also, an Account of the Number of new Ships then on Sale.

Ports.	Building on Contract.		Building on Speculation.		Ships launched and on Sale.		Observations.
	Ships.	Tons.	Ships.	Tons.	No.	Tons.	
London - -	1	409	1	60	9‡	2596	‡ These ships were built at the out-ports, and sent to the Thames for sale. See also list of other ships on sale there, P. 130.
Wells, Norfolk -	1	140	......	......	......	......	
Chepstow - -	......	......	2	470	1	190	
Stockton - -	1	180	......	......	......	......	
Lynn - - -	1†	120	1	300	......	......	
Lancaster - -	3	223	3	1040	......	......	
Scarborough - -	......	......	6	1327	3	365	
Boston - -	......	......	2	170	......	......	
Bristol - -	2	900	2	735	......	......	† It is not certain whether this ship is on contract or not.
Leith - - -	1	70	3	665	......	......	
Newcastle, North and South Shields	3	600	16	3755	2	508	
Sunderland - -	4	527	21	2776	......	......	
Kirkaldie - -	1	130	2	200	......	......	
Portsmouth and other places within the Isle of Wight -	......	......	......	......	......	......	
Harwich - -	......	......	......	......	......	......	
Whitehaven - -	1	400	2	300	......	......	
Blyth - - -	1	122	3	476	2	462	
Bridgewater - -	1	60	1	125	......	......	
Dartmouth - -	2	170	1	140	2	270	
Topsham - -	......	......	......	......	......	......	
Yarmouth - -	1	110	10	880	......	......	
Teignmouth - -	2	230	2	280	......	......	
Port of Barnstaple, viz.							
Bideford - -	6	547	1	80	......	......	
Appledore - -	4	330	1	24	......	......	
Cleaverhouses -	......	......	2	76	......	......	* See letter from Boroughstonness; by which it is presumed these small vessels are building on speculation.
Barnstaple - -	2	215	......	......	......	......	
Weymouth - -	......	......	4	462	......	......	
Whitby - -	......	......	8	1866	......	......	
Boroughstonness -	1	330	2*	94	......	......	
Arbroath - -	1	56	1	158	......	......	
Bridlington - -	......	......	1	175	......	......	
Hull, including Gainsborough and other places adjoining	3	572	8	1793	3	334	*Vide* the three letters from Hull.
Chester - -	4	1500	2	460	......	......	
Poole - - -	......	......	3	433	......	......	
Peterhead - -	......	......	2	140	......	......	
Port Glasgow -	2	800	4	410	......	......	
Dundee - -	1	170	2	245	......	......	
Liverpool - -	......	......	5	1242	......	......	
Totals - - -	50	8961	124	21,337	22	4725	

N. B. No returns have been as yet received from Maryport, Bridport, and Berwick, and some minor ports; but it is understood there are very few ships or vessels building there, and those principally small ones, and on speculation.

At a meeting of the committee of ship-owners for the port of London, held at Wills' Coffee-house, 6th of May, 1806:

Mr. BARNES in the Chair:

Resolved, THAT a letter be written by the secretary to the lords of trade, on the subject of opening the blockade of the Elbe and Weser to neutral ships, and to entreat their lordships to adopt the same regulation which prevailed during the former blockade of those rivers.

(Signed) T. BARNES, Chairman.

Letter addressed to the Board of Trade agreeably to the preceding Resolution.

MY LORDS, Austin Friars, May 6, 1806.

I AM instructed by the committee of ship-owners for the port of London, to state to your lordships the deep regret they feel from an apprehension which is entertained that it is in your lordships contemplation to permit the navigation of the rivers Elbe and Weser from this country to be open to *neutral* vessels only, for the accommodation of the export merchants, or rather the foreign consumer, but which will operate to the manifest injury of the British shipping interest. They humbly presume to state to your lordships, that in the *late* blockade of those rivers, other adjacent ports *were open*, by which the manufactures of this country, and the produce of the East and West Indies, found their way into the interior. The *British* ship-owners had then an equal chance with the *neutral*; and although the former had even then cause to lament the preference shewn to the latter, in direct prejudice to their own interest, still they did not complain, as their ships were employed, *in part*, of the carrying trade to that part of the continent. The committee flatter themselves your lordships will not consider it indecorous in them to express their fears of the serious consequences which must arise, should the application made to your lordships on this occasion be admitted and countenanced; for it will not only raise the neutral flag, but will materially injure the shipping interest of Great Britain, which, at present, requires all the care and protection which your lordships can bestow upon it.

The committee are well assured that the *British* merchants

would *not* press a matter so injurious to any set of individuals, especially the shipping interest, if they were truly apprised of its ultimate tendency and effect. For although it may be thought that few British ships are employed in the trade alluded to, yet when the number is considered, not only from this port, but also from Liverpool, Bristol, Hull, Newcastle, and Leith, it will be found to give not only employment to the vessels built expressly for that trade, but it also enables the vessels in the Baltic trade to bring home naval stores at much less expence to the country than they could possibly afford,. had they not had the advantages of freight to Tonning or Varel in their passage to the Baltic.

The committee are well convinced of the absolute necessity of keeping up a communication with the continent for the exportation of the produce and manufactures of this country, and most assuredly would not have complained of the *partial* passing by *neutrals* of the present blockade, had *no other means* been left for that purpose; but convinced that a *similar* medium might be adopted on this as on a *former* occasion, and which gave satisfaction to all parties, they cannot refrain from submitting it to your lordships consideration, namely, to permit the passage of goods over the Watten in small craft from Tonning into the Elbe, and from the Jade into the Weser, and which, if now sanctioned, and its protection is insured to this country by your lordships, will, they presume, answer every reasonable wish, and remove the difficulties which may now appear, whilst it gives relief to the foreign exporter, and will not so much injure the British ship-owner. Under all these circumstances, the committee most earnestly intreat your lordships *not* to sanction a measure which will militate so materially against the shipping interest of the country; and they wait your lordships decision with a firm reliance on your lordships patriotism and justice, which they are thoroughly convinced will be paramount to every partial consideration.

I am,

My Lords,

&c. &c. &c.

NAT. ATCHESON, Sec.

To the right hon. the lords of the committee of his majesty's privy council for the affairs of trade and foreign plantations.

Office of Committee of Privy Council for Trade,
SIR, Whitehall, May 13, 1806.

HAVING laid before the lords of the committee of council for trade and foreign plantations your letter, received the 8th instant, stating the great injury which will result to the interests of the British ship-owners if the Elbe and Weser are opened to *neutral* ships, and *not* to those of Great Britain, &c. I am directed by their lordships to desire you will assure the *society of ship-owners* of Great Britain that *their interests* will, at all times, be as much attended to as the *general commercial* interests of the kingdom will permit *.

I am, Sir,
Your most obedient
Humble Servant,
To Nat. Atcheson, Esq. (Signed) W. FAWKENER.

At a meeting of the committee of ship-owners for the port of London, held this 19th day of June, 1806:

ROBERT CURLING, Esq. in the Chair:

Resolved unanimously, THAT the thanks of this meeting be given to the fifty-six members of parliament who have expressed their opinion of the necessity of maintaining and supporting the principles of the navigation system of Great Britain.

Resolved unanimously, That it is the opinion of this committee that no necessity whatever exists to justify the American Intercourse Bill, in support of which no evidence has been adduced; and that the shipping of Great Britain and Ireland is more than sufficient to insure, at all times, both in peace and in war, when properly protected, the carriage of a regular and constant supply of provision and lumber to the British West Indies, from whatever country it may be purchased; and, consequently, there is no occasion to yield to America, or any other neutral nation, that lucrative branch of trade which would annually, in the article of freight only, realise to the shipping interest of Great Britain, and of her settlements in America and the West Indies, upwards of 300,000*l.*

* See Yorke's Political Review, vol. i. col. 413, for observations on the *partial* opening of this blockade.

Resolved unanimously, That the adoption of this bill at the present moment is highly objectionable and impolitic, as it cannot fail to encourage claims on the part of America to allow a free intercourse between the United States and the king's dominions in the West Indies, *which was declared by his majesty's privy council* in 1791 to be inadmissible, *even as a subject of negotiation*, and which will likewise tend to expel from that part of the colonial trade, which is left for British shipping, a greater number of them, which will increase the accumulated distress already felt by the owners of British ships in the European trade, from neutrals being allowed to break the blockade of the Prussian and other ports, in consequence of which many British ships usually employed therein are now actually in the want of employment.

Resolved unanimously, That it is the opinion of this committee, that in consequence of the suspensions of the Act of Navigation, there is not at present building throughout the empire a sufficient number of *new* ships to meet the annual decrease and consumption of shipping; for whilst such temporary and fluctuating systems of suspending the Act of Navigation are adhered to, the great body of British ship-owners will not extend their capitals in shipping, as no certain or adequate protection and encouragement is afforded them.

Resolved unanimously, That it is the opinion of this committee that it is now more than ever important that the exertions which were begun by this committee in 1801, and continued in the years 1802 and 1803, to obtain attention to the interests of British shipping, should be renewed with increased activity, *as the good effect of the measures adopted in Mr. Pitt's last administration in* 1804, for gradually regaining the inestimable advantage this country must at all times derive from the Navigation Act when enforced, began to be manifested; and if those measures had been followed up, with others dictated by wisdom, which there is good reason to believe was intended, the carrying trade between America and the West Indies would soon have been restored to British ship-owners.

Resolved unanimously, That the principle of this bill unequivocally evinces an intention of an abandonment of a fundamental law of Europe, universally acknowledged and acted upon, and of the colonial system of Great Britain, as established by the Act of Navigation, and a total dereliction of those principles which our ancestors cherished for the maintenance of the maritime power of the nation, and by which the British navy has attained that superiority which is so essentially necessary, at this time, to preserve the independence of the empire.

Resolved unanimously, That it is the opinion of this committee that the ship-owners of Great Britain and Ireland ought not to relax in their endeavours to obtain, through the medium of their representatives in parliament, the future, full, effective, and beneficial operation of the Act of Navigation, by which means only we can "rear and retain our seamen, the grand support of our present pre-eminence, and preserve our country from falling below the level of surrounding nations," but which never can be done if a discretionary power is lodged with the privy council to suspend its operation at their discretion.

Resolved unanimously, That these resolutions be printed in the Morning and Evening Newspapers, and distributed in all the out-ports.

Resolved unanimously, That the thanks of this committee be given to the chairman for his indefatigable and unwearied exertions to support the shipping interest of the country, and thereby promoting the landed and manufacturing interests of the empire.

(Signed) R. Curling, Chairman.

At a meeting of the committee of ship-owners for the port of London, held this 31st day of July, 1806:

Ralph Keddey, Esq. in the Chair:

Resolved unanimously, That the thanks of this meeting be given to the right hon. John Lord Sheffield, for the eminent services rendered by him to the shipping interest of the united kingdom, and for his zealous exertions on all occasions to maintain, unimpaired, the maritime strength of Great Britain.

Resolved unanimously, That the thanks of this meeting be given to the other peers of parliament, who have expressed their opinion of the necessity of supporting, inviolably, the principles of the navigation system of Great Britain.

Resolved unanimously, That the thanks of this meeting be given to Sir Charles Price, Bart. Sir William Curtis, Bart. and to Mr. G. B. Mainwaring, for their steady and manly opposition to a bill likely, in the opinion of a respectable meeting of persons concerned in the building, fitting, and owning ships in this metropolis, to be seriously injurious to their interests, as well as to the general interest of the country.

Resolved unanimously, That the thanks of this meeting be given to the right hon. George Rose, the right hon. Sir William Grant, the right hon. Sir William Scott, Lord Castlereagh, the right hon. George Canning, the hon. Spencer Perceval, Mr. Staniforth, and the several other *members of the House of Commons, who have expressed their decided opinion, formed on the fullest and coolest reflection, against any further departure from the navigation and colonial system of Great Britain (relaxed partially and temporarily in the late war, for reasons, whether justifiable or otherwise, not necessary to be entered on), but which system the experience of the *late* government had induced them to adopt measures *for completely restoring*, and which, in part, had been effected.

Resolved unanimously, That a petition be presented to parliament early in the next session, for the repeal of the West-India and American Intercourse Act recently passed; this meeting being convinced of the highly injurious ten-

* The following are the names of the other Members of the House of Commons who voted against the American Intercourse Bill, and in support of the Navigation Act, referred to in this resolution, viz. Lord Charles Manners, Lord Robert Manners, Lord Edward Somerset, Lord Charles Somerset, Lord Arthur Somerset, Lord De Blaquiere, Lord Rendlesham, Lord Lovaine, Lord Garlies, General Phipps, Mr. Chute, Sir Henry Mildmay, the Right Honourable John Foster, the Honourable Henry Lascelles, Colonel Sibthorpe, Mr. Bankes, the Honourable Rich. Ryder, Sir Robert Buxton, Sir Robert Preston, Sir A. S. Hammond, Sir V. Gibbs, Mr. Spencer Stanhope, Sir J. D. King, Mr. M'Naghton, Mr. Charles Long, Mr. Samuel Smith, Mr. George Smith, Mr. Huskisson, Mr. Fellowes (Huntingdon), Mr. G. H. Rose, Mr. Rutherford, Mr. Bagwell, Mr. Wm. Bagwell, Mr. Baker (Hertford), Mr. Barne, Mr. Bootle, Mr. Ashley, Mr. Fitzhugh, Mr. Steele, Mr. Wallace, Mr. Leycester, Mr. Dent, Mr. Hammett, Mr. Brodrick, the Honourable W. Wellesley Pole, the Hon. R. S. Dundas, Mr. W. Dundas, Mr. Holt Leigh, Mr. Claude Scott, Mr. Samuel Scott, Mr. Holford, Mr. Thoroton (Grantham), Mr. S. Bourne, Mr. G. Johnstone, Mr. Ainslie, and Mr. Longfield.

dency thereof to the general interest of the country, as well as to that of the ship-owners: it having been established beyond all possibility of doubt, that the islands in the West Indies are inundated with the produce and manufactures of the East Indies and of other countries by the Americans, to the prejudice of British merchants and manufacturers.

Resolved unanimously, That it is the opinion of this committee, that the merchants, ship-owners, and manufacturers of Great Britain and Ireland ought not to relax in their endeavours to obtain a full and effectual operation of the navigation and colonial system of the country, by securing the freight to the colonies to British ships exclusively, and the monopoly of supplies of manufactures of all sorts to the Mother Country, which it appears to this meeting can be best done by dutiful and respectful applications to parliament, and by the persons who are interested availing themselves of the earliest and best opportunities of awakening the attention of the *representatives of the sea ports and manufacturing counties* to the true and most important interests of their constituents; and also, by the attention of those who may be desirous of becoming representatives of such places being called to the same object.

Resolved unanimously, That the thanks of this meeting be given to the sub-committee, who were appointed to superintend the application to parliament, during the late session, against the American Intercourse bill, for their uniform attendance and perseverance in pursuing the measures previously adopted by this committee, to give effect to the maritime interest of this country.

Resolved, That the preceding resolutions be inserted in the Morning and Evening Newspapers, and transmitted to the out-ports, and to the principal manufacturing towns in Lancashire, Yorkshire, Cheshire, Staffordshire, Warwickshire; to Edinburgh and Glasgow; and to Dublin, Cork, Waterford, Limerick, and Belfast.

Resolved unanimously, That the thanks of this meeting be given to the chairman, for his great attention to the shipping interest.

(Signed) RALPH KEDDEY, Chairman.

At a Meeting of the Committee of Ship-owners for the Port of London, held this 23d day of October, 1806:

RALPH KEDDEY, Esq. in the Chair:

RESOLVED unanimously, That it is the opinion of this committee, that the ship-owners of Great Britain and Ireland ought, at the present crisis, to express unequivocally their grateful sense of the patriotic conduct of those peers and members of the legislature who publicly declared, during the last session of parliament, their opinion of the impolicy of relaxing the maritime principles of the country, and the absolute necessity of maintaining inviolably in future the navigation and colonial system of Great Britain.

Resolved unanimously, That the thanks of this committee be given to Sir Charles Price, Baronet, for his constant and unremitted attention to the interests of British ship-owners, for his uniform support of the maritime principles of the nation, and for his manly and independent opposition, in the last session of parliament, to a bill, which this committee are still convinced will prove highly injurious to the general interests of the Empire.

Resolved unanimously, That the thanks of this committee be given to Sir William Curtis, Baronet, for his attention and readiness to support the petition presented by them last session against the American Intercourse Bill, and for the manly and spirited sentiments expressed by him on that occasion.

Resolved unanimously, That it is the opinion of this committee, that, unless the navigation and colonial system of Great Britain be strictly adhered to in future, the most ruinous consequences will result to the country; the committee, therefore, trust, that an early investigation will take place in parliament on that important subject, in order to ascertain the actual state of the shipping and navigation of the Empire—the present state of the loyal British colonies in America—and the great increase of foreign shipping employed in the trade of this country and its dependencies; so that the public may no longer be deluded with speculative theories in political economy, which cannot be supported by the test of experience and truth.

Resolved unanimously, That these resolutions, and those which were entered into by this committee on the 31st day of July last, be inserted in the Newspapers; and which, at this critical and important juncture, are most earnestly recommended to the serious attention and consideration of the public.

Resolved unanimously, That the thanks of this committee be given to the chairman, for his attention and judicious conduct on this occasion.

(Signed) Ralph Keddey.

No. VII.

Rates of Freight of Sugar and Rum from 1780 to 1806, both inclusive, in the Trade from the British West Indies to Great Britain.

	Jamaica.						Leeward Islands.					
Years.	Sugar.			Rum.			Sugar.			Rum.		
	l.	s.	d.	l.	s.	d.	l.	s.	d.	l.	s.	d.
1780	0	8	0	0	0	9	0	7	0	0	0	9
1	0	8	0	0	0	9	0	7	0	0	0	9
2	0	8	0	0	0	9	0	7	0	0	0	9
3	0	8	0	0	0	9	0	7	0	0	0	9
4	0	4	0	0	0	6	0	3	6	0	0	6
5	0	4	0	0	0	6	0	3	6	0	0	6
6	0	4	0	0	0	6	0	3	6	0	0	6
7	0	4	0	0	0	4	0	3	6	0	0	4
8	0	4	0	0	0	6	0	3	6	0	0	6
9	0	4	0	0	0	6	0	3	6	0	0	6
1790	0	4	0	0	0	6	0	3	6	0	0	6
1	0	4	0	0	0	6	0	3	6	0	0	6
2	0	4	0	0	0	6	0	3	6	0	0	6
3	0	5	6	0	0	8	0	5	0	0	0	6
4	0	8	0	0	1	0	0	7	0	0	0	10
5	0	9	0	0	1	0	0	8	0	0	0	10
6	0	9	0	0	1	0	0	8	0	0	0	10
7	0	9	0	0	1	0	0	8	0	0	0	10
8	0	9	0	0	1	0	0	8	0	0	0	10
9	0	10	0	0	1	0	0	9	0	0	0	10
1800	0	10	0	0	1	0	0	9	0	0	0	10
1	0	10	0	0	1	0	0	9	0	0	0	10
2	0	6	0	0	0	8	0	5	0	0	0	6
3	0	5	0	0	0	6	0	4	0	0	0	6
4	0	9	0	0	0	10	0	8	0	0	0	8
5	0	9	0	0	1	0	0	8	0	0	0	10
6	0	9	6	0	1	0	0	8	6	0	0	10

(Signed) John Blacket.

No. VIII.

Rates of Freight from 1782 to 1806, both inclusive, in the Baltic Trade.

Years	Petersburgh, &c. to London. Hemp & Flax.	Petersburgh, &c. to London. Tallow.	Petersburgh, &c. to London. Deals.	Timber from Riga to London.	Timber from Memel to London.
	per Ton.	per Ton.	per Hund.	per Load.	per Load.
	s. s.	s. s.	s. s.	s. s.	s. s. d.
1782	85 to 105	75	120 to 160	48 to 60	43 to 52 6
1783	35 to 45	28	80	24	19
1784	32 6d.	25	50	20	16
1785	do.	do.	do.	18	15
1786	do.	do.	do.	do.	do.
1787	do.	do.	do.	do.	do.
1788	do.	do.	do.	do.	do.
1789	do.	do.	do.	do.	do.
1790	do.	do.	do.	do.	do.
1791	do.	do.	do.	do.	do.
1792	do.	do.	50 to 60	do.	15 to 16
1793	65	42 6d. to 45	90	32 6d.	25 to 32 6d.
1794	do.	45	do.	do.	do.
1795	80	30	120	36	32 6d. to 36
1796	80 to 85	60	125	40	30 to 35
1797	60	40	70	25	21
1798	60 to 75	40 to 50	80 to 95	25 to 45	20 to 35
1799	90 to 125	60 to 82 6d.	160	50	44
1800	100	60	155	55	43
1801	90	55	140	40	35
1802	45 to 50	30 to 35	67 6d.	24	19
1803	90 to 100	50 to 55	125 to 130	35 to 60	30 to 45
1804	75	50	105	40	33
1805	75.	50	115	40	33
1806	85	55	110 to 120	38	30 6d.

(Signed) JOHN AKENHEAD.

No. IX.

Rates of Freight from 1780 to 1806, both inclusive, in the Trade between Great Britain and Portugal.

	Lisbon.		Oporto.	
Years.	Out.	Home.	Out.	Home.
	War. *l. s. d.*	*l. s. d.*	*l. s. d.*	
1780, 1, 2, 3	2 5 0	4 10 0	1 13 9	£ 5 per Ton.
4, 5, 1790, 1, 2	Peace. 1 2 6	2 10 0	1 2 6	£ 2 per Ton.
3, 4, 5	War. 2 5 0	4 10 0	1 13 9	£ 5 per Ton.
1800, 1	2 5 0	5 0 0	1 13 9	£ 6 & 7 per Ton.
2	Peace. 1 10 0	2 10 0	1 13 9	£ 3 to June 1803.
3	War. 1 10 0	2 10 0	3 0 0	£ 6
4	2 10 0	5 0 0	3 0 0	£ 6
5	2 10 0	4 10 0	2 0 0	£ 5
6	2 10 0	4 10 0 and 4 0 0	2 0 0	£ 5 per Ton.

(Signed) John R. Sherman.

No. X.

WEST-INDIA TRADE.

Cost and Charges of a new British-built Ship, called the Ann, of London, 236 Tons (Register), together with Expences and Loss to her Owners, on two Voyages from London to Jamaica and back to London in 1803 and 1804.

	Dr.	£	s.	d.		Cr.	£	s.	d.
1803	To cost of the ship, with masts, yards, &c. £4864 3 7				1803	By amount of the ship's freight from London to Jamaica	£1077	7	5
	Cost of outfit and expences for the first voyage	£3339	10	10		Ditto, from Jamaica to London	2663	13	1
	Premium of insurance on ship and freight out and home	834	19	9		Loss to the owners	1149	5	10
	One year's interest on £4864 3 7 at £5 per cent.	243	4	0					
	Commission of £ 2½ per cent on £ 3339 10 10	83	9	9					
	Depreciation on ship and stores for one voyage, say £8 per cent. on £ 4864 3 7	389	2	0					
		£4890	6	4		N. B. The ship was fully loaded this voyage out and home.	£4890	6	4

THE SECOND VOYAGE.

	Dr.	£	s.	d.		Cr.	£	s.	d.
1804	To outfit and expences for the 2d voyage	£2856	8	6	1804	By amount of freight from London to Jamaica	£423	19	8
	Premium of insurance for ditto	700	0	0		Amount of freight from Jamaica to London	2879	13	9
	One year's interest on £ 4864 3 7 at £ 5 per cent.	243	4	0		Loss to the owners	956	9	4
	Commission of £ 2½ per cent. on £ 2856 8 6	71	8	0					
	Depreciation on ship and stores	389	2	0					
		£4260	2	6		N.B. The ship was about half loaded out, and fully loaded home.	£4260	2	6

	£	s.	d.
Loss on the first voyage	1149	5	10
Ditto second	956	9	4
Total loss	£2105	15	2

Cost and Charges of a British-built Ship, the Sir Edward Hamilton, of London, 500 Tons (Register), together with Expences and Loss to her Owners, on two Voyages from London to Jamaica and back to London in 1804 and 1805.

FIRST VOYAGE.

Dr.

		£	s.	d.
1804	To first cost, outfit, and expences, clear to sea, after deducting outward-bound freight.... .... £10,524 17 7			
	Disbursements for this voyage..............	£4377	15	2
	Premium of insurance on ship out and home..	1431	12	0
	One year's interest on £10,524 17 7 at £5 per cent..........................	526	4	9
	Premium of insurance on freight home, to cover expences in Jamaica	148	15	6
	Commission of £2½ per cent. on £6535 6 2 freight..........................	165	17	6
	Depreciation on ship and stores for one voyage, say £8 per cent. on £10,524 17 7	841	19	6
		£7487	4	5

Cr.

		£	s.	d.
1804	By amount of ship's freight from Jamaica to London	£5800	18	8
	By ditto, from London to Jamaica	734	7	6
	Loss to the owners........................	951	18	3
		£7487	4	5

N. B. This ship had only made one voyage to India *before* 1804, when she was purchased by her present owners.

"Mr. Anderson's compliments to Mr. Barnes, and upon "reference to the accounts of the ship Sir Edward Hamilton, "finds that the first cost, outfit, and disbursements of her from "Gravesend, amounted to £18,162 4 11, independent of "the insurance out and home, and the expences during the "voyage. Old Pay Office, 21 May, 1806."

[Y]

THE

THE SECOND VOYAGE.

Dr.

		£	s.	d.
1805	To outfit and expences for the voyage	£ 4720	2	6
	Premium of insurance on ship out and home, on the depreciated value, say, £9682 18 1..	1180	9	9
	Do. do. Freight home to cover expences in Jamaica, £ 2000........	143	15	6
	One year's interest on £ 9682 18 1, at £ 5 per cent..........................	484	2	9
	Commission of £ 2½ per cent. on £ 6261 15 6 freight............................	156	10	0
	Depreciation on ship and stores for one voyage; say, £ 8 per cent. on £ 9682 18 1........	774	12	3
		£7459	12	9

N. B. The depreciation in the value of this ship, the insurance and interest might fairly be charged in this instance on the original cost of £ 10,524 17 7, instead of £9682 18 1. —Vouchers are ready to be produced to substantiate the above accounts.

26 May, 1806.

Cr.

		£	s.	d.
1805	By amount of freight from Jamaica to London	£5701	14	3
	Do. do. London to Jamaica..........	560	1	3
	Loss to the owners..........................	1197	17	3
		£ 7459	12	9

	£	s.	d.
Loss on the first voyage....	951	18	3
Ditto, second	1197	17	3
Total loss	£ 2049	15	6

No. XI.

TRADE TO ST.

A Statement of the Loss incurred by the Employment of the Shi]
between April, 1802, and

Dr. The Owners of the Ship Nelson, in Account Current wit

1802.		l.	s.	d.	Voyage.	l.	s.	d.	18
April 30.	Amount postages, &c.				1	0	6	10	Mar
	Balance due at this date to the owners				1	77	19	5	
						78	6	3	
Aug. 20.	Cash paid, Thoyts and Co.				1	536	14	1	Apri
Oct. 19.	Stanley, provisions				1	174	15	0	Nov.
Jan. 15.	Fletcher and son, shipwrights				1	448	17	0	
March 26.	S. Reed, rope-maker				1	105	8	2	
April 5.	J. Morrison, sail cloth				1	22	4	7	Dec.
9.	Capt. Lennon, for disbursements outwards; viz. London	86	14	10					
	Downs	19	4	9					
	Torbay	7	9	9					
	Madeira	30	5	5					
	St. Kitts	87	6	10					
					1	231	1	7	18
	His disbursements homewards, viz.								
	Expences of discharge and negro hire	145	13	0					Jan.
	in London river	50	14	11					Feb.
	Portledge bill	388	10	8					
	Cabin allowance	30	0	0					
	Island pay and horse hire	28	7	0					
	Primage out	17	12	0					
	Do. home	14	2	0					
	Privilege	37	3	0					Marc
	This sum paid J. Blackett	31	10	0					April
					1	743	12	7	
	John Blackett's account, outwards:								
	Register	3	10	6					

Dr. The Owners ofANDERDON, and BOSANQUET. Cr.

		Voyage.	l.	s.	d.
1803.					
May 1.	To balance due, Marceived from Brickwood and Co.	2	65	9	5
	date............den......................	2	28	0	6
July 5.	Cash paid, Davison, his Dawson................	2	13	9	2
23.	Lennon's bill to Wm. and Co......................	2	45	14	0
26.	Paid Lyon and Co...ner......................	2	27	6	4
Aug. 29.	Paid Spraggon for ha and Co. homeward bound....	2	1024	4	3
Sept. 6.	Port charges at and Co. outward bound......	3	583	3	9
28.	Stanley, for pro and Co......................	2	104	1	0
Nov. 18.	Paid Blackett on accMann......................	2	43	17	0
Dec. 12.	Pickering and and Co......................	2	9	0	0
	voyage.....ft.........................	2	75	17	0
	Smith, primage est-India Dock Company......	2	54	10	1
1804.	freight...... wine, C L and D G..........	2	6	7	2
Jan. 18.	Marman, butcher .. non for, as follows:				
	Blackett's acceptance bill to Wallace from				
Feb. 4.	Do. for apprentices w................ 77 1 0				
10.	Do. paid Taylor, cotly for wages...... 9 3 4				
March 7.	Blackett, butcher's bine received in Saint				
17.	His acceptance of S................ 18 12 11				
April 30.	JohnBlackett, for sundes out............ 71 11 3				
	ments, viz. enter s shipped by himself 28 5 9				
	duty, fees, &c..... puncheons sold in				
	Assistance from Do................. 31 7 0				
	pilotage, 8l. 8s....	2	231	1	3
	Hire 3 men from Grato Manning and Co. at this date		560	11	3
	reporting, 3l.....				
	James Solly, wages,				
	Thomas Jerry, pilo				
	Dock rate, 114l. 17s.				
	and dues, 44l. 19s.				
	Lights				
	Paid Ship Bellona, fo				
	Deduct 60 fathoms c				
	Ditto for amount of				
	bills as follow				
	A. Hooper, sail-mak				
	John Forrest, mast-m				
	Thomas Davidson, b				
	Wm. Forrest, chandl				
	Thomas Reuilby, iro				
	James Herbert, coope				
	S. Reed, rope-maker				
	R. S. Stanley, baker.				
	J. Karnock, painter.				
	R. Lewis, ironmonge				
	A. Morrison, sail-ma				
	H. Taylor, rope-mak				
	R. Whales, blacksmis				
	Fletcher and Son...				
	Commission on recei				
	at 2 per cent....				
	Charges, coffee-ho				
	king's weighers,				
	John Lennon for dis				
	London, outwar				
	Downs and Lyming				
	Madeira........				

No. XI.—Co[iii]

Dr. The Owners of the Ship NELSON, in Account Current Cr.

Date		Voyage.	*l.*	*s.*	*d.*
1804.					
April 30.	To balance due Manning and Co. brought forward	3	560	11	3
June 15.	Cash paid Blackett's order to Lyon for beer	3	16	16	0
July 5.	Paid Stanley provisions	3	149	11	8
Aug. 18.	Paid Blackett on account	3	300	0	0
Aug. 29.	Paid Blackett on account	3	200	0	6
Sept. 13.	Paid Blackett's acceptance to Smith	3	157	17	10
18.	Paid Blackett	3	200	0	0
Nov. 13.	Paid do. on account balance last year	3	400	0	0
1805.					
Jan. 5.	Paid do. for survey on shore	3	2	2	0
16.	Paid do. for provisions	3	134	5	7
26.	Paid do. balance of his account. Blackett's account against the ship, including tradesmen's bill, third voyage 1647 5 11; Received by him at sundry times 1100 0 0; 547 5 11	3	447	5	11
29.	Paid do.	3	100	0	0
April 3.	Paid Granger for lighterage	3	16	2	0
March 30.	Paid Lennon's order to Forrest for battering tops	3	5	14	0
	John Blackett, for amount Smith's primage	3	15	1	0
1806.	Charges, portage, stamps, &c.	3	2	8	9
March 24.	Perry and Co. carpenter's bill, repairing damage, in August, 1804	3	21	6	0

Statement of Loss on a Vo|itish Ship of 329 Tons, Register

Dr. | Cr.

		l.	s.	d.
	London charge / f Freight and Port Charge, viz.			
April 1.	Agreement, seaman 17s. 6d.; / t charge	17	5	6
	house, clearing in ballast, 5l / oak plank at 37s.	162	12	3
	190 Tons of ballast 6l. 5s. hea / deals, 36s.	357	16	9
	Crimpage for carpenter, co / timber, 35s.	155	17	0
	3l. 3s. each / d, 4 feet, 6 feet,	8	16	0
	Wages and / s, 10s.	13	0	0
	To 3½ months' wages, at 74 /	5	0	0
	Statement, No. I.)			
	To provisions for 14 peop			
	per do. man per day			
	Dantzick			
	One third port charges and l			
	Sundry small charges for ball			
	Sound C			
	Sound charges up, 3l. 11s. 7d			
	Pilot up and down, 3l. shore,			
	London,			
	Pilot, 3l. 3s. boats, assistance,			
	Reporting*, 1l. 5s. tonnage a			
	38l. 12s.			
	Lights, 8l. 1s. 6d. clearing, fe			
	Delivering cargo, 24l. measu			
	Charter and stamp, 2l. 2s.			
	6s. 6d. at 2 per cent. 14l.			
	Wear and tear on this voy			
	lation, to supply the ship w			
	the hull in repair			
	Insurance on 4500l. the valu			
	ment, No. II.)	722	6	
	nce, loss on this voyage	174	7	
	To loss on th	896	13	

No. I. above | above referred to.

Insurance.

1805.	Monthly Statement of W	l.	s.	d.
	Master per month / l value of the ship at Lloyd's 8l. 8s. per	378	0	0
	Mate, do.			
	Carpenters, do. / t. policy 5l.	9	0	0
	Cook, do.			
	Downs and Lyming			
	Madeira			

No. XIII.—BA

A Statement of the Expences of a Ship of 300 Tons on a Vo
Average of *three Months* to comp

Dr.

1806.	*l.*	*s.*	*d.*
To wages for 14 people for 3 months, at 67*l.* 7*s.* 6*d.* per month. (See Statement, No. I.)	202	2	6
Wages for ditto, the same time, at 1*s.* 6*d.* per man, per diem,	96	0	6
Wear and tear on this voyage for the support of hull, rigging, and materials, supposing her to make three voyages annually, which is seldom effected, at 12*l.* per cent. per annum,	120	0	0
Port charges and expences at Dantzic and the Sound. (See No. II.)	66	9	0
Custom-house and port charges, duties, delivery, &c. at London, out and in. (See No. III.)	100	14	7
Insurance for this voyage on 3000*l.* the estimated value at 8 guineas per cent., with 4*l.* per cent. returns for convoy. See No. IV.	139	15	0
	725	11	7
To loss on this voyage,	78	11	7

N. B. It must be evident to every man conversant with shipping, that many
general head, and yet on such a voyage would amount to 30*l.* or 40*l.* at a moder

	l.	s.	d.
1804, January.			
To first cost..	348	17	0
Outfit, viz.	812	10	8
To Farmer, joiner	232	0	0
Elstob, shipwright	287	18	1
Hopkins, carver			
Burn, sail-maker			
Brett, plumber			
Oliver, brazier			
Dowding, ship chandler			
Reid, rope-maker			
Wheatly, for an anchor ..			
Lake, blacksmith			
Cabin furniture..........			
Willan, for 2 guns			
Hawkins, for patent to windl			
Cherty, painter			
Claughton, mast-maker			
Harington, for junk			
Welsh, for twice laid rope ..			
March.			
To disbursements, London, outw			
Do. Gravesend			
Thompson, for provisions ..			
Haden, cheese-monger.....			
Groceries			
Smalls, butcher			
Sap, brewer			
Salmond, for coals........			
Thurlby, for candles......			
Blackburn, water casks			
Pilot to the Downs			
Richard Danters, for longbo			
Disbursements at Portsmout			
Do. at Lymington.........			
Do. at Falmouth			
Do. at Quebec			
Do. at London, inwards			
Postage bill			
Messrs. Dawsons, custom-ho			
Insurance on 2500*l.* from Lo			
8 guineas, to return 4*l.* pe			
Do. from Quebec to London			
Insurance on freight, at do.			
Interest of money on ship val			
Wear and tear, 8 per cent...			
	1661	5	9
To loss on			

	l.	s.	d.
1805, January.			
First cost and outfit	534	18	0
To Elstob, shipwright	750	0	0
Greig, for earthenware	230	0	0
Hill, for paint ....ge	448	5	5
Syeds, for compasses........			
Brett, plumber			
Groceries			
Dowding, ship chandler ...			
Charles and Steel, coopers .			
Haden, cheese-monger.....			

No. XV.—CO

An estimated Statement of the Expences incurred by an averag Port of Newcastle-upon-Tyne to London, shewing the Loss v Prices. December 3, 1806.

Dr.	l.	s.	d.
To wages for 11 men and boys. (See Items annexed, No. I.)......	66	19	6
To provisions for ditto, say at 40 days (averaged times at 9 voyages in the year) at 1s. 6d. per day, per man, ...	33	0	0
Fitter's bill for 128 Newcastle chaldrons of Wallsend coals, with keel dues, expences, and custom-house charges. (See Items annexed, No. II.)	223	15	0
Factor's bill for duties, charges, delivery, &c. (See Items annexed, No. III.)	208	10	11
Sundry small charges which always occur that do not come under any general head. (See Items annexed, No. IV.)	11	12	6
Wear and tear on this ship for a voyage which, supposing her to make nine in a year, will give 270*l.* annually for the supply of masts, rigging, sails, cables, materials, &c.	30	0	0
Insurance on this ship, moderately valued at 2000*l.* at 3¼ guineas per cent. per voyage, with duty, ...	76	0	0
	649	17	11
To loss on the voyage, ...	89	17	11

N. B. *Wallsend* are the most beneficial coals to load for the *London* market. these coals, which is rarely performed, and it is necessary to observe that the estim

No. I. above referred to.

Statement of the Wages paid on a ship of 16 Keels, or 240 London Chaldrons, for *a Voyage* in the Coal Trade, from Newcastle to London and back.

	l.	s.	d.
Master's wages, ...	9	9	0

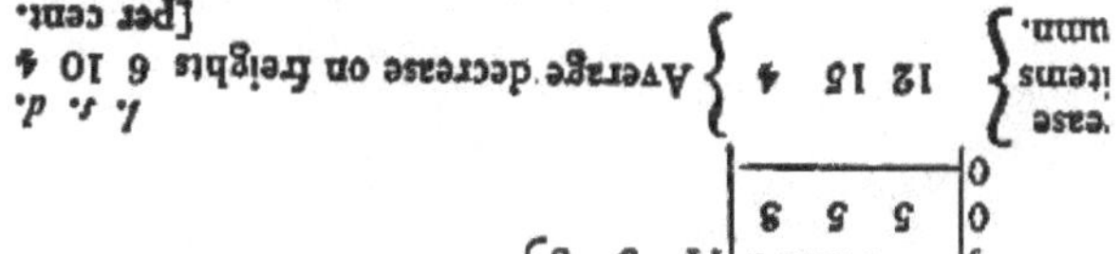

Statement of the Prices of Shi 1780—1795, compared with the Prices and Rriods of War.

PROVISIONS.

Irish beef, per cwt. -		
Ship bread, ditto - -		
Flour, per sack - -		
Peas, per bushel - -		
Beer, per barrel - -		
Salt beef, per tierce -		*l. s. d.*
Salt pork, per barrel -	lvance on all in this class	84 8 2 per ct.

MATERIALS, STORES,

Rope, per cwt. - -		
Masts, per load, fit for an a sized ship - -		
Sails made up of No. 1 canva yard - - -		
English oak timber, per load		
Quebec, ditto ditto		*l. s. d.*
Builder's price in the river, p measurement for average ships - - -	vance items s	122 10 2 per cent.

SEAMEN'S WAGES

Mates and carpenters to the Indies, per month -		
Seamen, ditto dit		
Ditto, Mediterranean, dit		
Ditto, Baltic, ditto		
Shipwright's wages, per day		*l. s. d.*
Caulkers, ditto di	vance on all in this class	39 7 1 per ct.

RATES OF FREIGH

West-India Leeward Islands per cwt. - - -		
Ditto, Jamaica, ditto		*l. s. d.*
Baltic freight, Memel timbe load - - -	Average decrease on these 4 items	19 5 8 per ct.
Riga timber - -		
Deals, per hundred -		

Charles and Steel, coopers .
Haden, cheese-monger.....

No. XVII.

Statement of the Difference of the first Cost, Outfit, and Expences on a Voyage to *St. Petersburgh and London*, betwixt a *British* and a *Dantzic* Ship, supposing each to be four Months on the Voyage, at an equal Freight and of an equal Tonnage, say 304 Tons per Register Measurement.

Suppose the British Ship cost 4772*l*.	*l.*	*s.*	*d.*
Outfit, including provisions,	100	0	0
Crimpage for 9 men at 3 guineas each, ...	28	0	0
Loading, &c. at St. Petersburgh, in which the sailors will not assist, ...	190	0	0
Port charges, &c. at Elsineur, ...	17	6	9
Pilotage and assistance up the river to her moorings,	5	5	0
Discharging the cargo, ...	35	0	0
Tonnage duty and dock dues, ...	33	8	0
Lights and reporting, ...	8	13	3
Wages, of which about 60*l*. must be paid in advance, previous to the ship's sailing, ...	329	0	0
Insurance on 4800*l*. at 8 guineas per cent. with policy, 415*l*. 4*s*. less, return at 4 per cent. 192*l*.	223	4	0
	970	4	0

Suppose the Dantzic Ship cost 3200*l*.	*l.*	*s.*	*d.*
Outfit, including provisions,	60	0	0
Crimpage, none.			
Loading at St. Petersburgh, in which the sailors assist,	140	0	0
Post charges, &c. at Elsineur, ...	17	6	9
Pilotage and assistance up the river to her moorings,	17	0	0
Discharging the cargo, ...	25	0	0
Tonnage, duty, and dock dues, ...	33	8	0
Lights and reporting, ...	16	5	6
Wages without any advance, ...	218	0	0
Insurance on 3200*l*. at $2\frac{1}{2}$ guineas per cent. with policy, ...	92	0	0
	619	0	3
Difference in favour of the Dantzic ship, ...	351	3	9
	970	4	0

No. XVIII.

An Account of the Number of Ships and Vessels belonging to the British Empire *which appear from Lloyd's Lists* to have been lost, stranded, and got off, captured and re-captured from the Year 1789 to 1800, inclusive.

Years.	Lost.	On Shore.	Got off.	Captured.	Recaptured.
1789	163	61	7		
1790	167	47	11		
1791	213	82	8		
1792	195	59	11		
1793	201	38	5	357	62
1794	246	64	4	701	86
1795	222	42	2	646	56
1796	181	44	1	534	67
1797	193	59	6	751	135
1798	165	61	6	447	91
1799	210	46	3	451	86
1800	229	49	6	457	122
	2385	652	70	4344	705

652 on shore. — 705 Recaptured.

3037 — 3639 Total lost by capture.

70 got off.

2967 Total lost by perils of the sea.
3639 Total lost by capture.

6606 Total loss by perils of the sea and capture in twelve years.

N. B. There is no doubt but that many ships belonging to the British empire have been lost and captured, which are not mentioned in Lloyd's lists.

No. XIX.

An Account of the Number of Vessels, with the Amount of their Tonnage, which have been annually built and registered, in the several Ports of the British Empire, between 5th of January 1793, and 5th January 1805.

	Vessels.	Tonnage.	Average Rate of Tonnage.
In the year 1793	800	75,085	$93\frac{685}{800}$
—— . 4	714	66,021	$92\frac{333}{714}$
—— . 5	719	72,241	$100\frac{341}{719}$
—— . 6	823	94,972	$115\frac{327}{823}$
—— . 7	727	84,195	$115\frac{590}{727}$
—— . 8	833	89,319	$107\frac{188}{833}$
—— . 9	858	98,044	$114\frac{116}{429}$
—— 1800	1,041	134,198	$128\frac{950}{1041}$
—— . 1	1,065	122,593	$115\frac{113}{1065}$
—— . 2	1,281	137,508	$107\frac{441}{1281}$
—— . 3	1,407	135,692	$96\frac{620}{1407}$
—— . 4	991	95,979	$96\frac{843}{991}$
Total 12 years	11,259	1,205,847	$107\frac{1134}{11259}$

Custom-House, London,
Office of the Register General of Shipping,
January 28, 1806.
} T. E. WILLOUGHBY,

N. B. This account was printed by order of the House of Commons, on the 1st of April, 1806, and contains a return of ships and vessels *of all sizes*, from *three tons upwards*, for which see subsequent account, No. XX. ordered to be printed by the same authority, on the 24th of June, 1806. The calculation of the average tonnage has been *since* added to the above account.

By sect. 3d, 26 Geo. III. chap. 60. Every ship or vessel *having a deck*, or being of the burthen of *fifteen tons or upwards*, is required to be registered.

By sect. 6. Except lighters' barges, boats, or vessels of

No. XIX.—Continued.

any description whatever built in, and used *solely* in rivers, and in inland navigation.

By sect. 15. Bond from 100*l.* to 1000*l.* penalty that the certificate shall not be sold, lent, or otherwise disposed of; and that in case the ship shall be lost or taken by the enemy, burnt or broken up, or otherwise prevented from returning to the port to which she belongs, the certificate, *if preserved*, shall be delivered up within one month after the arrival of the master in any port or place in his majesty's dominions, to the collector or comptroller, in order that the same may be cancelled.

Therefore, Owners ought to give notice to the comptroller of the customs where registered, when the ship is either lost or captured, whether the certificate of registry be preserved or not. At present there is great reason to believe many ships are continued on the entries at the register-general's office, although not in existence; consequently the general returns of tonnage cannot be accurate.

No. XX.

RETURN to *an Order* of the Honourable House of Commons, *dated 20th May*, 1806,—for an Account of the Number and Tonnage of the Ships and Vessels built in Great Britain, from 5th January 1790 to 5th January 1806; distinguishing each Year, and the Tonnage of each Ship or Vessel, and also the Ports or Places where they were respectively built.

PORTS.	Year 1790.	1791.	1804.	1805.
	Tons	Tons	Tons	Tons
LONDON	1 Ship - 229	1 Ship - 1,210	1 Ship 52	1 Ship 50
	— - 38	— - 463	— - 58	— - 840
	— - 34	— - 40	— - 57	— - 858
	— - 157	— - 58	— - 18	— - 858
	— - 243	— - 189	— - 61	— - 864
	— - 105	— - 173	— - 46	— - 862
	— - 29	— - 64	— - 49	— - 175
	— - 238	— - 41	— - 18	— - 52
	— - 52	— - 183	— - 54	— - 43
	— - 52	— - 286	— - 52	— - 52
	— - 246	— - 57	— - 192	— - 40
	— - 364	— - 416	— - 45	— - 52
	— - 280	— - 346	— - 11	— - 48
	— - 1,255	— - 300	— - 16	— - 50
	— - 1,246	— - 257	— - 21	— - 45
	— - 369	— - 36	— - 7	— - 50
	— - 36	— - 525	— - 48	— - 29
	— - 342	— - 313	— - 34	— - 50
	— - 305	— - 28	— - 7	— - 43
	— - 255	— - 52	— - 23	— - 49
	— - 573	— - 31	— - 43	— - 9
	— - 1,233	— - 9	— - 38	— - 46
	— - 1,246	— - 53	— - 43	— - 50
	— - 47	— - 18	— - 47	— - 45
	— - 81	— - 3	— - 36	— - 48
	— - 12	— - 63	— - 64	— - 30
	— - 12	— - 5	— - 55	— - 46
	— - 14	— - 39	— - 11	— - 45
	— - 12	— - 8	— - 26	— - 43
	— - 16	— - 5	— - 60	— - 7
	— - 9	— - 52	— - 25	— - 48
	— - 8	— - 7	— - 249	— - 48
	— - 15	— - 91	— - 179	— - 46
	— - 45	— - 49	— - 8	— - 44
	— - 16	— - 48	— - 28	— - 4
	— - 6	— - 12	— - 253	— - 12
	— - 28	— - 6	— - 285	— - 134
	— - 16	— - ½	— - 633	— - 134
	— - 63	— - 11	— - 403	— - 360
	— - 79	— - 4	— - 302	— - 33

PORTS.	Year 1790.		1791.		1804.		1805.	
		Tons		Tons		Tons		Tons
LONDON *continued*	— -	45	— -	5	— -	26	— -	54
	— -	10	— -	24	— -	470	— -	27
	— -	15	— -	10	— -	869	— -	79
	— -	36	— -	14	— -	861	— -	8
	— -	28	— -	4	— -	51	— -	8
	— -	45	— -	12	— -	53	— -	22
	— -	4	— -	41	—		— -	25
	— -	35	— -	50	—		— -	38
	— -	24	— -	25	—		— -	24
	— -	29	— -	84	—		— -	48
	— -	7	— -	34	—		— -	19
	— -	33	— -	47	—		—	
	— -	5	— -	14	—		—	
	— -	20	— -	2	—		—	
	—		— -	59	—		—	
	—		— -	38	—		—	
	—		— -	13	—		—	
	—		— -	24	—		—	
	—		— -	100	—		—	
	—		— -	75	—		—	
	—		— -	100	—		—	
	—		— -	55	—		—	
	—		— -	170	—		—	
	—		— -	175	—		—	
	—		— -	152	—		—	
ABERYSTWITH	1 Ship	19	1 Ship	86	1 Ship	54	1 Ship	50
	— -	38	— -	18	— -	132	— -	45
	— -	20	— -	15	— -	91	— -	51
	— -	70	— -	20	— -	58	— -	42
	— -	18	— -	20	— -	82	— -	56
	— -	48	— -	24	— -	58	— -	75
	— -	32	—		— -	31	— -	35
	— -	146	—		— -	22	— -	59
	— -	24	—		—		— -	43
	—		—		—		— -	88
	—		—		—		— -	75
	—		—		—		— -	23
	—		—		—		— -	126
	—		—		—		— -	53
	—		—		—		— -	265
ALDBRO' -	None.		1 Ship	5	1 Ship	4	1 Ship	13
ARUNDEL -	1 Ship	32	1 Ship	27	1 Ship	81	1 Ship	227
	— -	107	— -	114	— -	95	—	
	—		—		— -	205	—	
BARNSTAPLE	1 Ship	11	1 Ship	58	1 Ship	66	1 Ship	52
	— -	38	— -	37	— -	97	— -	104
	— -	142	— -	59	— -	187	— -	92
	—		—		— -	53	— -	51
	—		—		— -	186	— -	61
	—		—		— -	167	—	

PORTS.	Year 1790.	Tons	1791.	Tons	1804.	Tons	1805.	Tons
BEAUMAURIS	1 Ship	15	1 Ship	33	1 Ship	81	1 Ship	35
	— -	35	— -	25	— -	20	— -	56
	— -	10	— -	18	— -	46	— -	90
	— -	72	— -	5	— -	140	— -	43
	— -	34	— -	32	— -	52	— -	29
	— -	35	— -	19	— -	19	— -	125
	— -	52	— -	27	— -	51	— -	101
	— -	17	— -	45	— -	35	— -	28
	— -	19	— -	7	— -	37	— -	17
	— -	32	— -	8	— -	31	— -	32
	— -	91	— -	13	— -	58	— -	52
	— -	16	— -	21	— -	17	— -	59
	— -	15	— -	28	— -	29	— -	40
	— -	28	— -	56	— -	29	— -	27
	— -	120	— -	31	— -	17	— -	52
	— -	233	— -	29	— -	38	— -	137
	— -	99	— -	35	— -	73	— -	21
	— -	15	— -	17	— -	68	— -	16
	— -	18	— -	36	— -	105	— -	93
	— -	39	— -	119	— -	107	— -	93
	— -	70	— -	119	— -	39	— -	159
	—		—		— -	100	— -	137
	—		—		— -	54	— -	61
	—		—		— -	18	— -	94
	—		—		— -	125	— -	47
	—		—		— -	82	— -	11
	—		—		— -	32	— -	61
	—		—		— -	30	— -	21
	—		—		— -	25	— -	22
	—		—		— -	64	— -	59
	—		—		— -	60	— -	35
	—		—		— -	29	— -	8
	—		—		— -	131	—	
	—		—		— -	57	—	
BLACKNEY and CLAY	None.		None.		None.		1 Ship	5
BERWICK -	1 Ship	63	1 Ship	84	1 Ship	186	1 Ship	336
	— -	62	— -	12	— -	51	— -	183
	— -	16	— -	116	— -	83	— -	58
	—		— -	136	— -	166	— -	82
	—		—		— -	61	— -	21
	—		—		— -	125	— -	116
	—		—		— -	80	— -	112
BIDEFORD -	1 Ship	39	1 Ship	67	1 Ship	207	1 Ship	44
	— -	42	— -	44	— -	82	— -	46
	— -	24	— -	61	— -	134	— -	90
	— -	45	— -	28	— -	73	— -	175
	— -	149	— -	18	— -	137	— -	187
	—		— -	34	— -	59	— -	84
	—		—		— -	60	— -	149
	—		—		— -	76	—	
	—		—		— -	57	—	
	—		—		— -	164	—	
	—		—		— -	101	—	
	—		—		— -	119	—	
	—		—		— -	165	—	

PORTS.	Year 1790.	Tons	1791.	Tons	1804.	Tons	1805.	Tons
BOSTON	1 Ship	6	1 Ship	44	1 Ship	44	1 Ship	43
	—	34	—	27	—	46	—	46
	—	46	—		—	42	—	73
	—	41	—		—	251	—	37
	—	37	—		—	35	—	42
	—	11	—		—	6	—	23
	—	24	—		—	119	—	
	—	29	—		—		—	
	—	40	—		—		—	
	—	48	—		—		—	
	—	8	—		—		—	
	—	42	—		—		—	
	—	49	—		—		—	
	—	47	—		—		—	
	—	44	—		—		—	
	—	30	—		—		—	
	—	42	—		—		—	
BRIDGWATER	None.		None.		1 Ship	83	1 Ship	68
	—		—		—	59	—	
	—		—		—	278	—	
BRIDLINGTON	None.		1 Ship	160	None.		None.	
	—		—	204	—		—	
BRISTOL	1 Ship	237	1 Ship	7	1 Ship	123	1 Ship	44
	—	207	—	32	—	10	—	401
	—	22	—	27	—	494	—	428
	—	80	—	227	—		—	50
	—	458	—	236	—		—	73
	—	16	—	14	—		—	
	—	8	—	12	—		—	
	—	12	—	10	—		—	
	—	18	—	90	—		—	
	—	176	—	280	—		—	
	—	11	—	60	—		—	
	—		—	249	—		—	
	—		—	56	—		—	
	—		—	14	—		—	
	—		—	229	—		—	
	—		—	11	—		—	
	—		—	55	—		—	
	—		—	13	—		—	
	—		—	11	—		—	
	—		—	233	—		—	
CARDIFF	1 Ship	60	None.		1 Ship	59	1 Ship	176
	—	20	—		—	59	—	45
	—	60	—		—	64	—	47
CARDIGAN	1 Ship	20	1 Ship	50	1 Ship	124	1 Ship	28
	—	12	—	13	—	30	—	46
	—	24	—	37	—	28	—	22
	—	14	—	21	—	26	—	23
	—	19	—	53	—	28	—	25
	—	23	—	22	—	83	—	29

PORTS.	Year 1790.	Tons	1791.	Tons	1804.	Tons	1805.	Tons
CARDIGAN *continued*	1 Ship	23	None.		1 Ship	2	1 Ship	15
	—	2	—		—	4	—	27
	—	40	—		—	7	—	
	—	22	—		—	30	—	
	—	70	—		—		—	
	—	90	—		—		—	
	—	27	—		—		—	
	—	48	—		—		—	
	—	175	—		—		—	
CARLISLE	1 Ship	12	None.		1 Ship	61	1 Ship	73
	—		—		—	59	—	14
CHEPSTOW	1 Ship	193	1 Ship	36	1 Ship	169	1 Ship	76
	—	129	—	25	—	434	—	129
	—		—	126	—	60	—	60
	—		—	82	—	23	—	40
	—		—		—	125	—	45
	—		—		—		—	74
	—		—		—		—	113
	—		—		—		—	70
	—		—		—		—	49
	—		—		—		—	315
CHESTER	1 Ship	73	1 Ship	127	1 Ship	156	1 Ship	116
	—	19	—	20	—	163	—	80
	—	335	—	19	—	55	—	76
	—	13	—	11	—	47	—	234
	—	49	—	87	—	96	—	411
	—	73	—	99	—	78	—	58
	—	147	—	82	—	77	—	328
	—	141	—	197	—	72	—	
	—		—		—	78	—	
	—		—		—	28	—	
	—		—		—	174	—	
	—		—		—	171	—	
COLCHESTER	1 Ship	21	1 Ship	6	1 Ship	16	1 Ship	17
	—	8	—	18	—	25	—	33
	—	46	—	11	—	25	—	22
	—	6	—	59	—	82	—	30
	—	20	—		—	22	—	17
	—	20	—		—	19	—	
	—	88	—		—		—	
	—	7	—		—		—	
	—	16	—		—		—	
	—	23	—		—		—	
	—	12	—		—		—	
	—	14	—		—		—	
	—	16	—		—		—	

PORTS.	Year 1790.	Tons	1791.	Tons.	1804.	Tons.	1805.	Tons.
CHICHESTER	1 Ship -	26	1 Ship	141	None.		1 Ship	21
	— -	36	— -	286	—		— -	106
	— -	132	— -	62	—		— -	28
	— -	12	— -	19	—		— -	9
	—		— -	24	—		—	
COWES	1 Ship -	78	1 Ship	33	1 Ship	53	1 Ship	12
	— -	32	— -	32	— -	53	— -	28
	— -	24	— -	32	— -	33	— -	10
	— -	36	— -	14	— -	47	— -	23
	— -	60	— -	43	— -	63	— -	10
	— -	7	— -	27	— -	27	— -	25
	— -	26	— -	25	— -	15	— -	8
	— -	31	— -	33	— -	11	— -	22
	— -	70	— -	21	— -	105	— -	14
	— -	16	— -	11	— -	39	— -	14
	— -	19	— -	14	— -	70	— -	52
	— -	21	— -	23	— -	26	—	
	— -	14	— -	14	— -	76	—	
	— -	15	— -	12	— -	27	—	
	— -	128	— -	30	—		—	
	— -	11	— -	34	—		—	
	—		— -	23	—		—	
DARTMO'	1 Ship -	33	1 Ship	44	1 Ship	245	1 Ship	116
	— -	32	— -	77	— -	71	— -	38
	— -	60	— -	29	— -	118	— -	75
	— -	42	— -	30	— -	39	— -	41
	— -	31	— -	45	— -	40	— -	39
	— -	34	— -	30	— -	77	— -	31
	— -	105	— -	35	— -	64	— -	40
	— -	32	— -	33	— -	39	— -	15
	— -	30	— -	88	— -	57	— -	74
	— -	16	— -	31	— -	155	— -	82
	— -	29	— -	29	— -	47	— -	15
	— -	32	— -	30	— -	38	— -	79
	— -	31	— -	34	— -	16	— -	17
	— -	31	— -	28	— -	17	— -	40
	— -	3	— -	36	— -	36	— -	53
	— -	155	— -	32	— -	102	— -	73
	— -	52	—		— -	45	— -	80
	—		—		— -	117	— -	31
	—		—		— -	38	— -	166
	—		—		—		— -	14
	—		—		—		— -	180
DEAL	1 Ship -	18	1 Ship	34	1 Ship	72	1 Ship	25
	— -	19	— -	18	— -	66	— -	21
	—		— -	49	— -	16	— -	18
	—		—		— -	51	—	
	—		—		— -	60	—	
	—		—		— -	31	—	
	—		—		— -	57	—	

PORTS.	Year 1790.	Tons.	1791.	Tons	1804.	Tons.	1805.	Tons.
DEAL continued	—		—		1 Ship	47	—	
	—		—		—	77	—	
	—		—		—	36	—	
DOVER	1 Ship	34	1 Ship	20	1 Ship	75	1 Ship	89
	—	71	—	36	—	29	—	16
	—	13	—	28	—	16	—	89
	—	71	—	20	—	132	—	23
	—	18	—	33	—	66	—	110
	—	47	—	17	—	82	—	38
	—	40	—	43	—	47	—	19
	—	42	—	42	—	16	—	81
	—	69	—	16	—	60	—	19
	—	25	—	19	—		—	18
	—	20	—	92	—		—	108
	—	57	—	38	—		—	40
	—	45	—	20	—		—	51
	—	48	—	45	—		—	
	—	60	—	38	—		—	
	—	23	—	21	—		—	
	—	47	—	131	—		—	
	—		—	58	—		—	
	—		—	29	—		—	
	—		—	22	—		—	
	—		—	34	—		—	
	—		—	19	—		—	
	—		—	18	—		—	
	—		—	62	—		—	
	—		—	21	—		—	
	—		—	21	—		—	
	—		—	22	—		—	
EXETER	1 Ship	131	1 Ship	269	1 Ship	84	1 Ship	209
	—	91	—	148	—	78	—	20
	—	78	—	14	—	78	—	126
	—	85	—	17	—	23	—	26
	—		—	63	—	137	—	111
	—		—	124	—	139	—	80
	—		—	34	—	141	—	41
	—		—	75	—	43	—	48
	—		—		—	22	—	59
	—		—		—	25	—	85
	—		—		—	36	—	79
	—		—		—	37	—	59
	—		—		—	59	—	
	—		—		—	53	—	
	—		—		—	42	—	
	—		—		—	41	—	
FALMOUTH	1 Ship	26	1 Ship	15	1 Ship	40	1 Ship	186
	—		—		—		—	48

PORTS.	Year 1790.		1791.		1804.		1805.	
		Tons.		Tons		Tons.		Tons.
FEVERSHAM	1 Ship	12	1 Ship	43	1 Ship	6	1 Ship	26
	— -	5	— -	31	— -	6	— -	7
	— -	5	— -	5	— -	6	— -	8
	— -	6	— -	7	— -	6	— -	8
	— -	14	— -	39	— -	44	— -	8
	— -	10	— -	15	— -	27	— -	8
	— -	5	— -	62	— -	5	— -	31
	— -	10	—		— -	5	— -	8
	— -	11	—		— -	4	— -	8
	— -	11	—		— -		—	
	— -	6	—		— -		—	
	— -	7	—		—		—	
	— -	28	—		—		—	
FOWEY	1 Ship	28	1 Ship	15	1 Ship	48	1 Ship	96
	— -	55	— -	106	— -	15	— -	48
	— -	53	— -	12	— -	78	— -	96
	— -	25	— -	14	— -	56	— -	46
	— -	68	— -	60	— -	123	— -	107
	— -	34	— -	53	— -	79	— -	59
	— -	17	— -	16	— -	93	— -	29
	— -	57	— -	19	— -	33	— -	138
	— -	13	— -	89	— -	36	— -	45
	— -	101	— -	115	— -	57	— -	112
	— -	38	— -	121	— -	67	— -	81
	—		—		— -	49	— -	49
	—		—		— -	94	— -	101
	—		—		— -	75	— -	18
	—		—		— -	59	—	
	—		—		— -	99	—	
	—		—		— -	111	—	
	—		—		— -	70	—	
	—		—		— -	70	—	
GLOUCESTER	1 Ship	35	1 Ship	60	1 Ship	4	1 Ship	111
	— -	28	— -	16	— -	65	— -	145
	— -	39	— -	57	— -	14	— -	58
	— -	16	— -	37	— -	64	— -	120
	— -	17	— -	20	—		— -	125
	— -	47	—		—		— -	59
	— -	12	—		—		— -	54
	— -	12	—		—		— -	60
	— -	6	—		—		— -	24
	— -	36	—		—		— -	65
	— -	15	—		—		— -	54
	— -	8	—		—		— -	88
	— -	12	—		—		— -	58
	— -	52	—		—		— -	57
	— -	52	—		—		— -	63
	—		—		—		— -	55
	—		—		—		— -	55
	—		—		—		— -	27
	—		—		—		— -	53
	—		—		—		— -	58
	—		—		—		— -	59

PORTS.	Year 1790. Tons	1791. Tons	1804. Tons	1805. Tons
GWEEK	1 Ship 15	1 Ship 15	None.	None.
GRIMSBY	None.	None.	None.	None.
HARWICH	1 Ship 114	1 Ship 20	None.	1 Ship
	— - 42	— - 22	—	— - 75
	— - 22	—	—	— - 53
	—	—	—	— - 31
HULL	1 Ship 216	1 Ship 318	1 Ship 192	1 Ship 48
	— - 43	— - 227	— - 46	— - 39
	— - 45	— - 346	— - 315	— - 223
	— - 45	— - 13	— - 254	— - 263
	— - 60	— - 15	— - 91	— - 298
	— - 108	— - 105	— - 287	— - 46
	— - 324	— - 13	— - 47	— - 35
	— - 44	— - 320	— - 305	— - 47
	— - 45	— - 164	— - 271	— - 46
	— - 298	— - 301	— - 246	— - 47
	— - 30	— - 118	— - 45	— - 158
	— - 48	— - 110	— - 144	— - 183
	— - 45	— - 105	— - 172	— - 45
	— - 9	— - 74	— - 46	— - 231
	— - 51	— - 44	— - 44	— - 182
	— - 44	— - 45	— - 45	— - 46
	— - 155	— - 46	— - 143	— - 46
	— 37	— - 44	— - 46	— - 146
	— - 66	— - 277	— - 47	— - 44
	— - 83	— - 111	— - 47	— - 137
	— - 15	— - 41	— - 45	— - 46
	— - 181	— - 149	— - 610	— - 81
	— - 45	— - 45	— - 111	— - 131
	— - 44	— - 151	— - 71	— - 72
	— - 42	— - 45	— - 153	— - 82
	— - 163	— - 12	— - 342	— - 68
	— - 9	— 218	— - 155	— - 69
	— - 70	— - 109	— - 403	— - 46
	— - 104	— - 102	— - 123	— - 46
	— - 47	— - 101	— - 148	— - 18
	— - 43	— - 195	— - 45	— - 613
	— - 119	— - 112	— - 46	— - 225
	— - 41	— - 225	— - 336	— - 157
	— - 6	— - 46	— - 69	— - 71
	— - 113	— - 114	— - 152	— - 48
	— - 110	— - 46	— - 79	— - 191
	— - 111	— - 7	— - 69	— - 112
	— - 49	— - 46	—	— - 46
	— - 48	— - 46	—	— - 45
	— - 236	— - 7	—	— - 51
	—	— - 49	—	— - 45
	—	— - 62	—	— - 98
	—	—	—	— - 102
	—	—	—	— - 293
	—	—	—	— - 75

PORTS.	Year 1790.	Tons	1791.	Tons	1804.	Tons	1805.	Tons
ILFRAÇOMBE	1 Ship	24	1 Ship	60	1 Ship -	48	1 Ship	48
	—		—		— -	138	— -	138
	—		—		— -	40	— -	40
IPSWICH -	1 Ship	337	1 Ship	59	1 Ship	57	1 Ship	69
	— -	9	— -	25	— -	26	— -	9
	— -	19	— -	22	— -	10	— -	342
	— -	27	— -	17	—		—	
	— -	64	— -	259	—		—	
	— -	52	— -	27	—		—	
	— -	20	—		—		—	
	— -	7	—		—		—	
LANCASTER	1 Ship	74	1 Ship	95	1 Ship	275	1 Ship	300
	— -	10	— -	44	— -	102	— -	48
	— -	182	— -	127	— -	121	— -	99
	— -	24	— -	310	— -	267	— -	69
	— -	21	— -	85	— -	75	— -	31
	— -	76	— -	35	—		— -	82
	—		— -	30	—		—	
	—		— -	20	—		—	
	—		— -	45	—		—	
	—		— -	77	—		—	
	—		— -	78	—		—	
LIVERPOOL	1 Ship	41	1 Ship	168	1 Ship	273	1 Ship	63
	— -	141	— -	148	— -	60	— -	63
	— -	33	— -	14	— -	33	— -	77
	— -	100	— -	165	— -	112	— -	75
	— -	230	— -	71	— -	196	— -	78
	— -	186	— -	25	— -	254	— -	216
	— -	26	— -	153	— -	75	— -	27
	— -	92	— -	28	— -	604	— -	32
	— -	97	— -	173	— -	276	— -	33
	— -	35	— -	106	— -	282	— -	145
	— -	405	— -	25	—		— -	76
	— -	47	— -	103	—		— -	76
	— -	77	— -	159	—		— -	147
	— -	46	— -	111	—		— -	7
	— -	72	—	6	—		— -	26
	— -	123	— -	129	—		— -	8
	— -	127	— -	226	—		— -	194
	— -	190	— -	10	—		— -	71
	— -	11	— -	71	—		— -	20
	— -	116	— -	230	—		— -	24
	— -	307	— -	149	—		— -	401
	— -	176	— -	258	—		— -	82
	— -	46	— -	208	—		— -	9
	— -	150	— -	58	—		— -	14
	— -	54	— -	49	—		— -	25
	— -	45	—		—		—	
	— -	110	—		—		—	
	— -	225	—		—		—	
	— -	397	—		—		—	
							—	

PORTS.	Year 1790. Tons	1791. Tons	1804. Tons	1805. Tons
LIVERPOOL *continued*	1 Ship 304	—	—	—
	— 140	—	—	—
	— 57	—	—	—
	— 59	—	—	—
	— 162	—	—	—
LOOE	None.	None.	1 Ship 22	1 Ship 98
	—	—	— 47	— 82
	—	—	— 116	— 80
	—	—	— 120	— 60
LLANELLY	1 Ship 18	1 Ship 68	1 Ship 76	1 Ship 114
	— 82	— 31	— 22	— 28
	— 24	— 30	— 40	— 44
	— 38	— 25	— 49	— 55
	— 54	— 17	— 107	— 60
	—	— 30	— 50	— 103
	—	—	—	— 27
	—	—	—	— 225
LYME	1 Ship 12	1 Ship 32	1 Ship 67	1 Ship 42
	—	— 38	—	— 75
	—	— 10	—	— 84
	—	—	—	— 41
	—	—	—	— 68
	—	—	—	— 31
LYNN	1 Ship 65	1 Ship 20	1 Ship 138	1 Ship 93
	— 7	— 171	—	— 127
	— 162	—	—	—
	— 6	—	—	—
	— 119	—	—	—
MALDON	1 Ship 11	1 Ship 10	1 Ship 84	None.
	— 11	— 8	— 8	—
	— 8	— 9	— 4	—
	— 6	— 20	— 16	—
	— 5	— 10	— 16	—
	— 16	— 20	— 13	—
	— 7	— 20	—	—
	— 4	— 21	—	—
	— 14	— 63	—	—
	— 8	—	—	—
	— 11	—	—	—
	— 8	—	—	—
MINEHEAD	1 Ship 31	None.	1 Ship 45	None.
MILFORD	1 Ship 15	1 Ship 58	1 Ship 52	1 Ship 22
	—	— 14	— 28	— 109
	—	—	— 131	—
	—	—	— 25	—
	—	—	— 32	—
	—	—	— 190	—

[A a]

PORTS.	Year 1790.		1791.		1804.		1805.	
		Tons		Tons		Tons		Tons
NEWCASTLE	1 Ship	253	1 Ship	291	1 Ship	344	1 Ship	108
	— -	116	— -	86	— -	207	— -	422
	— -	16	— -	55	— -	328	— -	368
	— -	148	— -	216	— -	112	— -	413
	— -	142	— -	148	— -	77	— -	341
	— -	320	— -	324	— -	176	— -	111
	— -	162	— -	167	— -	193	— -	231
	— -	293	— -	25	— -	214	— -	160
	— -	370	— -	344	— -	164	— -	103
	— -	288	— -	209	— -	102	— -	366
	— -	320	— -	317	— -	139	— -	148
	— -	272	— -	82	— -	155	— -	208
	— -	121	— -	247	— -	524	— -	412
	— -	281	— -	73	— -	253	— -	199
	— -	285	— -	150	— -	303	— -	341
	— -	164	— -	300	— -	250	— -	673
	— -	284	— -	303	— -	399	— -	227
	— -	239	— -	166	— -	232	— -	361
	— -	281	— -	274	— -	320	— -	60
	— -	253	— -	187	— -	471	— -	251
	— -	224	— -	120	— -	252	— -	60
	— -	99	— -	232	— -	387	— -	114
	— -	282	— -	348	— -	232	— -	192
	— -	37	— -	214	— -	179	— -	70
	— -	293	— -	448	— -	142	— -	24
	— -	166	— -	250	— -	60	—	
	— -	174	— -	268	— -	403	—	
	— -	41	—		— -	230	—	
	— -	317	—		— -	224	—	
	— -	88	—		— -	346	—	
	— -	186	—		— -	415	—	
	— -	133	—		— -	227	—	
	—		—		— -	171	—	
	—		—		— -	248	—	
	—		—		— -	229	—	
	—		—		— -	374	—	
NEWHAVEN	None.		None.		None.		None.	
PADSTOW	None.		None.		None.		1 Ship	70
	—		—		—		— -	5
PEMBROKE	1 Ship	17	None.		1 Ship	20	None.	
	— -	23	—		— -	52	—	
	—		—		— -	82	—	
PENRYN	None.		1 Ship	19	None.		None.	
PENZANCE	1 Ship	16	1 Ship	26	None.		1 Ship	46
	— -	19	—		—		— -	57
	— -	18	—		—		—	
	— -	19	—		—		—	

PORTS.	Year 1790.	Tons	1791.	Tons	1804.	Tons	1805.	Tons
PLYMO'	1 Ship	70	1 Ship	154	1 Ship	214	1 Ship	67
	—	24	—	87	—	65	—	78
	—	30	—	14	—	115	—	158
	—	31	—	68	—	53	—	25
	—	210	—	73	—	23	—	80
	—	65	—	60	—	33	—	38
	—	10	—	55	—	88	—	29
	—	72	—	50	—	44	—	40
	—	28	—	129	—	116	—	
	—	34	—	68	—		—	
	—	36	—	29	—		—	
	—	47	—	54	—		—	
	—	34	—	29	—		—	
	—	46	—	71	—		—	
	—	18	—		—		—	
	—	33	—		—		—	
	—	62	—		—		—	
	—	59	—		—		—	
	—	8	—		—		—	
	—	29	—		—		—	
	—	50	—		—		—	
	—	30	—		—		—	
	—	119	—		—		—	
	—	102	—		—		—	
	—	64	—		—		—	
	—	74	—		—		—	
	—	30	—		—		—	
	—	54	—		—		—	
POOLE	1 Ship	75	1 Ship	163	1 Ship	198	1 Ship	42
	—	20	—	15	—	9	—	177
	—	19	—	40	—		—	37
	—	106	—		—		—	278
	—	134	—		—		—	
	—	153	—		—		—	
	—	126	—		—		—	
	—	6	—		—		—	
	—	152	—		—		—	
PORTSMO'	None.		1 Ship	6	1 Ship	13	1 Ship	8
	—		—	6	—		—	24
	—		—		—		—	13
	—		—		—		—	8
PRESTON	1 Ship	50	None.		None.		1 Ship	99
	—		—		—		—	80
ROCHESTER	1 Ship	48	1 Ship	16	1 Ship	22	1 Ship	4
	—	49	—	33	—	63	—	14
	—	49	—	15	—	88	—	60
	—	57	—	5	—	35	—	73
	—	32	—	14	—	37	—	66
	—	58	—	23	—	35	—	52
	—	8	—	6	—	76	—	86

PORTS.	Year 1790.	Tons	1791.	Tons	1804.	Tons	1805.	Tons
ROCHESTER *continued*	1 Ship	116	1 Ship	30	1 Ship	32	1 Ship	7
	—	10	—	14	—	12	—	12
	—	28	—	42	—	25	—	59
	—	50	—	61	—		—	52
	—	10	—	8	—		—	23
	—	33	—	33	—		—	20
	—	70	—	22	—		—	53
	—	34	—	39	—		—	23
	—	7	—	11	—		—	70
	—	13	—		—		—	
	—	37	—		—		—	
	—	10	—		—		—	
	—	14	—		—		—	
	—	26	—		—		—	
	—	28	—		—		—	
	—	71	—		—		—	
	—	32	—		—		—	
	—	33	—		—		—	
	—	78	—		—		—	
	—	9	—		—		—	
	—	67	—		—		—	
RYE	1 Ship	31	1 Ship	9	1 Ship	27	1 Ship	91
	—	36	—	47	—	25	—	30
	—	97	—	9	—	81	—	
	—	56	—	38	—	75	—	
	—		—	64	—	90	—	
	—		—	19	—		—	
ST. IVES	1 Ship	18	None.		None.		1 Ship	51
	—	111	—		—		—	
SANDWICH	1 Ship	148	1 Ship	16	1 Ship	104	1 Ship	17
	—	274	—	18	—	11	—	
	—	26	—	8	—	32	—	
	—	31	—	15	—	177	—	
	—	20	—	118	—	164	—	
	—	149	—		—		—	
	—	9	—		—		—	
SCARBOROUGH	1 Ship	197	1 Ship	78	Ship	60	1 Ship	147
	—	141	—	209	—	206	—	212
	—	83	—	21	—	200	—	163
	—	121	—	326	—	72	—	219
	—	130	—	107	—	242	—	266
	—	143	—	316	—	478	—	138
	—	92	—	275	—	172	—	60
	—	174	—	57	—		—	55
SHOREHAM	1 Ship	9	1 Ship	84	1 Ship	58	1 Ship	64
	—	41	—	100	—		—	396
	—	44	—		—		—	251
	—	21	—		—		—	143

PORTS.	Year 1790. Tons	1791. Tons	1804. Tons	1805. Tons
SCILLY -	None.	None.	1 Ship 137	None
SOUTHAMPTON	1 Ship 215	1 Ship 28	1 Ship 199	1 Ship 13
	— - 218	— - 130	— - 15	— - 132
	— - 12	— - 11	— - 18	— - 14
	— - 29	— - 15	— - 50	— - 4
	— - 5	— - 134	— - 69	— - 66
	— - 38	— - 15	—	— - 13
	— - 44	— - 15	—	— - 15
	—	— - 276	—	—
	—	— - 15	—	—
SOUTHWOLD	1 Ship 79	None.	1 Ship 107	1 Ship 24
	— - 75	—	—	— - 135
STOCKTON	1 Ship 320	1 Ship 124	1 Ship 296	1 Ship 50
	— - 116	— - 318	— - 69	— - 130
	— - 16	— - 73	— - 52	— - 70
	— - 64	— - 73	— - 263	—
	—	— - 68	— - 68	—
SUNDERLAND *	1 Ship 6	1 Ship 157	1 Ship 333	1 Ship 130
	— - 112	— - 194	— - 203	— - 123
	— - 170	— - 159	— - 109	— - 152
	— - 43	— - 350	— - 112	— - 195
	— - 212	— - 222	— - 157	— - 130
	— - 139	— - 123	— - 217	— - 127
	— - 76	—	— - 124	— - 152
	— - 168	—	— - 121	— - 111
	— - 131	—	— - 139	— - 137
	— - 104	—	— - 228	— - 160
	— - 172	—	— - 179	— - 209
	— - 94	—	— - 119	— - 223
	— - 95	—	— - 239	— - 108
	— - 274	—	— - 130	— - 172
	— - 177	—	— - 144	— - 261
	— - 113	—	— - 171	— - 150
	— - 112	—	— - 110	— - 182
	— - 312	—	— - 192	— - 167
	— - 230	—	— - 200	— - 164
	—	—	— - 130	— - 234
	—	—	— - 51	— - 151
	—	—	— - 105	— - 84
	—	—	— - 186	— - 148
	—	—	— - 119	— - 189
	—	—	— - 53	— - 119
	—	—	— - 146	— - 152
	—	—	— - 124	— - 102
	—	—	— - 193	— - 122
	—	—	— - 231	— - 121
	—	—	— - 52	— - 257
	—	—	— - 148	— - 147
	—	—	— - 145	— - 123
	—	—	— - 108	— - 185

* Nearly the whole of the Ships built at this port in 1804-5 were built *on Speculation* in order to employ the apprentices, and preserve *men* for repairing Ships.—See *Letters ante* from the out-ports.

PORTS.	Year 1790.	Tons	1791.	Tons	1804.	Tons	1805.	Tons
SUNDERLAND *continued*	None.		None.		1 Ship -	193	1 Ship	337
	—		—		— -	137	— -	157
	—		—		— -	134	— -	189
	—		—		— -	349	—	
	—		—		— -	130	—	
	—		—		— -	139	—	
	—		—		— -	139	—	
	—		—		— -	131	—	
	—		—		— -	318	—	
	—		—		— -	125	—	
	—		—		— -	184	—	
	—		—		— -	135	—	
	—		—		— -	192	—	
	—		—		— -	110	—	
	—		—		— -	125	—	
	—		—		— -	204	—	
	—		—		— -	96	—	
	—		—		— -	347	—	
SWANSEY -	1 Ship	10	1 Ship	48	1 Ship -	57	1 Ship	60
	— -	25	— -	125	— -	77	— -	154
	— -	281	— -	17	— -	38	—	
	— -	20	— -	47	— -	6		
	— -	25	— -	35	—			
	— -	44	— -	28	—		—	
	— -	216	—		—		—	
TRURO -	None.		None.		None.		None.	
WELLS -	None.		1 Ship	107	1 Ship	110	1 Ship	77
	—		— -	130	— -	106	— -	77
	—		—		— -	129	—	
WEYMOUTH	1 Ship	17	1 Ship	82	1 Ship -	36	1 Ship	230
	— -	10	— -	6	— -	67	— -	68
	— -	6	—		— -	42	—	
	— -	37	—		— -	108	—	
WHITBY	1 Ship	367	1 Ship	317	1 Ship	279	1 Ship	269
	— -	188	— -	280	— -	377	— -	296
	— -	113	— -	363	— -	92	— -	103
	— -	72	— -	113	— -	135	— -	77
	— -	79	— -	84	— -	68	— -	365
	— -	353	— -	164	— -	373	— -	127
	— -	281	— -	267	— -	60	— -	219
	— -	287	— -	284	— -	58	— -	242
	— -	292	— -	230	— -	70	— -	194
	— -	165	— -	139	— -	244	— -	160
	— -	208	— -	83	— -	81	— -	182
	— -	284	— -	238	— -	431	— -	482
	— -	68	— -	364	— -	132	— -	400
	— -	313	— -	233	— -	61	— -	330
	— -	142	— -	341	— -	337	— -	375
	— -	370	— -	184	— -	124	— -	389

PORTS.	Year 1790.		1791.		1804.		1805.	
		Tons		Tons		Tons		Tons
WHITBY *continued*	1 Ship	108	1 Ship	294	— -	401	— -	250
	— -	193	— -	319	— -	81	— -	418
	— -	164	— -	353	— -	163	—	
	— -	193	— -	380	— -	325	—	
	— -	339	— -	320	— -	344	—	
	—		— -	263	— -	125	—	
	—		— -	306	— -	447	—	
	—		— -	320	— -	73	—	
	—		— -	51	— -	198	—	
	—		— -	261	—		—	
	—		— -	302	—		—	
	—		— -	306	—		—	
WHITEHAVEN	1 Ship	112	1 Ship	113	1 Ship	182	1 Ship	193
	— -	35	— -	146	— -	156	— -	343
	— -	22	— -	116	— -	202	— -	172
	— -	12	— -	223	— -	157	— -	301
	— -	212	— -	216	— -	209	— -	159
	— -	107	— -	11	— -	153	— -	80
	— -	133	— -	114	— -	185	— -	175
	— -	11	— -	221	— -	207	— -	188
	— -	89	— -	103	— -	176	— -	210
	— -	65	— -	247	— -	35	— -	195
	— -	116	— -	132	— -	93	— -	122
	— -	46	— -	65	— -	204	— -	168
	— -	158	— -	105	— -	201	— -	47
	— -	197	— -	29	— -	64	— -	138
	— -	136	—		— -	241	— -	44
	— -	158	—		— -	151	— -	216
	— -	180	—		— -	211	— -	169
	—		—		— -	246	— -	97
	—		—		— -	100	—	
	—		—		— -	60	—	
	—		—		— -	161	—	
	—		—		— -	158	—	
	—		—		— -	183	—	
			—					
WISBECH -	None.		None.		1 Ship	41	1 Ship	42
	—		—		— -	50	— -	41
	—		—		—		— -	37
	—		—				— -	41
WOODBRIDGE	None.		None.		None.		1 Ship	50
	—		—		—		— -	14
YARMOUTH	1 Ship	136	1 Ship	126	1 Ship	229	1 Ship	116
	— -	161	— -	86	— -	92	— -	78
	— -	14	— -	108	— -	84	— -	69
	— -	106	— -	52	— -	85	— -	121
	— -	127	— -	167	— -	106	— -	26
	— -	115	— -	60	— -	37	— -	34
	— -	121	— -	92	— -	26	— -	150
	— -	12	— -	71	— -	93	— -	117

PORTS.	Year 1790.	Tons	1791.	Tons	1804.	Tons	1805.	Tons
YARMOUTH *continued* -	1 Ship	89	1 Ship	108	1 Ship	125	1 Ship	26
	— -	114	— -	103	— -	242	— -	93
	— -	122	— -	108	— -	115	— -	47
	— -	132	— -	91	— -	290	— -	122
	— -	104	— -	109	— -	79	— -	30
	—	10	— -	126	— -	84	— -	87
	— -	94	— -	105	— -	191	— -	47
	— -	116	— -	17	— -	113	— -	79
	— -	104	— -	71	— -	46	— -	87
	— -	88	— -	107	— -	15	— -	105
	— -	92	— -	23	— -	94	— -	26
	— -	139	— -	84	— -	113	— -	35
	— -	102	— -	89	— -	24	— -	96
	— -	120	—		— -	93	— -	116
	— -	104	—		— -	80	— -	97
	— -	46	—		—		— -	298
	—		—		—		— -	84
	—		—		—		— -	24
	—		—		—		— -	91
	—		—		—		— -	51
	—		—		—		— -	47
	—		—		—		— -	109
	—		—		—		— -	81
	—		—		—		— -	52
	—		—		—		— -	19
	—		—		—		— -	22
	—		—		—		— -	49
	—		—		—		— -	75

PORTS OF SCOTLAND; viz.

PORTS.	Year 1790.	Tons	1791.	Tons	1804.	Tons	1805.	Tons
ABERDEEN	1 Ship	134	1 Ship	60	1 Ship	110	1 Ship	132
	— -	90	— -	138	— -	87	— -	120
	— -	51	— -	24	— -	290	— -	33
	— -	48	— -	53	— -	564	— -	122
	— -	53	— -	62	— -	106	— -	69
	— -	83	— -	39	— -	165	— -	85
	— -	84	— -	72	— -	186	— -	127
	— -	75	— -	67	— -	65	— -	63
	— -	95	— -	100	— -	68	— -	127
	— -	24	— -	69	— -	161	— -	169
	— -	29	— -	50	— -	314	— -	85
	—		— -	12	— -	148	— -	[illegible]
	—		—		— -	127	— -	52
	—		—		— -	135	— -	121
	—		—		— -	51	— -	64
	—		—		— -	124	— -	179
	—		—		— -	65	— -	132
	—		—		— -	370	— -	116
	—		—		— -	17	— -	132
	—		—		— -	26	— -	102

PORTS.	Year 1790.	Tons	1791.	Tons	1804.	Tons	1805.	Tons
ABERDEEN *continued*	—		—		1 Ship	90	—	
	—		—		—	110	—	
	—		—		—	128	—	
	—		—		—	68	—	
AIR	1 Ship	177	1 Ship	59	1 Ship	126	1 Ship	121
	—	45	—	16	—	159	—	130
	—	155	—	219	—	61	—	153
	—		—	73	—	325	—	
ALLOA	1 Ship	40	1 Ship	53	1 Ship	58	1 Ship	79
	—	66	—	51	—	89	—	139
	—	16	—	100	—	80	—	64
	—	75	—	52	—	153	—	74
	—		—	57	—	82	—	86
	—		—		—	47	—	33
	—		—		—	68	—	75
	—		—		—	82	—	
	—		—		—	76	—	
ANSTRUTHER	1 Ship	41	1 Ship	21	1 Ship	57	1 Ship	42
	—	37	—	45	—	45	—	120
	—	37	—	102	—	35	—	30
	—	146	—	30	—	58	—	
	—		—	37	—		—	
	—		—	38	—		—	
BANFF	None.		None.		1 Ship	51	1 Ship	16
	—		—		—	57	—	64
	—		—		—	21	—	19
	—		—		—	91	—	29
	—		—		—	56	—	111
	—		—		—	49	—	
BOWNESS	1 Ship	65	1 Ship	53	1 Ship	82	1 Ship	82
	—	47	—	30	—	30	—	51
	—	34	—	72	—	44	—	162
	—	49	—	56	—	64	—	62
	—	16	—	75	—	27	—	41
	—	51	—	68	—	74	—	33
	—	19	—	73	—	76	—	
	—	64	—	48	—		—	
	—	84	—		—		—	
CAMBLETOWN	1 Ship	39	1 Ship	50	1 Ship	61	1 Ship	43
	—	13	—	20	—		—	
	—	12	—		—		—	
DUMFRIES	1 Ship	35	None.		1 Ship	45	1 Ship	4
	—	40	—		—	21	—	43
	—	16	—		—	35	—	57
	—		—		—		—	31
DUNBAR	1 Ship	74	1 Ship	220	1 Ship	34	1 Ship	116
	—	53	—		—	56	—	61
	—		—		—		—	97

[B b]

PORTS.	Year 1790.	Tons	1791.	Tons	1804.	Tons	1805.	Tons
DUNDEE	1 Ship	37	1 Ship	118	1 Ship	75	1 Ship	82
	— -	18	— -	60	— -	73	— -	61
	— -	160	— -	18	— -	32	— -	152
	—		—		— -	76	— -	144
	—		—		— -	113	— -	82
	—		—		— -	23	— -	65
	—		—		— -	68	— -	75
	—		—		—		— -	68
	—		—		—		— -	45
	—		—		—		— -	38
	—		—		—		— -	71
FORT WILLIAM	None		None.		1 Ship	16	None.	
GLASGOW	1 Ship	71	1 Ship	220	Ship	226	1 Ship	61
	— -	75	— -	207	— -	52	— -	45
	— -	58	— -	248	— -	49	— -	79
	— -	25	— -	11	— -	80	— -	215
	— -	58	— -	325	— -	69	— -	59
	— -	57	— -	77	— -	78	— -	80
	— -	62	— -	55	—		—	
	— -	55	— -	142	—		—	
	— -	40	— -	102	—		—	
	— -	168	— -	23	—		—	
	— -	39	— -	13	—		—	
	— -	56	— -	48	—		—	
	— -	86	— -	70	—		—	
GREENOCK	1 Ship	71	1 Ship	29	1 Ship	396	1 Ship	388
	— -	14	— -	31	— -	57	— -	22
	— -	40	— -	45	— -	74	— -	20
	— -	19	— -	624	— -	189	— -	279
	— -	12	— -	69	— -	188	— -	16
	— -	29	— -	20	— -	15	— -	66
	— -	13	— -	59	— -	15	— -	551
	— -	30	— -	103	— -	65	— -	16
	— -	62	— -	30	— -	80	—	
	— -	29	— -	30	— -	185	—	
	— -	35	— -	69	— -	72	—	
	— -	16	— -	61	— -	79	—	
	—		— -	16	—		—	
	—		— -	56	—		—	
	—		— -	65	—		—	
ISLE MARTIN	None.		1 Ship	35	None.		None.	
INVERNESS	1 Ship	67	1 Ship	60	1 Ship	40	1 Ship	68
	— -	95	— -	45	— -	45	— -	38
	— -	63	— -	214	— -	167	— -	34
	— -	50	— -	63	— -	45	— -	64
	— -	25	— -	20	—		— -	24
	— -	33	— -	31	—		— -	79
	— -	57	— -	58	—		— -	65
	— -	23	—		—		—	

PORTS.	Year 1790.	Tons	1791.	Tons	1804.	Tons	1805.	Tons
IRVINE -	1 Ship	226	1 Ship	73	1 Ship	141	1 Ship	144
	— -	149	— -	92	— -	102	— -	15
	— -	63	— -	101	— -	80	— -	95
	— -	83	— -	79	— -	113	— -	95
	— -	186	— -	78	—		—	
KIRKALDY	1 Ship	236	1 Ship	262	1 Ship	52	1 Ship	54
	— -	7	— -	42	— -	70	— -	30
	— -	178	— -	253	— -	28	— -	50
	— -	115	— -	53	— -	52	— -	206
	— -	75	— -	62	— -	245	— -	157
	— -	136	— -	82	— -	17	— -	55
	— -	143	— -	111	— -	26	— -	29
	— -	44	— -	262	— -	47	— -	158
	—		— -	338	—		— -	77
	—		—		—		— -	71
	—		—		—		— -	61
KIRCUDBRIGHT	1 Ship	87	1 Ship	55	None.		None.	
	— -	21	— -	19	—		—	
	— -	11	— -	54	—		—	
	—		— -	17	—		—	
KIRKWALL	1 Ship	76	1 Ship	58	1 Ship	19	None.	
	— -	33	—		— -	76	—	
LERWICK -	1 Ship	23	1 Ship	16	1 Ship	15	1 Ship	11
	—		— -	14	—		—	
	—		— -	15	—		—	
LEITH -	1 Ship	82	1 Ship	55	1 Ship	140	1 Ship	106
	— -	81	— -	15	— -	80	— -	199
	— -	77	— -	10	— -	142	— -	168
	— -	30	— -	28	— -	309	—	
	— -	72	— -	197	— -	53	—	
	— -	32	— -	118	— -	106	—	
	— -	219	— -	172	— -	68	—	
	— -	149	— -	229	— -	267	—	
	— -	42	— -	144	— -	201	—	
	— -	122	— -	134	— -	48	—	
	— -	16	— -	121	— -	201	—	
	— -	124	— -	85	—		—	
	— -	108	— -	60	—		—	
	— -	49	— -	34	—		—	
	— -	54	— -	38	—		—	
MONTROSE	1 Ship	38	1 Ship	29	1 Ship	40	1 Ship	119
	— -	13	— -	39	— -	102	— -	122
	— -	43	— -	52	— -	50	— -	92
	— -	49	—		— -	137	— -	66
	— -	60	—		— -	100	— -	63
	—		—		— -	57	— -	270
	—		—		— -	102	— -	50
	—		—		— -	117	— -	80
	—		—		— -	15	— -	23
	—		—		— -	58	—	

PORTS.	Year 1790.	Tons	1791.	Tons	1804.	Tons	1805.	Tons
OBAN - -	1 Ship	21	1 Ship	49	1 Ship	41	1 Ship	64
	— -	18	—		— -	13	— -	11
	— -	145	—		—		—	
PERTH -	1 Ship	83	1 Ship	115	1 Ship	73	1 Ship	79
	— -	85	— -	64	— -	70	—	
	—		— -	231	— -	82	—	
	—		—		— -	72	—	
	—		—		— -	26	—	
PORT PATRICK	1 Ship	50	None.		None.		None.	
PRESTON-PANS	None.		None.		None.		None.	
ROTHSAY -	1 Ship	28	1 Ship	37	None.		None.	
STORNOWAY	1 Ship	27	1 Ship	58	1 Ship	20	1 Ship	36
	—		—		—		— -	20
STRANRAER	1 Ship	27	1 Ship	45	1 Ship	56	None.	
	—		— -	85	—		—	
	—		— -	51	—		—	
THURSO -	1 Ship	44	1 Ship	42	None.		None.	
TOBERMORY	None.		None.		None.		1 Ship	21
WIGTOWN	None.		1 Ship	30	1 Ship	45	None.	
	—		— -	61	—		—	

T. E. Willoughby.

Custom-House, London,
Office of the Register General of Shipping.
23d June, 1806.

N. B. The above account was ordered to be printed the 24th of June, 1806. It is observable that it contains only a return of *four* years instead of *sixteen* years, which was ordered pursuant to a motion made by sir Charles Price, bart. in the words set forth at the head of this account. To form a correct idea of *ship-building* in Great Britain, in 1805, a reference must be added to the letters from the out ports, page cxxxiii; by which it will be seen that there is a *general* decline of *ship-building*, and not merely a *removal* of it from one port to another from cheapness of wages, &c. It therefore becomes a subject of the highest importance for *immediate legislative* inquiry into the causes which have led to it, and to consider of the most effectual means to regain it. Had the old maritime principles of the nation been adhered to, and such burthens on shipping as those imposed by the tonnage duty bill, which passed in the peace of 1801-2, there is good reason to believe the country would not have had cause, at this moment, for alarm on this interesting subject, and that the same spirit of enterprize which theretofore characterised the shipping interest would have continued; but which, unhappily for the nation, is at present nearly extinguished.

24th December, 1806.

eat the Year 1790, at the several Ports mentioned in
shin:rent Rates of Tonnage of *each* Ship, Vessel, and
ar.

1790.							
. of ips.	Amount of onnage.	No. of Ships.	Tonnage of each.	Amount of Tonnage.	No. of Ships.	Tonnage of each.	Amount of Tonnage.
5	11915	136		19262	172		28353
1	157	1	215	215	1	292	292
2	316	2	216	432	2	293	586
1	160	1	218	218	1	298	298
1	161	1	219	219	1	304	304
3	486	1	223	223	1	305	305
[illegible]	163	1	224	224	1	307	307
2	328	1	225	225	1	312	312
	165	1	226	226	1	313	313
	336	1	229	229	1	317	317
	170	2	230	460	3	320	960
	172	1	236	236	1	324	324
	348	1	237	237	1	535	335
	175	1	238	238	1	337	337
5	176	1	239	239	1	339	339
7	354	1	243	243	1	342	342
78	178	1	246	246	1	353	353
80	180	2	253	506	1	364	364
81	181	1	255	255	1	369	569
[illegible]	[illegible]	[illegible]	[illegible]	[illegible]	[illegible]	370	740

Vessels from four tons to 99 a
Ships from 101 tons to 551, av
East Indiamen, from 613 tons
Do. lighters

, the Year 1805, at the several Ports mentioned in
:r to shew the *actual* Number of *Ships* fit for the

1805.

Amount of Tonnage.	No. of Ships.	Tonnage of each.	Amount of Tonnage	No. of Ships.	Tonnage of each.	Amount of Tonnage.
19401	187	16355	29356	East	Indiamen.	
188	1	278	278	1	613	613
378	1	279	279	1	673	673
191	1	293	293	1	840	840
192	1	296	296	2	858	1716
193	2	298	596	1	862	862
338	1	300	300	1	864	864
390	1	301	301	Light-		
398	1	315	315	ers		5568
206	1	328	328	2	268	
208	1	330	330			268
413	2	341	682	9		
210	1	342	342			
212	1	343	343			
215	1	360	360			
432	1	361	361			
438	1	365	365			
446	2	366	732			
450	1	368	368			
454	1	375	375			
230	1	388	388			
462	1	389	389			
468	1	396	396			
242	1	400	400			
250	2	401	802			
502	1	411	411			
257	1	412	412			
261	1	413	413			
262	1	418	418			
263	1	422	422			
265	1	428	428			
266	1	482	482			
270	1	551	551			
29356	223		42512		Ought to be	42562

No. XXIII.

EAST INDIA TRADE.

East India House, 12th June, 1806.

Sir,

THE court of directors of the East India Company having referred to the consideration of the committee of shipping your letter of the 10th ultimo, requesting to be furnished, for the information of the committee of ship owners, with an account of the quantity of tonnage employed by the company in their export and import trade, from the year 1780, to 1805, inclusive, *and also the average rate of freight per ton, with the war contingencies in those years* *, I have the committee's commands to transmit you an account of the number and tonnage of the ships employed by the company in their export and import trade, from the year 1780, to 1804, inclusive.

I am,

Sir,

Your most obedient servant,

James Coggan.

Mr. Nathaniel Atcheson.

* It is to be regretted that the rates of freight in their service for those years were not given with the statement of tonnage.

No. XXIII.—Continued.

An Account of the Number and Tonnage of regular and extra Ships engaged for the East India Company's service, from the season 1780, to 1804, inclusive.

		Regular and Extra.	Tons.	Ships for an outward bound voyage only.
Season .	1780	20 Ships.	14315	
	1781	26	19655	3 ships, 2043 tons.
	1782	23 .	17504	1 —— 864
	1783	13 .	9978	
	1784	27 .	20424	
	1785	43 .	31643	
	1786	34 .	26795	
	1787	31 .	25824	
	1788	32 .	26905	
	1789	31 .	26332	
	1790	25 .	22556	
	1791	28 .	23522	
	1792	43 .	37583	
	1793	46 .	40665	
	1794	34 .	28896	
	1795	46 .	41721	
	1796	46 .	36464	
	1797	26 .	21601	21434 tons of shipping, not in the Company's regular employ, were engaged this season for special purposes.
	1798	39 .	35754	1 ship of 778 tons.
	1799	34 .	30517	
	1800	49 .	42396	
	1801	39 .	34593	
	1802	52 .	45466	
	1803	54 .	46562	
	1804	50 .	42603	

The season 1805 is not yet concluded.

East India House, 12*th June*, 1806.

James Coggan.

No. XXIV.

Statement of Ships employed in the Trade between *Great Britain* and *America*.

Extract from Lord Sheffield's Strictures.

"THE navigation laws of Great Britain, among other objects, have recently experienced the effect of the changeful and temporising policy that has lately prevailed. Those laws were long considered as involving the permanent, commercial, and political interests of the state. But on too many occasions of late they have been viewed, or pretended to be viewed, in a very different light; and they are relaxed, or suspended, not because they are defective in principle, but because it is thought necessary to yield to the pressure of immediate circumstances and interests: on these occasions they are estimated, perhaps, by some casual and partial effect which they are said to produce, and instead of being considered as they refer to the general interests of the empire, they are frequently discussed with a reference to some particular object, as may suit the purpose of the moment, or perhaps the interested views of individuals. General inferences, therefore, are frequently deduced from most *partial statements* *; and thus in parliament, and out of parliament, delusion is sometimes abetted and diffused."

* There are instances enough before me on other subjects of management of this kind; I shall merely glance at two of them. The tonnage duty bill during its progress through the House of Commons gave rise to much debate, and it was asserted in support of the bill, that the tonnage of England was well able to bear the duty, having lately flourished beyond all former example. To sustain an assertion so strong, it was attempted to be proved by figures that this tonnage had actually increased since the year 1792 to a great amount. But it was not stated that this tonnage was not all British built; that it was principally increased by the number of prize vessels, which had been taken during the war; and that if it had been all British built, it would not thereby have authorised the conclusion which was drawn, because it remained in a great proportion utterly unemployed, and because the British tonnage which was actually employed in the year 1792 was greater, comparatively considered, than the British tonnage so employed, even in the year 1802, the boasted period of the highest prosperity of the shipping trade of Great Britain.

The other case to which I would advert is almost equally plausible, and equally delusive. During the three years ending in 1802, inclusive, many

No. XXIV.—Continued.

An Account of the Number of Vessels with their Tonnage, which cleared inwards and outwards, between *Great Britain* and the *United States* of *America*, in the following years.

	British.		American.	
	Ships.	Tonnage.	Ships.	Tonnage.
1790 Outwards . .	245	50079	218	39441
Inwards .	312	64197	246	46234
1791 Outwards .	253	55328	291	55806
Inwards .	247	53102	318	62253
1792 Outwards .	223	50963	285	59414
Inwards .	197	42035	313	64035
1799 Outwards .	57	14627	354	78683
Inwards .	42	9796	343	75225
1800 Outwards .	62	14381	507	112596
Inwards .	77	27144	550	124015

Thus in the course of a very few years, the number of *British* vessels employed *inwards* in one branch of trade has *declined* from 312 to 77. And the number of *American* vessels so employed in the same branch has *increased* from 246 to 550, and which clearly shews the deep and well digested policy of America, in imposing a duty on *British* manufactures exported into America in *British* ships, which is not counteracted by any adequate duty on American produce, &c. exported into *Great Britain* in *American* bottoms.

arguments tending to prove the rapid progression of British commerce were deduced from papers laid before the house, purporting to state the clear amount of the annual exports and imports of Britain. That these papers were accurately drawn up, the sound understanding and indisputable correctness of the inspector-general leave no doubt. But the fallacy lay not in the accounts, but in the deductions from the accounts. The sum total became the grand topic of ministerial arguments, and as that sum was great, the hearers were satisfied. But it was not stated, that, of the imports and exports exhibited in the accounts, a considerable part was brought in foreign vessels, and had been merely landed and warehoused in England to be re-exported without payment of duties; and that a deduction of the value of this property should have been made from the sum total of the account, in order to shew the true balance by which the prosperity of British commerce was to be estimated.

No. XXV.

INCREASE OF AMERICAN TONNAGE, &c. &c.

Extract from a Publication in 1802.

AMERICAN POPULATION, NAVIGATION, COMMERCE AND REVENUE.

WE have, on former occasions, found it necessary to endeavour to direct the attention of *our countrymen* to the interesting scene exhibited on the other side of the Atlantic, and we were not a little surprised to perceive our endeavours treated, not only with neglect, but with contempt. We were told, that "a country so *distant*" could be little interesting to Englishmen; but it has required only a very short time to show, that "a country so distant" may be, and already has been found to be, of more importance to Englishmen *than any other country*, England only excepted. It is, therefore, with the hope of attracting a somewhat greater degree of attention, that we revive this *uninteresting* subject, with the insertion of some facts relative to the population and commerce of the United States.—A census was taken in 1800, and returned to Congress in the autumn of 1801, according to which the population of the several States was found to be as follows:

States.	Total Population.	Slaves.
New Hampshire	183,858	8
Rhode Island	69,122	380
Massachusets	422,845	
Maine	151,710	
Connecticut	254,002	951
Vermont	154,465	
New York	504,195	15,602
New-Jersey	211,149	12,422

Carried over

[C c]

States.	Total Population.	Slaves.
Brought forward		
Pensylvania	602,365	1,706
Delaware	64,273	6,154
Maryland	329,704	100,393
Virginia	878,950	345,796
North Carolina . . .	478,103	133,296
South Carolina . . .	345,591	146,151
Georgia	162,686	59,699
Kentucky	220,955	40,843
Tennesse	109,960	14,022
Territory of Mississippi . .	59,857	3,615
District of Columbia . .	14,093	3,244
Grand Total in 1800 .	5,214,801	876,790
Population in 1790 .	3,929,326	697,697
Increase in 10 years .	1,285,475	179,093

TONNAGE.

	Tons of Shipping.	Men.
In 1800	939,000	56,340
In 1790	450,000	27,000
Increase in 10 years . .	489,000	29,340

COMMERCE AND REVENUE.

	Dollars.
The American produce exported in 1800, amounted to	32,000,000
Ditto, in 1790	14,000,000
Increase in 10 years . . .	18,000,000

	Dollars.
The * foreign commodities brought into the country for re-exportation, in 1800, amounted to	30,000,000
Ditto in 1790	2,000,000
Increase in 10 years	28,000,000
The revenue in 1801, is estimated at . .	11,359,000
Ditto in 1790, amounted to . . .	6,124,000
Increase in 11 years	5,235,000

It will be perceived, that the *commerce* and *revenue* of the United States have increased in a proportion much greater than that of the *population*. We shall subjoin here an extract from a debate, in the lower house of Congress, on the 16th of December, 1801, which will enable our readers to form some judgment of the motives, from which the bill † now before *our own* legislature has been requested by the American government.

"*Gen. Smith* differed from the gentleman who spoke last, as to the effect which he seemed to apprehend from the repeal of this law. The effect he knew would be the very contrary, and was of so much importance to the commercial interests of the United States, that it was for that very reason he wished that no delay might take place in adopting measures for commercial security. It was found, very early after the establishment of our government, expedient to adopt a system pursued by other nations, in laying such duties as would discriminate between our own and foreign tonnage; at that time *our ships* were not adequate to *carry one half of our produce* to foreign markets; when discriminating duties were laid, the measure appeared to act as a charm, and beyond the expectations of the most sanguine calculations of commercial

* The very great increase of this branch of the *American* trade appears to have taken place since the subjects of that country were allowed a *free* trade to the *British* settlements in *India*, under the *first* Treaty between Great Britain and America, and which, it is seriously apprehended, will *continue* to increase under the ruinous and impolitic concessions since made to that country by the *British* government, and particularly from the relaxation of the rule of the war, 1756, allowing the Americans to bring the produce of the *belligerent* colonies to *Europe*, &c.—To form a correct estimate of the designs of the United States, see Mr. *Tench Coxe*'s View of America, reprinted by Johnson, in 1796.

† See the debate on the *American* treaty bill, 5th March, 1802, in the Parliamentary Register.

men, *our tonnage doubled* in a short period, we were not only very soon able to carry all our own produce, but to enter *largely into trade abroad.* Other nations, affected by our success, *particularly Great Britain*, devised means to enter into a competition with us in their own markets, and enacted countervailing laws, or devised duties equal to the amount which we had laid on to protect our own commerce. The war *that has lately ceased* gave us great advantages; for although new countervailing duties, and to an extent perhaps not authorised by existing treaty, were laid, yet as *their* tonnage was subject to a high war insurance, from which ours was exempt, we retained our advantage during the war; which having now changed the relative state of things, as well *with Great Britain* as with other nations, it is incumbent on us to provide new means to guard our trade, and retain it in our own hands. *By the operation of the existing laws of Great Britain laying countervailing duties they possess an advantage so great*, as to make a difference of 18 dollars *in their favour* upon the freight of every hogshead of tobacco shipped from our ports in a British vessel; they will therefore have the whole difference of the market price in their favour against American shippers; and of consequence, if we do not make provision to guard against the contingency, the whole of our carrying trade may go into their hands, for every man will ship his goods for a market where he can effect it on the most advantageous terms. We were circumstanced in the same way with regard to France, where her regulations were never more disadvantageous to us than the British, though the state of her tonnage did not leave room to apprehend so much. He had it from high authority, that the difference in favour of the French tonnage in their ports over ours amounted to 10 livres in the 100, or about 190 on the hogshead of tobacco only; from whence it was evident that this step was necessary to be taken to bring us upon more equal terms of trade. The commerce in tobacco to that country is very important to us; to Great Britain we export only 14,000 hogsheads, we export to France 40,000 hogsheads. The present was the season to make use of our fortunate situation, and to provide such regulations as would secure to us that important branch of trade; no time could be lost with propriety on the subject, and the measures proposed by the resolution would give us the best opportunity to use the advantage. *We are now in a very different situation* from that in which we stood on the passing of the discriminating law: at that time we had an *insufficiency of tonnage*, and it was necessary to create a competent quantity; that has been effected, and we have *now tonnage sufficient to carry on all our* trade under judicious regulations, and it is our interest to seek the means by which we can start upon equal terms *with them* in our own and *in their ports*. We are competent to enter into such an amicable contest. Our spirit of enterprise and the skill of *our maritime citizens* are equal, if not superior, to any in the world; and it is becoming our circumstances and situation to shun a mercantile warfare, while we seek a generous emulation of skill, industry, and enterprise. *We want* to enter the ports of *other* nations much more than they want to enter ours. *He that can carry cheapest and best will have the advantage. We not only build cheaper than other nations, but we build better, and sail with fewer hands.* We need, therefore, no other than * *equal terms* to start upon."

* That the government of *America* is particularly attentive to its *carrying trade*, and feelingly alive to future advantages which it may derive, is obvious from the following passage in Mr. *President Jefferson's* address to Congress on the 15th December, 1802:—"We find in some parts of Europe, monopolising discriminations, which, in the form of duties, tend effectually to prohibit the carrying thither our own produce in our own vessels. From existing amities, and a spirit of justice, it is hoped that friendly discussion will produce a fair and adequate reciprocity. But should false calculation of interest defeat our hope, it rests with the legislature to decide whether they will meet inequalities abroad with countervailing inequalities at home, or provide for the evil in any other way.

"It is with satisfaction I lay before you an act of the British parliament; *anticipating* this subject, so far as to authorise a mutual abolition of the duties, and countervailing duties, permitted under the treaty of 1794. It shews on their part a spirit of justice and friendly accommodation, which it is our duty and *our interest* to cultivate with *all nations*. *Whether this will produce a due equality in the navigation between the two countries, is a subject for your consideration.*"

It is evident from the *subsequent* concessions made to the government of the United States by Great Britain, that those in 1802 were deemed insufficient, and not finding the *yielding* system which pervaded lord Sidmouth's administration adopted by the *late British* government, the Non-importation act passed the Congress. and it is to be *apprehended* it has produced on our *present ministry* the effect intended; and although lord Auckland and lord Holland were only appointed commissioners to negotiate with the American ministers in September last, yet it appears from lord Howick's letter to the lord-mayor that the differences between the two countries have been adjusted within a period of less than *four* months. It will of course afford *great* exultation and triumph to Mr. *president* Jefferson, though he may be *surprised* at the *facility* with which the claims of his country have been acceded to by Great Britain, as it is evident, by the following message to Congress, he did not expect the differences between the two countries would have been so *speedily* adjusted.

"*Mr. Griswold* was still unsatisfied by the reasons given by the General. He agreed that it was desirable to secure as much of the foreign trade as we could to our own vessels, and if he could be persuaded that a repeal of the discriminating duties would effect that purpose, or that their continuance would exclude us from our own carrying trade, he would assuredly vote for the resolution. But he had heard nothing to satisfy him on that point. With Great Britain, he believed, no such measure could be effected in that way, and he questioned if it would prove more advantageous with other nations, as they pursue their own measures, whatever laws we might adopt or repeal. It was true, that in Great Britain our tobacco trade was subjected to the disadvantage of heavy duties; but it should be recollected that comparatively little tobacco is consumed in Great Britain: in the north and other parts of Europe the consumption was much greater. Tobacco landed in England, therefore, was not all subjected to their heavy duties, *because whatever was exported* had the duties returned by way of drawback; so that our tobacco trade thither in American bottoms stood exactly upon the same charges to which the British bottoms are sub-

SPECIAL MESSAGE FROM THE PRESIDENT TO THE CONGRESS.

To the Senate and House of Representation of the United States of America.

"I have the satisfaction to inform you that the negotiation depending between the United States and the government of Great Britain is proceeding in the spirit of friendship and accommodation which promises a result of mutual advantages. Delays, indeed, have taken place, occasioned by the long illness and subsequent death of the British minister charged with that duty. But *the commissioners* appointed by that government to resume the negotiation *shew every disposition* to hasten its progress; *it is however a work of time*, as many arrangements are necessary to place *our future harmony* on stable grounds. In the mean time, we find by the communication of our plenipotentiaries, that a *temporary* suspension of the act of the last session, prohibiting certain importations, would, as a mark of candid disposition on our part, and of confidence in the temper and views with which they have been met, have a happy effect on its course. A step so friendly would afford farther evidence that all the proceedings have flown from views of justice and conciliation, and that we give them willingly, that which may best meet corresponding dispositions.

"Add to this, that the same motives which produced the postponement of the act till the 15th November last are in favour of its further suspension. And *as we have reason* to hope that it may soon yield to arrangements of mutual concert and convenience, justice seems to require *that the same measures may be dealt out* to the few cases which may fall within its short course, as to all others preceding and following it. I cannot, therefore, but recommend the suspension of this act for a reasonable time, on considerations of justice, amity, and the public interests.

"Dec. 3, 1806. (Signed) THOS. JEFFERSON."

jected. If we repeal the law laying discriminating duties, then we permit British ships to come into our ports upon equal terms with our own, and the consequence will be that they will then become our carriers. In France, likewise, there is little likelihood of advantage accruing by the repeal. In that country the tobacco trade was a monopoly of the Farmers-General, and no one but them could import tobacco into France: it was probable that the same regulations would exist in one shape or another in future, and that we should not be likely to obtain better terms by the repeal of our law. If we could secure the carriage of our own commerce by any reasonable measures, it would make him very happy; but he did not believe the measure proposed to be calculated for such an effect, and he was not disposed to run rashly into the repeal; he was not prepared to give his consent to the resolution, and particularly as it was not much detailed; it was constructed so loose as to render it impossible to say how or by whom the regulation is to be defined, or its extent ascertained. The *carrying trade* of our own country was to us all *important*, none, not all the other was so much so. The British carrying trade was certainly much less so to them, *it was of little value to them;* but with us it is otherwise; our articles of home production are all *bulky* and require *large tonnage*, such as rice, flour, tobacco, fish, &c. and it was requisite to retain duties which gave them a decided preference. He was not prepared to agree to the resolutions, and would rather *prefer the appointment of a committee to investigate and report upon the subject.*"

N. B. Since the year 1800 there has been a further alarming increase of *American tonnage*: endeavours have been made, but in vain, to obtain the statements of it, *which are laid before Congress.* Had they been successful, the publication of them might probably have dispelled the infatuation which pervades at this time the government of Great Britain, *ere the whole of its carrying trade is lost*, and with it the *naval* power of the empire: It is *reported* that the *United States* of *America* have now *above one million of tons* of shipping, and above *eighty thousand* seamen.—See an admirable letter on this subject, signed *Civis*, in Yorke's Political Review, 17th January, 1807, and many others in the former numbers of that work.

April, 9, 1806,

Read and ordered to lie on the table *.—A Letter from the Secretary of the Treasury, transmitting a *Statement* of Goods, Wares, and Merchandise, *exported* from the United States, *during one Year*, prior to the 1st day of October, 1805.

SIR, TREASURY DEPARTMENT, *April* 8, 1806.

I HAVE the honour to transmit herewith a statement of goods, wares, and merchandise, exported from the United States during one year prior to the 1st day of October, 1805, and amounting to 95,566,021 dollars. The goods, wares, and merchandise of *domestic* growth, or manufacture, included in this statement, are estimated at . . . . *dollars*, 42,387,002
And those of *foreign* growth, or manufacture, at 53,179,019

95,566,021

Those foreign goods may be divided into three classes, viz.

1st. Articles, on the importation of which no duty had been collected, they being free of duty by the laws of the United States, and amounting to . . . . . . *dollars*,	1,641,725
2d. Articles liable to duty, and which were, on re-exportation thereof, entitled to drawback, ...	42,119,498
3d. Articles liable to duty, but which were not, on re-exportation thereof, entitled to drawback, ...	9,417,796
	53,179,019

The duties collected on the importation of the articles of the 3d class, and which not being paid by consumers within the United States, are derived directly from *the carrying trade*, amount to dollars 1,581,618, exclusively of the additional duties, which constitute the Mediterranean fund.

* Of the House of Representatives.

It appears by the additional statement (A) that the articles of domestic growth, or manufacture, exported during the period aforesaid, may be averaged under the following heads, viz.

Produce of the Sea, . .	*dollars,*	2,884,000
Forest, . .		5,261,000
Agriculture, . .		31,562,000
Manufactures, .		2,525,000
Uncertain, . .		155,000
		42,387,000

I have the honor to be,

With great respect, sir,

Your most obedient servant,

ALBERT GALLATIN.

The honorable the SPEAKER
Of the house of representatives.

[Dd]

CCXX

Statement of Exports, the Produce and Manufacture of the United States, commencing the 1st of October, 1804, and ending the 30th September, 1805, before referred to.

SPECIES OF MERCHANDISE.		Quantity or Value.
Fish, dried or smoked,	quintals	514.549
Pickled,	barrels	56.770
Ditto,	kegs	7.207
Oil, spermaceti,	gallons	72.624
Whale and other fish,	do.	626.089
Whalebone,	pounds	21.335
Spermaceti candles,	do.	180.535
Wood, staves and headings,	M.	42.062
Shingles,	do.	74.854
Hoops and poles,	do.	5.523
Boards, plank, and scantling,	m. feet	94.939
Hewn timber,	tons	18.063
Lumber of all kinds,	dollars	53.380
Masts and spars,	do.	25.546
Oak bark and other dye,	do.	61.512
All manufactures of,	do.	223.142
Naval stores, tar,	barrels	72.745
Pitch,	do.	13.977
Rosin,	do.	9.057
Turpentine,	do.	95.640
Ashes, pot,	tons	3.557
Pearl,	do.	1.575
Skins and furs,	dollars	967.534
Ginseng,	pounds	370.932
Beef,	barrels	115.532
Pork,	do.	57.925
Hams and bacon,	pounds	903.924
Tallow,	do.	13.681
Butter,	do.	1.656.724
Cheese,	do.	843.005
Lard,	do.	1.308.287
Hides,	number	5.692
Horned cattle,	do.	5.822
Horses,	do.	4.046
Mules,	do.	481
Sheep,	do.	6.091
Hogs,	do.	2.808
Poultry,	dozens	3.302
Wheat,	bushels	18.041
Indian corn,	do.	861.501
Rye,	do.	1.474
Oats,	do.	35.400
Barley,	do.	7.185
Buckwheat,	do.	90
Beans,	do.	22.700
Peas,	do.	56.086
Potatoes,	do.	62.995
Apples,	barrels	5.654
Flour,	do.	777.513
Meal, rye,	do.	23.455
Indian,	do.	116.131
Buckwheat,	do.	98

Statement continued.

SPECIES OF MERCHANDISE.		Quantity or Value.
Bran and shorts,	bushels	104
Shipstuff,	cwt.	1.301
Biscuit or shipbread,	barrels	90.737
Ditto,	kegs	23.962
Rice,	tierces	56.830
Indigo,	pounds	97.184
Cotton, sea island,	do.	8.787.659
Other,	do.	29.602.428
Tobacco,	hhds.	71.252
Flaxseed,	bushels	179.788
Flax,	pounds	340
Hops,	do.	134.606
Mustard,	do.	6.540
Wax,	do.	248.394
Household furniture,	dollars	141.008
Coaches and other carriages,	do.	20.279
Hats,	do.	95.098
Saddlery,	do.	23.516
Beer, porter and cider in casks,	gallons	80 225
in bottles,	dozens	7.070
Boots,	pairs	10.128
Shoes, silk,	do.	1.120
Leather,	do.	101.382
Candles, tallow,	pounds	981.446
Wax,	do.	3.091
Soap,	do.	1.815.775
Starch,	do.	4.990
Hair powder,	do.	1.326
Snuff,	do.	23.531
Tobacco manufactured,	do.	404.929
Leather,	do.	203.231
Lead,	do.	8.000
Maple and other brown sugar,	do.	251.827
Bricks,	m.	1.043
Spirits from grain,	gallons	67.092
Linseed oil,	do.	9.690
Spirits of turpentine,	do.	26.247
Canvas and sail cloth,	pieces	100
Cables and cordage,	cwt.	3.010
Cards, wool and cotton,	number	1.338
Iron, Pig,	tons	365
Bar,	do.	927
Nails,	pounds	278.051
Castings,	dollars	25.821
All manufactures of iron or iron and steel,	do.	40.559
Spirits from molasses,	gallons	929.658
Sugar refined,	pounds	138.618
Chocolate,	do.	5.008
Gunpowder,	do.	349.300
Copper or brass, and copper manufactured,	dollars	12.977
Medicinal drugs,	do.	13.644
Merchandise and other articles not enumerated,		
Manufactured,	do.	225.410
Raw produce,	do.	155.415
Total value of the foregoing statement	dollars	42.387.002

Statement of Exports,—the Produce and Manufacture of *foreign* Countries, commencing the 1st October, 1804, and ending the 30th September, 1805.

SPECIES OF MERCHANDISE.	QUANTITY OR VALUE.		
	Entitled to Drawback.	Not entitled to drawback.	Total.
Value of goods free of duty,.... dollars	- -	1,641,725	1.641.725
at 12½ per cent. .... do.	7.090.600	4.711.286	11.801,886
15 do............ do.	727.762	860.039	1.587.801
20 do. .... do.	43.382	46.564	89.946
Wines,			
Malmsey, Madeira, &c. gallons	46.617	7.256	53.873
All other Madeira,........ do.	61.379	11.384	72.763
Burgundy, Champaign, &c. do.	245	1.060	1.305
Sherry and St. Lucar, ... do.	27.503	9.374	36.877
Claret, &c. in bottles or cases, do.	252.557	50.230	302.787
Lisbon, Oporto, &c. ...... do.	65.110	4.208	69.318
Teneriffe, Fayel, &c. ...... do.	184.506	20.073	204.579
All other, ... do.	2.572.950	205.328	2.778.278
Spirits,			
from grain, ... do.	237.392	43.399	280.791
other materials,...... do.	1.408.982	122.443	1.531.425
Molasses,.................... do.	20.640	27.834	48.474
Beer, ale, and porter,........... do.	41.615	19.156	60.771
Teas,			
Bohea,................ pounds	91.055	7.904	98.959
Souchong, and other black, .. do.	853.077	73.681	926.758
Hyson, Imperial, &c. .... do.	259.456	72.712	332.168
Other green, ... do.	382.518	48.485	431.003
Coffee,...................... do.	44.881.367	1.878.927	46.760.294
Cocoa,............... .... do.	2.280.285	145.395	2.425.680
Sugar,			
Brown, ... do.	91.345.257	4.273.059	95.618.316
White, clayed, or powdered, do.	20.319.150	6.841.899	27.161.049
Candy, ... do.	28.436	941	29.377
Loaf, ... do.		251	251
Almonds, ... do.	37,316	21.116	58.432
Prunes and plumbs, ... do.	40.749	10.661	51.410
Figs,............ .... do.	8.070	2.101	10.171
Raisins,			
in jars, boxes, and muscadel, do.	167.900	40.057	207.962
All other, ... do.	131.297	21.736	153.033
Candles,			
Tallow,................ do.	36.723	1.473	38.196
Wax or spermaceti, ... do.	1.766	1.123	2.889
Cheese,...................... do.	380.439	15.681	396.120
Soap, ... do.	1,063.853	261.403	1.325.256
Tallow, ... do.	3.631	5.335	8.966
Spices,			
Mace, ... do.	771	812	1.583
Nutmegs,................ do.	928	500	1.428
Cinnamon,.......... ... do.	13.244	3.465	16.709
Cloves, ... do.	14.169	17.038	31.207

STATEMENT CONTINUED.

PECIES OF MERCHANDISE.	QUANTITY OR VALUE.		
	Entitled to drawback.	Not entitled to drawback	Total.
Spices,			
Pepper, ... pounds	5.368.344	2.190.880	7.559.224
Pimento, ... do.	147.955	889	148.844
Chinese Cassia, ... do.	282.517	127.670	410.187
Tobacco, manufactured other than snuff and segars, ... do.	1.104	126.278	127.382
Snuff, ... do.	7.998	1 598	9.596
Indigo, ... do.	295.765	62.749	358.514
Cotton, ... do.	1.712.121	280.223	1.992.344
Powder,—Hair, ... do.	17.318	250	17.568
Gun, ... do.	70,569	72,830	143,399
Starch, ... do.	567	126	693
Glue, ... do.	289	1.307	1.596
Iron,—Anchors and sheet, ... do.	1.372	47.115	48.487
Slit and hoop, ... do.	25.403	38.477	63.880
Nails, ... do.	527.126	99.601	626.727
Spikes, ... do.	9.786	1.426	11.212
Quicksilver .... do.	1.050	4,702	5.752
Paints,—Ochre, yellow in oil, ... do.	4.985	11.249	16.234
dry yellow, ... do.	34.839	3.025	37.864
Spanish brown, ... do.	3.219	3.175	6.394
White and red lead, ... do.	35.251	12.839	48.090
Lead, and manufactures of lead, .. do.	58.023	290.319	348.342
Cordage,—Tarred, ... do.	190.575	68.125	258.700
Untarred, ... do.	7.193	1.517	8.710
Cables, ... do.	- -	2.395	2.395
Steel, ... cwts.	22.226	- -	22.226
Untarred yarn, ... do.	1	- -	1
Twine and packthread, ... do.	49	103	152
Glauber salts, ... do.	3	344	347
Salt,			
weighing more than 56lbs per bushel, ... pounds	217.065	20.916	237.981
weighing 56lbs. or less, .. bushels	8.559	2.550	11.109
Coal, ... do.	500	993	1.493
Fish,			
Foreign caught dried, .. quintals	2.125	17.875	20.000
Pickled, Salmon, ... barrels	130	896	1.026
Mackarel, ... do.	- -	2.077	2.077
All other, ... do.	126	2.896	3.022
Glass,—Black quart bottles, .. gross	3.996	796	4.792
Window not above 8 inches by 10, ... 100 sq. ft.	1.065	438	1.503
Ditto 10 inches by 12, ... do.	27	1	28
Segars, ... M.	324	664	988
Foreign lime per cask of 60 gal... casks	15	- -	15
Boots, ... pairs	296	131	427
Shoes and slippers,—Silk, ... do.	4.442	5.449	9.891
Kid, Morocco, and all other for men and women, .. do.	14.235	10.571	24.806
All other for children....... do.	2.711	254	2.965
Cards playing, ... do.	- -	480	480
Value, ... dollars	42.119.498	11.059 521	53.179.0[illegible]

A Summary of the Value and *Destination* of the Exports of the United States, agreeably to the preceding Statement.

	Domestic produce.	Foreign produce.	Total value to the dominions of each power
Russia,	12.044	59.328	71.372
Prussia,	145.727	244.093	389.820
Sweden,	35.834	55,214	
Swedish West Indies,	209.707	105.288	406.043
Denmark and Norway,	435.926	1.481.767	
Danish West Indies,	1.523.106	575.149	
Danish East Indies,	13.770	7.736	4.037.454
United Netherlands,	1.783.503	14.959.380	
Dutch West Indies,	454.645	138.785	
Dutch East Indies,	48.734	224.776	
Cape of Good Hope,	56.339	169.054	17.835.216
England, Man and Berwick,	10.603.302	1.401.830	
Scotland,	1.939.823	49.919	
Ireland,	1.230.598	19.889	
Guernsey, Jersey, Sark and Alderney,	165.940	962	
Gibraltar,	134.379	40.704	
British African ports,	5.439	23.603	
British East Indies,	14.267	274.212	
British West Indies,	5.473.218	518.189	
Newfoundland and British fisheries,	183.380	34.687	
British American colonies,	787.230	138.704	
Other British colonies,	7.111		23.047.386
Hamburgh, Bremen, the other Hanse Towns, &c.	893.591	2.338.917	3.232.508
French European ports on the Atlantic,	2.852.708	9.260 724	
Do. do. on the Mediterranean,	227.154	624.878	
French West Indies and American colonies,	2.876.384	4.455.599	
French East Indies,	4.926	2.656	
Bourbon and Mauritius,	66.552	638.436	
Other French African ports,	13.452	49.478	21.072.747
Spanish European ports on the Atlantic,	1.729.973	1.469.214	
Do. do. on the Mediterranean,	597.182	187.098	
Teneriffe and the other Canaries,	114.110	85.110	
Manilla and Phillipine islands,	33.430	9.081	
Floridas,	95.181	39.057	
Honduras, Campeachy and Mosquito shore,	203.255	418.539	
Spanish West Indies and American colonies,	2.806.112	4.884.776	12.672.768

CCXXV

Summary continued.

	Domestic produce.	Foreign produce.	Total value to the dominions of each power
Portugal, ...	508.284	851.647	
Madeira, ...	479.182	160.238	
Fayal and the other Azores, . . .	16.060	24.057	
Cape de Verd Islands, ...	13.029	24.161	
Other African ports, ...	7.941	20.760	2.105.409
Italy, ...	142.475	2.320.099	2.462.574
Trieste and other Austrian ports in the Adriatic, ...	6.665	322.992	329.657
Turkey, Levant and Egypt, ...	11.984	134.741	146.725
China, ...	145.573	176.502	322.075
East Indies, (* generally)	348.290	1.459.266	1.807.556
West Indies, do.	2.128.774	1.368.173	3.496.947
Europe, do.	179.608	628.608	808.216
Africa, do.	591.690	421.356	1.013.046
South seas, do.	3.643	2.000	5.643
North-west coast of America, . .	25.922	276.937	302.859
Total, ...	....	....	95.566.021

* Not before particularized; and it is to be regretted *their* destination is not shewn, whether to the *British* or other settlements in the East and West Indies.

A Summary of the Value of the Exports from each State.

	Domestic.	Foreign.	Total.
New Hampshire, ...	389.595	218.813	608.408
Vermont, ...	101.997	67.405	169.402
Massachusetts, ...	5.697.051	13.738.606	19.435.657
Rhode Island, ...	1.065.579	1.506.470	2.572.049
Connecticut, ...	1.353.537	90.190	1.443.727
New York, ...	8.098.060	15.384.883	23.482.943
New Jersey, ...	20.633	110	20.743
Pennsylvania, ...	4.365.240	9.397.012	13.762.252
Delaware, ...	77.827	280.556	358.383
Maryland, ...	3.408.543	7.450.937	10.859.480
District of Columbia, ...	1.135.350	184.865	1.320.215
Virginia, ...	4.945.635	660.985	5.606.620
North Carolina, ...	767.434	12.469	779.903
South Carolina, ...	5.957.646	3.108.979	9.066.625
Georgia, ...	2.351.169	43.677	2.394.846
* Territory of the United States, .	2.651.706	1.033.062	3.684.768
Total, . . .	42.387.002	53.179.019	95.566.021
* Detroit, ...	65.328	....	65.328
Michilimakinac, ...	247.895	....	247.895
New Orleans, ...	2.338.483	1.033.062	3.371.545
Total *, . . .	2.651.706	1.033.062	3.684.768

TREASURY DEPARTMENT,

REGISTER'S OFFICE, March 29, 1805.

JOSEPH NOURSE, Register.

* It is understood that the *exports* from the United States between the 1st Oct. 1805, and 30th Sept. 1806, *far exceeded* those of the preceding year, and particularly the export of *West-India* produce.

(A.)

A Summary Statement of the Value of the Exports of the Growth, Produce, or Manufacture of the United States, Year ending on the 30th September, 1805.

THE SEA, ... 2.884.000			
1 Fisheries,			
Dried fish or cod fishery, ...	....	2.058.000	
Pickled do. or river fishery, herring, shad, salmon, mackarel,........	....	348.000	
Whale (common) oil and bone, ..	315.000		
Spermaceti oil and candles, ...	163.000		
		478.000	
			2,884.000
THE FOREST, .. 5.261.000			
2 { Skins and furs, ...	967.000		
Ginseng, ...	148.000		
		1,115.000	
3 Product of Wood,			
Lumber, (boards, staves, shingles, hoops and poles, hewn timber, masts, &c.)	2.607.000		
Oak bark and other dyes, ...	61.000		
Naval stores, (tar, turpentine, pitch, rosin,)	702.000		
Ashes, pot and pearl, ...	776.000		
		4.146.000	
			5,261.000
AGRICULTURE, .. 31.562.000			
4 Product of animals,			
{ Beef, tallow, hides, live cattle, ..	1.545.000		
Butter and cheese, ...	415.000		
		1,960.000	
Pork pickled, bacon, lard, (live hogs,)	....	1,190.000	
Horses and Mules, ...	220.000		
Sheep, ...	1.500	235.000	
			3.385.000
5 Vegetable food,			
Wheat flour and biscuit, ...	....	8.325.000	
Indian corn and meal, ...	....	1.442.000	
Rice, ...	....	1.705.000	
All other, (rye, oats, pulse, potatoes, apples, &c.)	....	280.000	
			11.752.000
Carried forward, ...	....	.. Dollars,	23.282.000

SUMMARY STATEMENT CONTINUED.

Amount brought forward,....	....	....	23.282.000
6 Tobacco, ...	....	....	6.341.000
7 Cotton, ...	....	....	9.445.000
8 All other agricultural products,			
Indigo, ...	....	146.000	
Flaxseed, ...	....	360.000	
Brown sugar, ...	....	25.000	
Hops, ...	....	13.000	
Wax, ...	....	75.000	
Various items, (poultry, flax, mustard,)......	....	20.000	
			639.000
Manufactures,.. 2.300.000			
9 Of domestic materials,			
Soap and tallow candles, ...	414.000		
Leather, boots, shoes, saddlery,..	221.000		
Hats,....................	95.000		
Grain, (spirits, beer, starch),....	86.000		
Wood, (including furniture, coaches, and other carriages, }	384.000		
Cordage, canvass, linseed oil, ..	57.009		
Iron,....................	198.000		
Various items, (snuff, silk shoes, wax candles, tobacco, lead, bricks, turpentine spirits, wool and cotton cards), ...	124.000		
		1.579.000	
Of foreign materials,			
Spirits of molasses,..........	558.000		
Sugar refined,..........	30.000		
Chocolate, ...	1.000		
Gunpowder, ...	105.000		
Brass and copper, ...	13.000		
Medicinal, ...	14.000		
		721.000	
Uncertain, ... 380.000			2.3000.000
10 Articles not distinguished in returns,			
Manufactured, ...	....	225.000	
Raw produce,..........	....	155.000	
			380.000
Total,........	....	Dollars,	42.387.000

(B.)

A Statement of the Duties collected on the Importation of Articles which were afterwards re-exported, without being entitled to Drawback.

SPECIES OF MERCHANDISE.	Amount of duty.	
	Dollars.	Cts.
At 12½ per cent.	588.910	75
15	129.005	85
20	9.312	80
Malmsey Madeira,	4.208	48
All other do.	5.692	
Burgundy,	477	
Sherry,	3.749	60
Claret,	17.580	50
Lisbon,	1.262	40
Teneriffe,	5.620	44
All other wine,	47.325	44
Grain spirits,	12.151	72
Other spirits,	34.284	04
Molasses,	1.391	70
Beer,	1.532	48
Bohea,	948	48
Souchong,	13.262	58
Hyson,	23.267	84
Other Green,	9.697	
Coffee,	93.946	35
Cocoa,	2.907	90
Brown Sugar,	106.826	47
White,	205.256	97
Candy,	108	21
Loaf,	22	59
Almonds,	422	32
Prunes,	213	22
Figs,	42	02
Raisins in jars,	801	14
All other,	326	04
Candles, tallow,	29	46
Wax,	67	38
Cheese,	1.097	67
Soap,	5.228	06
Tallow,	80	02
Mace,	1.015	
Nutmegs,	250	
Cinnamon,	693	
Cloves,	3.407	60
Pepper,	131.452	80
Pimento,	35	56
Chinese Cassia,	5.106	80
Carried forward,	1,468.917	68

STATEMENT, CONTINUED.

SPECIES OF MERCHANDISE.	Amount of duty. Dollars.	Cts.
Brought forward,	1.468.917	68
Tobacco,	7.576	68
Snuff,	159	80
Indigo,	15.687	25
Cotton,	8.406	69
Powder, Hair,	10	
Gun,	2.913	20
Starch,	3	72
Glue,	52	23
Anchors and sheet iron,	706	72
Slit and hoop,	384	77
Nails,	1.992	02
Spikes,	14	26
Quicksilver,	282	12
Ochre, yellow in oil,	168	73
Dry yellow,	30	25
Spanish brown,	31	75
White and red lead,	256	72
Lead,	2.908	19
Cordage, tarred,	1.362	50
Untarred,	37	92
Cables,	47	90
Twine,	412	
Glauber salts,	688	
Salt,	584	60
Coal,	49	65
Dried fish,	8.937	50
Pickled fish, Salmon,	396	
Mackarel,	1.246	20
All other,	1.158	40
Bottles,	477	60
Window glass, at 160,	700	80
at 175,	1	75
Segars,	1.328	
Boots,	98	25
Shoes, Silk,	1.362	25
Men and womens,	1.585	65
Childrens,	25	40
Cards, playing,	120	
Total amount of duties on merchandise exported, not entitled to drawback, dollars,	1.531.618	32

No. XXVI.

The following Extracts have been selected from recent Publications, as they relate to some of the Proceedings of the Society of Ship-Owners of Great Britain.

Extracts from a work intituled " A Vindication of the " Principles and Statements advanced in the Strictures " of Lord Sheffield, on the Necessity of inviolably " maintaining the Navigation and Colonial System of " Great Britain." Edition 1806. By the Rev. I. Alley.

INNOVATIONS thus direct, contributed, in a most essential manner, to impair the interests of British shipping. The extravagant prices, in this country, of all the necessaries of life; the weight of taxes; the rapid advance of wages; the high rate of ship's provisions and stores; and various other depressing circumstances, tended, already, sufficiently to discourage speculation in shipping; and it was admitted, that a foreign vessel might be sold in the Thames, on considerably cheaper terms than a vessel British built, of the same species, and same tonnage. These difficulties are of a permanent nature, and the rates of freight have been such as to afford little compensation. The hire of the vessel should naturally have borne a due proportion to the expences of outfit; but according to the following table, the freight on two great articles, for five years, ending in 1784, was nearly equal in sum, and much superior in value, to that which was paid in the five years, ending in 1804.

Rates of Freight on Sugar and Rum.

DATE.	SUGAR.		RUM.	
	s.	d.	s.	d.
1780	8	0	0	9
1	8	0	0	9
2	8	0	0	9
3	8	0	0	9
4	4	0	0	6
1800	10	0	1	0
1	10	0	1	0
2	6	0	0	8
3	5	0	0	6
4	9	0	0	10

Under these circumstances, with all the disadvantage of dearness on the side of the British ship-owners, and all the advantages of cheapness on the side of the foreign; and with rates of freight, which, *even without competition*, would have afforded *inadequate* compensation to the former, for the increased expences of his outfit, the suspension of the Navigation Acts deprived the English ship-builder of the protection, which he had hitherto experienced in his own ports. What was the result? Every tide bore neutral bottoms into the harbours of England. Speculation in English shipping, instead of being stimulated by the full enjoyment of the English market, was checked and deterred by the intervention of foreign competition; and our own naval artizans were, consequently, deprived of occupation, and, in many instances, dispersed abroad, in search of the employment which they should have found at home.

That these statements are by no means exaggerated, it would be abundantly easy to prove, by a more minute reference to facts. There are now before me copies of memorials, which have been presented to ministers, and of various letters, and other documents, which would enable me fully to detail the mischiefs that have been here imperfectly enumerated. For more ample evidence on this subject, however, I shall here refer but to the following extracts from authentic papers, relative to one branch of our trade, furnished by merchants of unquestionable authority on subjects of this nature.

"It is obvious to every man who has ships trading to the ports in the Baltic, or the White Sea, that provisions, cordage, sails, masts, tar, pitch, &c. are much cheaper in them than in England, and wages to navigate neutral ships, is 3l. 10s. per month, for each seaman; and British ships are at present paying from 5l. 5s. to 5l. 10s. per month, with the addition of from three guineas to four for procuring them. By the suspension of the Navigation Act, foreign ships have got our trade, and the *foreign seamen*, which in former wars manned our ships, *followed it*; and the reason why they will sail for less wages in foreign ships than in English is, they are not liable to be taken by the enemies of Britain, nor impressed into her navy*. The crews of foreign ships can abide on board, to deliver and take in their cargoes, and complete their rigging for another voyage; when a British ship-owner must hire riggers at six shillings per day, and labourers to load and discharge his cargo at five shillings per day. Besides, the insurance of a British ship and cargo will be one half more than that of a neutral in time of war; added to which, the British ship has a detention in getting her seamen, and waiting for convoy, which time may, in general, be computed at one third of a Memel voyage from London and back. Considering, therefore, the whole of the disadvantages which the British ship sails under, it may be asserted that the neutral ship, in time of war, sails under a protection of from 35 to 40 per cent.; and what is stated here respecting a ship from the Baltic will hold good as to American ships, except in cordage and sails."

From all these circumstances, the ship-owners throughout the country are, at this moment, labouring under great depression; and unless the Navigation Act in future is strictly enforced, and means are adopted to put the British ship-owner on a level with the neutral owner, the maritime interests of the country in a very few years will be annihilated. Indeed, in a memorial recently presented to the Board of Trade by the ship-owners at Sunderland, they intimate that many of them are apprehensive of

* This observation is peculiarly worthy of notice. At a period when so many of our seamen are required for our navy, it is obvious how injuriously every measure must operate which enables the foreign seamen employed in our service to find, so readily, safety and occupation in foreign bottoms. In such measures there is irresistible temptation: in such temptation there is the greatest mischief to English trade.

insolvency, from the losses they have sustained, by the improvident employment of their capital in shipping."

The other extract which I shall insert here, is selected from * a memorial presented in June 1801, to the Privy Council, by a great number of respectable ship-owners, whose names were subscribed.

"By an order of his Majesty in Council, dated the 21st of May 1801, and issued, ostensibly, in consequence of the Nothern Confederacy, it was rendered lawful, from and after the date of the said order, and until six weeks after the commencement of the then next session of Parliament, to import into any port of the united kingdom, in foreign ships belonging to the subjects of any kingdom, or state, not then at war with his Majesty, any hemp, flax, iron, tallow, masts, timber, square or otherwise, deals, oak-staves, linens, isinglass, bristles, ashes, hides, masts, tar, pitch, linseed, and rosin, &c., upon payment of such duties (if any) as were by law payable upon such articles, when imported in any foreign built ships."

Not long, however, after this order had been issued, the Nothern Confederacy was dissolved. It was natural, therefore, to expect that the order should be withdrawn: but the council were of opinion, that it could not be rescinded without an act of parliament; and it was, therefore, left to expire by efflux of time, six weeks after the commencement of the ensuing session †.

In consequence of the injurious operation of this order, the memorial of which I have spoken was laid before the council, and represented, amongst others, the following grievances.

"Your petitioners also beg leave to state, that neutral ships are daily arriving in great numbers, at all the ports in the Baltic, in order to bring into Great Britain and Ireland, merchandise, &c. which would have been brought in British bottoms, but for the order before recited, and that the trade to and from Hamburgh is at present almost wholly carried on in neutral vessels, to the manifest prejudice of your petitioners, and the shipping interest of Great Britain; so that

* Vide ante, p. liii.

† The usual words "or until further order" had been omitted in the order; and no remedy, therefore, was left.

a very great number of British vessels are now unemployed from the circumstances before stated."

This statement is abundantly confirmed by particular facts. Scarcely had the order of council been heard of on the continent, when multitudes of neutral vessels were employed to supply the demands of Great Britain; and the following copy of a letter from the port of Riga, addressed to a very eminent merchant in London, may serve to show how much of the carrying trade of England was, at that period, assumed by foreigners.

"*Riga*, { *19th June*, / *1st July*, } 1801."

"The ships which were under embargo here are daily leaving us, but none are yet arrived from England. About 440 neutral vessels, however, are already arrived here, some of which begin now to be at a loss for freights, owing *to the high prices* of most of our articles*."

These vessels were in search of freights for this country; and *similar efforts were made, at the same period, in the other ports of the Baltic.* But, if the order of council, already recited, was thus injurious in its direct, it was no less mischievous in its reflex, operation. For, in proportion to the number of vessels which it encouraged to enter into the trade, the demand for produce and stores was quickened, and the price, therefore, as above stated, enhanced; and the British ships, which had been detained in Russia, during the embargo, and which, in consequence of the order, had not been chartered in sufficient time, were precluded, not to say more, from all the advantages of speedy freight.

When these circumstances are considered, and when it is considered also, that, at this very period, the *unemployed* tonnage of Great Britain was thought to exceed *one fourth* of the whole tonnage of the empire, it will not be denied that the ship-owners of England had some cause to complain. But let me be understood: I do not mean to condemn the order, nor do I presume to censure the wisdom from which it flowed. Lord Glenbervie especially appears to have considered the memorial already said to have been presented on the occasion with all that coolness and candour

* The substance of this letter was stated at the time to the Committee of Council for Trade.

which he is known to possess; and his answer to the memorialists evinces a sound judgment, and a perfect knowledge of the subject. I see, therefore, in that nobleman, too decided an attachment to the genuine maritime interests of this country, to impute to him a wish unnecessarily to enforce or multiply orders hostile to the navigation laws, which he so well understands; and my only design, in alluding to these circumstances, is to show how easily *the suspending powers of privy councils* may divert the shipping and carrying trade of Britain into foreign channels; and how necessary it is to maintain, firmly and inviolably, that proud and ancient system which has so long protected and encouraged, in every national view, the commerce and navigation of the empire.—P. 11 to 20.

From the right, then, of restriction and regulation, we turn to the policy of the question. It is contended, with an affected parade of commercial knowledge, that the Suspending Acts of 1795, &c. have actually *enlarged, beyond all former experience, our means of trade; have increased more than ever the number of our mercantile seamen; have more than ever promoted our shipping interests;* and, therefore, should be continued, even if the peace had been likely to be permanent, and sailors not wanted for the defence of the country*. These paradoxes of temerity are sufficiently bold. I presume to assert, nevertheless, that they are, *in every instance*, untenable and false; and I should scarcely insult the understanding of my reader by referring to them particularly, if they did not lead to discussions of national import.

Various circumstances have obviously contributed, since the year 1795, to increase the exports and imports of Britain; and with those circumstances the suspension of the navigation laws had as obviously little to do. A revolution, in its nature and violence unprecedented, perhaps, in the annals of the world; a consequent war extending in its effects from one end of Europe to the other; and an utter derangement of the commerce of almost all the countries endangered by the contest, or engaged in it, eminently conspired to favour the mercantile pursuits of England†. There was no safety elsewhere to be found for assignment, and no market else-

* Answer to Lord Sheffield by Mr. Cock, p. 29, 30.

† "We absorbed at this period," says Chalmers, "almost all the commerce of Europe." Estimate of comparative Strength, &c. p. 207.

where, which was calculated to supply the demands of the countries disturbed. To Britain, accordingly, during a certain period, the wants of other nations looked for supply, and the fears of other nations brought their investments. Foreign capital was poured into the British funds; foreign speculation was directed to British ports; foreign wealth was remitted for British produce and manufacture; and, thus, the commercial prosperity of this country, *whatever it was*, resulted, *not from the suspending acts*, to which it has been attributed, but from the struggles, operations, and wants, of foreign necessity.

It was not the monopoly of European trade alone that was thus secured, for a season, to Great Britain. We enjoyed, at the same time, almost the whole commerce of the East, together with the trade of most of the French and Dutch settlements, in the West Indies. Surinam, Berbice, Demerara, Essequibo, St. Lucia, Martinico, Tobago, Trinidad, St. Eustatia, and, at one period, St. Domingo, added, by their demands and their produce, in a degree which the annexed table will show, to the trade and affluence of England; and this country, *whether the navigation laws had been suspended or not*, would have alike been rendered the mart of all those great East and West India articles, which have become so connected with the enjoyments, and so essential to the wants of Europe.

An ACCOUNT of the Quantity of Sugar, Rum, Coffee, and Cotton, imported into Great Britain from the Colonies of Surinam, Berbice, Demerara, and Essequibo; as also from the Islands of Martinico, St. Lucia, Tobago, Trinidad, and St. Eustatia, for Three Years previous to January 1st, 1802, as far as the same can be made up, distinguishing each Year.

YEARS	SUGAR.			RUM.	COFFEE.			COTTON.
	Cwt.	qr.	lbs.	Gallons.	Cwt.	qrs.	lbs.	lbs.
1799	517,296	1	5	276,068	80,774	1	21	6,030,299
1800	465,043	0	16	295,885	232,105	0	13	10,740,620
1801	753,376	1	25	446,641	359,761	3	4	11,959,612

Inspector General's Office, Custom-house,
London, 13 April, 1802.

WILLIAM IRVING, Inspector-General of the Imports and Exports of Great Britain.

The suspending acts, therefore, can, at best, be said to have afforded, *amid all the evils which they produced*, some facility of carriage from the nations with which we were at war. But, even in this contracted view, they were, probably, of little ultimate use. The commodities of the nations at war would, sooner or later, have found their way to the British ports, if the suspension had never been permitted to exist, because, I repeat it, in Britain alone were to be found safety for consignment, and a reasonable certainty of sale; and the suspension, consequently, it might be almost said, was effectual only in depriving England of a considerable portion of that very trade, which is most intimately connected with her best commercial and political interests*.

The fact is, in a great degree, allowed, where we should expect it would be most earnestly resisted or denied. "I fully admit," says the writer lately quoted †, "that *a very considerable increase of American shipping in the British carrying trade*" (and, consequently, a very considerable diminution in British shipping,) "*resulted from the acts*," and "I am by no means insensible that the *shipping interests* of England have a *right* to complain that cargoes which, *under the acts in question*, might be imported in a *neutral* vessel, *could not* be imported in a *British* ship; and that the former was excepted from a duty to which the latter was liable ‡." These admissions, uttered by a writer who is the most professed panegyrist of suspension, will be considered both as strong and strange. But what shall we say, when we find that his forgetfulness of what he had admitted is yet more curious than the admission itself; and when we hear him maintain, notwithstanding the mischiefs which he had taken pains to state, that "the alledged objections to the acts," the diminution of the carrying trade and the losses of the ship-builders and ship-owners of the country, "are *totally* groundless § ?"

To fortify the last opinion against the first, he produces an immense table, which, as far as is necessary to this argument, is here annexed.

* The carrying trade. † Mr. Cock.

‡ Cock, p. 50—58. § Ibid. p. 58.

An ACCOUNT of the Number of Vessels, with the Amount of their Tonnage, which entered Inwards and cleared Outwards, in the several Ports of Great Britain, in the Years 1791, 1792, 1793, and in the Years 1799, 1800, 1801, distinguishing British from Foreign vessels.

	INWARDS.				OUTWARDS.			
	BRITISH.		FOREIGN.		BRITISH.		FOREIGN.	
Years.	Vessels.	Tonnage.	Vessels.	Tonnage.	Vessels.	Tonnage.	Vessels.	Tonnage.
1790	12,141	1,423,376	2,321	277,599	12,560	1,399,233	1,130	148,074
1791	12,494	1,452,498	2,686	321,684	13,514	1,511,294	1,306	184,729
1792	12,030	1,587,645	2,477	304,074	13,891	1,563,744	1,138	175,556
1799	10,557	1,575,169	3,012	476,596	11,085	1,302,551	2,392	414,774
1800	10,496	1,379,807	5,512	763,236	11,866	1,445,271	4,893	685,051
1801	10,347	1,678,620	5,497	780,155	10,282	1,345,621	5,626	804,880

On this table the author relies, with implicit confidence, for a victorious defence of the suspension acts of 1795, &c. and of the general principles of suspension; and he proceeds to deduce the inferences already mentioned, with all the zeal of anticipated triumph. "In the latter of the periods here specified (1799, 1800, 1801), *our ships and tonnage were* GREATER *than in the former* (1790, 1791, 1792), *our own carriers at the same time were* FULLY *occupied**; *our shipping*

* Cock, p. 27, 29, 35, &c.

interest was MORE *than ever promoted; and our mercantile sailors* MORE *numerous than ever.*" And "it might, therefore, have reasonably been presumed, that Britain would "continue," by suspending the acts of navigation, "not only to allow, but to encourage such a beneficial traffic, *even if the peace had been likely to be permanent,* and *sailors not to be wanted for the defence of the country**."

By these evidences and inferences he fancies the inutility and folly are sufficiently demonstrated of what he scoffingly and ignorantly terms "the rules of the 17th century†;" and, as he has chosen *his own mode and his own periods* for his calculations, he has availed himself, it will be supposed, of every means in his power, to strengthen and sustain his opinions. If, therefore, his arguments shall be found to be very suicides; and, if in his *own* statements exist his *own* refutation, what is the public to conclude?

Now, it appears from the table produced, that, instead of the great augmentation of which he speaks, there was a great comparative decline, in the shipping and tonnage of England actually employed, during the very period when the acts of suspension were in the fullest operation. According to that table, "the number of British vessels, outward and inward bound, in the several ports of Great Britain," at the different periods *selected* for the calculation, may be stated as follows‡:

Years.		British Vessels.
1790	Navigation Laws in force - - - - -	24,701
1799	Navigation Laws suspended - - -	21,642
	Decrease of British Ships under suspending system	3,059

* Idem, p. 29, 35.

† Idem, p. 32. The great principle of the navigation laws was derived from the early wisdom of the Italian republics, and was introduced into our maritime code in the year 1381, by the law which declares, that "none of the king's subjects shall carry forth, or bring in, merchandise, but only in ships of the king's allegiance." See 5 Richard II. ch. 3. 6 Rich. ch. 8. It is singular that the famous law should have been passed in the same reign which declares, "that all the king's subjects may carry corn out of the realm when they will." 17 Rich. II. ch. 7.

‡ It must be recollected that I argue solely on facts stated by Mr. Cock, and that I do not make myself answerable for the accuracy of his assertions.

Years.		British Vessels.
1790 1791 1792	Navigation Laws in force - - - -	76,630
1799 1800, 1801	Navigation Laws suspended - - -	64,633
	Decrease of British Ships under suspending system	11,997

I look to the table again, and I find that while the number of British vessels, inward and outward bound, in the ports of Great Britain, thus declined, that of foreign vessels proportionally increased. The statement is as follows:

Foreign Vessels inward and outward bound, &c.

Years.		Foreign Vessels.
1790	Navigation Laws in force - - - - -	3,451
1799	Navigation Laws suspended - - -	5,404
	Increase of Foreign Vessels under suspending system	1,953
1790 1791 1792	Navigation Laws in force - - - - -	11,058
1799 1800 1801	Navigation Laws suspended - - -	26,932
	Increase of Foreign Vessels under suspending system	15,874

In this manner the shipping of England, occupied in the British ports, declined, and the foreign shipping, occupied in the British ports, increased, under the operation of those acts of suspension which have been so much extolled, as *promoting* the interests of British shipping, and *increasing* the number of British seamen.

But this subject demands farther consideration. At the close of the year 1792, "the number of prize ships, which had been registered in England, and appeared to be in existence, was 601; and the number in the year 1801 was 2779*." If, then, we deduct these numbers and quantities, in their order, from the number and quantity of the British vessels, stated to have been inward and outward bound, &c.

* I still follow the tables of Mr. Cock.

in each of the years above mentioned, it will be evident, that the number of British *built* vessels, so bound, in the year 1792, was 25,320, and that the number of British *built* vessels so bound in 1801, was 17,850; that is, the number of vessels British *built*, which is stated to have been employed in *one* year, under the *boasted* influence of the suspended acts, was *less* than the number employed in *one* year, under the protection of the navigation and colonial system, by 7,470 vessels*.

I shall make but one observation more on this, to the shipping interest of Great Britain, most important subject. From the causes which have been assigned (the events accompanying, or resulting from, the French revolution), the value of the imports and exports of Great Britain, for the three years † ending in 1801, exceeded those of the three years ending in 1792, to amount of £30,753,620. If, therefore, the counteracting influence of suspension had not been called forth, would not the shipping trade of England have augmented in the same proportion? would not the British ship-builder have been ready to exert himself to meet the increased demand, and the British carrier to benefit by the occasion? And if, on the contrary, the carrying trade was greatly contracted; if the ship-builder was, in many instances, impoverished by the speculations; if British vessels of considerable value were left, from want of employment, to rot in port; and this, too, at the very period when the exports and imports of Britain had increased as above stated, and when the foreign tonnage employed in the British service was, as is admitted, *more than doubled*‡;" there is, surely, but little reason to extol those relaxations of our maritime systems, which have produced with such rapidity such mischievous effects.

* The whole number of British vessels said to be employed in the year 1792, for instance, was - - - - - 25,921
Of this number the registered *prize* ships amounted to - 601

The remainder, therefore, 25,320
was the number of British *built* vessels, &c.

† See the 1st and 2d Vols. of Cobbett's Political Register for several documents on this subject.

‡ Mr. Cock's Answer to Lord Sheffield.

That many vessels were built in the British ports, in the years 1799, 1800, and 1801, I mean not to deny. The opportunities of extending the trade of England having increased, the British ship-builder speculated *for the moment*, and several vessels were accordingly built. These vessels, however, were found, in the various cases, to be supernumerary and superfluous. The Commercial Marine of England may have appeared to *advance*, but we have seen that the number of British vessels *actually* employed considerably *declined*; and the preceding statements abundantly testify, that a shipping *numerically* extended may be easily rendered, by the policy of suspending acts, very different from a shipping *profitably* employed*.

These speculations, indeed, in ship-building were worse than idle. Merely to build vessels, in the moment of enterprise, is not always to afford a proof of the prosperity of the trade of ship-building; and, in the present instance, capital was hastily and wildly lavished without profit and without return. Many British vessels remained unemployed, not merely at home, but in foreign ports†; and it was soon discovered that the carrying trade, which is once lost, is not so speedily to be regained; that the enterprise of the ship-builder, unprotected by the navigation laws, may destroy the individual, but not benefit the nation; and that to open the British ports, by acts of suspension, to the vessels of foreigners, is, in a very alarming degree, to close them against our own.

Under these circumstances I lament to add, that multitudes of our sailors were dispersed abroad, from want of sufficient employment at home. They turned for bread to any nation that would pay them; and it is even said, that, in six months, from the period of the signature of the preliminaries of peace, in the year 1801, they migrated to the number of nearly ten thousand, to America and France‡.

* I refer to the table so often quoted.

† Above 60 vessels, I am informed, remained unemployed in the port of Lisbon, and similar accounts were received from other ports.—See also the case of the owners of *British* ships lent to the Dutch.

‡ The fact, at least, was stated in a letter, which I have seen, to a gentleman in a highly confidential situation; and an offer was made, at the same time, to substantiate the fact by proof.

[Gg]

ccxliv

On a dispersion of this nature, a dispersion of those brave men who had contributed to the preservation of the empire, I shall not comment; but it should not be forgotten, that they who are thus driven abroad are generally lost to their country for ever, and are so scattered among the vessels of the nations which employ them, and not unfrequently of our enemies, as to have little left but to remain and to obey.—Page 44 to 56.

No. XXVII.

Extracts from a Work * *intituled*—"*Remarks on the probable Conduct of Russia and France towards this Country, also on the Necessity of Great Britain becoming independent of the Northern Powers for her Naval Supplies, and recommending (as the only Means of attaining that most important Object), the Encouragement of the British Shipping Interest, and the Cultivation of Naval Stores in Upper and Lower Canada, &c.*"——Edition 1805.

But far distant, we hope, is the day, when our naval pre-eminence will be obliged to strike its colours to our enemy; for the privileges we enjoy at sea are the very life, and soul of our naval superiority, skill, and discipline, the great stimulus to the heroic actions of our brave tars, and the fundamental principle of all our greatness. Destroy them, and then indeed will the Sun of Britain be set—never to rise again. Let us therefore rally round the great pillar of the State, and let us not be trifling away our time in party squabbles and dissensions, but unite with one hand and heart in adopting the best means to support our hitherto invincible Navy, and to defy the united attacks of our most malicious and inveterate foes.

Having thus far shewn that the great aim both of France and Russia, as well as every other naval power in their interest, is not only to rival but destroy our naval dominion, the object of these remarks will now resolve itself into two distinct heads—First, the necessity of alleviating the oppressed state of the British Shipping Interest, and encouraging by every possible means the carrying trade of this country. Secondly, supplying the navy with stores from our own Colonies and other parts of the British Empire, in order to render ourselves independent of the Northern Powers. Previous, however, to any observation on the first point, it may

* The name of the author of this Tract is unknown.

perhaps be not unnecessary for the clearer elucidation of the subject to lay before our readers an extract from the minutes of the proceedings at a general meeting of the Society of Ship-owners of Great Britain, held at the London Tavern, on Thursday the 22d day of March, 1804*.

It must appear to every unprejudiced mind, on viewing the preceding report of the Committee of Ship-owners, how very beneficial their exertions and enquiries must prove to the general interests of British shipping; and that very important objects have not only already been investigated by them, but that many, equally momentous, still remain to be enquired into. *Great praise is due to the Society* for their indefatigable exertions to overcome *the prejudices* of certain *interested* individuals, as well as recommending to his Majesty's Ministers the repealing of many obnoxious and oppressive duties which, though but of trifling consideration to the revenue, is a most material object to the Shipping Interest in its present depreciated state.—"The Committee," say they, "forbear commenting on the present depressed state of the Shipping Interest and the causes which have occasioned it, because they are already too obvious to need enumeration." These causes are evidently the oppressive taxes for various purposes, which have hitherto and still continue to burthen the British Shipping; and it is a lamentable fact that, from those causes, the freights for our ships become so extravagant, that the merchants naturally enough employ neutral foreigners, so that our vessels, excepting coasters and those for the colonies, remain in the river unemployed, till at length the owner, despairing of their being taken up, sells them to the ship-breakers, while, at the same time, foreign vessels in great numbers are daily bringing and carrying away freights to an enormous extent.

Every man concerned with shipping confesses, that it is at present a most ruinous concern, and will not pay the insurance; few ships are building in the River, except for Government, but numbers are daily broken up; and so profitable is the latter employ, that new ship-breakers are starting up every day, and lining their wharfs alongshore with the wrecks of our commercial Marine. It being a much safer venture to "turn the penny" upon copper bolts, fastenings, old

* *Vide Report of the Committee of Ship-owners for the port of* London. *Ante page* xcii, *which this writer inserts at length in his work.*

iron, knees, planks, timber, &c. than upon cargoes of merchandise, coals, or timber, while subject to heavy duties, insurance, damages, and a variety of losses. Thus our Mediterranean, Levant, East Country, and other trades that train our seamen, *are rapidly on the decline*, and will, ere long, be totally lost, unless some measures are speedily adopted to enable our Ship-owners to navigate their vessels *upon an equal footing with foreigners.*

Another evil of the greatest magnitude likewise attends the depreciation of these trades, which is the "emigration of many brave native seamen, who are either now in the employ of America, or in the service of the enemy;" not that we can suppose there are any great number of our seamen in the enemy's fighting ships, although every inducement is held out by Napoleon to make them enter his service; but there are no doubt many in their merchants' service, and neither is that service so despicable as this country endeavours to represent it; for notwithstanding our vast superiority at sea, they still contrive to carry on a considerable traffic in different parts of Europe, especially in the Mediterranean; and it is a fact, that no less than 200 merchant vessels entered the port of Bourdeaux in the course of one of the last months; the greatest part of which were French. But if the number in the enemy's service is upon the whole inconsiderable, and which, for the honour of British seamen, we hope is the case; yet we much fear that their numbers are great in the American service, particularly as it is difficult to distinguish one from the other; and in several instances we have known of English sailors being impressed in the river, but were discharged under the idea of their being Americans, particularly if they happened to have an American pass, which is not difficult to procure if they have been a voyage to that country. It is therefore evident, that the depreciation of our shipping not only impoverishes the nation, but destroys the nursery of our finest seamen on whom we depend for the protection of the Empire.

The next important object pointed out by the Committee, and which they fortunately attained, was the exemption from the Bell Rock Light-house Duties, which would have produced upwards of £10,000 *per Ann.* to that Light-house, and this enormous tax too would have been levied entirely on the Baltic trade*, although that very trade to the Baltic and East Country is more rapidly falling off than any other, except the Mediterranean. But thanks to the Committee for their timely interference, which happily relieved the most important branch of our Shipping Interest from such an impolitic and oppressive tax. Can Ministers suppose that our Merchants and Ship-owners will be able much longer to withstand such exorbitant imposts ? Can they think it possible that men will continue to send their ships to sea at a certain loss ? For such is now, with very few exceptions, the case. It is astonishing that men of sense, and of more than ordinary abilities, will continue so blind to the interests of their country, and at a time too when they are calling forth all its resources, yet they still will neglect and impoverish one of its most productive and important supplies.

* The Duty proposed to be levied, by the Bell Rock Light-house bill in 1803, upon all *British* Ships crossing the *Line of the Latitude* of the *intended Light-house*, altho' it would not have been in the Track of any Ship coming from or sailing to the *Baltic* which theretofore had never paid any Lights to the Northward of the Spurn—was one penny halfpenny per Ton out, and the like Duty *home*: and on *Foreign* Ships threepence per Ton *out*, and threepence per Ton *home*: and the Tonnage of British and Foreign Ships clearing outwards and entering inwards to and from Great Britain, in 1801, to the *Baltic* and other Places mentioned in the Bill, were as follows, viz.

British Ships *inwards*	345,315		
——— *outwards*	259,113		
Tons	604,428	at 1½d. per Ton is	£3777 : 13 : 6
Foreign Ships *inwards*	377,386		
——— *outwards*	440,244		
Tons	817,630	at 3d. per Ton is	£10,220 : 7 : 1
Amount of Lights Dues on the above Tonnage if the Bill had passed as originally proposed.			£13,998 : 0 : 7

This calculation is on the aggregate Tonnage of 1801, including all the Ships and their repeated Voyages to the above Places: therefore it is calculated on the British Ships at 1½d. per Ton instead of 3d. per Ton, and on the Foreign Ships at 3d. per Ton instead of 6d. per Ton—and which was made at the particular request of the late Sir William Pulteney, who introduced the Bill, and who was well satisfied with the propriety of the Exemption claimed by the Committee for Ships employed in the Baltic Trade, &c. which he agreed to and which was inserted in the Act, viz.—" Provided also, and it is hereby further enacted and declared, that nothing in this Act contained shall extend " or be construed to extend to subject or charge any Ship or Vessel trading to " or from that part of Great Britain called England, to the Baltic, Denmark, " Sweden, or Norway, or to any of those Countries, or to or from any of " them to Ireland when going South about, to or with the Payment of any " of the Rates or Duties of Tonnage by this Act imposed, but that all such " Ships so trading shall be wholly freed, &c."

On another subject also, the Committee say, they are sorry to observe, that the Lords Committee of Trade have refused to make any alteration in the regulations of the Commissioners of the Customs. As we are unacquainted with their Lordships' reasons for such refusal, it would be improper to make any remarks thereon; but it is to be hoped that no prejudice against innovation, or partiality in favour of ancient usage, should deter them from rendering so important a service to the shipping interest.

The next objects to which the Committee direct our attention are, the several duties which have arisen out of the Act for the Improvement of the Port of London, passed in the year 1799; of these they have obtained an exemption from a small part, about £4000 *per Annum*, which was levied on vessels entering inwards or clearing outwards from the Port of London, *in ballast**. While we deprecate the whole system of taxation with which the Shipping Interest is burthened, we must, in a still more forcible manner, deprecate and abhor the enormous dues levied on every vessel arriving in the Port of London, contrary to the practice or necessities of our other ports. These taxes have chiefly arisen out of the before-mentioned Act, which was passed for the purpose of making Docks for West India shipping, and a canal in the Isle of Dogs; the latter was to prevent the great injury which frequently happened to shipping in the circuitous and dangerous passage round that place. The Act at the same time created an establishment of Harbour Masters, who were to regulate the shipping and keep the navigation of the river clear and open, which had hitherto been in a very dangerous state, for though almost every petty harbour in Europe has some officer to regulate it, yet the Port of London, reckoned the largest in the world for commerce, had not till this period any officer to regulate its shipping and navigation, unless the Water Bailiff may be so called, but his capacity was better adapted to the seizing of unlawful nets, and picking up whaifs and strays, than regulating the mooring of ships.

* Total Tonnage of British and Foreign Ships *in ballast* entering inwards and clearing outwards from and to Foreign ports from the port of London between the 5th of Jannuary 1802, and the 5th of January 1803, viz. 183,446 Tons the several Duties on which under the Act referred to was *only* £1601 2 7½ and there mainder of the sum above mentioned were Custom-house fees and Brokerage.

The duties collected under this Act for the before-mentioned purposes, we have been informed, amount to more than £40,000 *per Annum*. Out of this large sum we find the Society has been able to procure an exemption from *Four Thousand Pounds* only. The West India Dock Proprietors having a capital of their own, very little if any of that sum could be appropriated to that extensive concern. The principal part therefore of those duties were entirely applicable to various improvements of the Port, under the direction of the Corporation of London.

With respect to the West India Docks, we shall only remark upon them as they affect the Shipping Interest in the Port of London. The Society of Ship Owners observe—"*that from the explanations recently given by the Directors, they were lead to believe, that the many inconveniences which had arisen, from several of the regulatisns adopted at the West India Docks, would in future be avoided.*" What those inconveniences are the Committee do not say; but, besides the very general disgust that pervades the Captains, Officers, and Seamen, belonging to West India Ships, in consequence of the severity of the Dock Regulations, a more important grievance presents itself—a grievance that goes very near, if not shortly checked, to annihilate, bad as it is, even our West India nursery for seamen: as soon as a ship enters the Docks, no person whatever is allowed to remain on board; masters are consequently under the necessity either of taking their apprentices to their own houses, which is generally very inconvenient, or else boarding them out at a very great expence, whereas, if the ship was lying in the river, they could remain on board for a mere trifle. This vast inconvenience has now so much discouraged the owners and masters of ships from taking apprentices, that they will rather trust to the chance of procuring foreigners and others to navigate their ships than be at the expence of maintaining them ashore. The grievance of such harsh regulations, and impolicy of suffering them to continue, are so very obvious, that it is needless to make any further remarks on them; we can only hope that they will soon be removed, either by the Directors of that Company or by the strong arm of Government.

Whether the West India Docks are beneficial to the Port of London is another point of consideration; they may possibly be so in some instances, but we believe they will be found to be more hurtful than otherwise. Innovations ought very carefully to be admitted, we have heard of an iron bridge with only one arch, to be substituted for London Bridge, &c. and a thousand other schemes which would produce no other effect than distressing our traders, impeding the commerce of the Country, and loading our Shipping with taxes to defray the enormous expences attending the execution of such wild projects. If money is so very plentiful, there are numerous other plans which might be adopted for facilitating commerce than those proposed, but we are of opinion that the shipping Interest of this Country is already too much burthened with imposts to allow of any further addition to what it at present bears. It is the support of the country; and experiments of every kind which tend to oppress it ought carefully to be avoided: *foreigners already trade with more advantage than we do,* it is therefore our interest to decrease its burthens, and enable it to trade with equal profit and success; but while our Shipping are obliged to support the expences attending Canals, Docks, and other schemes, besides various duties in aid of the necessities of the State, it is impossible that our shipping can ever trade upon equal terms with foreigners; and in the course of a few years we shall find that *they will ultimately engross the whole of our carrying trade.*

If Ministers conceive that the Tonnage Duty is necessary, they should at the same time be very scrupulous in suffering our shipping to the burthened with taxes for the support of ignorant schemes and experiments which tend only to fatten a few interested individuals, while they distress most severely the public interest. Docks have been said to save our Merchants a great sum, merely from the prevention of plunder in various articles. This may be allowed in part, but we are not willing to allow it to the extent supposed. But what is the plunder of a part of the Merchants' property, even snpposing it to be equal to their calculation, when put in competition with the annihilation of our naval pre-eminence? For though we may possess abundance of ships, yet if we cannot procure men to man them, our navy is of very little service to us; and it is clear to every one at all acquainted with the subject, that Wet Docks, upon the plan of those in the Isle of Dogs and at Blackwall, are highly injurious to the nursery of seamen.

With regard to other alterations or improvements in the

[Hh]

Port of London we have very little to observe; we leave it to those in whose hands the power of carrying them into execution is placed, how far such may be necessary or conducive to the prosperity of Commerce; we wish it was in our power to commend their abilities or economy, but that we understand will very shortly become the subject of an enquiry before the House of Commons, many Members of which begin to feel the necessity of strictly examining the expenditure of money drawn from the Shipping Interest of this Country. They now perceive *the rapid decay of British shipping*, and that foreigners are rapidly usurping the carrying trade of Great Britain; and while the latter can carry goods for a less sum than British ships, even British as well as foreign merchants will employ them in preference to our own ships.

It appears even by the Report of the Society of Ship Owners, respecting the Bell-Rock Light-house Dues, how very neglectful we must have been to the interests of British Shipping, when we could allow above £10,000. *per Annum* to be levied on the Baltic trade for a purpose that was ultimately dispensed with. It is indeed sincerely to be wished, that the Legislature would clearly see the benefits and advantage this country must derive from a proper attention to its Shipping Interest, and from cultivating the immense resources we possess to increase the number of our ships and seamen, without whom this country will never be able to counteract the machinations of her most inveterate and eternal foes.

It is indeed full time that some notice should be taken of this great expenditure, particularly as it is drawn from the Shipping interest, which unfortunately is now in a state that requires the utmost exertion of Ministers to support, instead of adding to its distresses. It is at the same time requisite that the merchants and owners of British shipping, who are now labouring under such heavy burthens, should know in what manner, and for what purpose such large sums of money coming from their pockets are applied, in order to prevent their being expended in childish experiments and unnecessary contracts. It is also necessary that Government should "watch with the most scrutinising eye the application of so large a revenue arising from the very vitals of the Country," for if duty upon duty is to be laid on British shipping without consulting the interests of the Owner and merchants, and if the money arising from those duties is suffered to be indiscriminately applied in the prosecution of ignorant schemes and experiments, who can be surprised that our ships are empty, and are daily having brooms stuck up at their mast heads for sale? Who can be surprised that vessels of every description *should prefer discharging at Bristol, Liverpool, and other ports, to the Port of London?* Who then can blame the Foreigners from taking advantage of the burthens that distress our shipping, and carrying away the trade of this country? Who can say where this abuse will end, or what will ere long be the state to which these oppressions will reduce the Naval Power of Great Britain?

The depreciated state of our Commercial Marine, on which principally depends the existence of our Naval superiority, has unavoidably led us into rather more detail than was originally intended; but the necessity of elucidating the causes of such depression, and pointing out the urgency of speedily removing them, will, we hope, excuse us for having availed ourselves so often of the opinions of others, in order to substantiate our arguments on this most important subject. It is of the last importance that British shipping should trade on equal terms with those of other powers, and that every encouragement should be afforded by the legislature for that purpose; but so long as it continues to be burthened with Tonnage, Convoy, Port Duties, and Insurance, Taxes for Docks, Canals, Tunnels, and a thousand other schemes, it will continue to drag on a miserable existence, till even the profitable concern of ship-breaking shall be no more.

The Committee of the Society of Ship Owners observe, that their investigations have been influenced by no other motive than a due sense of justice to their Country, and to themselves; a high sentiment of the national importance of the Shipping interest, and the remembrance that to it is to be attributed the glory and greatness of the British Empire. This we sincerely believe, and so must *every impartial man* who has read their report. It is also true indeed, that to the Shipping Interest is to be attributed the glory and greatness of the British Empire. It disperses over the whole world the produce of British industry, it rears and cherishes our brave defenders, it gives us a superiority and power which other nations do not possess, and it assists, by a considerable revenue, in relieving the necessities of the state. It must consequently appear evident, that the less this most essential part of our strength and resources, which we may call the stamina of our

Country, is burthened with taxes, the more prosperous and powerful it will become; not that we recommend every impost and duty to be taken off, but only such as are applied to frivolous and almost unnecessary purposes, which, from want of proper direction, are likely to continue as permanent taxes, though otherwise their duration was intended to have been confined to short periods. We have also shewn, that many grievances of a different nature continue to exist, and greatly retards, if not destroys the prosperity of our shipping; to these we wish likewise to direct the attention of Government, as the principal means by which we can become independent, not only of the Northern, but of all the other powers in Europe.

It will probably be recollected by some of our readers, that about a twelvemonth ago, two letters* appeared in *The Morning Chronicle* on the subject of East India shipping; these were afterwards published by the Proprietors of India Property, and (as the writer observes in his second letter), produced a sensation in every quarter which he trusted would be attended with the happiest effects; not that he imputed that sensation to any exertion of his own powers, but to that hold which undisputed truths will naturally take of the feelings of men, when conveyed even in the plainest language. These truths which he ventured to lay before the public, and which he asserts to be undisputed, are nothing less than the *absolute loss of Sixty-eight thousand Pounds* to the *owners of one* East India ship of *Eight Hundred Tons*, after she had been *six* voyages to sea. This loss he clearly displays, by a very accurate and convincing statement of every voyage, and which has hitherto been confuted by no one. If, therefore, such is the immense loss on a description of shipping which possess greater advantages than any other part of our mercantile marine, can the present distressed state of the British Shipping Interest be wondered at? Surely if this is not an exaggerated estimate of East India depreciation, our Commerce and Navy must be in a most alarming situation, and we must not only tremble for our Empire in the East, but also for that in the West; and what is of greater consequence than either, for the very existence of Great Britain and Ireland.

In support of our arguments on British shipping, we might bring forward *numberless letters* that have appeared in

* Vide post No. xxviii.

the public prints on that subject; but as that would be deviating too much from the intention of this Pamphlet, we shall only notice the observations of one of those writers, whose arguments on the Suspension of Navigation Laws are so pertinent and convincing that we hope they will be a sufficient apology for its insertion:—'In reviewing this very important subject, it is necessary to look back to the early periods of our History; from them we shall learn the high value our ancestors set upon the Shipping Interest of the country. From the infancy of our trade, it was fostered by them with the greatest care and attention, by enacting at different periods of time a series of wise and salutary regulations called the Navigation Laws, for the express purpose of preserving to British ships (under certain conditions) sundry portions of our trade with foreign countries, together with the whole of our coasting and colonial trade. The great benefits which have resulted from this wise system are too obvious to require a detail; it is sufficient to observe, that it has encreased the wealth and naval strength of old England to a high pitch of prosperity and power, and placed it in the most distinguished and pre-eminent situation as a great and maritime nation. Happy would it be for us—happy for our posterity, to maintain the glorious result unimpaired; but alas! it is already obscured with threatening clouds! From the *inattention* and *indifference* which is now shewn to these invaluable Laws of Navigation; and from their *frequent* suspension, on the most weak and frivolous pretexts; the most serious inconveniencies have ensued to the Shipping interest of Great Britain, which, if not remedied, will soon be felt by the whole country, by extending their fatal effects to the British Navy, in the destruction of its natural resources of men and money, which have hitherto arisen, and must still be supported, by means of our carrying trade.'

'To avert a calamity which threatened our existence as a powerful maritime state, many Ship Owners, residing in the principal sea-ports of the kingdom, in the year 1802, formed themselves into a Society, for the purpose *of promoting the interest of British shipping*, and of preventing, by their united efforts, any *infringement* of a body of laws which had stood the test and experience of ages, in raising their Country to a state of prosperity and greatness unrivalled by surrounding nations. It is, however, a lamentable fact, that hitherto all their endeavours have proved ineffectual, for they have failed in their attempts to impress conviction in the minds of the king's ministers of the necessity which exists, consistent with the welfare of our country, of preserving entire and unbroken a system of Laws, which had been founded and reared by the policy and wisdom of our wise and patriotic ancestors. Nay from this powerful quarter, I am sorry to observe, there is not any reasonable prospect of support or assistance in their laudable exertions, a leading Member of the present administration having declared—' That, however wise and salutary the Navigation Laws might have been in the infancy of our commerce, he did not perceive the efficacy of them at present, and the necessity of strictly adhering to their original provisions.'—But surely this opinion ought to be reversed, and read thus—' That, however wise and salutary the Navigation Laws might have been in the infancy of our commerce, they are become now more imperatively so, not only from the amazing and alarming encrease of foreign shipping, but likewise from the heavy expences and duties at present imposed on British shipping;' for it is evident that in the first essays of trade, the competition between us and other maritime states depended on the respective exertions which each made in industry and good management. Our ships were not then fettered with heavy duties, which have since been imposed on them from the exigencies of the state, and which our rivals in trade do not bear in the same proportion.'

' British ships now stand charged with heavy duties on every article necessary to their equipment, amounting to upwards of seven *per cent.* on their whole value, exclusive of a *double* duty on their gross tonnage; the first is permanent, the other is now denominated a *War Tax*, although it *originated* during what was termed a *profound peace* *. Added to these burthens, they have to contend with the high price of provisions, great wages, and *war* premiums of insurance. Under all these disadvantages united, is it a matter of wonder that British Ship Owners are no longer able to continue the contest with their rivals at the same rate of freight? Compare their situation with the ships of Denmark, Norway, Sweden, and Prussia: naval stores are the original produce of those countries; they are not burthened with heavy duties, provisions they have cheap, and seamen's wages are low. By these advantages, foreigners are enabled to take freight at a *lower* rate; and as the smallest difference in that respect

* In 1802, during lord Sidmouth's administration.

determines the preference of the merchants, *the carrying trade of Europe is almost entirely wrested from us.*'

'By these causes, indeed, we have arrived at a new æra in the history of British commerce; that at the end of March 1804, there is scarcely a single offer of trade for a *British* bottom, except such as are employed in coasting or colonial branches, and these are only held by the tenure of such parts of the Navigation Laws as still remain unbroken.—What a lamentable prospect for every lover of his country! It surely cannot be known *to the wise and public spirited Legislators of Britain* that our ships, and all those who depend upon them for support, are actually in a state of ruin.—Yet that is an undeniable fact. If it is doubted, look at the mooring places in the river Thames, which should be the emporium of *British* traffic in *British* bottoms; they are crowded with *foreign* ships in *full employ*, whilst those of our country cover the shores, and fill the Wet Docks, in a state of inactivity and decay. So effectually have the evil consequences taken root, that foreign seamen, on whom we chiefly depend in time of war for manning our merchantmen, finding the alteration that has taken place in that respect, no longer resort here for employment as formerly; therefore, it is evident that the whole system of our carrying trade and its connections is (for some time at least) *lost* to our country.'

'Happy should I be, if I could arouse my countrymen to a just sense of the danger which threatens them, from such inattention to our vital interests! Certainly the great importance of the subject deserves the most *serious consideration of the Legislature;* for it requires very little argument to demonstrate, that we depend on our carrying trade for support as a great maritime nation. Let us, then, endeavour to promote this interest by all justifiable means; it is not too late to retrieve that which has been lost by a few years' impolicy and indifference to the subject. Revise the Navigation Laws, and either increase the alien duties, or decrease the duties on imports in *British* shipping, that they may trade with equal advantage with *foreign* carriers. I am aware of the old objection to this suggestion, that foreigners will retaliate with countervailing duties. But there are many cases in which it could have no weight, even under the spirit of our Navigation Laws as they now stand. The produce of Poland ought not to be imported in Prussian bottoms, but confined to our own. The same rule ought to hold good with the commodities of the little states of the *Mediterranean*, who are not carriers themselves. It is surely no injustice to say to the Northern states, our rivals in shipping—'The balance of trade between our Countries is very considerably *against us*—we take the greatest part of all your produce, whilst you receive very little, if any, of ours in return; and it is neither just nor necessary that England should support the *continual* and *double* drain of money, by purchasing *your* produce, and paying for the *transit* of it in *your* own ships; we, therefore, are under the necessity of revising the duties, to place *British* shipping on an *equality* with *yours*.' Except some such mode be adopted for their relief, the carrying trade, at least during the war, must be inevitably lost to us, when the resources of our Navy are indispensable; and surely Britons will not resign a matter of such great importance to their interest and welfare, without a single struggle!'

'There is another point which I cannot pass over in silence, because it is laying the axe to the root of our nurseries for British seamen. I allude to the impolitic practice which now prevails of *impressing* sea apprentices, in the most arbitrary manner, and on the most frivolous pretences. By this system, and the frequent want of employment, the owners of British shipping have entirely lost every inducement to take *sea apprentices*. The bad effects of it are already severely felt in the British navy; and if it be not averted by salutary remedies, the most serious consequences must follow: for it is a *notorious fact*, that the *British trade does not produce half the number of seamen which it formerly did*; and it may not be improper to notice that the *regulations at the West India Docks* greatly discourage the owners and masters of ships in that trade from taking sea apprentices as they did formerly.'

'If, then, the public spirit which actuated our forefathers is not entirely fled—if we are not totally absorbed in the consideration of selfish pursuits, without regard to the public good, let me conjure my countrymen to rally round the bulwark of our carrying trade—the navigation laws; let us endeavour, by strenuous exertions, to maintain them in *their full and pristine vigour*; nor let us stop here, but unite our efforts to revive and amend them, that we may preserve to our country, and to our posterity, the *empire of the seas*, that invaluable legacy which has been handed down to us by our brave ancestors, founded and nurtured by their foresight and wisdom, and by which we may still be enabled to contend, *single handed*, with the colossal power of our *old inveterate and natural* enemy, for all we hold dear to us as men and Britons*.'

Such are the arguments of this very able and well informed writer, which to every man at all concerned with shipping must be convincing, without the intervention of a doubt. His observations on the arbitrary and injurious system of impressing sea apprentices are indeed too true; and we are sorry to add that a similar case exists with regard to watermen's apprentices, who are liable to be impressed after they have served three or four years of their time, just at a period when they are useful to their masters, for it seldom happens that during the first three years they earn sufficient to maintain themselves. This mistaken grievous policy is at the same time ruinous instead of being beneficial to the navy—It checks the nursery of watermen on the river Thames, which has hitherto considerably augmented the number of our sailors, and which has always proved a great advantage *at the breaking out* of a war, by affording a large supply of skilful hands so near home. At some periods there have been at work on the river Thames between Westminster-bridge and Gravesend more than 30,000 watermen, riggers, and other nautical men, exclusive of the British and foreign seamen on board the shipping; but at present there is not a sixth part of that number, and even that is daily decreasing in consequence of the improvident system of locking up our ships in Wet Docks, the baneful effects of which will plainly appear by the following simple statement, *that when five or six hundred ships at a time are shut up in those Docks, twice that number of lightermen are thrown out of employ, because the goods are carted from the Docks to the Merchants' warehouses in town; and watermen, three or four of whom, and sometimes more, that used formerly to be in constant attendance upon each of those vessels while lying in the river, are now unemployed, because there is no occasion for them according to the present regulations in the Docks:* and when the East-India Docks are completed how much more severe will this evil be felt amongst those watermen, lightermen, and riggers, whom that class of shipping entire-

* The letter from which this extract is made, and many others, at different periods, have appeared under the signatures of Amator Patriæ and Nauclerus, and are attributed to one of the committee of ship-owners for the port of London, to whom the public are indebted for his unwearied exertions to support the shipping interest of the country.

ly support. These men, most of whom have large families, it is very true, may go into the Navy rather than starve: but here ends the policy of this argument, as well as all future supply from this hitherto productive and excellent nursery of seamen.

The abettors of the Wet Dock system may perhaps say that the expence which the ship owner and merchant before experienced, from employing these men, is now saved to them; but we would ask, are the Dock duties nothing? Is the detention of ships in Dock nothing? Is the maintenance of apprentices and seamen ashore, who are not suffered to live on board, no expence to the owner? And again is it nothing, that the risk of fire is a thousand times greater when ships are collected together in Dock, than when they are lying in the river afloat? But it is unnecessary to argue further on the injurious and pernicious tendency of the Dock system, since the impropriety is clear to all but those who are concerned in its establishment, and by which they expect to realise splendid fortunes. Friendly as we are to any plans that are likely to add to the grandeur and dignity of the nation, yet when they possess obnoxious qualities that overbalance the beneficial effects expected to be derived from them, it is the duty of every man to point them out, and for this reason we would rather see the money of patriotic individuals employed in objects that are more likely to encourage and promote the prosperity of British shipping and the empire of the seas, than speculations in Wet Docks, Tunnels, and Canals. Page 79.

No. XXVIII.

Letters on the new System of East-India Shipping, and its destructive Consequences to the Public, and to the Commanders and Officers in the Service.

Extracted from the Morning Chronicle and other Newspapers.

LETTER I.

MR. EDITOR,

WHEN a man enters into a contract which is to subsist even for a short period of time, we readily give him credit for having called in the aid of preliminary calculation, founded on the variety of contingent circumstances which may operate for and against the undertaking, and on the magnitude of the capital which that undertaking will call into activity.

But this becomes more imperatively necessary, where the duration of the contract may extend to even beyond the term of fifteen years, certainly to not less than twelve years; and when the adventure is not only liable to casualties, of the most unforseen and unbounded nature, but where, *inevitably*, it will be affected by a most powerful and destructive agent; an agent, however, which, I trust, will long continue to operate with increasing energy in this country, because it is the best proof of the prosperity of the country—I mean the gradual and progressive decrease in the value of money. This reflection, sir, I am drawn into by understanding the general terms of the tenders made to, and accepted by, the East-India company within these few days back; and I must beg leave to preface any thing further I may have to say on this subject by the unqualified declaration, that I am in no shape whatever, either directly or indirectly, concerned as an owner in any of the East-India Company's ships, or desirous of being so. My sole reason for taking up the question I most solemnly avow to be a desire to check, if possible, imprudent and destructive speculation, ultimately tending (and not in my individual opinion only) to the most serious private injury and public wrong.

The grounds for that opinion I now beg leave to submit to the consideration of those concerned, soliciting, and anxiously inviting gentlemen, acquainted with the nature of the service, to convict me of any inaccuracy that is not in favour of my general position. To those unacquainted with the service, it may appear extraordinary, that there should exist such a wide difference of opinion, on a matter which may be thought, and undoubtedly is, as easily reducible to a mercantile certainty as any other shipping speculation whatever. But the wonder will vanish, in some respect, when we presume to hint, that the scale of calculation is in most, if not all, of these cases, biassed by the eager anxiety of men bred in the service, or their friends, to procure the only possible means, by the only possible way, of remunerating the sacrifice of a life hitherto wasted in that particular line and unfit, from habits, as they are, for almost any other. This I say will operate in a degree to bias the adventuring owner as to the expectations of emolument to be derived from his tender; still, however, that bias will operate but to a certain extent, regulated by the strength of friendship, or, in a moderate degree, by the depth of purse. A friend taking a sixteenth share to serve a friend, may be willing to risk, on the event of the concern, the loss of £500, £600, or even £1000, but here I conceive friendship might be reasonably expected to pause. To what then can I impute the extraordinary nature of the late tenders, which I am induced to think, from the following statement, can have been founded on no previous calculation, far less on a knowledge of the nature of the adventure?

As I do not write for fame, but take up my pen solely to exhibit the folly and destructive tendency of such engagements, both to the individual and the public, I beg leave at once to appeal to the common sense of that public by a calculation sufficiently in detail, founded on the tenders lately accepted by the Directors; and I repeat my challenge to any man to controvert my statement, or to show it defective, except in favour of the general result.

For the better understanding it, I have only these prefatory observations to make, viz.—That I take it up as a mercantile adventure, on common mercantile principles; that I allow two years only for each voyage, with the small interest of only 5 per cent. per annum; that I take the freight at £19 net (rather above the late tenders), in order to avoid fractions, making a large allowance for surplus freight; that I take no notice of the impress, except on the first and last voyages, as in fact immaterial to the calculation; and that I invariably, through the whole six voyages and twelve years, admit not the idea for a moment, that any untoward accident shall occur to disturb the harmony, or *precipitate the uniform tendency* of the adventure.

There is no man, I believe, who will obstinately dispute, that the building, at the present advanced rate, and the outfit at the present enormous price of every principal naval store, can amount on a ship of 800 tons, properly equipped for the Company's service, to less than £35000, but I am willing to allow every possible advantage which the most rigid economy can procure, and I will fix the

First cost and outfit, at only			£32,000
Deduct the impress			2,000
Leaving the cost to sea, first voyage,			30,000
Interest, two years, at 5 per cent. per annum,			3,000
Insure, to cover the same, £35,000 at seven guineas per hundred, with half per cent. and policy,			2,800
Cost on return from first voyage			35,800
Now the freight of 800 tons, at £19 per ton, is		15,200	
Surplus 100 tons, at £10		1000	
Less charges on the voyage, viz.			
Wages	2,300		
Captain's disbursements on the yoyage,	2,200		
Damage and short delivery	500		
Discharging in the river homeward	800		
		5,800	
Outfit on the second voyage I shall fix at what is well known to be far under the mark		9,000	
		14,800	
Leaving dividend to owners of			1,400
Cost to sea on second voyage,			34,400
Interest two years, and insurance £41,000 to cover			6,720
Cost on return from second voyage			41,120
And taking the freight and disbursements in the same favourable way, there will remain a dividend for the owners, as on the first voyage, of			1,400
Cost to sea on the third voyage			39,720

It is necessary here to remark, that on the third, or usual repairing voyage, I have made no alteration in the cost of outfit, allowing the idea of extraordinary and unprecedented success to prevail through the whole, and of course that the ship shall not need her thorough repair till the fourth outfit, which will enable her to complete her contract for six voyages.

Cost to sea on the third voyage - - - - - - -	£39,720
Interest for two years and insurance to cover 47,000l. - -	7,732
Cost on return from third voyage - - - - - - -	47,452
Here the outfit on her fitting voyage will, on the lowest possible estimate, exceed the former outfit by 3,000l. and of course, instead of a dividend arising on the concern to the owners, they will have to advance the sum of - - - - - -	1,600
Cost to sea on the fourth voyage - - - - - - - -	49,052
Interest for two years, and insurance to cover 58,000l. - -	9,540
Cost from sea, fourth voyage - - - - - - - -	58,592
And supposing the same favourable result on this as on former voyages, the ship will be fitted out on the ensuing voyage, and the owners will receive as before - - - - - - -	1,400
Cost to sea, fifth voyage - - - - - - - - - -	57,192
Interest two years, and insurance to cover 68,000l. - - -	11,159
Cost from sea, fifth voyage - - - - - - - - -	68,351
Less the dividend supposed as before to arise on the voyage -	1,400
Cost to sea, on sixth voyage - - - - - - - -	66,951
Interest two years, and insurance to cover 80,000l. - - -	13,095
Cost on return from sixth voyage - - - - - - -	80,046

Now let us wind up the concern.

The gross freight on the voyage, as before - -	16,200	
Less, the impress now to be deducted - - -	2,000	
	14,200	
Add value of the ship and stores - - - -	3,000	
	17,200	
From which deduct the amount of wages, disbursements, &c. as before - - - - - - - - - -	5,800	
		11,400
And there will remain the enormous, and, I will venture to say, indisputable loss to the owners of - - - - - -		£68,646

Will any man (even in the direction) among the most

sanguine admirers of the new system, for one moment contend, that there must not lie, behind this impenetrable curtain, this speculation which sets common reason at defiance, some object in perspective, some twig which may, in the time of need, save them from drowning: for, that that time must come, and speedily, cannot be denied; and let the East India company beware of the period. The barrier of a 10,000l. penalty will not protect the company against a conviction of loss to such an enormous amount—that conviction will most inevitably come in all its horrors—it has already visited the first speculators in this system, though, at the time they enlisted under its banners, building was eight pounds per ton less, and many other charges in proportion; and *I know it to be a fact*, that, with all the advantages which war contingencies could confer on these concerns, for the first two voyages (if war contingencies do confer advantages), they are, at this moment, in a most miserable and alarming state of deficiency.

But it is proper here to remark, that the late tenders are made by men unacquainted in a great measure with what has passed lately, and certainly strangers to the situation of the first adventurers; who, smarting under the losses they have already sustained, have not dared to come forward at a rate any thing like that proferred by these *Fresh men.*

In order, as much as possible, to prevent cavil at the above statement, I beg leave to observe that I take no credit whatever for demurrage, as it is well understood in the service to be barely adequate to the increased expence by the detention, and in the wear and tear of the ship and stores; nor do I take into consideration the probability of hostilities, and the benefits to be derived from war contingencies; for I am clear, and *I appeal to facts*, that there are no benefits to be derived, in that case, which are not fully met by the increased risk and increased annual value of an increased capital. But, in regard to the present tenders, I am perfectly clear that any war contingencies to those owners will be very trifling indeed, except in the articles of insurance, manning, and guns and shot, unless a miracle is performed on the twenty-four directors, or it is agreed at once to abandon the system; for I contend, without fear of contradiction, that the meaning of the present system is (and that meaning has hitherto been acted upon), that, in regard to war contingencies, owners of ships shall be allowed the difference in naval stores, &c. caused by war, as opposed to the prices and charges during peace; and the company best explain their sense of the matter during the present season, by refusing to allow war contingencies to the existing ships, notwithstanding the very advanced rate of cordage, &c. above the rates of 1792, on which these tenders were made and accepted. The company, in case of future hostilities, will naturally and readily answer any application on the part of the owners lately contracting, by asking how they could reasonably expect to be allowed war contingencies, on cordage, provisions, &c. while the war price of those articles is only 50l. per ton, and 8l. per tierce, recollecting that they thought themselves justified in coming forward with the tender of a ship at 19l. per ton, when these articles were at 60l. per ton, and 10l. per tierce, as they are at this moment, with little prospect of alteration? That this argument will be used by the company, no doubt can be entertained; for, otherwise, there is no meaning in the term *peace freight*; and although the ships, now actually in the service, on the new system, were tendered and accepted during the war on the peace prices antecedent to that war, yet, peace having again taken place, a new ground is formed on which to estimate peace freight, unless the company, by their advertisements, had held a different language, and agreed to admit the prices of 1792 as the standard for peace freight.

That peace, it is true, has taken place, finding the nation burdened with a heavy addition of debt, and at the same time individual riches more than ever extended and increased, the inseparable consequence of which is, that the value of money is proportionably decreased; or, in other words, that every man must contribute to enable his neighbour to pay his proportion of the additional public burden. Labour, therefore, and of course every description of manufacture, becomes affected. This the first speculators in the new system feel most deeply, though in little more than the first dawning of their adventure; but in the progressive state of accumulation, and of course the progressive diminution in the value of money, which may be expected in this country in the subsequent twelve years, what must the situation of the late contractors with the company be towards the end of this term, deprived, as they are, of the advantages the former possessed; saddled, at the same time, with all the disadvantages the former now experience, on account of the depreciation of money, and having in prospect those which the succeeding period of their long-winded engagement will inevitably expose them to? I will venture to assert, that even the strongest advocates for the new system in the direction were far from expecting to see tenders at so low a rate, convinced, as they must be by the inspection of the accounts of their own ships, that the matter is impracticable, at many pounds per ton more.

For my own part, I see only one way of relieving these new speculators from some part of the accumulation of loss which my statement entails on their contract. This is, that when the ship is fitted out complete to sea, on the first voyage they should place the whole cost and outfit to the debit side of profit and loss. Thus they will save the trouble of keeping the account, and the pain of seeing such a miserable business on the wrong side of their ledger every time they turn it over to look for funds to meet their engagements, and by continuing to watch the progress of the concern, and wiping off occasionally in the same way 8000l. or 10,000l. they may at last wind up with not only an *appearance*, but a *certainty*, of profit on the adventure.

For the present I beg leave to withhold further observation, anxiously expecting that my estimate will be either subverted or admitted;

And am, SIR,

Yours &c.

NO OWNER.

London, Jan. 9.

LETTER II.

MR. EDITOR,

I FIND that my letter of the 9th instant has produced a sensation in every quarter, which I trust will be attended with the happiest effects. In saying that this sensation was on my part by no means unexpected, I beg I may not be understood as imputing it to any exertion of my very inadequate powers of mind, but to that hold which undisputed truths will naturally take of the feelings of men, when conveyed even in the plainest language. That the truths I have ven-

[Kk]

tured to lay before the public on this subject *are* undisputed, I am fully warranted in asserting; for, although some trifling objections have been made on both sides of my statement, they are too immaterial in their nature to shake the foundation; and I may fairly conclude, as, indeed, it is allowed, that, on the whole, it is unanswerable.

The only objection which is at all deserving of notice is made against my charge of compound interest, with all its accumulating mischiefs; and to this I answer, that, as every man on such an adventure expects to derive from his capital at least the common return for the use of his money, I must charge the concern with interest, and insure that interest; otherwise the adventurer, in case of loss of the ship, loses the use of that capital, which he is equally entitled to as to the capital itself. This is surely the only mode of adventuring which can justify a mercantile man. But I am supported in this mode of drawing my statement by more respectable authority than some gentlemen are aware of who make this objection. I am supported by the uniform practice of the court of directors and their officers, and I appeal to their printed proceedings; and, if I had assumed six, or even seven, per cent interest, instead of five per cent. as I have done, I should have more closely adhered to their practice; for the court of directors have always admitted that five per cent. is not an adequate return for money vested in their shipping service. This question, however, in my opinion, is set at rest, by the consideration that the contract is a *whole*, from its commencement to its close. The result is at no period separable from the transaction, and the profit or loss must be judged of by the event. I am willing, however, to make every sacrifice which may be demanded of me *when trifles only are concerned;* and, as the accumulation of compound interest and insurance thereon may amount to somewhere about 3000l. I beg leave to adjust all disputed points between us, by drawing off, by way of free gift, 10,000l. or even 20,000l. from the loss which my statement winds up with. Allowing, therefore, my adventurers to retain the full benefit of the very weighty advantages I give them, in keeping them clear of those untoward circumstances, which we well know every ship does encounter in the course of her term in the service, I trust any reasonable man will content himself with the *decided and undisputed loss of the remainder*.

During that sensation which my last letter produced, I confess I did not expect that some men, though professing to act upon fair mercantile competition, would have shrunk from that duty which they owe even to themselves; and, instead of endeavouring to refute my principles, or controvert my statement, would have had recourse to the puerile threat of prosecuting the author. What the grounds for prosecution are, it is not easy to guess. If I am not founded in my ideas, let my pretensions be fairly canvassed; but I shall not by the *wincing of the galled jade* be deterred from doing, what I conceive to be the duty of every man, to protect the public, and, in doing that, to protect the individual.

I will not, Sir, unnecessarily take up your valuable columns in reminding that public, and the court of directors, as, in this case, the agent of the public, of what must be sufficiently obvious to every man—That *public good* can never be founded on *private wrong*; and that it is under no circumstances consistent with the real interest of the public to enter into contracts on grounds which render it more than doubtful that they can ever be brought to a termination in the regular and fair course of things.

The contracts now in question must be closed in some shape before their natural period of existence arrives; and, although the company, and, through that body, the public, may be temporary gainers by the forfeitures to which the owners must submit, rather than proceed in their contract, yet all these forfeitures, with all the accumulation of losses which have been sustained by the adventurers on the new system, may be fairly expected to fall eventually on the public, in the increased compensation which owners will find it necessary to require for the use of their capital; and accordingly I find that one gentleman, I believe, without exception, as well informed on the subject as any man can be, and possessing the advantage of full experience in that new system, has tendered, on the late occasion, at somewhere about 30l. per ton, instead of 19l. or 20l. and which, after all, would barely yield seven per cent. on the adventure.

After what has been said, I hope, Sir, I shall no longer be told, that the best test which can be furnished at any period of the solidity and efficacy of the present system of East India Shipping, and of the incorrectness of my assertion, that the concerns of ships lately admitted on that system are in a miserable state of deficiency, is the readiness with which the public come forward with tenders at rates even lower than before. No man will, I think, venture to say, that the late tenders accepted by the company are the result of very minute investigation, and, at any rate, after the conviction which, I trust, I have impressed on the minds of my readers, these tenders ought not to be, as I hear they are, held up by way of answer to the very reasonable and just representation which has been made to the company on the part of the new owners. This representation regards the impracticability of fulfilling their original contract, unless some allowance is made to them for the very great and (certainly with them) unexpected increase in the value of labour, and of necessity in naval stores, and every expence attached to outfit of shipping concerns which has followed, and ever will follow the increase of the debt of the country. The consequences of this increase are felt *in every other branch of mercantile shipping;* and are East India Shipping exempted from the general calamity? I have declared myself most solemnly no owner, or desirous of being so; but I sincerely feel for, because I truly know, the situation in which public events have placed these first adventurers; and, although the interests of the public are at all times to be preferred to those of the individual, yet there ought ever to be, in the breasts of those appointed by that public as conservators of its interests, a feeling for the individual as well as for the public: a feeling that should stimulate them on all occasions to consider themselves in their proper character, as *arbitrators* between both, and, as far as possible, to conciliate the two interests; for I repeat my position, that *public good* can never be founded on *private wrong.*

I am no advocate, Sir, against the present system, if it were placed under proper restraints, which I shall take the liberty of suggesting; but, in its present state, I see it in no other view than promising to be a productive source of misery and loss to those who may be induced to venture in it, until time and experience shall have made commanders and their friends better acquainted with the nature of these concerns, exposed as they are, and ever will be, as contracts of long duration, not only to the effects of that powerful agent I have already noticed—the progressive decrease in the value of money—but to a variety of losses and disasters to which this shipping service is exposed more than any other, and for which I have made no kind of provision whatever in my statement.

The restraints, or checks, which I would suggest on the present system, are two, either of which may be adopted with effect. The first is, that the company shall appoint a certain number of captains in the service, sufficient for the ships employed, who shall be entitled by seniority to the command of such ships as may be built for the service by public contract, the owners having no voice in the nomination of such captain, but possessing a power, by means of a supercargo, or purser, to controul the expences of their ship while abroad.—Thus the competition among the public bidders for the company's freight-service will be limited to the employment of capital solely, and the system will be relieved from the slur which the ill-disposed have now too much ground for throwing on it, by asserting, that the savings in that article to that respectable body, the East India Company, and of course to the public, are drawn from the hard earnings of commanders in their service, anxious to make any sacrifice rather than close a laborious life without obtaining the only chance of reimbursing themselves for the loss of their earliest years, and best blood spent in the service.

The second check which I propose is probably more readily attainable every way. It is that the court of directors shall have a discretionary power of accepting or rejecting tenders made to them, according as they are convinced, on mature deliberation, that the proposal is, or is not, practicable; and it will be allowed that there cannot be better judges, assisted by the able men in their different offices, to whom they will refer, and aided likewise by the documents with which their own ships annually furnish them.

These, Sir, appear to me the only means by which both the interests of the public and the individual may be secured; and I will, for the present, take my leave of the subject, with repeating my assurance, that my sole view in requesting the indulgence you have granted me was to render some service, by guarding individuals against a dangerous speculation; and by enabling any man to become his own calculator on such an adventure, before he fills up his tender with terms to which he is to be bound for twelve or fifteen years to come, and on which the fortunes of his family may depend; I flatter myself, my labour and your indulgence will not be thrown away. At any future period I shall be as ready as now to step forward in pointing out the expectations which may be derived from tenders accepted by the Company; for I repeat, that I think it a public duty, when such tenders carry on the face of them no rational prospect of a regular termination;

And am, SIR,

Yours, &c.

NO OWNER.

London, January 19, 1803.

The following ironical Letter, in allusion to the preceding, appeared in the TRUE BRITON *of* January 22d, 1803, *as addressed to the Commanders and Officers in the Service.*

MY EVER DEAR CHILDREN!

YOU, whom, I may say, I have reared from the shell, nursed like the pelican with my own entrails, and whom I gather every day under my wings, as a hen does her chickens, will naturally expect that I should be alive to every thing which, either in its present or remote tendency, may affect your interests.

With a poignancy of sorrow which I cannot express, which convulses me to my centre, and even palsies the sinews of my servant Charles, as he hands you your respective pittances of coffee, I have heard a statement read, and commented on, which appeared in the *Morning Chronicle*, of the 13th instant, signed *No Owner*, followed up by another letter, in the same paper of this day, and which statement, if only tolerably accurate, alarms me for your safety, even more than did the first introduction of the Shipping of *India-commission Dealers* among you. But what renders my affliction more severe, is the hearing it asserted, that the statement of this *No Owner* is incorrect, though incorrect on the wrong side—that the sums he assumes for charges are, on the whole, inadequate—that his credits are on too liberal a scale, and, what is worst of all, that he takes it for granted (God help his ignorance), that you, my dear children, lead the most comfortable fresh-water lives; that you go to, and return from, India without even a wet jacket—that (to use an expression of one of your early friends, Mr. BROUGH), your voyages resemble those of Cleopatra down the Silver Cydnus—that you have not sufficient practice in naval matters, to enable you to conduct yourselves with propriety under the circumstances of even the parting of a cable, the splitting of a sail, the loss of a yard, the springing of a bowsprit; far less, if subjected to those tremendous consequences, which certain lying navigators have impudently imputed to things called *hurricanes*, *tiffoons*, &c. and which, they pretend to say, even happen in the Indian and China Seas, as well as elsewhere between the Tropics—such little accidents I mean as the sweeping of a ship's masts by the board—the entire loss of a rudder, or the straining of the hull, by means of a heavy cargo, to such a degree as to compel the Company's Surveyors at home to shew their zeal for the service of their Honourable Masters, by turning it inside out for the benefit of the Owners. This *No Owner* knows nothing of such things, and I begin to think myself, from what I have heard within these very few years back of the transactions in Leadenhall-street, that really the seasons and the weather beyond the Cape are wonderfully altered for the better; in which opinion, indeed, I am supported by the uniform contempt with which the Court of Directors and their servants abroad have treated both the seasons and elements. I cannot think after all, however, that the woeful risks, dangers, and losses to which I have heard all your predecessors, my departed children bear witness—so often both in their persons and purses, are so thoroughly annihilated as this *No Owner* would have it.

I well remember the time, my Children!—it is about twenty-eight years ago, when a strong contest, between the Court of Directors and the then Owners had reduced the freights to 21l. and 22l. per ton, and I well remember that they were then such very bad concerns, and such serious losses were sustained, that, about the commencement of the French-American war, it is a well-known fact that the United East-India Company, your lords and masters, my Hearts!

were entirely indebted to you, and your predecessors, assisted now and then by the thirty-second share of a tradesman down the river, for every ship furnished for the purpose of bringing the surplus revenue to Europe, and of defending their Indian possessions.—This, however, was all well enough for you, because you depended on a regular system, which enabled you to look forward to futurity with comfort, and a tolerable certainty of seeing the sacrifice of your early youth and maturer years crowned eventually with success, and rewarded with some competency at the close of life.—What, my dear children, is the prospect now? for I fear this *No Owner* is a shrewd fellow, and knows something of the matter—he really, I must say, somehow convinces me that all is not right.

Your situation appears to be this—you were first attacked in the little profits of your petty commercial warfare, on which your very existence depended, by a set of *Commissioners from India*, who began by overturning what they called a most infamous system of corruption established among you, in passing a sum of money from the succeeding to the retiring Commander, and which the party paying suffered no further by, than in the money lying unproductive while he held the command, for he again received it from his successor. These *Commissioners* succeeded in doing away this gross system, by the establishment of one, it must be confessed, in no one degree yielding to the former: —for, what did they do, my Children, in the first instance, but compel you, who held commands, to take a sum by way of remuneration, by no means adequate, in most cases, to what you paid; and then passed a law, compelling you to refund that remuneration by the payment of five hundred pounds every voyage, not out of your profits, my Infants; but, profit or loss, you must pay, and this seems now entailed on you in perpetuity, for your comfort. What did they then do?—I well remember to have overheard a short conversation, in my neighbourhood, one day, between a very respectable Director and a person tolerably well versed in East India Shipping concerns. It was during the first agitation of the question regarding remuneration for commands; and this person gave it as his opinion, that the best plan for the Company to adopt, would be to sell the commands themselves, by public sale; or, in other words, to open the Shipping Trade to the best bidders; little dreaming, at the time, that what he then said in jest would be, not virtually only, but really and fully, adopted by that respectable body, *the United Company of Merchants of England, trading to the East Indies.*

This system was adopted—a system which opened the door, not to competition among yourselves, for that might be fair enough; nor have you a right to complain, because it admits the public as speculating owners in the trade. But what you have a right to complain of, is, that this system, whose benefits have been so much amplified by the *India Commissioners*, effectually cuts up your very existence; —for the East India Company's savings, in the article of freight, are no longer, as they used to be, dependent on an agreement, entered into annually, between the Company and Owners, founded on the circumstances of the times; but *these savings are now, by the new system, unequivocally drawn from your hard-earned wages and precarious profits.*—It requires no deep investigation to prove this, for you all know, my Children, and it will not be denied by your friends, that, in order to procure a ship in the service (the goal to which all the efforts of all your laborious lives tend) you must set out with either making heavy sacrifices yourselves, or being reduced to the alternative, painful to a feeling mind, of requesting your friends to part with so much of their property for your benefit—for it is a well-known truth, that no rational Owner, now-a-days, expects to see his first advance. Now, in the various ways in which this matter is managed, I appeal to all of you, whether many of your friends have not forsaken you, smarting, as they do, under the severity of their losses:—whether many of yourselves are not encumbered with engagements, on account of your ships, from which even the universal physician, death, will not relieve you?—Whether some of you are not driven, like jaded post-horses, by virtue of the spur, bestrode by your Owners, to whom you are compelled to be brokers and clerks, and whether you have now any ground of reasonable expectation that, even after you have, with all these disadvantages, procured a command, you are not likely to spin out the remainder of a hard life in that command, exposed as you are to a competition in the market to which you are going, by the very parties who profess to support, you, and under whose orders, as Owners, you act? I acknowledge, with pleasure, that there are men in the present list of

[L l]

Husbands and Owners, familiar with the old, as well as the concerned in the new system, who employ their fortunes and talents in the relief and support, at their own charge, of many respectable young men in the service, to avoid the pain of seeing an old friend starve. To such, and we all know there are such, I will ever hold out the palm of the highest merit; but we all likewise know that there are others of a different description, and I can see only one further step (after what the last three weeks have produced) that can be taken for the complete degradation of the service, and the total demolition of the hopes your little bosoms cherished when, for the first time, you found yourselves strutting a quarter-deck in all the pride of boyish vanity. This step is—the next tenders made to the Company will be by a combination of the Taylors, Drapers, Shoemakers, Glass and Music-sellers, Perfumers, Butchers, Cheesemongers, &c. &c. &c. whose families have been supported in affluence, and whose fortunes have been made out of the risks, hardships, disappointments, broken rest, and hard earnings you have suffered in the service. These men, I say, will now think it their turn to participate with others in the little adventures which used to yield a meed for your faithful exertions, for the sweat of your brows under many a scorching sun. These men will entertain you as only their pursers or stewards, subject to all the petty tyranny of this democratic ownership, and to the consequences of a bond of resignation, whenever you call down, on your devoted heads, the displeasure of any one of your little lords—your Cork-cutter or Toothpick-maker—and you will even hold by the like precarious tenure the little bit of solitary lace, which, by that time, you may possibly be able to afford, as the only remaining distinctive mark between what you were and what you are.

Oh, my Children! before that event crushes my parental heart, may I drop a shapeless ruin into my own cellars.

All the eyes of an Argus shall be on the watch to prevent this most alarming result of any further combined efforts of ignorance and wild senseless speculation; for while I exist, I hope it will be for the purpose of continuing to be a shelter to you with unbroken spirits—untrodden upon—undegraded.

THE JERUSALEM.

Cooper's-Court, Cornhill,
Jan. 20, 1803.

LETTER III.

To the Commanders and Officers in the East India Service.

From the TRUE BRITON, February 25th and 26th.

GENTLEMEN,

HAVING, by my former Letters on East India Shipping, endeavoured, and I trust, not unsuccessfully, to rouse the attention of the public from the lethargic state in which the bustle of hostilities had kept the general mind on the score of the new system and its destructive effects, it was not my intention so immediately to have followed up my original plan by an address to you, had not some recent circumstances concurred to render it highly proper that I should lose no time in calling upon you to step forward in your own defence.—You, on whom, and on whose friends solely, the accumulated and accumulating evils of this system fall—you, whose hard-earned wages and precarious commerce form the foundation on which the superstructure of the East India Company's freight-savings is built; and give me leave to add, you, with whom alone it lies to administer some remedy to check this overwhelming mass of corruption, if a thing in itself radically rotten can admit of remedy, and if you are still to continue unfortunately condemned by your Honourable masters to linger out your lives in hopeless misery and fruitless exertion.

I have been accused, gentlemen, of presumption, in obtruding my sentiments on the world unasked and unexpected—I have even been accused of being actuated by malicious motives in volunteering my services, where I am unconnected with the matters in dispute. To these accusations I answer, that it is because I am unconnected with East India Shipping, it is because my opinion was unasked and unexpected, that I am the more entitled to a fair and candid hearing. Had I any part of my capital at present embarked in concerns of this nature, as used to be the case fifteen years ago, it might with justice have been urged, that my opinions were biassed by other considerations, than that only of the attachment I declare myself to feel for the fate of deserving men; bred to the service, and originally entering into it with the honest hope of acquiring a decent competency, many of whom I have still the pleasure of being on terms of intimacy with, though our pursuits are now widely different; and many of whose characters I am no stranger to, though I am personally unknown to them. I confess, that the imputation of malicious motives gave me at first some pain, because the possibility of the charge had never occurred to me; but I very soon consoled myself with the reflection, that those who are acquainted with me, *and I am not perfectly unknown*, will not, for one moment, countenance the charge. To those who are strangers to me, it may be proper for me to say, by way of repelling such an unjust imputation, that I have pointed my observations at no individual—that I am even well acquainted with one of the parties, and slightly with another gentleman, whose tenders have been lately accepted; and I am sure that the former is well convinced of my disposition to do him every service —nor has the latter any the smallest reason to entertain a contrary opinion of me. The fact is, had my own brother been in that list of contractors, I should have spoken of the measure with the same freedom, for it is the *sin*, not the *sinner*, I attack; and those parties, in accusing me of malicious motives, may, with equal propriety, direct their accusations against their parish pastor, and assert, that on every sabbath he disseminates malice and scandal from his pulpit, in warning the ignorant, and guarding the deluded, against the arts of their more designing fellow-creatures.

To proceed, gentlemen, with some degree of regularity in this address, it will be necessary to go into a very short review of the Freight-service of the company—to unveil some of the evils attendant on the present system, and, if possible, to suggest some alleviation of the mischiefs flowing from it. —To many of you a great deal of this is rendered useless, by the sad experience of the few last years; but to others, who are at present in subordinate situations, though looking forward to their ultimate hope, a command, and who may be but little versed in the nature of such concerns, it is absolutely indispensible.

The East India Company, till within these few years, were supplied with such shipping as they required in a very different way from the present.

Not desirous, for very obvious reasons, of employing any part of their capital stock in their own freight-service, permission was given to certain persons to build ships of the necessary dimensions, calculated solely for this service, and capable of acting in the double capacity of men of war and merchantmen. With adventurers in these concerns, a freight, for the use of the ships, was annually settled by the Court of Directors, according to the current rates of naval stores, and other incidental charges; and thus the Company and Owners had jogged on for a century, without much cause for complaint on either side, except what originated in that mutual desire which naturally existed, to reduce on the one side, and augment on the other.

On this system you, gentlemen, stood fairly and honourably independent of both parties, except as to your personal obligations to the Owners, who intrusted you with their property. The trade you were allowed to carry on was deemed by both a just and proper compensation for your services; and merely as *Captains* and *Officers*, it was of no kind of importance to you at what rate of freight your ships were entertained in the service. In process of time, however, a practice had crept in among you, certainly indefensible in every point of view, however it may be at this moment practised, and of course justified, by the Company themselves. This practise originated in a certain compliment, by way of a lumping sum paid for cabin furniture, by the succeeding to the retiring Commander—this sum, from small beginnings, and as the value of commands in the service came to be developed, increased in the course of time to £500, £1000, £2000, £5000, and I have even heard of £10,000!

About the period at which these compensations arrived at such an enormous pitch, the Direction came under the influence of a superior control, and several gentlemen, who had been engaged in commercial pursuits in India, having procured seats in Leadenhall-street, were called upon, together with their brother directors, by the controlling power, to use every exertion to convert this country into a great European emporium for Indian commerce.

The idea was patriotic, it was proper, it was the conception of a great mind; but the object of our present enquiry is to investigate one branch of the means which were adopted to accomplish it. These compensations for commands, paid by you to each other, were certainly, with strict justice, stigmatised as monstrous corruptions; but it was not with equal justice asserted, that they were the cause of the high freights which, it was said, the Company paid to the Owners; for every body now knows that there was no connection whatever between the two, and that instead of each of you absolutely paying £5000, or £8000, or any sum for your commands, you only passed such a sum into the hands of your predecessor, receiving it again from your successor; by this means in fact paying no other compensation for your command than the use of that money, so lying dead, would amount to, and of course not even paying so much as you now do to the Company every voyage for such command. These compensations, however, became the stalking-horse of the day, and it was suggested (I by no means say with any other than disinterested views) that the destruction of the established system, and the adoption of another, founded on public competition, would remove that great preponderance in favour of *foreign* freights, which it was said existed against our charges on the importation from India. I have no objection, before I proceed farther, to allow, that the views of these gentlemen were founded in a justifiable jealousy of *foreign* trade, and in a determination to strike at the root of it in an honourable and justifiable way; I am far from accusing them of sinister, or even selfish motives, but I accuse them of want of information on the subject; for want of foresight in forming their plan. If they really meant, that fair and open competition should be resorted to, they have completely *failed in establishing it*—if they meant that the proposed public benefit should result from the effects of that sanguine desire which every man feels to render himself independent of the world, and which they concluded might, in this case, induce you to involve yourselves, your friends, your dearest interests, in the blind attempt, at any rate, and against all reasonable chances, to grasp at this independence, they have as completely *succeeded in establishing it.*

It ought to have been known, and doubtless these very men did know, that the freight paid by our East India Company on their importations from India, was by no means a fair object of comparison with that paid on *foreign* ships by individuals, and for this simple reason, that nearly the whole weight of the British freight is thrown on the homeward voyage, while the foreigner receives an adequate outward freight, which enables him to lessen very considerably his charges homeward; and every man knows the effect which a sum of money paid on the outset of a ship on her voyage has in reducing the burthen of the concern. I beg leave to add to this my opinion, that, taking the out and home voyages together, *more charges* were incurred on *foreign* than on British bottoms, and I am supported in this opinion by information I procured in the year 1789, on my way through Ostend, at the table of a very respectable merchant there, largely embarked in the India trade. From the facts he adduced, nothing could be more clear than that the charges and incidents on the *foreign* trade far exceeded our own. Without attending however to the effects of outward freight, or at least without appearing to do so, these gentlemen only fixed their eyes on the striking difference of probably one-third between the homeward freight of foreigners and British; and they argued solely on the necessity of diminishing the charges on the *importation*, in order to attain the object proposed; not perhaps recollecting, or not perhaps choosing to recollect, that the charges of exportation as well as importation fall in one shape or other on the trade generally; for it is to be considered as a gaining or a losing trade to the country on the whole, not in its parts, and on this broad basis must the result of every branch of trade be invariably taken. In this view of the matter, they represented the existing system of shipping as irremediably defective in its constitution, not only as encumbered with the abuses attached to commands, but as exposed to what they were pleased to call the impositions of Owners in the annual adjustment of the freight, and concluded that the only proper and equitable way of securing to the company the lowest possible terms of freight would be, by public contract; very *justly* thinking that if commands were really worth what was understood to be paid for them, the competition thus created would in fact reduce the terms of freight by so much as they were worth.—Some benevolent and considerate characters at that time in the Direction, headed, if I recollect right, by a gentleman well known to you, and in his own person no stranger to your situations, immediately saw the dreadful ruin thus impending over your heads; and, I believe, after encountering no small share of obloquy for advocating the defence of those who had committed such flagrant abuses in the service, on the score of illegal compensations for commands, these gentlemen succeeded in establishing a plan of remuneration to such of you as had paid such compensations, founding their arguments, in its favour, on the presumption that, although the first disbursement by the Company might extend to £300,000, or

£100,000, yet that the competition now to be adopted would very soon, by a reduction of the freight, repay that advance; and I will venture to say that these gentlemen had at this time no idea of the mischiefs which have since resulted to you from this competition.—The reformers, however, dissatisfied with this prospect of return, felt their consciences revolt at the idea of throwing away so much of the public money, without being able to produce a more substantial evidence of their attention to the public interest, and lulling their recollection of the degree of infamy they had attached to the old system on the score of compensations for commands, or probably thinking, as is too often the case in Leadenhall-street, that a public body may stand excused in matters where an individual would be expelled from society, they withheld their consent from the plan of remuneration, unless with the condition attached to it, that every Commander of a regular ship should, on his return from every voyage, pay to the Honourable United Company of Merchants of England trading to the East Indies the neat sum of five hundred pounds (£500.) clear of all deductions, unquestionably as a consideration to such company for the liberty of commanding his ship during that voyage. To wind up the regulation to a still more ridiculous, more culpable point, it was stipulated, that both Owners and Captains should be restrained by the sanction of an oath, to be taken at the outset on every voyage, from receiving or paying compensations for commands, doubtless holding it no breach of your oaths as commanders, that, at the very moment you took such oath, you actually entered into an agreement to pay the Company this £500. for that very command.

If some of these reformers had not been remarkable for their professions, and I firmly believe practice, on the score of moral rectitude, I should have doubted the bias which led them into so strange an absurdity; but I am willing to attribute it to oversight in the first instance, though I cannot now allow them that excuse, since the payment of compensations for commands is so generally known to prevail, and to an infinitely more mischievous extent, as you too well experience; and yet this disgraceful and disgracing oath still exists, which, like a magnet with two repelling poles, keeps conscience and interest constantly asunder. Indeed, I have heard, that it was once in contemplation to wipe off this stain from the service—not, gentlemen, out of any tenderness to your religious prejudices, but in consequence of an opinion delivered by a certain legal character, that the oath would be a bar to any proceedings in Chancery, which the Company might at a future period have occasion to resort against delinquents—and on the plain ground, that a man cannot well be brought forward to prove, by a second oath, that he has already incurred the heavy penalties of the law of perjury, by the breach of an oath formerly taken by him.

Thus, gentlemen, in addition to the other burthens imposed by the new system, was this tax, this heavy tax, on your industry, established; and thus, in defiance of all decorum, of all propriety, of all feeling for your situations, (far from being mended by the extension of the Commission Trade to India) are you compelled, by the Company and Public, surely on no justifiable or liberal foundation, to contribute from £20,000. to £25,000. per annum, to the necessities of that Public and that Company, out of your hard-earned wages and precarious profits; and, however desirous you may be to pay your way among your creditors, however liberal the tradesmen who supply your investments, and every man will cordially assign them that praise, yet it certainly is hard that you may suffer in your credit, and they in their fortunes, because the Company must first be satisfied out of whatever comes in your privilege—*Their five hundred pounds must first be paid.* In vain do you look for the surplus which your fond fancy painted would result from the sale of your investment outwards at fifty per cent. Your duties in India, your insurance, interest, wastage, breakage, and loss by remittance, at once sweep away above 30 per cent. and the poor remainder is absorbed by this £500. and the *guarantees that you have entered into with your Owners, that the concern shall yield them five per cent.*

These regulations thus obtained and fixed, the new system was launched, and a glorious and proud day it was deemed: not by you, gentlemen, for you began at a very early period to apprehend the ill effects of it. Tenders were made by many, some by yourselves and your friends, and some by speculators, whose sole object was to acquire the honour of being ranked among East India Husbands, with the usual courtesy of an *Esquire* at the end of their names. So far their ambition was innocent, however puerile; I have good reason even for thinking, that in some cases, in the infancy of this system, commands were obtained upon very easy terms to Captains, and even their friends. In other cases, these speculators, in adopting their commander after their tenders were accepted, dictated their terms to that commander and his friends, which bound them, as owners of the ship, to the allowance of what was never before known in the service, that is, a commission of two and a half per cent. on all receipts and payments, instead of a small compensation, short of £100. for a voyage, which used to be made to the Husband for his trouble. Exclusive of this, the speculator insisted on deriving certain advantages from the insurance of the individual concerns of the Owners and the Captain's investment—he was to become the agent, broker, and banker of the commander, drawing his per centage as such, and this agreement was to ſubsist *durante vita* of the ship.—So that, whether the concern became profitable or otherwise, whether the contract became even tenable or otherwise, if even their accumulating losses should determine the Owners to pay any reasonable forfeiture to the Company, rather than continue to the ruin of their fortunes, the husband was still securely sheltered behind his agreement; by virtue of which, before any such step could be taken by these unfortunate adventurers for their mutual relief, he would claim, and doubtless establish his claim to a full compensation for the loss of commission and other advantages, which their efforts to escape from destruction would expoſe him to. It may be said that he, as an Owner, is equally a sufferer as the others—To this I answer, by *what I have seen*, that in a case of that nature, the commissions to the Husband on the first voyage falling something short of £1800. of course covered half the concern of one-eighth part he held in the ship. In all this, gentlemen, we must not reflect on the individual—every merchant who advances his capital, or contributes his knowledge or exertions in an adventure, is entitled to the fair mercantile compensation for that capital, that knowledge, and those exertions; we can only reflect on the system, which confessedly does expose you and your friends to such misfortunes, and even to the worst designs of the worst men—for, in considering this subject, I have a right to assume any case that is within probability, and in doing this, I shall detail, not what has happened, but what may happen, and I am sure, will even become very common, if the present itch for speculation in East India Shipping is not by some means checked. I beg, gentlemen, your attention to what I am going to state, because I may possibly hit upon some strong truths which may not be perfectly obvious to you, unacquainted as you, in genera may be with the nature of the shipping laws. Here I ai much disposed to invoke the spirit of our immortal HOGARTH to assist me in delineating the progress of a *Husband*, in th fine colouring of his *Rake's* Progress; but the ſerious natui of the subject repels the playful illusions of fancy, and chair my faculties, absorbed as they are in the magnitude of th mischief to you, your families, and friends. Let us the proceed.

On some future occasion of tenders to be made fo ships to the Company, some man, already on the brir of ruin, with little credit, and no pecuniary resource may throw in such terms as *must* be accepted, (for tl Court *must* accept the lowest offer). His next step will b to bring his tender among you, with a view to stimulate son worthy fellow, anxious for bread, and possessing wealth friends, to step forward with thoſe friends, and take 15-1 of the ship off his hands, exclusive of a handsome doucei made privately to him by some of this worthy ſellow's friend for singling out *him* as the object of his paternal solicitude Due care is here taken by the Husband to ſecure to himse not only the management of the concern, and fingering of cash, but likewise the *cash and concerns of the Commande* With money drawn from the holders of the 15-16 share he builds his ship, and as a sufficiency must be contributed advance by the Owners to enable him to pay the outfit, thus gets possession of a large sum of money in hand, ai takes the usual credit for what is due to the tradesmen w have supplied the ship. He now, with renovated vigoı returns to those speculations which had already reduced h to the verge of bankruptcy; and if his decline is not very rap he may contrive to spin out probably the length of the t first voyages, receiving as much, and paying as little as pos ble, both on account of the Owners and Captain, and, tha God! in this country there are ways and means *by which n may at all times secure their persons*, at least from the importu ate molestation of creditors. At this critical period his Sou Sea bubble bursts, and it is found that very little of the seco outfit, probably even not all of the first, is paid, and none the third, though incurred; and at the same time that homeward freight on the second voyage (the usual sm balance excepted) together with the impress on the third received and gone, leaving "not a wreck behind."

Here it is proper to remark, that in any shipping concern the law is, that if there is only one individual owner holding in that ship a single stick, and who is capable of discharging the debts of the concern, he must pay them to the last farthing. This is probably little known, and less adverted to among you and your friends—yet, such is the law; and as some late acts of parliament have wisely required a faithful register of the names of the owners of every British ship to be lodged at the Custom-house, any person having supplied such ship with stores or necessaries, and experiencing difficulty in procuring payment, may, for 2s. 6d. obtain from the Custom-house a copy of that register, forming a legal document for him to proceed upon against any of the parties he may therein discover to be owners, and whom he may think most competent to answer his demand; and, as I have already mentioned, if that man is the only competent owner in regard to pecuniary circumstances, *he* must pay every debt of the ship contracted during the time he has been an owner.

Now let us take a view of the tempting situation of the concern at this period.—All the objections, Gentlemen, which have been made to the statement in my first letter, have been, as I expected, in favour of the general result—indeed, I have no hesitation in avowing, that my object was fully to avail myself of the advantage I had, and set those adventures in the strongest possible light, by a calculation not admitting of cavil, except on that side most favourable to me; for a calculation on fair and equitable principles, and on the experience of the service, would, instead of 68,000l. have left my result at least at 100,000l. But I will, notwithstanding, adhere to what I first laid down, and take the first cost and outfit at, as before, 30,000l.

15-16 parts of which, as the concerns of the Captain's friends, will be 28,125l. which, with interest and insurance on the 1st and 2d voyages, will amount, at the period of the 3d outfit, to - - - - - - - - - - -		£39,913
Now, taking my moderate outfit of 9000l. on each of these voyages, and admitting that it is found the husband has left only half the 2d outfit, and the whole of the 3d unpaid, the debts of the ship will be - - - - - - - - - - -	13,500	
Less the balance of freight, due by the Company on 2d voyage, say - - - - - - - - - -	2,500	
And there remains to be added by the Owners of the 15-16, a farther advance on their concern of - - - - - -		11,000
Cost to sea on the 3d voyage of 15-16 shares - - -		50,913

And I have already enabled you to trace the operation of this additional burthen upon the concern, bending under the weight of its oppressions.

At this dreadful period, however, what will be the situation of the poor commander?—Fifteen or twenty friends may little feel even these severe effects of the imprudence and improvidence of their engagement with this speculator; but the captain's all is gone; and from, perhaps, easy circumstances, probably comparative affluence, he is at once hurried down the precipice, and condemned to toil for many succeeding years, very possibly to the decline of life.

This picture, gentlemen, is not exaggerated.—It will not be disallowed by any man that the present system exposes both owners and commanders to such misfortunes, and I am very much concerned to add that you have not solely to guard against the imposing terms and speculative flights of the husband, for I have it from the best authority, that a tradesman in a certain line, though fully convinced of the destructive nature of the late contracts, actually applied to a friend to introduce him to a share in some of them, for the purpose of supplying the ship with his article; and I leave you to judge of the mode he would adopt to square his accounts at the end of the year—his friend, after endeavouring, ineffectually, to dissuade him, told him the door of admission was always wide open, and that he required no Sir CLEMENT COTTERELL.

All these mischiefs, however, might be still less to be regretted, if the consequences of them were confined to the parties themselves so becoming owners; but, in this case, the sins of the father are visited upon the children; for instances have occurred of parents, in the distribution of their property by will, having bestowed these concerns as specific legacies to particular children; and the consequence is, that, doubtless contrary to the intention of the testator, some of his children are in affluence, while the innocent legatees of such concerns are left upon the wide world without a shilling.

It is urged, gentlemen, by the advocates for the new system, that the fairness of open competition is undeniable, and that they cannot answer for the wild speculations which may be built on that system. But I most positively deny that, in this case, the competition can, in the most distant degree, be entitled to that character of fairness, which, in all other cases, is attached to open competition. It has one feature exclusively its own; and, until the commanders are rendered independent, as they used to be, of the terms on which ships are let to the company, it is no fair field for competition, it is only taking advantage of your anxiety for employment to pick your pockets under the specious pretext of public benefit; and for the truth of this, I may appeal to the experience of many of you. Until you are treated as the man of humanity and feeling would treat you, until you are released from the servile dependance you now hold on this wretched system, by the means I have suggested in my second letter, the nature of this competition must not only be exceptionable in the extreme, but the only one a great company ought *not to adopt*. We have heard much of the savings to the company and the public from this competition, and there is no man who will deny that those savings extend to 50,000l. or 60,000l. per annum, *bating heavy losses sustained by insufficient ships*. But although the transactions of the public ought to be on the strictest principles of economy, they ought at the same time to be on a liberal scale.—I am a strenuous advocate for the system of open competition; it is the only one which ought to be resorted to; but let it be stripped of this extraneous, crude, and dirty mass which encumbers it. In some shape or other, it must be allowed, that the company *must* pay an adequate compensation to those who export and import their merchandise. To use a vulgar phrase, they must pay it in meal or in malt. Gentlemen, you are, in this case, either the meal or the malt; and I leave it to abler heads than mine, abler even than those of its principal advocates in the direction, to justify the East India company in maintaining a system of shipping, the benefits arising from which they must acknowledge to be drawn out of your exertions, to raise yourselves to the honourable independence we all aim at, however different our pursuits. I have said that the company's savings are undoubted; and, allowing for extraordinary losses arising from bad ships, they may even pocket a clear annual sum of a few thousands. But is the mode adopted consistent with the high ground the East India company should take?—As well compare the honourable profits of general commerce to the excrementitious earnings of a nightman; and indeed the simile is not inapt between the Honourable United East India company drawing their profits from the sweat of your brows, and the nightman his gold from the less refined superfluities of your nature.

Let us not, however, throw indiscriminate censure on the direction—Many gentlemen in that body have, from the first, been fully sensible to what point this system tended; but, if there is *one black sheep* in the whole flock, the fleeces of the rest must of necessity in this case imbibe a dusky hue—for, though I pledge myself to prove that the company have paid proportionably higher freights under the new system than at any period under the old, *yet the charges on shipping concerns have so far exceeded those charges twenty years ago*, except in the article of insurance, that the losses I have stated have arisen. And as this system must be allowed, as I have said, to be beneficial to the public, *however foul the benefit*, it certainly is a very invidious task in any man, as a director, to oppose such public benefit. I have some reason, however, for thinking, that the advocates for this system in the direction are reduced from the plural to nearly the singular number; and if there is still an individual, either in or out of that direction, who, in the face of the conviction with which he must be impressed, can degrade himself so far as to continue the tool of a party of interested men—I envy not his portion of either mental comfort or public esteem. Had Pope been now writing his *Dunciad*, he would have assigned him the muddy honours in the race with *Lintot* and *Curl*.

If such an individual, or individuals, have enriched themselves by honourable traffic, either here or in India, how can they justify it to the world, how to their own consciences, that they should dedicate their very existence to the abridgement among you, of those fair and allowable means to which they have been themselves indebted; and only for the support of a system, which their own minds must now revolt at, however favourably they might have viewed it some time ago? This is of a piece with the characters we have of late years heard of in a neighbouring country, as rising to fame and power on the blood and ruin of their fellow-creatures. I am far from expecting that the observations I have made should have any effect upon such characters: I might as well expect they would have the effect of alluring the sow from her mire, or the crow from his carrion; for so long as a man can entertain such groveling ideas of the foundation on which the prosperity of a great company ought to be built, my mind can form no resemblance to him, but in the person who, furnished with a leather bag and a short stick, we see daily raking the gutters for the head of an old nail.

After thus detailing some of the evils poured out among you, from the well-furnished Pandora's box of this system, and after thus making some general observations on its nature, it only remains for me to point out some means by which it is possible to alleviate, in a small degree, the miseries flowing from it, though I do not pretend to say, that any means are practicable, generally speaking. For until a system of morality shall be emanated from the Divine Being, which shall not only embrace, but annihilate, all the failings and weaknesses of humanity, I cannot expect that you should be exempt from those weaknesses, particularly that one on which the proud pre-eminence of this country is built—*the desire to acquire riches in a fair and honourable way*—Until, Gentlemen, this system of morality can be established, by which you may be deprived of the wicked unprincipled desire of getting bread for your families, which you are now actuated by, the present plan ought to be laid on the shelf, so far as regards you—for, observe, it is to your interest alone I look. I am not, in the smallest degree, solicitous about the fate of monied men—they will always take care of themselves. If you are secured in the just and allowable compensation for a life spent in honourable exertions, I shall be satisfied. Let them even limit your privileges, if they only give you that fair play to which every industrious man is entitled. At present, if you earn *half-a-crown*, the Company steps in and claims *twenty-nine pence of it.*

The necessity, thus much, and in this manner, of premising my remedy, will be readily acknowledged, when I add, that the success of it depends on the exertion of the patience and fortitude of all of you, and on your forbearance to indulge those dreams of hope naturally enough founded on a command.

The remedy I propose is comprehended in a few words—avoid a speculator in tenders, as you would the deadliest reptile; he resembles nothing in nature; his only likeness is that of the arch-fiend, going about seeking whom he may devour.

You and your friends are the only parties who, under the present wretched system, ought to throw in tenders, and in order to enable you to do it without injury to yourselves, take this rule, which the experience of near thirty years in East India, as well as other shipping concerns, has furnished me with, and which, you may rely upon it, will only produce what adventures of that precarious nature ought to produce. It is this, ascertain with as much precision as possible, the expected amount of the nett cost and out-fit at such period as you make your tender, and a rate of freight, which will produce on the voyage a sum equal to three-fourth parts of this amount of cost and out-fit, ought to be inserted in your tender; any thing under that is a sacrifice out of your trade. And in calculating on war contingencies on ships now, or at any time to be, tendered, you ought to take it for granted that the company mean to allow only the difference during the war, exceeding the very great prices now paid for naval stores; for, although the company, with the usual insidious reserve of Leadenhall-street, are studiously inexplicit on this point in their advertisements, you may rely upon it that the current rate of naval stores will form the foundation for any grant they may in future make for contingencies on the ships, now, or at any time hereafter, to be tendered.

If they meant otherwise, they would so explain themselves in their advertisements; but as they lay themselves open for tenders at a permanent peace freight, they must be understood to mean a freight calculated on the *present rates* during the *present peace*, of every naval store requisite in those outfits; and as it must be understood in this point of view, it follows that, in case of future hostilities, there is very little chance of any considerable war contingencies on ships now tendered, except in the articles of insurance, guns, and manning; the prices of every other article of out-fit being at present as high as may be reasonably expected during future hostilities.

It is proper here to observe, that the ships required by the East India Company in their advertisements for the 9th of next month, are of a very different description from any hitherto taken up for six or eight voyages. Those required now are ships which have been built for some time, lying dead on the hands of the proprietors, and which, before the present advertisements, the owners would have been glad to sell at 12l. to 15l. per ton, ready coppered, with stores and every thing belonging to them. The freights, therefore, at which such ships, not expressly built for the service, may be tendered, can be no criterion for even the freight of irregular

[N n]

or small ships, built and fitted for the purpose, and of course you may expect to see tenders of such ships, at a pretty low rate; but my rule will still apply in ascertaining the value to be paid by you and your friends for such ships.

The company have adopted this plan in order to counteract that of the agents for India-built shipping, who are so solicitous, doubtless, for very disinterested motives, to strike at our shipping manufacture, the most valuable manufacture we have, and transfer it to India. For even those ships, now advertised for, will certainly be superior in every respect to India-built ships, manned and fitted as they are.

I am compelled by the limited privileges of a newspaper to compress my sentiments and narrow my arguments, otherwise, the field is so wide, that if my usual avocations admitted of it, I should not shrink from the most extended investigation of the subject; but having thus pretty well completed what I intended, and given you the only practicable, however fallible, means, of rendering palatable this despicable mass of corruption you are condemned to exist by, having originally taken up my pen with the desire of doing a general good, which might ultimately centre with you, with no applause to court, and no profit to seek, it may be allowable in me to mention that I have already met with a high reward.

I have the best reasons, Gentlemen, for knowing that my representations have had the effect of saving thousands to many—of even saving many from utter destruction. If there are any who, confident in their own superior abilities and knowledge, want faith in my calculations, and are dissatisfied with any thing short of experience, it would be the height of presumption in me to oppose my short-lived experience to theirs, and I cannot object to any mode they may think most eligible for the acquisition of wisdom.

But if there are others who hesitate to proceed, and probably will ultimately quit the pursuit in consequence of what I have said, I beg them to believe, that if they do, I shall think, when I pay the debt of nature, that the clod will lie lighter on my breast.

I have only now to add, that although it is not my wish to give offence, yet, as I have no idea of sacrificing a tittle of my subject to avoid giving that offence, it is possible I may have spoken so plain as to awaken the attention of certain framers and supporters of this vile system, and, though unwilling to have my name held up to the public at the foot o this address, I am equally unwilling to shelter myself behin an anonymous signature.

The Editor of this Paper* is therefore furnished with th means of satisfying such inquiries as have not for their bas impertinent curiosity.

Although I have at present no idea of renewing this subjec yet I shall keep myself open to defend any thing I have writter or attack the arguments of an opponent.—I beg leave to cor clude with repeating my first position, *that public good ca never be founded on private wrong*, and am with regard, and wit a deep sense of feeling for your situations,

Gentlemen,

Yours, &c.

NO OWNER.

London, February 22, 1803.

* True Briton.

No. XXIX.

A Sketch of the numerous Classes of the King's Subjects whose Trades are connected with, and in some Degree dependent upon, the Building, Equipment, and Employment of British Shipping, &c.

" The great trade of fishing imploying so many men and ships *at sea*,
" must likewise necessarily maintaine as great a number of tradesmen and
" artizans *on land*, as spinners, and hempwinders to cables, cordage, yarne
" twine for netts and lines, weavers to make saile cloathes, cecive, packers,
" tollers, dressers, and cowchers to sort, and make the herring lawful mer-
" chandize, tanners to tanne their sailes and netts, coopers to make caskes,
" block, and bowlemakers for shippes, keelemen, and labourers for carrying
" and removing their fish, sawyers for plankes, carpenters, shipwrights,
" smithes, carmen, boateman, brewers, bakers, and a number of others,
" whereof many are maimed persons and unfit to be otherwise imployed,
" besides the maintenance of all their severall wives and children and
" families." Extract from Sir John Borroughs' very valuable Tract " On the Sovreignty of the British Seas," which was written in 1633.—See Edition, 1651, which is now scarce. 1806.

A Ship-owner, in order to build a ship, must necessarily employ	Who derives his knowledge from the	Arts and Sciences.
	And who, in the construction of the ship, gives employment to	
	The shipwright, The sawyer, The caulker, The joiner, The blacksmith, } and these give encouragement to	Manufactures.
The Ship-builder.	The Baltic merchant for tar, pitch, iron, and other stores imported from abroad, which gives encouragement to.................	Shipping.
	The Canada merchant for timber, &c. which encourages the......	Loyal Colonies.
	The copper merchant and coppersmith, for copper, bolts, &c.....	Mines.
	The iron master, for iron knees, &c.	Foundries.
	The dealers in old rope, for oakum, which is generally made by infirm and old persons who are incapable of laborious employment	Industrious Poor.
	The landed interest for timber of all kinds, &c......................	Agriculture, &c.

Trade	Dependent on	Interest
The Mast and Block Maker.	The Baltic merchant, for masts, &c.	Shipping.
	The West-India merchant, lignum vitæ, &c.	Colonies.
	The landed interest, for elm for pumps, &c.	Agriculture, &c.
	The manufacturers of varnish, &c.	Manufactures.
	The journeymen block-makers	
The Sail-maker.	The sail-cloth manufactories for canvas	Manufactures.
	The rope-maker for bolt rope	Shipping and Revenue.
	The twine spinner for twine, lines, &c.	
	The Baltic merchant for tar, flax, hemp, &c.	
	The journeymen sail-makers	
The Rope-maker.	The Baltic merchant for hemp, tar, &c.	Shipping and Revenue.
	The blacksmith for iron implements	Do. and Manufactures.
	The iron wheel-maker for wheels	
	The carpenter for sledges	
	The journeyman rope-maker	
The Ship-chandler.	To the manufacturers of ivory-black, whitelead, &c.	Manufactures.
	To the brush-maker for brushes, &c.	Mechanics.
	To the turner for bowls, platters, spoons, &c.	Do.
	To the broom-makers for brooms	
	To the manufacturers of horn, &c.	Do.
	To the hardwareman for shovels, &c.	Manufactures.
	To the twine-spinner	Do.
	To the needle-maker for needles	Do.
	To the wire-maker for wire	Do.
	To the potter	Potteries.
	To the scale-maker for steelyards	Manufactures.
	To the lead merchant for sounding leads, sheet lead	Do.
	To the lamp-mak. for binnacle lamps	
	To the time-glass-maker for time-glasses	Do.
	To the tinman for lanthorns, speaking trumpets, copper pumps, &c.	Do.
	To the iron founder for cannon and shot	Manufactures.
	To the gunpowder-maker for powder	Do.
	To the gunsmith for muskets, pistols, &c.	Do.
	To the locksmith	Do.
	To the sword-cutlers for cutlasses	Do.
	To the mathematical instrument-maker for compasses, quadrants, and sextants	Do.
	To the manufacturers of bunting colours, &c.	Do.
	To the ironmonger for fish-hooks, nails, pump-tacks, &c.	Do.
	To the lead shot-maker for bullets	Do.

The Ship-chandler.	To the leather-seller for sheep skins, for hides	Manufactures.
	To the iron-monger and hardware-man for marlin-spikes, &c.	Do.
	To the Baltic merchants for pitch, tar, rosin, &c.	Shipping and Revenue.
The Boat-builder.	To the Baltic merchant for wainscoat, tar, and pitch	Do.
	To the land-holder for oak and elm, &c.	Agriculture, &c.
The Plumber.	To the lead merchant for lead, &c.	Mines.
The Glazier and Painter.	The glass manufacturer for glass ..	Manufactures.
	The oil manufacturers for oil	Fisheries.
	The colour-maker for colours, &c.	Manufactures.
The Cooper.	To the Baltic merchant for staves, iron	Shipping and Revenue.
	To the Canada merchant for ditto, wood	
	To the hoop bender for wood, hoops, &c.	Agriculture, &c.
The Tallow Chandler.	To the Baltic merchant for tallow	Shipping & Rev.
	To the West-India merchant for cotton	Colonies.
	To the tallow melter for tallow, &c.	Manufactures.
The Grocer.	To the sugar baker	Shipping. Colonies and Revenue.
	To the West-India merchant	
	To the Mediterranean and Portuguese merchants	
The Coal Merchant.	To the proprietors of coal mines ..	Shipping, &c.
	To lightermen, &c.	
	To bargemen, &c.	
The Butcher.	To the farmer, grazier, &c.	Agriculture, &c.
The Baker.	To the miller for flour, &c.	Do.
	To the farmer for peas, &c.	
The Cheesemonger	To the farmer for butter and cheese	Do.
The Brewer.	To the maltster for malt..........	Do.
	To the hop merchant for hops	
	To the back maker for backs......	Manufactures.
	To the cooper for casks	Do.
	To the copper-smith for coppers, &c.	Do.
The Brazier.	To the coppersmith for copper, &c.	Mines.

In addition to the various classes above described, might be added the numerous persons employed in the subordinate branches of the different trades, &c. enumerated, but which is not considered necessary to shew the importance of *ship-building* to the empire, as a manufacture of the first impression; not only from the employment which it affords, and the encouragement it gives to national industry, but from it producing the only *real defence* on which the country can rely for its protection and support, as an independent nation.

The ship being built and equipped for sea, the guidance of that wonderful machine through the trackless ocean depends upon a knowledge of the science of astronomy and of mathematics, together with a practical knowledge of the management and manœuvres it is capable of performing, which can only be obtained by practice and experience, from whence arises the superiority and excellence of *British seamen*, but which depends

upon the *employment* of the ship in transporting merchandise and ma
tures from one part of the globe to another, and is usually call
carrying trade, though Dr. Adam Smith has described it as " *A beggarly*
if this expression was used by its author for the inadequate return o
for capital employed in *British* shipping, he was correct; but if he
to convey that no *beneficial* effects resulted to the nation from the e
ment of *British* shipping, he was as *incorrect* as he is in many other p
his work, to which may be attributed, if the present temporising sys
gratuitous concessions to neutral nations is persevered in, the ulter
nihilation of the *naval* power of Great Britain.

FINIS.

Printed by T. DAVISON,
Whitefriars.

Zeitfracht Medien GmbH
Ferdinand-Jühlke-Straße 7
99095 Erfurt, Deutschland
produktsicherheit@kolibri360.de